RAISING THE BAR

In and Before Indian River County
A History of the Courts and Judges, 1513 through
1999

Eugene J. O'Neill

Raising the Bar

Copyright© 2025 Eugene J. O'Neill

Revision February 2, 2026

ISBN: 978-1-970153-58-3

Available Through Ingram Book Company

Library of Congress Control Number: 2025915593

Preface

I started this manuscript in 1993. I was the Indian River County Bar Association President for that fiscal year (July 1993 - June 1994). I recalled that my brother, Kevin O'Neill, when he was in college at Belmont Abbey in North Carolina, as a summer intern, had helped to write a history of the Courts in Gaston County.* Also, back in 1971, my sister, Anne O'Neill Schulte, had given me J. Noble Richards' book, Florida's Hibiscus City, Vero Beach, with several chapters on the local courts. I thought it might be a good idea to update some of that history, focusing on documenting the history of the Indian River County Courthouse, then on 14th Avenue, while there were still a few people around who remembered its beginnings, particularly before the opening of the new courthouse on 16th Ave, which was to open in 1994.

I mentioned this concept in passing to Mrs. Jean Callahan, the mother of American television presenter John Walsh. She did what I believe to have been volunteer work at the Indian River County Library, and before I knew it, she had furnished me with copies from microfilm of

---

*Tepper, Roberta L., Esq., and Art Bernardino, Art, Two Hundred Years of Justice: The Courts in Gaston County, Commission on the Bicentennial of the United States Constitution.

The beginnings of this 14th Ave courthouse, mostly, if not entirely, from the Vero Beach Press Journal. I felt committed to this endeavor after that!

Like many public works projects, there were delays, and the courthouse opened in late 1994. I had started this manuscript with this county's prior courthouses or courtrooms – Chapter 5. It also seemed apropos to preserve the histories of the now defunct municipal courts which had existed in this county and to tell of their judges, and even of the Fourth District Court of Appeal while it once (first) sat in Vero Beach. More recently, I discovered that we had justices of the peace, who are interwoven with the municipalities and addressed in the newly written Chapter 6.

I gave my draft of the initial missive to Sherman N. Smith, Jr., one of the well-deserving speakers (see more on his bio infra) for the ribbon-cutting ceremonies for the 16th Ave. courthouse on Nov 11, 1994. Sherman publicly alluded to my document, as it then existed, and said he would present it at the next county commission meeting, which he did.

Three to four generations of attorneys have practiced in the prior courts, for example, the Vocelles and Smiths. Upon the opening of the fourth courthouse in Indian River County, the Indian River County Bar Association wished to place this history in the new courthouse, with the hope that it will be updated periodically as the history of the courts in Indian River County continues.

I then went back to the drawing board to add what I could reconstruct about the courts and judicial life prior to 1925, which would have been applicable for this area, albeit at that time a very large and sparsely populated area.

The subtitle is a slight play on words with the way pleadings "In and For" the circuit and county courts are typically captioned. Nevertheless, it should accurately capture the time and place of this history.

I titled the book through the year 1999, as that date was reasonably close to the courthouse's opening, and was the end of the millennium. I cut it off with the judges who were then or were previously in office. Perhaps someone someday will add additional biographies of judges beyond that point in time.

Acknowledgments

While many of the people listed below are now deceased, I would gratefully like to acknowledge the assistance of Jean Callahan Walsh, former Associate Librarian, Technical Services, for the Indian River County Library, who started this research by looking for articles on the 14th Avenue courthouse from the microfiche of the Vero Beach Press Journal at the Indian River County Library. Her efforts were such that I had to complete this project. I regret the passing of this wonderful woman, who did not get to see this published.

I would also like to thank Pamela Cooper, the former head of the Archive Center and Genealogy Dept. at the Indian River County Main Library. Her knowledge of historical resources amazed me.

I would also like to thank the Honorable D. C. Smith, then a retired Judge of the Nineteenth Judicial Circuit, Honorable Sherman N. Smith, Jr., former Chief Judge of both the Second District Court of Appeal and the Fourth District Court of Appeal and my former partner and mentor, B. T. Cooksey, who were tremendously knowledgeable about the judicial and legal history of this county.

I would also like to thank the following who are a part of the history and gave personal interviews or information that were most valuable: David Albrecht, Esq.; David Andrews; Randi Bailey,

Library Technical Assistant to Florida Collection, State Library of Florida; Chuck Balnius, helpful and inveterate volunteer at the Archive Center and Genealogy Dept. at the Indian River County Main Library; Matilda Barnes; Jeffrey K. Barton, Clerk of Circuit Court of Indian River County; Barbara Bonnah, Clerk to the County Commission Board Supervisor; Mrs. Mary N. Boring; Lucy Brown of the office of St. Helen Catholic Church; John H. Cann, former Mayor of Fellsmere, Gladys Honeywell Cobb; Chester Clem, Former Small Claims and Municipal Judge; George Collins; Arnold Cooperman, Esq., Division of Statutory Revision, State of Florida; Spencer C. Cross; Cathy Daniel, the Indian River County Building and Grounds Division; Mrs. John (Jolene) Day; James M. Denham, Professor of History at Florida Southern College; Kelly Devlin, Digital Services, U.S. Court of Appeals for the 11th Circuit; Nancy Dobson, Executive Director of the Florida Supreme Court Historical Society; David Dowd, formerly of Holyoke, MA. for his edits, Nancy Dwinell, my legal assistant for most of the years of this writing effort; Frank H. "Speedy" Fee, III, Esq; Darrell Fennell, Esq.; Virginia Gilbert, Clerk, Town of Indian River Shores; Michael Gray, Esq., former Vero Beach attorney, now patent attorney for the U. S. Army, and great proof reader, Ryan Humm, Archivist/Public History Coordinator at the Florida Historical Society Library; Robert Jackson, Former Municipal Judge for City of Vero Beach; Carolyn

Jones of St. Lucie Village, Cindy Krupp, of the former Indian River County Law Library; Mrs. Linda Sample Kyser; Catherine Maccarone Lally, English Professor, Eastern Florida State College; Mrs. Diane Walker Lembo; Margaret Lyon, Assistant City Attorney for the City of Vero Beach; Margaret MacIntyre Mancini; Miles B. Mank, II, Former County Judge of Indian River County; Elizabeth Mason; Mrs. Linda (Baker) Metz; Kathryn Applegate O'Brien; William C. Owen, Jr.; Stephanie Petrulak, Former Clerk for the Fourth District Court of Appeal; Clarence Redstone; John A. Reed, Jr.; Linda L. Richardson, Administrative Assistant, Okeechobee Library, Lucille Rieley Rights; Janice Rutan, Indian River Shores Town Clerk, Rosalee Saunderson, University of Florida Law Library; Cora Sembler Sadler; James Scutti, writer, neighbor & former attorney; Carolyn Short, Indian River County Historical Society; Thomas Snell, Former Mayor of Fellsmere; Linda Steffee, Osceola County Historical Society and Museum, Mrs. Paul (Hazel) Stevenson; Graham W. Stikelether, Jr., Former County Judge for Indian River County; Maria F. Suarez-Sanchez, CMC, City Clerk, Fellsmere; John Sutherland; Mrs. David Swing; Marty A. Thomas; Richard B. Votapka, Fellsmere Historian; Michelle Wagner, Genealogy Librarian, Archive Center and Genealogy Dept. at the Indian River County Main Library; Honorable James Walden; Honorable Joe Wild, Judge of the County Court for Indian River

County; Jeanette Williams, MMC, City Clerk, City of Sebastian; Mr. Lynn Williams, Indian River County Building and Grounds Division; Richard Woodard, Recording Supervisor, Clerk of the Circuit Court. I would also like to thank the following for their editing help: Janie Gould, Caryn Maingot Toole, Lori Keeton, Marge Dyer, and Melly T. Nofal.

Lastly, I would like to thank my publisher, Janet Sierzant from La Maison Publishing, for her formatting and cover design services.

Table of Contents

Chapter 1 - Pre-United States

Cacique (Ais Indian) by artist Theodore Morris, donated by Indian
River National Bank, March 1, 1997
to the Florida History and Genealogy Room at the Indian River
County Main Library

A. Ais Indians

The initial known inhabitants of our area of Florida were the Ais
or Ays Indians. However, we know little about these Indians,
particularly their tribal system of justice. Our limited knowledge of
the Ais comes from their interaction with the Spanish, French,
English, and the United States. All four countries controlled at least

portions of Florida at various times. Thus, to a certain extent, the laws of the Florida frontiers were arguably governed by the laws of the particular ruling country at the time.

Most of our information on the Ais or Ays Indians comes from the Spanish and from Jonathan Dickinson, a Pennsylvanian Quaker, who was shipwrecked around Hobe Sound on September 23, 1696. He likely walked along what is now the beachside or barrier island in Vero Beach, within a few weeks thereafter. Obviously, the Indian tribes did not have three branches of government as we know it. Nevertheless, important tribal decisions were likely made by a chief, often in conjunction with some type of council. We know that when an Ais chief, called a casseekey by the English[1] (and cacique by the Spanish), and his council deliberated, it was often in conjunction with a Cassina Ceremony. This involved drinking a liquid which had been made by boiling the leaves of the Cassina shrub.[2]

Territory of the Ais People, Wikipedia

B. First Spanish Period (1513-1763)

Spanish rule began with Juan Ponce de Leon's discovering (sighting) of Florida near St. Augustine on approximately Easter Sunday, March 27, 1513. It is believed he landed on April 2 and claimed the land for Spain on April 8, 1513. Modern thinking has it that the discovery of Florida by de Leon was south of Melbourne Beach,[3] although theories vary as to the location, as far north as Jacksonville. This was after Ponce de Leon had conquered Puerto Rico and was still searching for the Fountain of Youth. (There is a lot more to the background of that story. See, for example, Fuson, Robert H., <u>Juan Ponce de Leon and the Spanish Discovery of Puerto Rico and Florida</u>, The McDonald and Woodward Publishing Company, Blacksburg, Va., 2000, Chapters 2 & 3.)

Spanish governors, commissioned by the King of Spain, largely governed Florida from 1513[4] to 1763. The Governor or Adelantado in early Spanish Florida made all the rules for the government of the province, subject only to such appeals from them as might be made to the King. In effect, the Governor was the Executive, Legislature, and Judiciary in one.[5]

Pedro Menendez de Aviles

Pedro Menendez de Aviles was appointed Adelantado, i.e., Governor and Captain-General for His Majesty the King of Spain, on March 20, 1565. He is considered the founder of the first permanent Settlement in the future United States – St. Augustine. Menendez appointed in his absence and in the absence of his Lieutenant General and Corps Commander (Pedro Menendez de Valdes), Captain Juan Velez de Medrano to govern the people of the River of Succor, also known as the Ays. Velez had been part of Pedro Menendez de Aviles' storming of Fort Caroline (now Jacksonville) in September of 1565. Those Spaniards marched southward from St. Augustine and defeated a group of Huguenot Frenchmen near Cape Canaveral. The Spanish then established the first of what would be several different locations of Fort St. Lucia, the first being in what is now the Orchid Island area in Indian River County.[6]

During this time frame, the French occupied certain portions of Florida. When the mother countries of Spain and France were at war on several occasions, portions of Florida, and particularly Pensacola, changed hands from the Spanish to the French and back to the Spanish a few times. There were also English and U.S. occupations interspersed in the Pensacola area at a later time.[7]

English incursions into Florida included Sir Francis Drake's raid on St. Augustine in 1586.[8] However, the most significant English period was in the 1760s and 1770s, described below.

The French and Indian War lasted from 1754 to 1763. In 1761, Spain disastrously allied with France against England. France lost all its New World holdings except for New Orleans. Spanish Havana, Cuba, and the Bahamas had been captured by the English and were given back to Spain in a humiliating exchange for Florida by Spain to England.[9]

C. English Period (1763-1783)

The English then divided Florida into East and West Florida on October 7, 1763.[10] East Florida extended west to the Apalachicola River, and West Florida extended farther west to the Mississippi

River. English governors ruled in both East and West Florida for almost the next two decades, but in conjunction with the courts.

The first British governor of East Florida, James Grant of Scotland, arrived in St. Augustine, the capital of East Florida, in 1764 and took the old Spanish governor's residence. The entire Spanish population, at the time of the transfer of East Florida, was 3,046.[11]

Land grants were given to soldiers and settlers who came from all over. Florida began to prosper, governments were established, laws were passed, and courts soon enforced the laws. New Smyrna, a colonial settlement which was established by a prosperous Scottish physician, Dr. Andrew Turnbull, and his English associates on February 3, 1768, had to be abandoned due to sickness and lack of food, clothing, and shelter, on top of many abusive conditions. When the settlement was abandoned in 1777, the survivors came to the St. Augustine courts for relief. Those courts, and particularly the Court of Sessions, addressed the indentured servitude arrangement of Dr. Turnbull with his Minorcan employees, servants, or slaves. The courts dealt with insurrection matters as well.[12]

Following an earlier rebellion in the colony in 1768, a trial was held in January 1769. Three men, including Elia Medici, who killed a cow, which was then a capital offense, were sentenced to death. However, because of the manpower shortage, Medici was given a choice of executing the other two to spare his life. He chose this option, and the scene of kissing his co-defendant friends goodbye was described as most moving.[13]

As would be expected, the British used court names and established subject matter jurisdiction emanating from England. However, what is a bit surprising is that they established so many courts on such a sparsely populated frontier.

There were at least eight courts: 1) the Court of Common Pleas; 2) the Court of Chancery; 3) The Court of General Sessions of the peace, Oyer et Terminer, Assize, and General Gaol (means jail) Delivery; 4) Special Court of Oyer and Terminer; 5) the Court of Vice-Admiralty; 6) the Court of Ordinary; 7) the General Court; and 8) a District Court.[14]

The last endnote cites Professor Mirow's article in which he also points out that records from those courts were only recently rediscovered in the National Archives in London (Kew), and only those pertaining to the Court of Common Pleas have been studied. He also refers to the Proclamation of 7 October 1763, which created British-type governments, with courts and English law and procedures, in the various parts of North America where the British controlled the territory. Another point he noted is that the governor was to create courts modeled after the other colonies, and particularly Georgia. Mirow also covers the Scottish influence in the judiciary in the southeast of our future country and generally outlines the nature of each of the courts listed above.

A further word about those courts:

The Court of Common Pleas was the most important court of general civil jurisdiction, which in East Florida included the jurisdiction of Common Pleas, The King's Bench, and Exchequer in England, and was presided over by the Chief Justice.

The governor was the chief official of the Court of Chancery. That court handled cases pertaining to partnerships, guardianships, more complex administration of estates of decedents, and the detention of slaves and appeals to the Privy Council.

The Court of General Sessions (short for The Court of General Sessions of the peace, Oyer et Terminer, Assize, and General Gaol Delivery) handled most of the criminal matters.

The governor served as Vice Admiral, but at times it was ruled by judges and handled admiralty-type cases.

The governor was in charge of the Court of Ordinary. One reference questions if it was ever held, and another reference indicated it handled probate matters.

The General Court was the successor to the Court of General Sessions, above. It also summoned grand jurors and petit jurors for criminal matters.

Mirow also notes that there were justices of the peace who handled lower-level criminal cases and procedures. This concept would continue throughout the time Florida was a U.S. Territory and even a state until around the 1950s, and is covered more in future chapters of this book.

Lastly, there were appeal possibilities for the various British Courts. These typically involved appeals to the governor or the Privy Council (in London).[15]

A list of the English judges, really Chief Justices, in East Florida is set forth below:[16]

James Moultrie. Appointed October 31, 1764; died August 6, 1765.

William Grover. Formerly Chief Justice of Georgia (suspended in 1762); appointed 1766, died in New Providence, November 9, 1766.

William Drayton. Appointed by Governor Grant on Moultrie's death; given mandamus dated February 10, 1767, on Grover's death; commissioned, February 1, 1768; suspended February 13, 1776; reinstated June 1776; suspended December 16, 1777; resigned June 1778.

Rev. John Forbes. Acting Chief Justice in Drayton's absences, 1776 and 1777-1779.

James Hume. 1779-1783.

The St. Augustine courts also included the following court officials:

Henry Cunningham, Assistant Judge. Appointed June 10, 1766; died February 24, 1771.

Martin Jollie, Assistant Judge. Appointed December 20, 1768; absent, 1771-1775; resigned, March 31, 1776.

Francis Levett, Sr., Assistant Judge. Appointed March 4, 1771; absent after December 1773.

Rev. John Forbes, Assistant Judge. Appointed December 15, 1772. He was also the Judge of the Court of Admiralty, appointed April 30, 1771, and resigned in 1776 when he succeeded Drayton as Chief Justice.

Robert Catherwood, Assistant Judge. Appointed June 20, 1776; suspended January 1783.

Dr. Lewis Johnston, Assistant Judge. Appointed 1783.

Spencer Man, Clerk of the Court of Common Pleas. Appointed June 20, 1765. Suspended and replaced by Collins, below. Man was also the Public Vendue Master in 1771 and Master in Chancery, the latter appointment on May 22, 1772.

Dr. Andrew Turnbull, Clerk of the Court of Common Pleas. Appointed August 21, 1766 (by warrant; never acted), & Justice of the Peace.

William Collins, Clerk of the Crown and Court of Common Pleas. Mandamus, May 22, 1767; sworn in October 4, 1768; resigned February 11, 1769.

John Holmes, Clerk of the Court of Common Pleas. Appointed February 11, 1769.

Florida remained loyal to England throughout the Revolutionary War. On June 16, 1779, Spain entered the war against England on the Patriot side, hoping to reacquire its Florida colonies of East and West Florida. The Governor of Spanish Louisiana, Bernardo de Galvez, attacked the British at Pensacola in May of 1781, which was reportedly the site of the largest battle ever fought in Florida. By 1781, Spain had recaptured all of West Florida. Two years later, with the treaty ending the Revolutionary War, East Florida was also returned to Spain. It is interesting to note that just before the return of East Florida to Spanish rule, the last naval battle of the Revolutionary War was fought off Cape Canaveral on March 10, 1783.[17]

D. Second Spanish Period (1784-1819)

During the first year of the Second Spanish Period, a dual government regime existed. Governor Tonyn ruled the English group, situated on one side of town, which was preparing for evacuation. Spanish Governor Zespedes (which today would be spelled Cespedes), while ruling the rest of St. Augustine, appointed two English figures as judges to handle disputes involving British subjects. The issues typically involved debts or the rights pertaining to slaves. Those judges were John Leslie, a/k/a Don Juan Leslie, and

Francis Philip Fatio, a/k/a Don Francisco Filipe Facio. The British weren't always happy with those judges, as they answered to the Spanish governor and were not as well-versed in British law.[18]

Under Spanish rule, there was no separation of civil and military authority. While there were court cases, and trials were held at the now famous Government House, it was the governor who was the ultimate decision maker on judicial as well as all other government matters.

With the departure of the British in 1785, the population of East Florida fell to under 2,000, and many plantations were abandoned. The Spanish, then, like the British, encouraged agricultural development extending into the interior of Florida. In earlier times, to own land, one had to prove adequate financial resources and swear an oath of allegiance to Spain. Further, unlike the official policy of the Spanish Empire, the Spanish crown permitted non-Catholics to settle in Florida.[19] In 1790, the Spanish King liberalized land grants in Florida. He invited aliens regardless of religious affiliation.

By the early 1800s, because of the Spanish land grants, plantations began to flourish in the region along the Halifax and Tomoka Rivers. These areas would soon be a part of St. Johns and subsequently Mosquito Counties during the U.S. Territorial Period. These plantations were settled by a number of hardy individuals who had come from the Bahamas and obtained Spanish land grants. They included owners such as Bunch, Dummett, Darley, and Addison, who would be connected to the judiciary in Florida, and who are discussed in more detail in the next chapter.

One of the Spanish titles, The Fleming Grant, was issued for land in what is now the Sebastian, Florida area. This grant, made in 1816, resulted from Fleming's services to the crown, as well as his marrying into the influential Francisco Fatio family. More information on the Fleming Grant litigation is set forth in the next chapter.

Spain subsequently lost interest in Florida during its war with France, which was fought against Napoleon in the early 1800s. In 1803, the United States purchased the Louisiana Territory for $15 million from Napoleon. In the years following the purchase, the question arose whether the Louisiana Territory included that portion of West Florida extending east to the Pearl River or further east to the Perdido River. Claims to the disputed area of West Florida were made by the United States, Spain, and various communities desiring independence. President Madison, on October 27, 1810, issued a proclamation that West Florida was a part of the Louisiana Territory.

President James Madison requested that Spain cede Florida to the United States, and Congress gave President Madison the power to take Florida in defense of America. At the same time, some Georgians and Floridians established the Republic of Florida on the St. Mary's River. Fernandina, on Amelia Island at the mouth of St.

Mary's River, was held by a Spanish garrison, but on March 17, 1812, the Spanish surrendered to the United States forces. Following several more defeats, primarily at the hands of Andrew Jackson, Spain lost interest in Florida by 1819, as set forth in the next chapter.

E. Biographical Information - Judicial Figures of East Florida 1764 – 1784

Robert Catherwood, British East Florida Vice Admiralty Court Judge, 1776-1783

Robert Catherwood arrived in East Florida in 1764. He was an initial appointee of Governor James Grant to the Council of East Florida, where he served for most of the British Period. He also served as a judge in British East Florida. He took the place of John Forbes in the Vice-Admiralty Court in 1776 when Forbes was appointed Chief Justice. Catherwood served until 1783, when he was suspended, which was just before the end of the British Period.

Catherwood was also a surgeon and served primarily as a military surgeon, at the same time fulfilling his judicial duties. He was also caught in a scandal involving the handling of the proceeds of sales of captured slaves through the Court of Vice Admiralty under his supervision. That suspended his council and judicial functions.

William Collins, British East Florida Clerk of the Crown and Common Pleas, 1768

William Collins was in the horse sales business in St. Augustine during the British Period. In 1768, he took the oath as Clerk of the Crown and Common Pleas. After serving for less than one year, he was succeeded by John Holmes in 1769.

Henry Cunningham, British East Florida Assistant Judge, Court of Common Pleas, 1766

Cunningham likely came from Scotland, and he studied medicine at the University of Edinburgh in the 1740s and was a surgeon for the 20th Regiment of Foot, 1744-1752. He came to East Florida in the mid-1760s. He petitioned the East Florida Council for a land grant in October 1765, and he was granted 100 acres in March 1766. His wife was Margaret.

Dr. Henry Cunningham was appointed assistant judge of the courts of Common Pleas, General Sessions of the Peace (criminal), oyer and terminer (treason and felony), assize and general gaol (jail) delivery in 1766. At one time, he and Chief Justice William Drayton were specifically ordered by a royal commission to hold a special session of the Court of Oyer and Terminer at St. Augustine on August 11, for the trial of runaway slaves. He was also a deputy commissary at the Fort in St. Augustine. Cunningham died in February 1771.

William Drayton, British East Florida Chief Justice, 1768-1776 and 1776-1777

William Drayton was born at Magnolia on the Ashley River in South Carolina on March 21, 1732. He came from a prominent family. His grandfather and uncle were Lieutenant Governors of South Carolina. He was the son of Thomas Drayton and his father's first wife, Elizabeth Bull, who was the daughter of Lt. Governor William Bull of South Carolina.

William Drayton received his legal education in London. He was admitted to the Middle Temple on October 6, 1750. By 1756, he was practicing law in South Carolina. On October 4, 1759, he married Mary Motte, the daughter of the public treasurer of the province. They were the parents of nine, including William, discussed below.

Drayton moved to Florida in the 1760s and acquired three hundred acres of land near St. Augustine. He named the location Oak Hill.[20] He lived there while he was Chief Justice of East Florida, which lasted from 1768 to 1778, except that he did not serve continuously in that capacity because of suspensions by Governor Tonyn. Drayton was appointed by Governor Grant to take the place of Chief Justice Moultrie, who died in 1765. However, Drayton's appointment was not confirmed. He commenced serving under the appointment, notwithstanding William Grover, a former chief justice of Ga., being approved by the crown, as Grover died in a shipwreck on the way to East Florida and arguably only served nominally. Drayton formally took office in February 1768, but was suspended and reinstated a couple of times before resigning.[21] The Governors did not want a General Assembly, which was at odds with Chief Justice Drayton and Dr. Andrew Turnbull.[22]

During Governor Grant's rule, Drayton was one of the few to protest a lack of an assembly, which Grant was authorized to organize, and which existed in the other American colonies of the British, including West Florida. In 1768, Drayton declared that proclamations of the Governor's malleable council might stay in effect until an assembly could be organized, but that they were not legal. Grant, who was popular and did not have an outcry for an assembly, ignored Drayton's protestation.

Governor Patrick Tonyn suspended Drayton from office in 1776 on account of Drayton's participation in a plan to lease Indian lands on the St. Johns River. Drayton was a friend of Tonyn's arch-rival, Dr. Turnbull of the New Smyrna Colony. However, upon a protest to London, the Governor of East Florida was ordered to reinstate Drayton and pay him back salary. The Governor later suspended Drayton again (in 1777) from his judgeship for Drayton's refusal to try a case involving Dr. Andrew Turnbull and refugees from the New Smyrna Colony. (Drayton had directed another magistrate to try the case).

Drayton went to London again, but resigned from office in June of 1778 before his latter suspension was reviewed. He returned to East Florida, where his wife soon died. He continued as a part-time planter until selling his Oak Forest estate to Panton and Forbes, and moved to Charleston, South Carolina.[23] His second wife was Mary Grote, whom he married in 1780. They had one child, a daughter.

In South Carolina, Drayton took the American side against the British. He was made an Associate Justice of the Supreme Court of South Carolina. In 1786, he received a degree from the College of New Jersey, now Princeton. Drayton also designed the courthouse in Charleston. Justice Drayton was appointed by George Washington as the first judge of the United States District Court for the District of South Carolina. He served in that capacity from 1789 until he died in 1790.

Drayton's son, William, was educated in England and admitted to the bar. William served as a colonel and inspector general in the War of 1812. He was the recorder of Charleston in 1819. He served in Congress from 1825 until 1833. William later moved to Pennsylvania and was briefly President of the (Second) U.S. Bank in 1839. He died in 1846.

Francis Philip Fatio, A Spanish Judge for the British, 1784

Francis Philip Fatio, a/k/a Don Francisco Felipe Facio, was a native of Switzerland, born by Lake Geneva in 1723. He moved to St. Augustine, where he was a planter. He had a house in St. Augustine, a 10,000-acre New Switzerland Plantation, and a 500-acre Castle Plantation on the St. Johns River. He was the father of what turned out to be a very prominent Florida family for generations to come. His wife was an Italian, Maria Magdalena Crispel, who was born in approximately 1728.

One of the Fatio daughters, Mary Magdalene, married Judge Dunham, who is discussed in the next chapter. Daughter Sophia Filipina, who was born in London in approximately 1767, married George Fleming, an Irishman born in approximately 1761, after whom a Spanish land grant in now Indian River County was named. See the next chapter.

As mentioned above, Fatio was appointed judge by incoming Spanish Governor Zespedes to handle British disputes during the transition period of the British vacating St. Augustine. While controversial with the British, he was trusted enough to be a secret straw man, taking title to properties which British subjects weren't yet able to sell prior to their mandatory vacating of East Florida, and holding title for the benefit of those British evacuees.

John Forbes, British East Florida Vice Admiralty Judge, 1771; Assistant Judge, Courts of Common Pleas and General Sessions, 1772; and Chief Justice, 1776 and 1777-1779

Rev. John Forbes was born in Scotland around 1740. He was the son of John Forbes of Newe. His mother was Anne Grant, the sister of the future East Florida Governor James Grant. Forbes' parents were married in 1735. Forbes' mother died in 1775.

John Forbes was educated at King's College in Aberdeen. In 1763, he received his Master of Arts degree from the University of Aberdeen and qualified as a minister.

In December of that year in London, his uncle, Colonel James Grant of Ballindallock, took the oath as the first Governor of East Florida. The following spring, Forbes was recommended by the Propagation of the Gospel in Foreign Parts to the position of Minister to St. Augustine. He was the first British clergyman licensed to officiate in East Florida. Grant and Forbes likely left together for St. Augustine in August 1764.

With Forbes' arrival, Protestant services were held in St. Augustine for the first time in two hundred years. In November 1764, Forbes was made a Justice of the Peace. In May 1765, he was made a member of the Governor's Council,[24] a position he would hold until returning to England in 1783.

In early 1766, Forbes received a land grant from the governor for property at Charlotte and Aviles Streets in St. Augustine. That summer, Forbes became ill from the hot weather and traveled north to recuperate.

A few years later, he went north again, this time to marry Dorothy or Dolly Murray, the daughter of James Murray. Mr. Murray was a planter and landowner in North Carolina, Boston, and Scotland, who had come to America from Scotland and England in 1735. Forbes and his wife were married outside of Boston, and more particularly, at her aunt's property at Brush Hill, outside of Milton, Massachusetts. Governor Grant was the godfather of the Forbes' firstborn, James Grant Forbes.

In 1770, Forbes acquired a land grant of 1,000 acres. In April of 1771, he acquired another lot. At the same time, he was appointed First Judge of the Court of Vice Admiralty, a post that Grant established at that time.

Wright, in his "British St. Augustine," has written:

Royal Navy warships and swift privateers brought in prizes to the East Florida capital for condemnation. Saint Augustine had a vice-admiralty court, for long periods, the only one on the Atlantic Coast in the south. Acting as vice-admiralty court judge, supplementing his salary from fees, and reaping the rewards of this world and the next, Rev. John Forbes handed down condemnation verdicts with gusto. Merchandise, powder, slaves, and especially foodstuffs made available to the citizenry from these prizes were a godsend.[25]

By 1772, Forbes was minister to the Turnbull Colony at the Mosquitoes; was assistant judge of two courts, Common Pleas and General Sessions; Grand Master of the Masonic Lodge, and a member of the Governor's Council. He was also the youngest minister in the area, preceding many Anglican ministers who were added to serve the growing military and civilian populations.

By 1773, the Forbes family had two sons, James Grant Forbes and John Murray Forbes, and the couple was expecting a third. Mr. Murray wanted his daughter in Boston, to which Rev. Forbes apparently agreed. However, Forbes insisted on keeping the older boy. April 27, 1773, was the last time Forbes would see his wife, who was then carrying their third son, Ralph Bennet Forbes.

Forbes acted for a period of time as Chief Justice of East Florida, in 1776 and 1777-1779. He was called on to fill the vacancies occasioned by the suspension of Justice Drayton.

During the Revolutionary War, religious ministerial duties were handled by others, as Forbes was preoccupied with his official positions at the capital of East Florida. He was also supervising his 6,000 acres and sixty slaves and was busy renting his other property in St. Augustine to refugees and enemy prisoners.

Forbes was a republican ideologue and suspected of being loyal to the American cause, so his appointments as Chief Justice were never confirmed. As a result, another chief justice, James Hume, was sent from England in 1779 or 1780. Hume was loyal to the royal cause.

Following the Revolutionary War, Dorothy Forbes, who had remained a loyalist to the crown, followed General Howe to Halifax. While Mr. Murray recommended that his daughter and her sons return to Florida, it never happened. On July 17, 1783, John Forbes returned to England with his son, James. James, then aged fifteen, was placed in a school near London. John Forbes died on September 17, 1783, in Norwich, England.

James Forbes subsequently attended Harvard, as well as his brother John Murray Forbes. Brother, Ralph Bennet Forbes, who married into the prominent Massachusetts merchant family, the Perkins, is best known for his son, Robert Bennet Forbes. A Milton, Massachusetts, National landmark, *The Captain Robert Bennet Forbes House*, was built in 1833 and is named after Rev. John Forbes's grandson. It has been written that, "If one excepts public office, there are few American families whose careers, individually and collectively, can equal those of the Rev. John Forbes of East Florida."[26]

William Grover, British East Florida Judge, 1766

William Grover was a former Chief Justice of Georgia who was suspended in 1762. In 1766, he was appointed a judge in British East Florida. He died in New Providence (Bahamas) on November 9, 1766, after being shipwrecked on his way to Florida.

John Holmes, British East Florida Justice of the Peace, 1764, and Clerk of the Court of Common Pleas and Royal Pleas, 1769

John Holmes was a member of the original Council of East Florida, being appointed by Governor Grant in October 1764. He served through the administrations of Governor Grant, Lt. Governor Moultrie, and most of Governor Tonyn's administration. Gov. Grant also appointed Holmes Commissioner of Peace (Justice of the Peace).

In 1765, Holmes obtained a grant of a town lot in St. Augustine. In February 1769, he was appointed as Clerk of the Common Pleas and Royal Pleas. In 1770, he obtained a grant of 300 acres, which property was subsequently the subject of two "Loyalist Claims" by him following the end of the British Period. He was successful in being awarded compensation.

James Hume, British East Florida Chief Justice, 1779-1783

James Hume was likely from Scotland. He practiced law in Georgia and was a member of its council and acting Attorney General there, but was a loyalist and expelled from Georgia in 1776 for not accepting the provisional congress's supervision of the courts.[27] He subsequently became the last British chief justice of the English twenty-year rule of East Florida. He was likely appointed Chief Justice of East Florida in 1779 when the acting Chief Justice, John Forbes's appointment, was not confirmed.

After a year as chief justice, Hume delegated the signing of writs to John Holmes, who was the clerk of pleas. Hume was on the Council in the upper house of the General Assembly and was involved in controversies over the power of the lower house usurping legislative power.[28]

In an early controversy involving the Spanish takeover of British East Florida, Hume thought that the turning over of the territory to the newly appointed Spanish Governor Zespedes was effective upon Zespedes' presenting of official papers from King George III to the outgoing British Governor Tonyn, which occurred on June 27, 1784. Zespedes, however, insisted upon the vacating of the Castillo de San Marcos[29] before he took control, which occurred on July 11, 1784.

A more heated controversy arose with Governor Zespedes over the Governor's proclamation on the Negro population dated July 26, 1784. The proclamation, *inter alia*, forbade any person from embarking as a passenger without a license signed by the governor. The proclamation also affected the ownership of Negroes and

Mulattos and provided for fines to be paid to informers and the judges appointed by Zespedes. The latter part particularly annoyed Hume, and, as a result, Zespedes did not vigorously enforce the proclamation.

Hume owned a sixty-acre estate located approximately four miles north of St. Augustine called "Oak Forest." It occupied the two miles between the North and San Sebastian Rivers (not to be confused with the river of the same name on the edge of Indian River County). It had parks, orange groves, swampy rice lands, and dairy cattle. However, most of the production came from the tall oaks that were sold for firewood. The estate was surrounded by a fence that had oriental-styled ornaments.

Hume died in Berwickshire, Scotland, in 1838.

Lewis Johnston, British East Florida Assistant Judge, 1783

Dr. Lewis Johnston was from Edinburgh and came to East Florida by way of Georgia. He was a merchant and may not have had a medical degree. He helped create settlements in St. Kitts and Georgia.

Johnston served as an assistant judge in St. Augustine from 1783 until the end of the British Period. His appointment came about when Robert Catherwood was suspended from the Court of Vice Admiralty. Dr. Johnston returned to Scotland via Jamaica. Jamaica, incidentally, was the initial destination of a number of loyalist refugees from Mosquito Inlet (present-day Ponce de Leon Inlet, between New Smyrna Beach and Daytona Beach) following the British Period.

Martin Jollie, British East Florida Assistant Judge, appointed 1768, absent 1771-1775, resigned 1776

Martin Jollie, the son of an Edinburgh tailor, spent time in Georgia and East Florida. He was an assistant judge, as well as a member of the Council in British East Florida. He was an agent of Lord Egmont's plantations consisting of thousands of acres, and particularly a tract on the St. Johns River, which Jollie found, which was called Mount Royal.

Jollie was loyal to Dr. Andrew Turnbull and Chief Justice Drayton while serving under Governor Tonyn. Jollie, as a Council Member, voted against a suspension of Turnbull as Clerk of the Council and Secretary of the Province by Governor Tonyn. Jollie resigned his seat from the Council as well as from the bench as assistant judge, because of the incident.

Carita Doggett, in her "The New Smyrna Colony in Florida," has written, "This was certainly the action of a brave man, as well as a loyal friend, for one does not find people who are participants in an unrighteous cause sacrificing themselves so promptly. Undoubtedly,

Mr. Jollie had reason to believe that Governor Tonyn's actions would not be upheld in England."[30]

For the reason above, Jollie gave up, or perhaps lost his jobs in Florida, both governmental and as a plantation agent, and by spending too much time in Ga.[31] He was also captured during the Revolutionary War when his plantation was invaded. He was taken prisoner to Savannah, from which he was released in 1778. Being a loyalist to the crown, Jollie took refuge on Exuma Island in the Bahamas following the British Period. He died in Edinburgh in 1806.

John Leslie, Spanish East Florida Judge, 1784

John Leslie, a/k/a Don Juan Leslie, was born in Scotland in approximately 1751. He was a British merchant in St. Augustine during the second half of the British period. By the end of the British period, his trading firm, known as Panton, Leslie and Company, enjoyed a monopoly and was referred to as a "trading colossus[32]" on account of its trading business with the Indians. The firm was started in Frederica, Georgia, in approximately 1774, but maintained a London office, with partner Thomas Forbes.

When the Spanish (again) took over East Florida after 1783, Leslie was one of the British subjects who stayed with his estate to make a new life under the Spanish regime.[33] He was then known as

Don Juan Leslie. The 1786 census shows Leslie as single and a merchant.[34]

Leslie was bilingual and could easily obtain tangible personal property, so useful for the mercantile trade business. He also had great influence with the Indians, and he showed great favor with the new Spanish Governor, Zespedes. In 1784, Zespedes appointed Leslie and Francisco P. Fatio as judges, to handle disputes among the British subjects. This typically involved questions of slave ownership.[35]

During the governorship of Zespedes, Panton, Leslie, and Company operated a store south of Lake George (south of Palatka). The firm was also dominant in the Pensacola region.

Leslie left St. Augustine in 1789 and died in London in 1803. He was survived by his wife, Elisabeth Cain of East Florida, who followed Leslie in death two years later.[36]

Francis Levett, Sr., British East Florida Assistant Judge, 1771-1774

Francis Levett, Sr. came to British East Florida in early 1769 with his son, Francis, Jr. The senior Levett stayed until June 1785. He was the brother-in-law of Gov. Tonyn and was sent to Florida as the plantation agent for Lord Egmont, replacing Jollie.[37] Thus, he was a planter and manager of plantations, as well as on the council and an assistant judge, serving from March 4, 1771, until 1774. He had a 10,000-acre plantation estate at Julianton Creek and the St. Johns

River, and a townhouse. (This area, originally named after his wife Julia, today is known as the Julington (yes, a difference in the spelling) Creek Plantation Park south of Jacksonville.)

Levett Sr. was accused of appropriating property for his own behalf and left the area in 1773 for the Carolinas and Rhode Island. He returned in 1774 to both resign his offices and straighten out his legal problems through arbitration. He died shortly thereafter and left his property to his son, who continued the plantation known as Julianton.

It is likely the younger Levett suffered a loss on board the schooner "Providence." He also asserted a claim in England for the loss of his lot, house, and servants in St. Augustine following the end of the British Period.

Spencer Man, British East Florida Clerk of the Court of Common Pleas, 1765; Master in the Court of Chancery, 1771; and Clerk of the Crown, 1772

Spencer Man was an English attorney who was commissioned as clerk of courts of common pleas, general sessions of the peace, oyer and terminer, assize, and general gaol delivery on June 20, 1765, at St. Augustine by Governor James Grant. He was also the clerk of the crown until the royal pleasure should be known. He was the Public

Vendue (auction) Master in 1771. On May 22, 1771, he was also appointed master in the court of chancery.

Man subsequently served as a Justice of the Peace. In that role, he was one of two to hear the twenty-one depositions between May 9 and 20, 1777, in connection with the grievances filed by the New Smyrna colonists against Dr. Turnbull. Man was subsequently placed on Governor Tonyn's list of traitors; that is, one of those loyal to Turnbull.

James Moultrie, British East Florida Chief Justice, 1764-1765

James Moultrie and his brothers were the sons of a distinguished South Carolina family. Their father, John Moultrie, was a physician who had emigrated from Seafield, Scotland, in 1728 to South Carolina. The father was born in 1702 and died in 1771. John's first wife was Divertia Cooper, to whom he was married in 1728. She died in 1747. His second wife was Elizabeth Mathews, whom he married in 1748. She died in 1787.

James' brother, John Moultrie, was born in 1720 and followed in his father's footsteps, obtaining a degree in medicine from Edinburgh University. John was persuaded to come to Florida by his friend, James Grant, the first British Governor of Florida. The Governor felt that these high-quality additions to the area would help to attract other planters as well as bring skilled labor and enslaved people to help make the colony a commercial success.[38] Brothers John and James Moultrie were present for Governor Grant's inauguration on October 31, 1764, and each was thereafter appointed to the governor's council. John Moultrie helped organize East Florida and, as Lieutenant Governor of East Florida, replaced Grant as governor when Grant returned to England for health reasons.

James Moultrie became chief justice of the court of common pleas and president of the council. James had two children, James Moultrie and Annabelle Havleston. Another Moultrie brother, William Moultrie, born in 1730 and died in 1805, was a general on the American side during the Revolutionary War and subsequently became Governor of South Carolina. Brother, Alexander Moultrie was a colonel on the American side during the Revolution and spent 18 months as a British prisoner in St. Augustine.

The Moultrie land grant on the Tomoka River was a plantation called "Rosetta." Seventy slaves worked the rice and indigo fields. The Moultries also had land grants elsewhere on the Tomoka and Halifax Rivers. John Moultrie's mansion was called "Bella Vista." Moultrie land would become famous in 1823 as a result of the first Seminole War. Not only was there a Fort Moultrie, but the treaty of peace with the Seminoles became known as the Treaty of Moultrie Creek.

Andrew Turnbull, British East Florida Clerk of the Court of Common Pleas and Clerk of the Crown, 1767, and Justice of the Peace

Dr. Andrew Turnbull, who has been called "Florida's first developer,"[39] was a wealthy physician from Dundee, Scotland. He was born on December 2, 1720, the son of Andrew Turnbull.

Turnbull had two partners, Sir William Temple and Sir William Duncan. On June 18, 1767, Turnbull obtained from the Privy Council a land grant of 20,000 acres at Mosquito Inlet. He arrived with his wife and family in November of 1767 to claim the land. In 1767, Governor Grant made Turnbull a member of the governor's council and clerk of the court of common pleas and clerk of the crown. Turnbull then left his family in St. Augustine, returned to Europe, and organized for his planned colony.

In 1768, Turnbull brought 1,403 Minorcans, Italians, and Greeks to New Smyrna as indentured servants to establish the largest private settlement in America and to run a plantation. Dr. Turnbull established New Smyrna Colony at Mosquito Inlet, sixty miles south of St. Augustine. He named the settlement in honor of the birthplace of his (second) wife, Gracia Dura Bin, who was born in the 1730s in Smyrna, Asia Minor. Turnbull had thirteen children.

Governor Grant and Justice Drayton were friendly to Dr. Turnbull, but future Governor Moultrie was not. Turnbull was also a Justice of the Peace. When Governor Grant fell ill, Moultrie took over the governorship and made life difficult for Turnbull. Moultrie's successor, Governor Tonyn, was also an enemy of Turnbull.

Over the nine years of the colony's existence, there were crop failures, political problems, revolts, punishments, sickness, and death. Because of irrigation problems, Turnbull created a canal system made from coquina stone, which still exists but is largely covered by Canal Street in New Smyrna Beach. The colony was ultimately abandoned, and the colonists retreated to St. Augustine.

Turnbull, who moved to South Carolina along with his good friend William Drayton, died on March 13, 1792, in Charleston, South Carolina. His wife followed him in death on August 2, 1798. They were buried in St. Philip's Church Cemetery in Charleston.

Andrew Turnbull – Courtesy of Florida State Archives

Chapter 2 - U.S. Territorial Florida

A. Territorial Florida (1819-1845)

Following the Battle of New Orleans, where he became a hero, General Andrew Jackson led invasions into Spanish Florida in 1814 and 1818. He tried to keep law and order, fighting on occasion with the Seminole Indians, the British, and the Spanish.

The 1818 incursion is known as the First Seminole War. On April 8, 1818, Jackson and his troops occupied the Spanish fort at St. Mark's (south of Tallahassee), despite the protest of the Spanish commander. Jackson's activities were instrumental in convincing His Catholic Majesty of Spain to cede Florida to the United States. The United States, in turn, exonerated Spain from all claims of citizens to an amount not exceeding $5 million. On February 22, 1819, the Adams-Onis Treaty was signed by the United States and Spain and ratified exactly two years later.

On March 10, 1821, Andrew Jackson became the first United States Commissioner and temporary (or military) governor of the territories of East and West Florida. Jackson was appointed by President James Monroe in connection with establishing the temporary government.[40]

On May 18, 1821, President Monroe named the first two federal judges. The Judge of East Florida was William DuVal, a member of the Kentucky Bar since the age of 20 and a representative of that state in Congress from 1813 to 1815. Eligius Fromentin, an ex-Catholic priest from France who had been a U.S. Senator from Louisiana from 1813 to 1819, was named as Judge of West Florida.[41] Prior to 1821, Florida had been generally divided into east and west, with what were essentially the province seats of Pensacola in the west and St. Augustine in the east.

On July 11, 1821, Major General Andrew Jackson formally accepted sovereignty over Florida on behalf of the United States. On July 21, 1821, General Jackson, via Ordinance, ordained that there were two counties, one named Escambia, lying between the Perdito and Suwannee Rivers, and the other falling east of the Suwannee River, called St. Johns,[42] after San Juan Bautista, a Catholic saint.[43] The ordinance established a county court in each county composed of five justices of the peace, any three of whom constituted a quorum.[44]

By a congressional act of March 30, 1822, the territorial government of Florida was established. William P. DuVal of Kentucky was commissioned by President James Monroe on April 17, 1822, as first governor for the permanent territorial government of Florida, whose duties he assumed on June 20, 1822. (There was a brief interim acting governor following Andrew Jackson, when Jackson may have appointed William G.D. Worthington to that position on May 27, 1822, the day Jackson gave his farewell address.[45] However, another source indicates that Worthington was appointed Governor and Secretary of East Florida by President Monroe in 1821.)[46] The congressional act also established that the judicial power in Florida was vested in two superior courts, each consisting of one judge appointed by the President of the United States, with the advice and consent of the Senate, and such lower courts and justices of the peace as deemed necessary by the Legislative Council of the territory.[47]

The superior court had the broadest jurisdiction, unlike in the existing U.S. states, where a number of issues, such as land claims, many different crimes, and contract issues, were typically state court matters handled in state courts. Remember, this superior court in Florida was a federal territorial court. Some thought at the time that there was too much power in one judge.[48] See a few pages below discussing the lower courts established not by the federal government, but by the Florida Legislative Council.

The Superior Court of East Florida was to meet on the first Monday of January, April, July, and October at St. Augustine, and at such other times and places as the Legislative Council was to direct. A Superior Court in West Florida held forth in a similar fashion at Pensacola.[49] Congress amended the act establishing the territorial government of Florida on March 3, 1823.[50] Each act allowed for direct appeals from the Superior Court to the Supreme Court of the United States. However, the amended act limited those appeals to controversies where the amount exceeded one thousand dollars.

The first session of Florida's Legislative Council met on July 22, 1822, at Pensacola. In order to attend, it took the members from St. Augustine 59 days of traveling by water. The session, *inter alia*, resulted in the formation of two new counties: Duval, which was carved from St. Johns County, and Jackson, which was taken out of Escambia County.

The second Legislative session met at St. Augustine the following year. This time, the western delegates were shipwrecked in the passage around the peninsula of Florida. At this session, the council decided to locate the capital halfway between St. Augustine and Pensacola. In fact, two individuals left at approximately the same time from Pensacola and St. Augustine, respectively, and met halfway to select the site, a small Indian village called Tallahassee.[51]

By the 1820s, a great deal of salvage activities permeated the Florida Keys. On May 7, 1822, a United States Custom District was established at Key West. On July 4, 1823, the Florida Legislative Council and Governor did not believe that the federal territorial courts possessed exclusive jurisdiction over admiralty matters and authorized a court to assemble juries, consisting of a notary and 5 jurors, to determine the disposition of salvage claims. This jurisdiction was successfully challenged before the District Court of South Carolina, and the salvage award was declared a nullity. However, it was reversed in the United States Court of Appeals. The Supreme Court of the United States reversed that decision, ruling that the Key West court created by the Florida Legislature could not possess admiralty jurisdiction. As alluded to, the case involved an award by a notary and five jurors in Key West, granting salvage of cotton from a ship that was wrecked off the coast of Florida.[52] The Supreme Court of the United States said that admiralty jurisdiction was only proper in a true federal court.

The federal act establishing the territorial government of Florida was further amended on May 26, 1824, to provide for three superior courts and to organize a court of appeals, composed of superior court judges.[53] The judicial territories of the superior court were then broken into the land west of the Apalachicola River, the territory between the Apalachicola River and the Suwannee River, and the land east and south of the Suwannee River.[54] The latter applied to this area and was the Superior Court of the Eastern District of Florida.

The third Legislative Council, which was the first legislative session convened in Tallahassee, occurred in November of 1824.[55] On December 29, 1824, the Legislative Council created four new counties: Alachua, Monroe, Mosquito, and Leon. This meant that the land which is now in Indian River County changed from St. Johns

County to Mosquito County. The initial county seat for Mosquito County was John Bunch's home in New Smyrna.

In 1826, to protect the interests of shipowners, Congress vested exclusive admiralty jurisdiction in the Superior Court at St. Augustine. On May 23, 1828, at the urging of shippers who sought a more convenient forum near the stream of commerce, Congress created a Southern Federal Superior Court with its seat in Key West. The act creating the Southern District included territory from that part of the Eastern District, "south of the line from Indian River on the east, and Charlotte Harbor on the west, including the latter harbor."[56]

While that description is vague on where the line intersected the Indian River, and it may have been referring to Indian River Colony which seemed to come a little later - under the Armed Occupation Act of 1842, discussed below), it is likely that the area which now comprises Indian River County, then being a part of Mosquito County, remained in the Eastern District. That would also seem plausible because the line would probably be horizontal across Florida. It is largely an academic question, however, as there was sparse activity in 1828 in what would become Indian River County. While it is later than the 1828 act, there is an 1837 map, as mentioned under the bio of John Lee Williams below, which shows an "Indian River" where the inlet area was in the Ft. Pierce vicinity.

I also found no appellate case where the appeal was from this area, aside from the Fleming's Grant, Fleming's Heirs case, discussed further herein, which did emanate from the Eastern District. The Eastern (Federal Judicial) District did not change throughout the balance of the Territorial Period ending in 1845.

The Judges of the Superior Court of the Eastern District, whose biographical information is set forth at the end of this chapter, were as follows:

William Pope DuVal	1821 to 1822
Joseph Lee Smith	1823 to 1832
Robert Raymond Reid	1832 to 1839
Isaac Hopkins Bronson	1840 to 1845

The appointment of the clerk of the federal court was initially very controversial. The first federal court clerk was named by the provisional governor, Andrew Jackson, on July 19, 1821. John Miller was named clerk of West Florida. This selection was made prior to a judge being appointed by Jackson or President Monroe, with Monroe having had the Congressional authority, to Jackson's dismay. The clerk's position was very important in connection with the Spanish handing over documents, particularly pertaining to land claims and the propensity for fraud with these records. Thereafter, the acting governor for East Florida similarly filled the clerk's position for the other federal court, which was in St. Johns County. Some references show that the first Superior Court Clerk in East Florida was an Englishman, George Gibbs.[57]

The first eastern district federal judge, former congressman William Pope DuVal, reacted angrily to the then-appointment under Jackson's authority of a clerk, although the judge's power to appoint a clerk was then unclear. Other references show a Virginian, James S. Tingle, appointed as clerk by Jackson in East Florida. That reference is in the same book just noted in connection with Gibbs being appointed clerk, described in the preceding paragraph.[58]

As previously noted, DuVal believed it was his duty to reject any clerk so appointed by Jackson (the governor), as opposed to a clerk appointed by the judge. Jackson's position seemed to prevail until DuVal went on to replace Jackson as territorial governor, which then made the controversy moot. Later, Congress acted and specified that judges of the federal court could designate the clerk. Other eastern district federal court clerks, prior to statehood, included Major John Beard, who served until 1842 and was followed by his future son-in-law, George Fairbanks (see his biographical information).

During the so-called Territorial Period, both Federal "Superior Courts" and a number of seemingly state-like territorial courts existed. Florida was not a state at that time, but as mentioned,

Congress authorized[59] the Territorial Legislative Council to create a number of courts that were in existence at various times. It has been written:

> During the Territorial Period, five courts functioned in Florida. One, the Circuit Court, existed for less than a year; three, the County Court, the Superior Court, and the Court of Appeals were abolished at the end of the Territorial Period; only one, the Justice of the Peace Court, survived the transition from Territorial to State Government.
>
> The territory court of appeals for the Territory of Florida was established by the U.S. Congress on 26 May 1824 (4 U.S. Stat. 45). The court was composed of five judges of the superior court of the districts of Florida (eastern and western established 1822; middle 1824, southern 1828, and Apalachicola 1838). The first (appellate) court met on 1 March 1825. The court heard appeals from decisions rendered in the superior courts. The judges examined... the territorial court of appeals was replaced by the Florida Supreme Court in 1845.[60]

There were many difficulties in the overlap or the exclusivity of jurisdiction between territory officials and officials appointed by the federal government. This exhibited itself not only in the appointment of clerks of court,[61] the jurisdiction of the courts over the subject matter,[62] but in the enforcement of the law by the U.S. Marshall and territorial sheriffs.[63]

Insofar as the law to be applied in Florida, the Governor and Legislative Council of the Territory of Florida in 1829 borrowed the common and statutory laws of England, of a "general" as opposed to "of a local nature," as they existed, down to July 4, 1776 (American Independence). These laws were to be in full force and effect so long as the common law was not inconsistent with the Constitution, the laws of the United States, and the acts of the Legislature of Florida brought forward by the first legislature after Florida became a territory.[64] Thus, while Florida was not yet a state in 1829, it then had laws dating back 1000 years.[65]

Prior to the adoption of the common law in Florida, which was imported from England, Florida law essentially was a colonial version of Spanish law. Spanish law rested on the Civil Law system that Spain had inherited from ancient Rome. Since the succession treaty with Spain required the United States and Florida to honor legal rights that had been adopted under the earlier Spanish law, for many years, lawsuits in Florida involved the interpretation of Spanish law. This occurred most commonly in disputes over land that had been obtained when Spanish law was in effect.[66] Jackson was a proponent of continuing with the colonial version of Spanish law, while DuVal pushed for the adoption of the common law of England.

As early as the 1830s, there was a land claim before the Superior Court of East Florida that affected property in what is now Indian River County, Florida. In that case, the Superior Court for the Eastern District of Florida ruled on a claim involving 20,000 acres of land situated on the banks of the St. Sebastian River adjacent to the Indian River, also known as the "Ys" River, between the eastern coast of Florida and the St. Johns River. The Federal District Court held that the title was granted on September 24, 1816, by a Spanish Governor, Governor Coppinger, to George Fleming, the ancestor of the Plaintiffs. The Eastern District decided that the title was valid and confirmed it in the Plaintiffs. The matter then went to the Supreme Court of the United States, and Chief Justice John Marshall delivered the brief opinion that affirmed the decision of the Superior Court of the Eastern District of Florida.[67]

The decision of the Supreme Court of the United States did not end all controversy involving the Fleming Grant. The ruling on the title did not address a surveyor's error, which, in effect, caused the deletion of valuable Indian River frontage property from the grant. A Spanish surveyor, Andres Burgevin, surveyed the property in February of 1820, which included a generous portion of Indian River frontage. The American government, which took over Spanish

Florida in 1821, did not survey the property until 1844. Because of the boundary problem, the title question really was not settled until 1926 when President Herbert Hoover signed a patent. During this lengthy period of the title dispute, a portion of the property was acquired by Dempsey Cain, a possible squatter, who carved out 20 acres and secured title to it. However, see this endnote.[68]

This 20,000-acre parcel is still known today as the "Fleming Land Grant" and is shown on the maps of the county, prepared by R. D. Carter, Vero Beach, Florida, in 1946, as Fleming's Grant, and forms an irregular diamond-shaped parcel running diagonally from the normal north-south sectional, quarter-sectional, and township and range lines.

The 1827 Map of Florida, according to the Latest Authorities by Finley,[69] shows Mosquito County extending as far west as Port Charlotte Harbor, although not including the Tampa Bay area, which was part of Alachua County. Mosquito County extended north on the east coast to meet St. Johns County near the north end of what is now Lake Como. The southeast boundary of Mosquito County was where it met Monroe County around present-day Ft. Lauderdale. By 1830, Mosquito County was, in large part, devoted to the cultivation of sugar. The population of this large county was approximately 1,000, of which half were slaves.[70]

It has been reported that the first Mosquito County officials were appointed by Governor William P. DuVal in 1833. There is evidence, however, that George Anderson, James Darby, and Duncan McCrae were named as Mosquito County judges and that James Ormond was named clerk in 1828.[71] However, those offices were vacated by the Laws of Florida, 1829, changing the organization of the county courts. The Judge of the County Court in 1833 was David R. Dunham of New Smyrna, and the clerk was Joseph Hunter, who had a plantation on the Mosquitos.[72] A later Mosquito County Presiding Justice was Douglas Dummett, commissioned on February 26, 1844. One of the Mosquito County Justices of the Peace commissioned that same year was Nathaniel C. Scobie. (Dummett's father, Thomas, a relative of Scobie, was buried near him in St. Augustine).

There were insufficient county courthouses during the territorial timeframe, especially as the number of counties increased. Court business was conducted in adjacent counties in those instances for both financial and security reasons. For example, court for Mosquito County, which should have taken place in New Smyrna in 1835, had to be moved to St. Augustine, the seat of St. Johns County, because of the threat of Indian attacks during the Second Seminole War.[73] Court business for St. Lucia County, and later Brevard County, was also moved to the courthouse in St. Johns County (St. Augustine). This may explain why, on a list of justices of the peace in the mid-

1830s, which justices had the power to hold court as county court judges, but which county judge positions were once abolished by an Act on November 9, 1829, does not list Mosquito County.[74] However, the 1833 list includes Benjamin A. Putnam, John C. Cleland, George Anderson, John Lee Williams, John J. Bulow, William Williams, Joseph Hunter, and Douglas Dummett in St. Johns County, who were known to have been connected to the Judiciary for Mosquito County and subsequently St. Lucie and Brevard County.[75]

By December of 1837, Florida's Second Seminole War was completing its second year. New Smyrna was still the Mosquito County seat. However, Fort Ann, near the future county seat of Titusville, was active. From that fort, some soldiers were sent south, which brought about the birth of "Ft. Pierce," another future county seat. More particularly, on January 2, 1838, blockhouses made of Palmetto logs on a bluff near the Indian River Inlet were named after the leader of an artillery unit which had just come from Fort Ann, that is, Benjamin K. Pierce. Pierce was the older brother of the future President, Franklin Pierce.[76]

Because of the financial drain of maintaining forts such as Fort New Smyrna and Fort Pierce, Missouri's senator, Thomas Hart Benton, commenced working on the passage of an armed occupation act to encourage hardy farmers to defend the Florida soil from

Indians. Passage of such a congressional act, however, took several years. The act is described below.

New Smyrna remained the county seat of Mosquito County, and the records remained in St. Augustine until 1843, when the legislative council directed that the records be turned over to the proper officials in Enterprise, which was then named the county seat.[77] Enterprise is located on the north bank of Lake Monroe, between present-day Debary and Deltona.

The first Florida territorial constitution was written in 1838 at St. Joseph in anticipation of statehood, which came in 1845. It provided in connection with a judicial department that, "[t]he state should be divided into at least four convenient circuits, and until other circuits shall be provided for by the General Assembly, the arrangement of the circuit court shall be the western, middle, eastern and southern circuits..." each one staffed by an appointed circuit judge to be paid not less than $2,000.00 per year.[78] It set forth the court's jurisdiction and provided for a majority of the circuit judges to comprise the Supreme Court, which, having no chief justice, would convene occasionally for the purpose of reviewing each other's decisions. The Constitution provided that the circuit judges were to be elected by the Legislature.

In 1840, there were no inhabitants of Mosquito County, except the military, which occupied the posts of Fort Pierce and New

Smyrna.[79] However, it has been noted that Mosquito County did have its own officials in 1840. Henry A. Crane was County Clerk. Douglas Dummett was the Judge. John C. Houston of Enterprise was the Sheriff. Henry Crane served as Clerk, not only in Mosquito County, but through St. Lucie County's initial formation up to the formation of Brevard County. However, another record indicates that only three votes were cast in the election of 1840 in Mosquito County.[80] By 1842, the number of county judges, auctioneers, justices of the peace, and public notaries in Florida had reached 418. In Mosquito County, there were four justices of the peace. (The total Florida electorate voting in 1843 for territorial delegates was 4,544).[81]

Another reference to the sparseness of legal and even "extralegal" (a euphemism for lynching) proceedings for this area, throughout the Antebellum years of 1821 through 1861, is the statistics for executions. There appear to be none or no statistics for Mosquito, St. Lucia, or Brevard Counties during that time frame, despite a number of executions in other counties (22 Whites plus 25 Blacks in the legal category and more than 12 Whites and more than 12 Blacks in the extralegal category).[82]

Congress passed the Armed Occupation Act, which took effect on August 4, 1842.[83] According to the Act, any head of family or single man age 1-99 or over was able to claim 160 acres of land south of the line running between Gainesville and Palatka. The Act provided that the claimant had to live on the land for five years and put at least five acres under cultivation. The act resulted in a number of hearty pioneer families settling along the Indian River, in what is now St. Lucie County. It has been referred to as the Indian River or St. Lucie Colony. The Newnansville office handled the registering of claims in the west and central sections of Florida, and the St. Augustine office handled those for the east coast area. (Newnansville is no longer extant – but was near Alachua, northwest of Gainesville)

The Armed Occupation Act required the applicant to be a resident of Florida and that he could not settle within two miles of any permanent military post. The first permit issued at the land office pertinent to this area was obtained by Frederick Whidden. The permit describes the deactivated Fort Pierce, which was near the permitted area. Permit #69 was issued to John Barker, who was William F. Russell's brother-in-law, the future Inspector of Customs at the Indian River Inlet.[84] Russell was a very prominent homesteader, and Barker became more famous or infamous in connection with a later Indian uprising, his murder, and through litigation following his death.

On February 24, 1843, the Seat of Mosquito County became Enterprise. (As mentioned, that is south of present-day Deland and on the north side of Lake Monroe). That area developed because of its proximity to the St. Johns River.

Mosquito County
Entered according to Act of Congress in the year 1836
by H.S. Tanner in the Clerk's Office of the
Eastern District of Pennsylvania

On March 14, 1844, one year before Florida became a state, Santa Lucia County (also called Santa Lucea) was formed. Generally known as St. Lucie County, it was formed from the giant Mosquito County, created in 1824. St. Lucia's boundaries started near Cape Canaveral on the north (12 miles South of Ft. Ann) and went south as far as Lake Worth. The western boundary was the Kissimmee River.[85]

The first legal system in the Indian River Colony may have been set up as a result of a convention called by Dr. Moses Holbrook, the colony's physician. It resulted in the appointment of a committee of arbitrators to settle disputes among the settlers. The arbitrators were J.S. Heermans, Mills O. Burnham, and C.L. Brayton.

Caleb Lyndon Brayton was elected the first County Clerk of the newly formed St. Lucie County in 1844.[86] This, however, conflicts with the information on Joseph Osborne (per Shofner, below). The Florida State Archives indicates that the first St. Lucie County Judge was John C. Cleland, appointed March 15, 1844. He was followed by Samuel H. Peck on March 11, 1845. (Florida became a state on March 3, 1845).

When St. Lucia County was created on March 14, 1844, the initial county seat was at the home of John Cleland on the Indian River.[87] Pam Cooper, the one-time Florida History and Genealogy Librarian at the Indian River County Main Library, reconstructed the location of the Cleland homestead via his homestead grant application under the Armed Occupation Act and by reference in Cleland's neighbors' deeds (Holbrook & Smith) as being adjacent to Cleland. She has found that the Cleland property was located at what is still known as Ankona, a town immediately south of Fort Pierce on the west bank of the Indian River.

Counties of which Indian River County was once a part, the time frames, and county seats are as follows:

1821	St. Johns	St. Augustine
1824	Mosquito County	1824 John Bunch's Home[88]
		1835 New Smyrna[89]
		1843 Enterprise[90]
1844	Santa Lucia or St. Lucie County[91]	House of John Cleland on the Indian River
1855	Brevard County[92]	Susannah/Ft. Pierce
		1864 Bassville
		It ended in 1866 when Bassville was annexed to Orange County.
		1874 Eau Gallie (Bovine)[93]
		1875 Lake View
		1876 Bassville
		1879 Savages' Store at Old Fort Taylor
		1879 Titusville
1905	St. Lucie County[94]	Fort Pierce
1925	Indian River Co.	Vero Beach

It is interesting to note that the name of Mosquito County was changed for the obvious reason of negative connotations.[95] However,

Mosquito County was known for a short time as Leigh Read County. Leigh Read was a colonel who commanded troops during the Seminole Wars and was a delegate to a 1837 convention lobbying for Florida statehood. On December 12, 1839, Read, a Whig leader, killed Democratic Party leader Augusta Halston in a duel near Tallahassee. The two-year political feud that followed led to Read's assassination. The feud itself helped establish multi-party politics in Florida and the practice of dueling. The territorial legislature voted in 1842 to change the name of Mosquito County to Leigh Read County.[96] However, the governor never seemingly signed that bill, and in 1844, the southern half of Mosquito County became St. Lucie County, and in 1845, the northern half of it became Orange County.[97]

In 1845, the County Seat for St. Lucia or St. Lucie County was referred to as St. Lucie.[98] At that time, one of the pioneers in the Fort Pierce area was Ossian Bingley Hart. He became a Florida Supreme Court Justice (1868-1873) and Florida's first native-born Governor (1873-1874).

The Federal Criminal Docket for the Eastern District of Florida, during the last year of the Territory prior to statehood, was not very active. It has been reported that the total cost to prosecute criminals during that period was $445.34.[99]

B. Biographical Information

1. Eastern District Federal Territorial Judicial Figures (1821-1845) - in order of service:

William Pope DuVal
Courtesy of the Florida State Archives

William Pope DuVal, Eastern District Superior Court Judge for East Florida, 1821-1822

William Pope DuVal was born in 1784 at Fort Comfort, Virginia. He was a descendant of Huguenots expelled from France by the revocation of the Edict of Nantes. He was the son of William and Ann

(Pope) DuVal. The father was an associate of Patrick Henry and served in the Revolutionary War.

DuVal left Virginia at age fourteen to become a hunter in Kentucky. He abandoned that to read law under Judge Broadnex of Bardstown, Kentucky, circa 1802. He was admitted to the Bar in 1804 and practiced in Bardstown until 1821, except that he served in the United States House of Representatives from 1813 to 1815. He later returned to practice in Bardstown from 1834 to 1836.

On October 13, 1804, DuVal married Nancy Hynes and likely had eight children: Burr, Thomas Howard, John Crittenden, Marsha (Price, Paschal), Elizabeth (Beall), Mary (Robinson, Hopkins), Laura Harrison (Randolph), and Florida (Everett, Howard). He served as a Captain of the Mounted Rangers in 1812, before leaving for Congress.

DuVal must have crossed paths with Washington Irving. The author was most impressed with DuVal as an outstanding frontiersman. Irving wrote several stories in which DuVal, called Ralph Ringwood, was the main character.

DuVal was the first Judge of the Superior Court for the Eastern District of the Territory of Florida from 1821 to 1822. He sought the judgeship through his friend John C. Calhoun, then Secretary of War. He was appointed by President Monroe. DuVal was also appointed by Monroe as the first civilian Governor of the Territory of Florida in

1822. Duval County, created in 1822, was named after DuVal. He was reappointed by Presidents John Quincy Adams and Andrew Jackson and served as governor until 1834.

On March 4, 1824, DuVal issued the proclamation of the decision that made Tallahassee the capital. He also established the state's first Board of Education. After returning to Kentucky, but returning once again to Florida, he practiced law in Tallahassee from 1836 to 1839 and was a member of the St. Joseph Constitutional Convention in 1838-1839. He served as a Senator for the Territory of Florida from 1839 to 1841 and became President of the Senate in 1840. He resumed his practice of law in Florida from 1843 to 1848, worked as a U.S. Boundary Commissioner, and ran as a candidate for the U.S. House of Representatives from Florida in 1848. He subsequently practiced law in Austin and Galveston, Texas, from 1848 to 1854.

DuVal died on March 19, 1854, in Washington, D.C., and is buried at Congressional Cemetery in Washington.

Joseph Lee Smith, Eastern District Superior Court Judge, 1822-1832

Joseph Lee Smith was born on May 28, 1779, in New Britain, Connecticut, the son of Elnathan and Chloe (Lee) Smith.

Judge Smith attended Yale College circa 1803 and read law under Tapping Reeve in Litchfield,[100] Connecticut, in 1804. Smith was admitted to the Connecticut Bar that same year. He then started to practice law in Litchfield.

In 1804, he married Frances Marion Kirby, who was born in Connecticut on April 6, 1785. She was the daughter of Revolutionary War patriot Ephraim Kirby. Judge Smith and his wife had four children: Ephraim Kirby-Smith, born in 1806; Frances Marvin Smith, who was born in 1812; Josephine Smith, who was born in 1818; and Edmund Kirby-Smith, who was born in 1824. The first two children were born in Connecticut. Mr. Smith practiced in Litchfield until 1812, where he was involved in defending politically controversial figures, including himself.

From 1812 to 1818, Judge Smith was a major and lieutenant colonel in the U.S. Army, and in 1819, he returned to practice in Connecticut until 1821. In 1823, after being recommended by the United States Senator from Connecticut, James Lanman, Smith was appointed by President Monroe as Judge of the Superior Court for the Eastern District, Territory of Florida. He served in that capacity until 1832.

Early in Judge Smith's career in Florida, he had been an associate of Benjamin Alexander Putnam (see next chapter). Mr. Putnam took an interest in Mrs. Smith's sister, Helen Kirby, and married her in 1830.

Smith was controversial on the bench. (See the Thomas Douglas quote below and Douglas's biographical section in the next chapter.) Smith also incurred the wrath of future Governor Richard Keith Call and other Middle Florida planters referred to as the Tallahassee Nucleus. This was prompted, among other things, by Smith siding with the small landowner in land disputes, as opposed to the powerful banking and development interests who were politically connected in the legislature.

Upon hearing from Edgar Macon, the district attorney with whom Smith had feuded, that Smith was receiving fees for work performed on vacation that had already been accomplished during the term of the court, Call rose against Smith in the U.S. House of Representatives. He stated, "his (Smith's) example in showing a disregard to the law...ignorance and corruption in your judiciary, is an evil not less to be lamented than apostacy in your religion...But, sir, it is your officer of whom we complain; you sent him to us, and we ask you to take him away." Smith, however, later responded that if Call had read the law with ordinary intelligence, he would have known that Smith was a territorial judge, not a district judge, where such conduct was allowed under a Florida Legislative Council Act of 1823.[101] Call didn't get his way just then. However, because Call was close to President Andrew Jackson, he saw that Smith did not receive a third 4-year appointment as a superior court judge in 1832.

After serving as a judge, Smith entered private practice in St. Augustine, Florida, until 1846. In 1832, he was Mayor of St. Augustine, Florida, and he was also a delegate to the Congress of the Territory of Florida in 1833 and 1834 from St. Johns - Mosquito County and in 1835 and 1836 from St. Johns County.

It has been noted that one of Judge Smith's greatest distinctions was being the father of General Edmund Kirby-Smith. General Edmund Kirby-Smith was one of seven full Confederate generals at the time the Civil War ended, and one of the last to surrender to Union forces. A statue of Kirby-Smith represented Florida in the Hall of Statues in our nation's capital in Washington, D.C.[102] (However, the statue was removed on Sept 4, 2021, because of Kirby-Smith's association with the Confederacy, and replaced on July 13, 2022, with the statue of African American educator and civil rights activist, Mary McLeod Bethune).

Judge Smith's oldest son, Ephraim, was a graduate of West Point, as was Edmund. Ephraim was a captain in the Mexican War, fighting with his brother, Edmund, then a junior officer under Ephraim. Edmund was a lieutenant at the time. Ephraim was killed while leading the attack on Mexico City in September of 1847.

Florida's first supreme court justice, Thomas Douglas, who practiced before Judge Smith, is quoted as describing Judge Smith as, "[a] gigantic man, both mentally and physically, who but for his unbounded prejudices and ungovernable passions, would have been qualified to fill any, even the most exalted station in the government. He had the advantage of an excellent education, was a sound lawyer, read much, had fine conversational powers, a highly discriminating mind, and could equally adorn the bench or the drawing room."[103]

Smith died on May 22, 1846, in St. Augustine, Florida. His wife, from whom he had previously been separated, died on August 3, 1875. Each is buried in the Huguenot Cemetery outside the gates of St. Augustine. Judge Smith's gravestone reads: "In Memory of Joseph L. Smith. Died 5/25/1846 at age 69. A Colonel in the Army of the United States in the War of 1812 and sometime Judge of the Superior Court of the United States in the Territory of Florida. To great assiduity in the performance of his duties, he united a dignity and learning, which adorned his office, and to a commanding presence were added the higher attributes of distinguished abilities."

It has also been written that Smith's "jurisprudential legacy was beneficial, for his decisions aided in unraveling the complexity of real property law, a prerequisite for subsequent Florida development. Politically, his alliance with (Joseph M). White against (Andrew Jackson's proteges referred to as the Tallahassee) Nucleus power presaged the evolution of the territory's Democratic Party. Finally, Smith's exercise of his judicial duties maintained independence from the dictates of the powerful, thereby lending credibility to a judicial system still aborning."[104]

Robert Raymond Reid
Courtesy of the Florida State Archives

Robert Raymond Reid, Eastern District Superior Court Judge, 1832-1839

Robert Raymond Reid was born on September 8, 1789, in Prince William Parish, South Carolina, the son of Robert and Joanna (Gardner) Reid. He attended school in Augusta, Georgia, for a time, while living with relatives, but returned to his family in South Carolina. Reid attended South Carolina College in Columbia, South Carolina, circa 1809. He was admitted to the Bar in 1810 and practiced law in Augusta, Georgia, from 1810 to 1816. In 1810, he married Anna Margaretta McLaws, who bore five children. She was the daughter of a lawyer under whom Reid studied.

Reid was a member of the U.S. House of Representatives from Georgia from 1816 to 1819 and 1823 to 1825 and a Judge of the Middle Circuit of Georgia (Burke County) from 1825 to 1827. He was the presiding Judge of the City Court of Augusta, Georgia, from 1819 to 1823, and the Mayor of Augusta from 1827 to 1832.

The first Mrs. Reid died in 1825. On May 8, 1829, he married Elizabeth Nepear Delphia Virginia Randolph, who passed away in 1831, and on November 6, 1837, he married Mary Martha Smith. He had additional children by his second and third wives. Reid suffered heartbreak and depression from the loss of his first two wives and the deaths of several of his children. As a result, his friends interceded for him for a possible territorial judgeship.

On May 23, 1832, President Andrew Jackson appointed Reid as judge of the Superior Court of the Eastern District Territory of Florida, where he served until 1839. Reid took the place of Judge Joseph Smith,[105] whom the president thought to be troublesome (for him and his colleagues). In 1838, Reid served as a delegate to the Constitutional Convention from St. Johns County. Reid was a territorial judge at a time of a great number of land claims and criminal matters, during the Second Seminole War.

Motte, in his Journal into the Wilderness, describes Judge Reid as accompanying him to Newnansville for the trial of two black men who were charged with the murder of Captain Gilliland of Alachua County. They confessed and, in a special session of the court, were convicted and hanged.[106]

Reid was President of the St. Joseph Constitutional Convention in Florida in 1838 and 1839. This came about by his defeating former Governor DuVal by one vote. Reid was considered to be pro-statehood, anti-bank, and could align himself with the powerful Middle Florida politicians as well as some of his East Florida colleagues. Reid was appointed Governor of the Territory of Florida on December 2, 1839, by President Martin Van Buren and served until 1841.

Reid succeeded Governor Keith Call. Call's biographer described Reid as follows: "Reid was a remarkable man: an urbane scholar, a gentleman, an intellectual who shrewdly evaluated his fellow men; he analyzed his own mind, dissected his vices with philosophic resignation, and wrestled with religious dogma, always wanting to believe but never quite able to do so. In his calm introspection, his tact, his discretion, his humanitarian impulses, and his shrinking from physical exertion, he presents a picture of a man quite opposite in temperament from Call.[107]

As Governor, Reid was caught in a national controversy. He offered General Zachary Taylor the use of two dogs for the U.S. Army in connection with the Seminole War. Taylor accepted but later refused to pay on the grounds that the dogs were ineffective. He said they were trained to track Negroes and could not be induced to "nose out" Indians. Abolitionists jumped on this, asserting the dogs were used to hunt runaway slaves. Former President John Quincy Adams then introduced a resolution in the House of Representatives, of which he was a member, inflaming the incident.[108]

Annie J. Reid, Reid's granddaughter, through his wife, Annie McLaws, who was also the daughter of his son Robert Raymond Reid, married William F. Forward, the son of Circuit Judge William A. Forward. (See Forward biographical information, infra). Reid died July 1, 1841, at Blackwood Plantation, Leon County, Florida, of yellow fever and further heartbreak over the then-recent loss of his son, a young naval officer who was commanding a vessel in the Wilkes expedition.

Isaac Hopkins Bronson, Eastern District Superior Court Judge, 1840-1845

Isaac Hopkins Bronson was born on October 16, 1802. He was probably born in Waterbury, Connecticut, but was raised in Rutland, Jefferson County, New York. He was the son of Rev. Ethel Bronson, who was also a Justice of the Peace in Waterbury, Connecticut, and a member of the Connecticut State Assembly. Issac Bronson's mother, Hepzibah Hopkins, was the daughter of a Connecticut lawyer, Joseph Hopkins.

Issac Bronson was married to Sophronia Louisa Beebe Bronson, and they had two daughters, Gertrude and Emma. Bronson read law under Micah Sterling in Watertown, New York. Sterling was a future congressman from New York and a brother-in-law to Bronson.

Bronson was admitted to the Bar in New York in 1822, where he practiced until 1834. He was elected to the U.S. House of Representatives in 1836, serving from March 4, 1837, to March 3, 1839, and was Chairman of the Committee on Territories from 1837 to 1839. He was not re-elected and thereafter pursued a legal career in New York from 1838 to 1840.

In 1840, Bronson became Judge of the Superior Court of the Eastern District of the Territory of Florida. He was appointed by President Martin Van Buren, who was trying to placate his New York constituency and satisfy East Florida Democrats. Bronson was reappointed by President Tyler in 1844 and served until 1845, when Florida became a state. Bronson then declined the appointment as the first circuit judge for the newly created Eastern Circuit Court. Instead, he became the State of Florida's first United States District Court Judge on August 8, 1846. He served in that capacity until 1847, when that single district was broken into two portions. He then became a judge in the Northern District of Florida from 1847 to 1855.

While Bronson sat as a judge primarily in St. Augustine, he was active in the community of Palatka. He drafted the town charter and petitioned for Palatka to be the county seat. He donated the land for the courthouse, was a part owner of a steam sawmill erected in 1853, and built an elegant home in 1854 with cypress from the Oklawaha region. The house is an example of simplified Greek Revival architecture of the antebellum period. It is a tourist spot today, called the Bronson-Mulholland House.

Bronson died on August 13, 1855, and is buried in Palatka, Florida. There is a grave to his memory in front of the Bronson Mulholland House, but there is some controversy about his being buried in the Oak Hill Cemetery in Palatka, which was apparently once the case, and some debate exists about whether at least some portions of his remains are still there.

A noted Florida historian dedicated his book "To the Memory of My Honored Friend, Isaac Hopkins Bronson, the First Judge of the United States District Court, Northern District of Florida, A Citizen Whose Private Life and Public Virtue Shed Luster upon the State of his Adoption, this Volume is Respectfully Inscribed."[109]

Following Bronson's death, his wife continued to live at the home in Palatka until the Civil War, when she returned to New York.

The home's attic was subsequently used by Rebel Soldiers as a lookout for Union Soldiers during the war. The house next door was used as a school for freed slave children. It also served as a Red Cross center during both World Wars.

2. Clerks of the Eastern District Superior Court

James S. Tingle, possible first Clerk of the Superior Court of East Florida, ca 1822-1824?

James S. Tingle may have been the first Clerk of the Superior Court of East Florida. I'm unsure whether it was he or George Gibbs. Each is noted in Cantor Brown's book as having that role.[110]

The Census records show that Tingle, who may have originally been from Virginia, was living in St. Augustine in 1822 and 1824. There are also court records showing him as a clerk in that timeframe.

He purportedly was a protégé of Jackson, with whom DuVal disagreed over Jackson's appointment of a clerk, but Tingle ironically likely once lived nearby to the future Governor DuVal in Virginia. Their names are each shown as petitioners in 1786 in connection with the Protestant Episcopal Church in Abington Parish and County of Gloucester, Virginia.

Gibbs, George, and Gibbs, K.B., possible first, second, and/or third Clerks of the Eastern District Superior Court starting in 1821.

Andrew Jackson, as provisional Governor of Florida, appointed the first Clerk of Court in Florida, John Miller, in 1821, for Escambia County (not covered here as that was West Florida). Soon thereafter, he arranged for the Clerk in St. Johns County (East Florida). It was purportedly an Englishman, George Gibbs, but see Tingle above. Jackson's power to appoint a Clerk, rather than being chosen by the judge, was controversial.[111] However, it was not challenged. Gibbs may have followed Tingle.

Thomas Douglas, whose biographical information appears in the next chapter, wrote,

"Our clerk, Mr. Gibbs, was well acquainted with his duties, and his son, Kingsley B. Gibbs, Esq., who was his deputy and afterwards succeeded him, was exceedingly expert and correct in making up records. Many land cases were carried up to the Supreme Court of the United States; as the law especially provided that an appeal should be taken in all cases where the decision was against the United States, and the claim exceeded a league square (3 miles by 3 miles), and authorized an appeal to be taken by the District Attorney in other cases, and by the claimant in cases decided against them. The Clerk of the Supreme Court, Mr. William T.

Carroll, has repeatedly said that the records sent up from the Superior Court at St. Augustine were made out better than those from any other court."[112]

Kingsley Beatty Gibbs was born in Brooklyn Heights, New York City, New York, in approximately 1810. His parents were George Gibbs and Elizabeth Isabelle Kingsley Gibbs (29 Apr 1772 - 22 Jan 1838), who were each from England. K. B. Gibbs was also the nephew of Zephaniah Kingsley, a prominent planter and territorial era politician who had an extensive plantation at Ft. George Island, northeast of Jacksonville. K.B. either purchased or inherited this plantation, which came with almost 50 slaves. The 1840 Census reflects him living in Duval County, and in the 1850 Census, with his wife, Laura, who was from South Carolina. His occupation is listed as farmer. His property was then worth $40,000.00. Laura Gibbs appears in the 1860 Census without Kingsley. He was also a member of the St. Johns Bar Association.

K.B. Gibbs was also a captain in the Seminole War and helped to defend the judicial figure James Darley's plantation in 1835. Gibbs was the first recording secretary and librarian for the newly formed Historical Society of Florida in 1855, which was then led by a Clerk of Court, subsequent to Gibbs, i.e., George Fairbanks, and a judicial figure, Benjamin Putnam. K. B. Gibbs died in 1859, and his estate went through probate in Duval County later that year.

<u>Beard, John, Clerk, Eastern District Superior Court, 1838 to 1842.</u>

Major John Beard was born in North Carolina in 1797. He was educated at Yale and served as a Federalist in the North Carolina legislature before moving to St. Augustine in 1838. He commenced serving that year as clerk of the United States District Court for the Eastern District of Florida in 1840. He served until 1842, when he was succeeded by George Fairbanks, who would become his son-in-law. Beard left the clerk's position to become United States Marshall, replacing the controversial Joseph Sanchez,[113] a position he held until Florida became a state in 1845.

In 1845, Beard was elected register of public lands and moved to Tallahassee. He ran unsuccessfully for Congress as a Democrat in 1850, being defeated by former Florida Territorial Governor and Whig, Richard Keith Call. However, Beard was elected Comptroller of the State of Florida, taking office on January 25, 1851, from which office he resigned in 1854 to become an agent of the Apalachicola Land Company.

In 1858, George Fairbanks' wife, Sarah, passed away. Beard had maintained his friendship with Fairbanks, whom he had known well from the court and through the Episcopal Church. In 1860, Fairbanks married Beard's daughter, Susan.

Beard was a representative from Leon County to the secession convention of 1861. He was reappointed to the office of Comptroller in 1866. Three years later, he suffered health problems and, after a long incapacity, died in Tallahassee in 1876.

To appreciate the times, consider that Beard reported as Comptroller for the year ending October 31, 1866, that revenues for the State were $25,596.00, while warrants had been issued for $127,821.00, nearly half of which was for past due salaries.

Beard had a son, William K. Beard, who was an adjutant general on the staff of General Braxton Bragg in the Civil War. William K. Beard was married to Letitia G. Shepard, a descendant of the well-known Breckenridge family of Virginia. Their son, John Shepard Beard, was educated at the University of the South at Sewanee, Tennessee, and went on to be a prominent attorney in Tallahassee and Pensacola around the turn of the century.

George Rainsford Fairbanks, Clerk, Eastern District Superior Court, 1842-1845

George Rainsford Fairbanks was born in Watertown, New York, on July 5, 1820. He was one of four sons born to Jason and Mary Massey Fairbanks. George's father was a native of Mendon (south of Natick), Massachusetts, and was in the saddle and harness business. They descended from Jonathan Fairbanks of Yorkshire, England, who came to America in 1633. George's grandfather, Sam Fairbanks, served in the Revolutionary War. Jason Fairbanks was a lieutenant in the War of 1812. Mary Massey was born in Vermont in 1796 and was the daughter of Hart Massey.

George Fairbanks attended public schools in Watertown, New York, until he was nine years old. He was then sent by his parents to a private school and, at age 10, was sent to Belville Academy. George and his brother, Samuel, subsequently attended Roman Catholic Petit Seminaire in Montreal, a minor seminary to prepare young men for the priesthood. George's father, an Episcopalian, did not intend for his sons to become Catholic priests, but desired a fine education for them. George graduated from Union College in Schenectady, New York, receiving a degree of B.A. in 1839. (Later, he received a Master of Arts degree from Union College and from Trinity College, Hartford, Connecticut.)

To prepare for the practice of law, he studied in the law office of W.A. Shumway, Esquire, and then transferred to the office of Joseph Mullin. Mullin was subsequently appointed to the Supreme Court of the State of New York.

George Fairbanks was admitted to the New York Bar in 1842, following an examination. He joined the New York State Militia and became acquainted with Miss Sarah Catherine Wright, the daughter of Judge Benjamin Wright of Adams, Massachusetts.

In 1842, Fairbanks married Sarah and took a position as clerk of the federal court (superior court) at St. Augustine, Florida. He accompanied the newly appointed federal judge, Isaac H. Bronson, who had a practice in Watertown and who had also been a congressman during the Van Buren administration. The opening for the clerkship arose by virtue of the then clerk (and future father-in-law of Fairbanks), Major John Beard, becoming the U.S. Marshall.

In the summer of 1843, Fairbanks returned from St. Augustine to Watertown, New York. He then brought back his wife in the fall and boarded with Mrs. Martha R. Reid, the widow of Governor and former Territorial Judge Robert Raymond Reid.

Fairbanks was a close friend of David Levy Yulee, who went on to become the first Jewish United States Senator. Fairbanks was also a friend of William P. DuVal, former federal judge and territorial governor of Florida.

In 1846, Fairbanks was elected to the state senate to represent the counties of St. Johns, Putnam, Volusia, Orange, and Brevard. He served for two years.

In 1850, Fairbanks developed an interest in Florida history. In 1855, he was part of the group that gathered in the upstairs hall of George Burt's St. Augustine store, which brought about the creation of "The Historical Society of Florida," where Benjamin Putnam was elected president. (Mr. Putnam's biographical information is set forth in Chapter 5). Fairbanks was the first vice president of the society from 1856 to 1861. Fairbanks lectured on Florida history and subsequently wrote "The History and Antiquities of St. Augustine, Florida," in 1858, among other history books.

Fairbanks was an orange grower and president of the Florida Fruit Growers' Association and its successor, the Florida Fruit Exchange. He helped to organize the Florida Horticulture Society and was its first vice president. He owned a large grove near Orange Lake in Alachua County.

In 1853, Benjamin Putnam decided not to run for Surveyor General of Florida. That job was considered the most influential position in Florida. Senator Yulee wished to see the post go to John Beard, a close friend of Fairbanks who, as mentioned, was to eventually become Fairbanks' father-in-law (Fairbanks' first wife passed away in Jacksonville in 1858). Beard would not accept the position, so Senator Yulee appointed Fairbanks. Senator Yulee's selection of Fairbanks was circumvented by President Franklin Pierce, who appointed another candidate. However, politics continued to beckon, and Fairbanks was elected mayor of St. Augustine in 1857.

Fairbanks helped found the University of the South at Sewanee, Lookout Mountain, Tennessee, in 1858. In 1862, he married Mrs. Susan Beard Wright, the widowed daughter of his friend, John Beard.

Following the Civil War, in which Fairbanks served as a major in the commissary department, and in connection with Fairbanks'

Episcopal church interests, he helped reconstruct the University of the South at Sewanee. He was on the Board of Trustees and, from 1867 to 1880, was Commissioner of Buildings and Lands. The Major's home at Sewanee, built in 1866, was called "Rebel's Rest."

In 1875, Fairbanks was instrumental in having his old friend, General Kirby Smith, join the staff of the college as a professor of mathematics. Fairbanks was well acquainted with General Smith, since Smith's father had practiced with Fairbanks in St. Augustine. In 1880, Fairbanks returned to Florida and settled in Fernandina, where he built a home. However, despite his lengthy absences from Tennessee, Fairbanks remained on the university's Board of Trustees.

While in Florida, Fairbanks continued to pursue his many interests regarding the state that had become his home. At the urging of David Levy Yulee in 1880, he edited a weekly newspaper, "The Florida Mirror." In approximately 1890, he was elected president of the Florida Press Association. In November 1902, Fairbanks was unanimously elected second president of the revived Florida Historical Society.[114] Additionally, in a tribute to his long and distinguished career, the University of Alabama awarded Fairbanks a Doctor of Laws degree in June 1906.

George Rainsford Fairbanks died at the age of 87 on August 3, 1906, two months after receiving this last honor. Fairbanks had one son and five daughters, three of whom predeceased him.

3. Biographies of County Territorial Judicial Figures in St. Johns, and subsequently Mosquito and then St. Lucia Counties (1821 – 1845) (in alphabetical order):

Thomas Addison, Mosquito County Justice of the Peace, 1827

Thomas Addison and his brother John came from County Carrickfergus, Ireland, via the Bahamas, and obtained a Spanish land grant for property in the New Smyrna area. They then established a plantation on 1,404 acres on the Tomoka River, called "Carrickfergus." This was over the period of 1807 to 1816.

In 1812, during the Patriot War, some American citizens tried to revolt against Spain and annex East Florida to the United States. The "Patriots" tried to attack the plantations along the Halifax and Tomoka Rivers but were ambushed by the Spanish at Addison's landing. All of the Patriots were killed in this attack.

On January 27, 1825, John Addison agreed to sell Carrickfergus to Colonel Thomas Dummett for $22,500.00, which was to be paid over time. Before the contract was fulfilled, John Addison died intestate (without a will). His brother, Thomas, took over the plantation, but he also died intestate. Dummett allegedly illegally transferred part of the Addison property to Duncan and Kenneth McCrea before fulfilling his contract with Addison.

Thomas Addison was appointed as a Justice of the Peace for Mosquito County in 1827. However, State of Florida Archives records indicate that he was dead when it came time for his appointment to be confirmed.

Several miles south of present-day Tomoka State Park are the ruins of what is referred to as the "Addison Blockhouse."[115] This structure was built by South Carolina soldiers during the Second Seminole War as part of Camp McRae. Nearby are the shallow depressions in the ground, surrounded by half-buried, moss-covered coquina rocks, containing the remains of Thomas and John Addison's graves and possibly some soldiers killed by the Seminoles.

George Anderson, Mosquito County Court Judge, late 1820s

George Anderson, a/k/a John George Anderson, was born on the banks of Scotland and later moved to the Bahamas. Subsequently, he moved to Florida and was the first Judge of the County Court of Mosquito County, being appointed by Governor DuVal on December 30, 1824. Anderson served as the presiding justice with associate justices Joseph Woodruff and James Darby. Anderson was reappointed in 1827 and 1829. He was shown as living in Mosquito County in 1830.

George Anderson acquired 450 acres on the west side of the Tomoka River, north of John Bunch's plantation. His wife, Sarah

Petty Dunn, had inherited the property from her mother, Mrs. Frances Kerr, who had bought it from Gabriel Perpall, a native of Minorca. The property was known during the British Period as the "Ferry Settlement" of Richard Oswald. Incidentally, John Addison, the brother of another judicial figure in this chapter, was the executor of Mrs. Kerr's will.

George Anderson and his brother James, grandsons of Mrs. Kerr, acquired a mill and plantation in 1832 called Dun-Lawton. It produced crude golden sugar syrup. (The ruins can be seen today off present Herbert Street in Port Orange). Dun-Lawton would become famous several years later, with the battle of Dun-Lawton, or Anderson's Plantation, in the Second Seminole War, when the "Mosquito Roarers" would experience their initial battle with the Indians in 1836. (See Dummett's and Putnam's bios in the next chapter.)

Caleb Brayton, St. Lucia County Court Clerk, 1844

Caleb Lyndon Brayton was born on July 11, 1816, in Cranston, Rhode Island. He married Mary Ann Paine at Plainfield, Connecticut, on July 8, 1838. They had four sons: Joseph Lyndon, born in Fall River, MA. on May 25, 1839, and died November 5, 1839; Thomas Lyndon, born in Augusta, GA. on August 8, 1841; Ellery Metcalf, born in Augusta on August 16, 1844; and William Paine, born in Augusta on September 17, 1850, and who died on April 19, 1877.

Mr. Brayton came to Florida for his health. He moved to Augusta first and went into the merchant business of wholesaling and retailing boots and shoes. In 1843, he left his pregnant wife and son to stake a claim under the Armed Occupation Act in the Fort Pierce area of Florida. From there, he wrote a series of letters to his absent wife when she lived in South Carolina and Massachusetts. These letters have been handed down and are the subject of an article appearing in the Florida Historical Quarterly.[116]

Brayton built a cabin on high ground south of the old Fort Pierce on property called "Brayton Bluff." It was south of what is now the St. Lucie County Courthouse. The home has also been described as located eight miles south of Fort Capron. Besides the various political offices Brayton held, he remained busy planting arrowroot, pumpkins, pineapples, and other fruits and vegetables. He also marketed poultry and fish, and green turtles in Key West.

Caleb Lyndon Brayton may have been the first County Clerk of the newly formed St. Lucia County in 1844. He was also one of three arbitrators appointed in connection with setting up a legal system in Indian River Colony that year. Public records show that Brayton was commissioned as a notary public on March 7, 1845. He was appointed Sheriff of St. Lucie County in 1850 and served until 1855.[117] His address was "Russell's Landing," which is the present-day St. Lucie Village. He was also the St. Lucie County Tax Appraiser and Collector by 1850. In 1852, he held the office of County Commissioner.

C. L. Brayton also served as Justice of the Peace, which, at that time, involved a wide range of responsibilities, from that of Coroner, Assessor of Revenue, Tax Assessor and Collector, Auctioneer, and Notary Public.

C. L. Brayton was the contract mail carrier along a route from New Smyrna through Indian River to Miami in 1851. Mail was supposed to be delivered twice monthly, but Brayton's job was a difficult one. He used a boat from New Smyrna to Indian River, but from that point southward, he attempted to ride a horse along the beach. It was difficult to find fresh water for the horse, and its feed had to be carried. Brayton complained that he had "ruined a horse each of the last two trips." Brayton is also an important historical figure because he witnessed the Indian attack against John Barker and his brother-in-law, Major Russell, and the burning of the home of E. H. Gattis.

Brayton was joined by his son in 1851, and finally by his wife, Mary Ann, in 1854, when Brayton was dying of tuberculosis. In 1854, the Commanding Officer at Fort Capron gave an account of the number of settlers he was protecting. He included a description of the occupants of C. L. Brayton's home: three men, one woman, two children, and one slave lived there, but two of the men were mail carriers, frequently absent.[118]

Brayton died of tuberculosis on June 9, 1854. Mrs. Brayton returned to Augusta, where she died on April 20, 1883. Son, Ellery, attended Brown University, graduated from Harvard Law School in 1866, and went on to somewhat follow in his father's footsteps. He became a Clerk of the Superior Court of Richmond County (Augusta, Georgia) from 1867 to 1871. He later moved to South Carolina and served in the Legislature. He died on March 6, 1907.

Son, Thomas, lived in Florida until at least 1861, returned to Massachusetts to join the Seventh Regiment, and then worked at a bank in Fall River, Massachusetts. Illness forced him to move to South Carolina, where he served as United States Marshal until he was murdered on July 20, 1881, by John McDowell, a moonshiner.

John Bulow, Mosquito County Justice of the Peace, 1833-1835

John Joaquin Bulow, a/k/a Von Bulow, was a Mosquito County Justice of the Peace from 1833 to 1835. The Bulows owned a plantation, reputedly the most glamorous and wealthy of all the plantations in the area. It was called "Bulow Ville" and was located four miles north of the Ormond Plantation.

The property was once owned by James Russell, who received four thousand acres from the Spanish Governor in 1812, in exchange for his schooner, Perseverance. (For details of the unusual ceremony connected with this particular title transfer, which at common law was called a livery of seisin, see Spanish Land Grants in Florida.)[119] Russell died in 1815, and his heirs sold the property to the wealthy Charles Bulow of Charleston for $9,944.50. The Bulows were descendants of a prominent German family.

Bulow brought slaves from South Carolina to develop cotton and sugar at Bulow Ville. Strickland, in her Ormond-on-the-Halifax, has written: "Charles Bulow lived only a few years after purchasing the plantation, and his marble tombstone is in the Huguenot Cemetery in St. Augustine. His sixteen-year-old son, John Joachim, inherited Bulow Ville and other valuable property, which included a dwelling house on Marine Street in St. Augustine, and six acres of land and an orange grove in the precincts of St. Augustine.

A trusteeship was formed until John Joachim reached his majority, and then he took over the plantation, which became one of the wealthiest in Florida. He had a large, slave-manned boat in which he went on long fishing trips with plenty of nets, fishing gear, guns, and a cook. On the riverfront at St. Augustine was his townhouse, and at Bulow Ville, John Joachim lived like a prince in the wilderness."[120]

Young John Bulow attended school with his neighbor, James Ormond III, during the winter for several years in St. Augustine.

They were each friendly with the Indians they would soon have to fight.

Bockelman, in his "Six Columns and Fort New Smyrna,"[121] describes plantation life in the early 1830s, with a reference to Bulow: "With the reconstruction of the King's Road completed by the U.S. Military about 1833, there existed for several years what might be called a plantation society with each of the larger plantations practically a social unit in itself. Those were the happy days of the Florida Plantation, with contests on the rivers between competing oared boats from their estates, including racing and the singing of boat songs. A familiar sight was that of young John Bulow traveling in his light-oared bark down the Halifax River with his oarsmen, cooks, and tents."

On December 28, 1835, Major Benjamin Putnam, in command of the Mosquito Roarers, took over Bulow Ville as a military post. They had to fight their way into the premises, as J. J. Bulow feared Indian reprisals and resisted Putnam with a four-pound cannon. Bulow was then arrested and confined. Putnam or Bulow tried to protect the plantation by placing Bulow's slave houses in a semicircle surrounding his palmetto fortification. Bulow later abandoned any idea of defending his land and buried his books, from his extensive library, and papers. However, the Indians were able to dig them up and scatter them on the grounds. Subsequently, troops were able to rescue some copies of Milton and Shakespeare.

Today, Bulow Ville or its ruins is a state park and on the National Register of Historic Places, as of September 29, 1970, and is located at 3501 Old Kings Highway in Flagler Beach.

John Bunch, whose house was the Mosquito County Seat, 1824

John Bunch was from Nassau in the Bahamas. He acquired 2,170 acres of land near New Smyrna, which included portions of the Moultrie and Moncrief British land grants. He later took over from his nephew, Patrick Dean, the grant of 995 acres opposite Pelican Island (now Port Orange), after Dean was killed by an Indian.

In 1824, the Territorial Legislature for Florida designated the seat of Mosquito County as John Bunch's house. (By 1835, the legislature had changed the seat to the more generic, "New Smyrna.") In 1825, Bunch sold a portion of his property to Colonel Thomas Dummett.

Bunch's daughter, Mary Dean Bunch, married a Scotsman, Robert McHardy, a merchant from Nassau. They acquired a plantation of 1,000 acres near New Smyrna. It was the site of the former "Rosetta" plantation of Lt. Governor John Moultrie of the British Period. McHardy was also a surveyor and planter. He surveyed many of the Spanish land grants.

Mills O. Burnham, St. Lucia County Arbitrator, 1843

Mills Olcott Burnham was born on September 8, 1817, in Thetford, Orange County, Vermont. His parents were English, and he moved with them when he was a boy to Troy, New York. After attending public schools, he apprenticed as a gunsmith at the Watervliet Government Arsenal, which was placed on the National Historic Landmark list in 1966.

On September 9, 1835, he married Mary McCuen, age 16, in Lansingburgh, New York. She was from Northern Ireland, having immigrated to New York with her parents. The couple had two children while living in New York: Frances and Mills O. In the fall of 1837, for health reasons, Burnham sailed south to the "Arsenal of the South" in Duval County in the Territory of Florida. After a winter in Florida, Burnham's health improved. He returned to New York but soon left with his family for Jacksonville to settle there on a permanent basis.

Burnham, who was strong and athletic, as well as an expert with guns, became a sheriff of Duval County in the Territory of Florida in 1840.[122] He was also elected from St. Lucia County to the Florida Legislature, serving from 1847 to 1851.

Lured by the Armed Occupation Act, Burnham and his family then settled on the west shore along the Indian River, approximately

8 miles south of Ft. Pierce. His land grant application is dated 1843. The property is described as being on Ankona Bluff and the former home of Samuel Peck, which was framed in Savannah, Georgia, and shipped by Peck's schooner to the site. The Burnhams had five more children, all born in Florida.

Captain Burnham, as he was known, and his son, George, explored by boat the Indian River north of the colony in the 1840s. They gave the Banana River its name after the bananas they found growing there. They also named George's Island after the son and Buck Point Island after the deer they found there, each island being in the Banana River. George died at the age of fourteen.

In the Indian River Colony, Burnham was appointed as an arbitrator to settle citizen disputes, which was one of the first steps in the colony's setting up of a legal system. Burnham not only raised citrus in the colony, but he was also one of the first to commercially raise pineapples. He is also noted for his exporting of green turtles from the Indian River to England, via Charleston. He was very innovative in that regard, purchasing a vessel, the Josephine, and carefully packing and shipping the live turtles.

The Burnhams, along with the other settlers, were driven from the area in 1849 as a result of the Indian attack on John Barker. Burnham was away when the attack occurred, and some authors have suggested that the colony wouldn't have fled if Burnham were there.[123] They initially went to St. Augustine, but soon Burnham became manager of a sugar-making operation at Dunlawton plantation. By 1853, however, the Burnhams were living by the Banana River as Burnham became the first permanent lighthouse keeper for the Cape Canaveral Lighthouse. This position came about in part due to the efforts of the Collector of the Port of New Smyrna, Captain Douglas Dummett. Later, with the assistance of buds from Captain Dummett's grove, Burnham budded orange fruit and raised citrus that was described as more delectable than Indian River citrus.

As a keeper, he followed orders to dismantle the lighthouse at the beginning of the Civil War. He buried the prisms, mirrors, and clock mechanisms in a wooden crate in his grove on the edge of the Banana River. At the end of the war, the materials were turned over to the government, but not reused at the Cape because of a total refurbishing of the lighthouse commencing in 1866. Burnham held the keeper position for over thirty years, from 1853 until his death in April 1886.[124] He is buried in the grove at the site of the lighthouse in Cape Canaveral. His wife, who followed Burnham in death two years later, is buried there as well. Photographs of the Burnhams are on display at The Brevard Museum of History & Natural Science in Cocoa, Florida.[125]

Henry A. Crane, St. Lucia County Court Clerk, 1850-1855

Henry A. Crane was born in approximately 1812 in New Jersey.[126] After working as a clerk in Washington, D. C., he moved to St. Augustine. In 1837, he married Sophia Allen and had a son, Henry Lafayette Crane, who went on to be a Confederate soldier, and six daughters. He became an Armed Occupation Act settler, permit # 10, applying for ownership of land which was located near Fort Mellon.

Crane was commissioned as a notary public for Mosquito County in 1843 and also as a Justice of the Peace. There is some information that he was a clerk of courts in Mosquito Co. in the 1840s and nominated to be a Probate Judge for Orange Co. in the 1840s. He subsequently became the last clerk of St. Lucia County, serving from 1850 until 1855, when the county changed to Brevard. In 1850, the clerk's duties for St. Lucia County were shared with the clerk of Orange County.

The 1850 census shows Crane living in Orange County with his wife, Sophia, and five children. They were all born in Florida. Crane's occupation was then listed as printer and farmer.

Crane, unlike his son, was a Union soldier and commanded a detachment of Federal troops in 1863 to disrupt the flow of cattle from Charlotte Harbor. He also served on the USS Sagamore, which patrolled the Florida Coast. This bio continues under his name in Chapter 3.

James Darley, Mosquito County Court Judge, 1828-1829

James Darley was one of the first two associate justices of Mosquito County, being appointed on December 29, 1824, to serve under George Anderson. Darley was also a Judge of the Mosquito County Court in 1828 and 1829. The 1830 U.S. census shows him living in Mosquito County.

Darley was an owner or lessee of property which was once owned by Surveyor Robert McHardy and his estate, which was also owned by Marquis de Fougiere, the French counsel at Charleston. The property was south of the Ormond sugar mill, off the King's Road. The plantation operated by Darley was called Mt. Oswald.[127] Darley's Plantation became a headquarters for General Hernandez and Major Putnam in November of 1835, during the Seminole War.

Strickland in her Ormond-on-the-Halifax says the following about Darley: "Another planter, James Darley, described by a contemporary as a "queer old Yorkshireman," was the owner of 500 acres, bounded on the north by John Bunch's plantation. Darley had made "continuous voyages of export and import which had benefitted the province and royal exchequer during the second Spanish occupation. He had also made several expeditions to Africa for slaves. Darley considered it fine sport to use puppies as bait to catch alligators in the Tomoka River." [128]

Douglas Dummett, Mosquito County Justice of the Peace, 1833, and County Court Judge, 1840-1844

Douglas Dummett, a/k/a Dummitt or Dummit, was born in Barbados in approximately 1806. He was one of 11 children of Colonel Thomas Henry Dummett, a British Marine officer and planter in the West Indies.

Thomas Dummett was born in Barbados on October 14, 1765, and was a British military officer with the rank of colonel and a wealthy planter. After an uprising in Barbados, he escaped in a sugar cask to the United States. After spending approximately five years in Connecticut, he established a plantation near New Smyrna in 1825. He purchased property for this purpose from the Addison estate and the Bunch plantation, which had then recently been the county seat. The property is in present-day Flagler County near Ormond Beach.

Thomas Dummett built a sugar mill, arguably the first in Florida. His contractor, Reuben Loring, was not happy with his payment, or lack thereof, and sued Dummett in Superior Court for assumpsit (for work done). The 1834 decision of the court jury was a finding for the plaintiff for $10.62 and court fees. The plaintiff then asked for a new trial.

Douglas Dummett, who was a captain in the Seminole War, commanded a force called the "Mosquito Roarers." They joined forces on January 17, 1836, with the St. Augustine Guard commanded by Major Benjamin A. Putnam (who became a circuit judge and is discussed in the next chapter) and fought the Seminoles at Dunlawton on the Halifax River. James Ormond III, in an addendum to his "Reminiscences," described Captain Dummett as the one man during the Battle of Dunlawton who didn't know fear.

On August 31, 1839, Dummet's father, Thomas, died. He is buried in the Huguenot Cemetery in St. Augustine.

In 1840, Dummett held the position of judge for Mosquito County. During this time, court records were kept at St. Johns County. Public records indicate that Dummett was a justice of the peace for Mosquito County on February 17, 1833, and presiding justice on February 26, 1844. He was also a member of the House of the Legislative Council, from St. Johns County, in 1843, and a member of that body from Mosquito County, in 1844 and 1845, but resigned before the legislature adjourned that year.

Douglas Dummett was the first Collector of Customs for the Port of New Smyrna. He married the daughter of a socially prominent family, but she promptly deserted him for another army officer. Another reference, however, is that the Florida Territorial Legislature enacted an Act on March 15, 1844, allowing Frances Dummett to divorce Duglas (sic) Dummett on the grounds of his abandonment and failure to support her and child.[129]

Douglas Dummett filed a claim under the Armed Occupation Act on March 16, 1843, for land near the site of Fort Ann in the Haulover portion of Merritt Island. He and his common law (second) wife, Leandra Fernandez, who was part African American and part Native American, developed orange groves at Dummett's Cove and on Merritt Island. He is noted for budding sweet oranges found in Turnbull Hammock in New Smyrna and establishing his (Dummett's) famous grove on Merritt Island. He is considered to be the Father of the Indian River citrus industry.[130]

Dummett moved to New Smyrna and built a home on an Indian mound, which he called Mt. Pleasant. Douglas had three daughters and a son, Charles, who was born in 1844. While home from school in April 1860, Charles was hunting near Mt. Pleasant when he tripped and accidentally discharged his gun, killing himself instantly. Douglas Dummett buried his son where he was killed. One hundred years later, developers worked around the grave, which still sits in the middle of Canova Drive, New Smyrna Beach. The marble slab on the sarcophagus reads, "Sacred to the Memory of Charles Dummett, Born August 18, 1844 - Died April 23, 1860."

According to the 1850 census, Douglas Dummett listed his occupation as a pilot and was living in St. Lucie County near N.C.

Scobie. Dummett went on to be a Collector of the Port of St. Augustine in 1853.

Following the Civil War, when economic times were difficult in Florida, Dummett was an exception to the rule because of his very successful orange groves nestled between the Indian River and Mosquito Lagoon. They were able to avoid freezes.[131]

The Last Will and Testament of Douglas Dummett was filed in Volusia County on May 7, 1887. His will was executed on April 4, 1874, with prominent pioneers Miles O. Burnham and Henry T. Titus as witnesses. The executrix named was his sister, Miss Anna Dummett. His handwritten will left his estate half to his sister and half to his illegitimate 3 children through Leandra. Dummett is reportedly buried in an unmarked grave on Merritt Island. His father is buried outside the city gates of St. Augustine.

In the 1960s, efforts were made to save what was known as the Dummett Castle in Brevard County. Those efforts were unsuccessful, and the castle was razed in 1967.

David R. Dunham, Mosquito County Court Judge, 1832-1833

David R. Dunham was the presiding justice of the Mosquito County court in 1832 and 1833. He was originally from New York, born in 1794. He has been referred to as the "Vanderbilt of his day."

Dunham's father, also named David, was a native of New Jersey, born there in 1770. Dunham's mother was Mary Shackerly of New York. Dunham's father started the construction of what became the famous steamship, The Robert Fulton. The father was knocked overboard and drowned before the ship was completed, which son David R. had to do. David R. Dunham sailed the ship to South Carolina and New Orleans and later sold it to the Brazilian Government.

In 1830, he moved to New Smyrna, Florida. In the early 1830s, he married Mary Magdalene Facio or Fatio, who was born in Hibernia on the St. Johns River. She was the daughter of Francis Philip Fatio, a/k/a "Philip, a native of Berne, Switzerland," who is mentioned as one of the Spanish judges during the Second Spanish Period. (See Chapter 1, supra).

In 1830, Mary and Caroline Dunham (David's mother and sister) purchased 575 acres from the estate of Ambrose Hull for $500.00. The property is located on the first block of South Riverside Drive in New Smyrna. It extended from the river to west of U.S. Highway # 1 to "Turnbull's back swamp." A stone mansion was built along the river by Mary Dunham, who conveyed it to David R. Dunham and his children by a deed of trust. David R. Dunham became an influential planter and prominent as the Judge of the Mosquito County Court. The premises described above were known as "Judge

Dunham's place." There is a sketch of this six-column home, which became the basis for the title of Bockelman's "Six Columns and Fort New Smyrna, in the back of the book."[132]

A post office was established at New Smyrna in connection with the Dunham residence on October 18, 1833. That post office was discontinued on August 30, 1837, but then reestablished in 1845.

The house was destroyed by the Indians during the Seminole War in 1835. Jacob Motte, an army surgeon, kept a diary entitled, "Journey into the Wilderness" and described the ruins from the explosion of Judge Dunham's princely mansion caused by the Indians' burning of the house, which had a keg of gunpowder in the basement.[133] This house was coincidentally located where Turnbull had established his Minorcan colony, and the coquina stones for the house were probably taken from the Hull house,[134] which stood on the Turnbull mansion foundation, but which fell into ruin by U.S. patriots in the Patriots' War of 1812.

The house had been described as the most beautiful home south of the Potomac River. After its destruction, its six tall, white, imposing Doric columns remained standing adjacent to the Hillsborough (now Indian) River. The pillars, soon thereafter, became a part of the newly constructed Fort New Smyrna in 1837 and the reconstructed fort in 1839.

Judge Dunham was blamed by his sister, subsequent to the fire, for failing to preserve the family silver and furnishings. In an ironic twist of fate, she sued her brother, the judge, in a suit in chancery entitled <u>Caroline Dunham v. David R. Dunham</u>, St. Johns Courthouse, 1837.

The 1850 U.S. Census for St. Johns County shows Dunham living with his wife, Marie or Mary Magdalene (nee Fatio), and their seven children, all of whom were born in Florida. They subsequently had two more children. David R. Dunham died in 1869.

Son, David L. Dunham, was a clerk of the circuit court, as was his father. David L. Dunham had a son, David R. Dunham (1886-1964), who was a prominent lawyer and judge in St. Augustine and was president of the St. Augustine Historical Society from 1932 to 1956. Another descendant of Florida Territorial County Judge David R. Dunham was Fatio Dunham, a clerk of courts for St. Johns County in 1874, appointed by Governor Ossian Hart.

Elias Gould, Mosquito County Justice of the Peace, 1828, County Court Judge, 1828-1845

Elias B. Gould was a descendant of John Gould, who was born in Dartmouth, England, in 1644. John Gould moved to New England from Devonshire, England.

Elias B. Gould was born in Westfield, New Jersey, in the 1780s. He started a printing business in Newark, New Jersey, and, in 1807 and 1808, he and a partner published Modern Spectator. Gould left Newark in 1810 for New York, where he remained until approximately 1818. He likely served in the U.S. Army in the War of 1812.

In 1822, Gould arrived in St. Augustine, via Charleston, South Carolina, and began publication of the East Florida Herald in August of that year. As editor, Gould had occasion to support Judge Joseph Lee Smith in the Smith-led efforts for the removal of District Attorney Edgar Macon. (See biographical information under Judge Smith in this chapter.)

Gould purportedly acquired 500 acres of land by the Big Bend of Durkin's Swamp from George Clarke, which was the subject of a claim or suit involving Clarke and the United States, and another claim involving one acre by Sanchez Creek & the St. Sebastian Creek. While it is unclear if Gould acquired a different property, many years following Gould's death, there was other land litigation that found its way to the Supreme Court of Florida. See the land case referenced below, which notes a couple of generations of Goulds.

Gould was way ahead of his time. As a county judge and newspaper editor, he decried the flaws in the law that deprived battered wives of protection.[135] He also addressed the outcry against sensational newspaper coverage that might increase crime by refusing to publicize acts of duels and fights.[136]

Gould's newspaper had its title shortened to the Florida Herald in 1829. In 1834, Gould's son, James, took over the paper. It was published until after Florida's statehood.

Elias B. Gould served four terms as mayor of St. Augustine. He was appointed a justice of the peace of Mosquito County in July 1828. In late November 1828, he was made judge of the Mosquito County Court.

It has been noted in Michael V. Gannon's introduction to Fairbanks' *The History and Antiquities of the City of St. Augustine, Florida* that Elias B. Gould copied several pages of correspondence of Spanish Governor, Manuel de Montiano (1737-1749), from the Archives of St. Augustine, Florida, which copies became a part of the appendix to the Annals of Florida, a manuscript written by Thomas Buckingham Smith which is located in the Library of Congress.

In the fall of 1837, Gould served at Ft. Marion, the then U.S. Territorial name for Castillo de San Marcos in St. Augustine. Gould was also a representative from St. Johns County to the Legislative Council in 1839. One of Judge Gould's sons, Ned, drowned as a result of an Indian attack during the Second Seminole War.

Judge Gould, as County Court Judge of then St. Johns County, has his name on the land grant application of John C. Clelland of

April 26, 1843, for property in what was the Ft. Pierce area, as to whom the application was sworn. Judge Gould continued in a judicial capacity for many years. He was still a county court judge in 1845.

Gould's other son, James M. Gould, the newspaper publisher and Elias's sole remaining heir, had 6 children. This lineage is discussed in the Supreme Court of Florida opinion in the case of Gould v Carr, 33 Fla. 523 (1894), which deals with a property acquired by Elias B. Gould and inherited by James M. Gould (in 1855). Incidentally, James Gould was a representative, like his father, but to the then State of Florida House of Representatives from St. John County in 1846.

Gould was preceded in death by his wife, Lydia F., who died on October 21, 1850, in St. Augustine. Gould died in St. Augustine on June 11, 1855.

Ossian B. Hart, first St. Lucie County lawyer, who helped organize its court, 1844

Ossian Bingley Hart was born in northeastern Florida on January 17, 1821. He was the son of Isaiah and Nancy (Nelson) Hart. Isaiah David Hart is credited with being the founder of Jacksonville in 1822, after opening one of the first village stores in Cow Ford, the predecessor name of Jacksonville, in 1821. The present-day Hart Bridge in downtown Jacksonville over the St. Johns River is named after him. He was also one of the early judges of the County Court for Duval County, being appointed in 1827. Isaiah, a Territorial Florida representative from Duval County in 1837 and 1838 and a senator from 1837 to 1845, may have been a bit of a wit. His tomb had the following inscription:

When I am dead and in my grave,
And these bones are all rotten;
When this you see, remember me,
That I may not be forgotten.[137]

Ossian Hart served as a volunteer soldier in the Second Seminole War from 1836 - 1837. After the war, he studied at a classical school for boys, Moses Waddell's Wellington Academy in Willington, South Carolina. Hart then read law with his father and a future justice of the Supreme Court of Florida, Joseph Lancaster. Ossian Hart was admitted to the Duval County Bar in 1842.

Ossian and his wife, Catherine Smith Campbell, of Newark, New Jersey, were married on October 2, 1843. They decided to take advantage of the Armed Occupation Act, a law that offered Florida frontier settlers 160 acres of free land. In 1844, the Harts moved to a farm outside of Fort Pierce. Fire destroyed their possessions ten days later. The Harts recovered in Key West and restarted soon thereafter in St. Lucie County.

Hart is listed as a voter in the John Barker/Precinct No. 2 district of St. Lucie County in 1844 and 1845. He emerged as a community leader and enjoyed early political success. He was named to the first board of county commissioners and served as St. Lucie County's first state representative in 1845. He was an East Coast Whig at the time of Florida's admission to the Union. He only served one term in the state legislature, however. Times were hard for the Harts in Fort Pierce. In three years, they suffered through their home burning down, a flood, and a hurricane destroying their orange grove in 1846. The couple then relocated to Key West, where Ossian enjoyed a lucrative admiralty practice.

In Key West, Ossian Hart was appointed Justice of the Peace and Notary Public. In 1849, he was elected as solicitor of the southern circuit, a position he held for four years.

During that time, and more particularly in April of 1850, he had occasion to be associated with a notorious case that would not likely happen today. A certain Cuban-born defendant was charged with murder. After a coroner's inquest, he was discharged by the Justice of the Peace for lack of evidence. Nevertheless, he was still charged and tried. An attorney was appointed at the beginning of the trial, who immediately moved for a continuance, which was denied. The defendant was convicted by a 12-man jury. After a motion for a new trial was denied and a Bill of Exceptions briefly delayed the case, Hart, as State Solicitor, moved that sentence be imposed. Judge Joseph B. Lancaster then on May 17, 1850, ordered that the defendant "shall hang by the neck until he is Dead! - Dead! - Dead!!!" The words "and the Lord have mercy on his soul" were scratched out from the Minute book. The defendant didn't hang, however. He escaped from prison and was shot by a soldier attempting to recapture him on May 20, 1850.[138]

Ossian took over his mentor, Joseph Lancaster's, law practice in Tampa in 1857. In 1859, he defended a slave who was charged with the murder of a white man and who was being prosecuted by future justice of the Supreme Court of Florida, Henry Laurens Mitchell. The trial was so acrimonious, and Mitchell appealed with such emotion, that despite a conviction, Hart was successful in having the Supreme Court of Florida grant a new trial. However, when news of the ruling reached Tampa, the defendant was lynched.[139] In 1860, Hart was named to the Tampa City Council.

Although Ossian was raised among slaves on his father's plantation, he openly opposed secession and suffered much hardship during the Civil War. He was considered a Union Loyalist. After the war, he took an active part in the reconstruction of the state government as a member of the Jacksonville Republican Party. He also organized a steamship company, which operated on the Indian River and St. Johns River after the Civil War.

In 1868, Hart served at the Constitutional Convention as a delegate from Nassau-Duval-St. Johns Counties and following the adoption of the Florida Constitution of 1868, Hart was appointed by Governor Harrison Reed as an Associate Justice of the Supreme Court. Hart, along with fellow justice James Diament Wescott, were the first native Floridians to sit on the Supreme Court of Florida.

Hart was defeated for Congress in a contested election in 1870 but continued on the Supreme Court through 1872 and founded Florida's Republican Party. In 1872, he was elected Republican Governor of Florida and is distinguished as the first Florida-born governor. Hart's administration as governor started Florida on a period of peace and progress. Hart had a reputation for integrity and had the support of black leaders and some white conservatives. Among the many constitutional changes he proposed was the concept of biennial, rather than annual, legislative sessions. One of the initial acts passed during his administration is considered Florida's first civil rights act.[140]

Ossian B. Hart had suffered from pneumonia while campaigning for governor and died in office on March 18, 1874, and is buried in the Evergreen Cemetery in Jacksonville. His grave notes, inter alia, "Elected Governor of Florida, September 1872" and notes "Patriot – Statesmen – Christian." He was survived at the time by his wife of 31 years, Catherine.

Moses Holbrook, St. Lucia County Physician, who helped set up a legal system

Dr. Moses Holbrook was likely the first physician in the Indian River Colony in the 1840s, being a settler under the Armed Occupation Act. His homestead was along the west side of the Indian River in Ankona.

Holbrook came to this area via Richmond County, Georgia. He had been described as an eccentric and very talented physician from a distinguished Charleston family. William Peck, the son of one of Dr. Holbrook's contemporaries, Samuel Peck, described Dr. Holbrook as obtaining great prominence in his profession in South Carolina and being polished, considerate, and tender with the settlers along the Indian River, but, because of "many misfortunes over the years," his brilliant intellect was affected. He lived in a primitive, large one-room cabin, loaded with books from Charleston and an "eight-keyed flute" on which he was very talented.

The crude legal system, which was in effect by 1844 in the Indian River Colony, was set up as a result of a convention called by Dr. Holbrook. That system initially called for the settling of disputes among the settlers by a committee of arbitrators.

Dr. Holbrook died in 1844 and is buried near the location of his cabin on Ankona Bluff, just south of Ft. Pierce.

Joseph Hunter, Mosquito County Court Clerk, 1833

Joseph Hunter was born in 1806 in Ballymere, Antrim County, Ireland. He was living in Mosquito County by 1830. He was appointed Clerk of the Mosquito County Court on February 17, 1833. He was also appointed justice of the peace at that time. He owned and cultivated a plantation that had once been cultivated by Dummett before the Second Seminole War, but was destroyed during the war. Hunter died on May 14, 1836, and is buried in the Huguenot Cemetery in St. Augustine.

Duncan McCrea, Mosquito County Court Judge, 1828, and Justice of the Peace, 1830

Duncan McCrea was a judge of the Mosquito County Court in 1828. He appears in the 1830 U.S. Census as residing in Mosquito County. He was named a justice of the peace in 1830. He and his brother, Kenneth, owned a plantation ten miles south of the Bulow plantation along the King's Road. The McCrea plantation was called "Carrickfergus," but this name was given to the land by a former owner, Thomas Addison, who came from County Carrickfergus, Ireland. Colonel Thomas Dummett's purchase of the Addison property was of questionable legality. He then conveyed to the McCreas.

At the time of the Second Seminole War, Kenneth McCrea had died, and Duncan occupied the plantation. The property subsequently became a military post in the Seminole War in 1836, called Camp McRae, or Fort McRae, or MacRae.

James Ormond, II, Mosquito County Court Clerk, 1828

James Ormond II was the son of Captain James Ormond, a Scotsman who immigrated to Florida via the Bahamas in approximately 1804. His father owned a brig, the Somerset, which traded between the West Indies and Europe, and Savannah and Apalachicola. His father retired from the sea, became a planter in Exuma, and then obtained two land grants in Florida. One was near New Smyrna and the other north of the McHardy Plantation, just north of present-day Ormond Beach. The latter grant became a plantation known as "Damietta," which was established in 1816. The plantation was one of the most productive in the Halifax region.

Ormond's father, while living at the New Smyrna grant, was killed, reportedly by a runaway slave, at the nearby plantation of General Williams. Ormond's widow and their son, Emanuel, went to Scotland to live with another of Ormond's sons, James Ormond II, who was born on one of the father's voyages and raised by an aunt.

James Ormond II was in the grain trade business in the Baltic, but the business failed. To escape debtor's prison, he, together with his mother and brother, went to Florida and developed the grant north of McHardy's plantation. They were later joined by James Ormond II's wife, Isabella, and their four children, Agnes, Russell, Helen, and James Ormond III.

When Florida became a U.S. territory, James Ormond II was active in civic affairs. Ormond was the Clerk of the Mosquito County Court in 1828. He died on September 30, 1829, and on his grave, his son, James Ormond III, had inscribed, "An honest man." The tomb is located on Old Dixie Highway in Ormond Beach. Mrs. James Ormond II died in Columbia, South Carolina, on November 5, 1836.

James Ormond III was born in 1815 at Mayfield, near Edinburgh, Scotland. He was raised in St. Augustine and subsequently moved to Charleston to become a merchant. He then returned to Florida and became an officer during the Seminole War in 1836. He commanded a platoon of "Mosquito Roarers" at the Battle of Dunlawton and was wounded.

On May 2, 1843, James Ormond III married Elizabeth Chaires, who had come to his attention after she had survived an Indian attack on her family while the family was living in Tallahassee. That same year, James Ormond III founded Newport (near Tallahassee), Florida, where he set up a business. Later, he established a business in Atlanta.

While too old to serve as a soldier in the Confederacy, he was a Confederate guard at the infamous Andersonville prison. The

Ormond family moved to Canada following the Civil War but ultimately returned to Atlanta.

The town where the Ormonds lived along the Halifax River was once called New Britain but was given the Ormond family name in 1880.

Joseph Osborne, St. Lucia County Court Clerk, 1845-1847

Joseph S. Osborne was the first clerk of St. Lucia County, serving from 1845 until 1847, when the legislature combined the clerk's office for both Orange and St. Lucie Counties.[141] His successor, for the combined counties, was J. C. Hemming.

While it may not be the same person, there is James Osborne, who married Mindora Odom (1823-1913) on June 15, 1847, in Duval County, Florida. He was born in Pennsylvania, and they may have had two daughters while living in Middlebury, Clay County, Fla., west of St. Augustine.[142]

Samuel Peck, St. Lucia County Arbitrator and Justice of the Peace, 1844

Samuel Peck was a banker from Augusta, Georgia. He worked as a cotton factor, but lost money because of the Panic of 1837 and the depression that followed. Peck then led several Houston County,

Georgia residents, who desired to settle under the Armed Occupation Act, to the Indian River Colony.

Peck owned and operated a schooner called the William Washington. It carried passengers and freight to and from the Indian River Colony and St. Augustine. It apparently was grounded in the Indian River in 1844 and salvaged by a Key West wrecker. Peck couldn't pay the salvage and abandoned his homestead in 1845.

Before abandonment, Peck's son, William, as a fourteen-year-old, joined his father in the colony. It has been noted that the Pecks brought some of the earliest non-escaping slaves to the area in early 1843, to help establish the Pecks' homestead in Susanna.[143] The Pecks were also engaged in clearing and planting citrus.

Samuel Peck was made a justice of the peace in St. Lucia County on March 15, 1844, the day after the county's creation. He was also one of three arbitrators initially appointed as a result of trying to set up a legal system in St. Lucia County. Peck served as the second St. Lucia County court judge, commencing in March 1845.

Son, William Peck, who was educated at Harvard, became a writer and later a settler at Courtney on Merritt Island. His recollection of his father and the early times in the Indian River Colony are documented in the Florida or Titusville Star on May 5, 1887. Samuel Peck's bio continues under his heading in Chapter 3.

Bernardo Sequi, Mosquito County Court Clerk, 1828-1829

Bernardo Sequi was a descendant of Minorcans who had migrated to Dr. Turnbull's colony in New Smyrna and then had moved to St. Augustine in 1777 when they were driven from the colony. Sequi's father, also Bernardo, was born in Minorca in 1742 and died in St. Augustine on November 5, 1813. Sequi's mother, Agueda Villalonga, was born in 1753. Bernardo Sequi was one of thirteen children.

The Sequis owned a home built of coquina rock at the corner of St. George and Artillery Streets in St. Augustine. That structure subsequently became the home of the St. Augustine Library and is now home to the St. Augustine Historical Society Library.

Bernardo Sequi was born in Florida in approximately 1784. He was prominent in St. Augustine and, in 1813, was a Spanish land grantee, along with several others, of what is known as the Hanson Grant of over 16,000 acres of land south of the St. Lucie River, which includes present-day Salerno, Sewall's Point, and St. Lucie Farms. Sequi was a Legislative Council representative for East Florida in 1822, but resigned. Sequi became a U.S. citizen in 1823. (Despite his being born in Florida, his birth was prior to Florida becoming a U. S. Territory).

On April 7, 1823, he was appointed by the United States to serve with Governor DuVal and Colonel James Gadsden on a commission to negotiate a treaty with the Indians following the First Seminole War. Conferences were held with the Indians at Moultrie Creek, where a treaty was entered, and more particularly accomplished at Fort Moultrie, approximately seven miles south of St Augustine, on September 18, 1823. It is known as the Treaty of Moultrie Creek.

Sequi was a clerk of the Mosquito County Court in 1828 and 1829 until the court was vacated by the Laws of Florida, 1829. Sequi continued to live in St. Johns County, as evidenced on the 1840 and 1850 U.S. Censuses. He was married and had a daughter. His wife and daughter were born in Florida.

John Lee Williams, Justice of the Peace, St. Johns County, 1833

John Lee Williams was born in Salem, MA, in 1775. He was first married to Mary Irwin, who died. They had one son. Williams' second marriage occurred in the Territory of Florida on March 9, 1829, in St. Augustine to Martha Lockhart Mackey. They had three children. Their first, Randolf John Lee Williams, died within a year, and his second son bore that same name. John Lee Williams was 58 when he started having these children. His daughter came 3 years later, in 1837, when John was 62.

John Lee Williams is noted for several things, besides being a Justice of the Peace for St. Johns County and possibly Mosquito County in the 1833 timeframe. He is credited with being one of the commissioners to select Florida's capital, which, of course, ended up being in Tallahassee. He also wrote a History of Florida, actually two, the second of which, "The Territory of Florida," stood for 40 years as the only history book about the state. His signature also appears on Florida Territory Papers, issuing Militia General Orders, such as on May 1, 1832, which he signed, John Lee Williams, Asst. Adj't General. He also created a map of Florida in 1837, which shows the gigantic Mosquito County. It also shows a break in the Indian River, around present-day Ft. Pierce, described as Indian River, which could be the northeast terminus of the Southern District of the Territory Superior Court, mentioned in this chapter.

On August 26, 1848, Williams conveyed property in Picolata, in St. Johns County, for $683.02. The deed is interesting as it is called "Conveyance of a Lot of Ground at Picolata." Williams died in Picolata, a town outside St. Augustine on the west side, but on the east side of the St. Johns River, on November 19, 1856.

William H. Williams, Justice of the Peace, Mosquito County, about 1833.

William H. Williams was a Justice of the Peace for Mosquito County. He was also a delegate to the Constitutional Convention from Mosquito County in 1838. He was also a member of the Legislative Council from Mosquito County from 1839-1842.

He is shown on the U. S. Census for 1840 as being in St. Augustine, St. Johns County, with his age being between 30 and 40 years old, and likely with a wife between the ages of 20 and 30 years old, and with a number of children.

Constitutional Convention Monument for 1838 – Port Saint Joe, Florida. Erected 1922. State Archives of Florida, Florida Memory.

Chapter 3 - Statehood - (1845) Through Pre-St. Lucie County (1905)

A. Statehood (1845)

Florida became the twenty-seventh state of the United States on March 3, 1845. Upon statehood, under the Florida Constitution conceived in 1838 at the St. Joseph Convention, circuit judges were to be elected by the legislature rather than the electorate. Circuit judges also served in the capacity of justices of the Supreme Court.

From this point forward, I am focusing on the courts of the State of Florida, to be distinguished from the federal courts and more particularly the United States District Courts in Florida, which in a sense sprang from the prior federal Superior Courts of the Florida Territory. I will say, however, that there was just one federal district court created initially in 1845 when Florida became a state. A second one was added two years later, creating the Northern and Southern (federal) District Courts, and the third and last, to this point, the Middle District of Florida in 1962.[144]

There were only four State of Florida judicial circuits initially in 1845. As alluded to, the circuit judges played a dual role as a trial-level judge (Circuit Court) and appellate judge (Supreme Court).[145] They also sailed or rode the circuit, traveling by boat, horse, or carriage to the major cities. Qualified jurists were deterred from becoming judges because of the physically arduous nature of the job. In fact, the circuit they traveled was not limited to within the circuit, but rather the judges rotated for a term in each circuit. The rotation only lasted two years, from 1846 to 1847, and was repealed because of the hardships of travel.[146]

The Act organizing the circuit courts of the State of Florida in July 1845 designated the area west of the Apalachicola River to constitute the Western Circuit. That part of the State lying east of the Suwannee River and north of the Southern Circuit was designated as the Eastern Circuit. The Middle Circuit consisted of all of the land between the Western and Eastern Circuits. All of that part of the State of Florida lying south of the northern line of St. Lucia County (then Cape Canaveral) constituted the Southern Circuit.[147]

St. Lucia County was thus initially a part of the Southern Circuit at the time when Florida became a state. However, shortly thereafter, the legislature transferred the county of St. Lucia from the southern circuit to the eastern judicial circuit. This Act was signed by the governor on December 20, 1845.[148] This was consistent with pre-statehood, when St. Lucia County, together with St. Johns and Mosquito Counties, were a part of the (federal) Eastern District of Florida.[149] For the preceding twenty-one months, the St. Lucia County seat or court site was John Cleland's house.[150] (The legislature spelled it with 3 "ls," but the signature on Mr. Cleland's Armed Occupation Act Application shows it with 2 "ls.")

The same Act that transferred St. Lucia County to the Eastern Circuit also consolidated Orange County and St. Lucia County for judicial purposes. Orange County, adjacent to St. Lucia County on the north, extended all the way to the East Coast of Florida.[151] Court for these counties was to be held at Mellonville in Orange County. The Act also provided that, "the judge of probate for the county of St. Lucia, until otherwise provided by law, shall record all instruments of writing required to be registered of record, and shall issue all licenses required to be issued, in said county, in the same manner and to the same effect that the territorial court of said county, was accustomed in this behalf to do previous to the state organization."[152]

Following statehood, the first judge of the Probate Court for then St. Lucia County was probably John S. Hermans. He was nominated by Governor William D. Moseley on July 26, 1845. The nomination was sent to the Legislative Assembly and subsequently approved. He is shown on the 1850 Census for St. Lucie County as "Judge Probate."

Between 1845 and 1854, several people served as justices of the peace. They included James P. Lightburn, Reuben H. Pinkham, William B. Davis, John Bullock, W. D. Ward, William F. Russell, C. L. Brayton, D.F. Jones, N.C. Scobie and George C. Stowell.[153]

Interestingly, at least four of these Justices were lighthouse operators at one time or another, at various locations in Florida.

The first Clerk of St. Lucie County was Joseph S. Osborne, who was permitted to keep records at his home, except when court was in session. In 1847, the legislature combined the offices of the Clerk of Court for St. Lucie and Orange Counties. J. C. Hemming was then elected to succeed Osborne. While J. C. Hemming apparently served as clerk until 1850, the records were kept in the home of D. H. Gettis until the home was destroyed in the Indian attack on the Russells and Barkers in 1849. Henry Crane, who was a Clerk of Mosquito County, became Clerk in 1850 and served through the change to Brevard County in 1855.

The combination of clerks for Orange and St. Lucie County, coupled with the maintenance of records at the clerk's home, may have triggered the creation of Volusia County from Orange County, east of the St. Johns River, on December 29, 1854.[154]

As mentioned, upon statehood in March of 1845, this area was initially a part of the Southern judicial circuit. However, during that brief period, until St. Lucia County's transfer to the eastern judicial circuit in December 1845, the southern circuit was without a judge. Great political dissension in the legislature existed on the election of a judge for the Southern circuit. While the legislature finally agreed in late 1845 upon Samuel Williams Carmack, a former Superior Court

Judge for the Apalachicola District in Florida, he declined to serve. Finally, George W. Macrae, a future justice of the Supreme Court of Florida, was temporarily appointed by Governor Moseley to the southern circuit, but that was after St. Lucie County's transfer to the eastern circuit.

The first term of the Supreme Court of Florida was scheduled for January 5, 1846. However, the matter of a circuit judge for the southern circuit was unresolved, and the circuit judge for the western circuit had not yet arrived. Thus, the Supreme Court of Florida commenced on January 6, 1846, with Thomas Douglas, the circuit judge for this area (Eastern Circuit) as chief justice, and with Thomas Baltzell and George S. Hawkins as justices. The first case, Charles D. Stewart v. Thomas Preston, Jr., found at 1 Fla. 1 (1846), involved an appeal that arose from Gadsden County Superior Court. In that case, the Supreme Court of Florida upheld its own jurisdiction to review cases pending in the former territorial Court of Appeals.

Probably the first case making it to the Supreme Court of Florida that emanated from our former Mosquito County was Taylor v. Baker, 1 Fla. 245 (1847). It did not involve an appeal from a circuit court because the newly created State of Florida had just come into existence the previous year. It involved an appeal from the Superior Court of the Territory of Florida sitting for the counties of St. Johns and Mosquito. Justice Thomas Douglas, who also sat on the Superior

Court, had to be recused (excused from the bench at the hearing of that matter). The case involved a contract for deed. The Supreme Court ruled that the contract superseded the Armed Occupation Act, which Congress approved on August 4, 1842, which provided that assignment of rights under the Act shall be null and void. This particular assignment was not under the Act. The land involved was a property near Lake Monroe, which is southwest of New Smyrna. The opinion was written by Justice Baltzell, and there was a dissent by Judge George S. Hawkins.

In 1851, the Florida Constitution did away with circuit judges sitting as Supreme Court justices. Rather, the Supreme Court was to be staffed by a chief justice and two associate justices elected by the state legislature for the term of their good behavior. (Incidentally, that same year, the legislature appropriated $1,000.00 for the construction of a wagon road from Indian River in St. Lucie County to what is today Miami!) Two years later, in 1853, an amendment to the Constitution provided for the election of Supreme Court justices and circuit judges by the people, and for six-year terms. William A. Forward was our first elected judge for the Eastern District.[155]

The 1850 census for St. Lucie County, primarily consisting of the Fort Capron area (just north of the present Fort Pierce), had 140 people, including 30 soldiers and 27 slaves.[156] One of the heads of families was John L. Herman, a/k/a John S. Heermans, Judge of

Probate. Judge Heermans seemed to have served as Probate Judge from 1845 to 1851 and again from 1853 to 1854. Heermans was succeeded by D. H. Gettis from 1851 to 1853. Heermans was actually elected and appointed in 1854 for another term, but declined to serve.

A couple of cases of the Supreme Court of Florida from the 1850s are of interest to attorneys and involve two of our Circuit judges sitting in for Supreme Court Justice Baltzell, who recused himself. The judges were William A. Forward and B.A. Putnam. The cases, which were connected, were Carter v. Bennett[157] and Carter v. Davis.[158] Each case involved compensation for attorneys under the theory of quantum meruit and the imposition of a lien for those services. Under the theory, a reasonable fee was to be allowed when no express agreement was made as to how the services were to be compensated. Reference is still being made to those decisions.[159]

In 1855, St. Lucie County's name was changed to Brevard, encompassing the same area as the older county.[160] At that time, the county site was permanently established and located at a place known and designated as Fort Pierce. The name of this county site was to be Susanna,[161] which was four miles south of Fort Pierce, although the map may have been wrong, and it could have been 4 miles north of Ft. Pierce, where St. Lucie Village is still situated.[162] At that time, Major William F. Russell was a state legislator and had a wife and daughter named Susan,[163] and it is thought that Susanna may have been named after them.[164] Another school of thought is that the name was a scrivener's error and that it should have been Savanna, the Spanish name for flat, wet, treeless grasslands.[165] At the time of the Armed Occupation Act settlement, and again in 1855, there were prominent settlers in what is now Ankona, which to this day is located next to a savanna, for which the settlement may have been named.

Another spin on the Susanna/Savanna County seat name is that a number of Armed Occupation Act settlers were from Georgia. In fact, the "most prestigious house erected up to that time" in the settlement was framed in and shipped from Savannah, Georgia. The house far overshadowed the other dwellings made of pine saplings and palmetto leaves. This house, incidentally, was owned by Col. Samuel H. Peck and sold to Capt. Mills Burnham (See biographies in chapter 2), who went on to be a keeper of the Cape Canaveral lighthouse in 1853.[166]

Colton Map with revisions through 1859
shows the new Brevard County
Courtesy of Brevard County Historical Commission Archives
Note how far south and west Brevard County is. However, note how
Orange County covers what is now the northern portion of Brevard
County. Note also, Susannah.

The naming by Major Russell seems the most plausible explanation because of his inherent power as Speaker of the House at the time the bill was introduced, and he sponsored the bill.[167] He is also credited with naming Brevard County after his friend and fellow legislator, Theodorus W. Brevard.

In 1858, Major James E. Paine arrived at Fort Capron. Shortly thereafter, he founded St. Lucie Village, where the Paine family became prominent. Mr. Paine served as a County Judge of Brevard during the late 1860s.[168]Judge James Paine's daughter, Gertrude Elizabeth, married Minor S. Jones, who was a Circuit Judge for this area from 1898 to 1911.[169]

From 1853 to 1857, Judge William A. Forward served as the circuit judge for the Eastern Circuit. He had been a well-respected lawyer and had served as a member of the General Assembly. Subsequently, he was made a Supreme Court Justice in 1859.

In January of 1859, the Eastern Judicial Circuit (one of the then four Judicial circuits of Florida) was scheduled to meet insofar as Volusia and Brevard counties on the second Monday after the fourth Monday in October and March. However, that law did not go into effect until the Fifth Judicial Circuit was organized and the judge duly selected and qualified (and until then, the courts were to be held at the time previously prescribed by the law in said counties).[170]

B. Secession & Civil War (1861-1865)

In January of 1861, Florida seceded from the Union. Its new government, as a confederate state, provided that Supreme Court justices and Circuit judges would be appointed by the governor, by and with the consent of two-thirds of the senate, and hold office for six years.

During the Confederate period, this area (then Brevard County) was a part of the Eastern Circuit, for which Benjamin A. Putnam was the Circuit Judge (from 1857 to 1868). This area was also under the command of the Fifth Commissary District, which was headed by Captain James McKay, a Scottish skipper and cattle driver. McKay replaced King of the Crackers, Jacob "Uncle Jake" Summerlin. The entire state was then under Chief Commissary of Florida Major Pleasant A. White, a lawyer and native of Quincy, Florida.[171]

Closer to what would again become St. Lucie County, several figures connected with the judiciary were active in securing this region. On August 28, 1861, a meeting of the citizens of Indian River, Brevard County, was held at the house of James Paine. William B. Davis chaired the meeting and, on a motion of John S. Herman, James Paine and Francis Ivey were appointed to draft a resolution which was sent to Gov. M.S. Perry relating to the protection of the Brevard Colony. The resolution noted that the citizens were without protection for one hundred miles, with their young men now in Virginia. The resolution affirmed that the citizens adhered to the Constitution of the Confederate States. The resolution further noted that James Paine was appointed Captain of the company on guard, and he was thanked, along with several others, for putting out the lights of Jupiter and Cape Florida lighthouses. Another archive record shows why Paine and others acted in connection with dismantling the lighthouses.[172]

In 1864, by an Act of the legislature, the Brevard County seat was moved to Bassville,[173] 65 miles west of the coast. We know little of what caused this relocation. However, this move was during the Civil War when the Union patrolled the coast of Florida, including the Indian River Inlet,[174] and the population in the Ft. Pierce area was sparse. The seat location was likely moved to a safer inland location and perhaps closer to a cattle trail. Moving cattle was one of the main activities of the Florida settlers who were not serving with the Confederacy.[175]

Before the Civil War, major cattle drives emanated from North Florida to Punta Rassa for shipment to Cuba. The drives passed near the east end of Lake Tohopekaliga. During the war, the direction of the drives reversed to the North Florida railheads.[176] By that lake, Needham Bass operated a ferry through the marsh. Bassville became a trading post along the trail that Jacob Summerlin and others followed. Coincidentally, Summerlin was later dramatically involved in the creation of another county seat, Orlando, for Orange County, including the financing of the Orange County Courthouse.[177]

Maps and records show that Bassville was southwest of St. Cloud in present-day Osceola County. A reference suggests that it was located between Kissimmee Park and Canoe Creek roads.[178] It would have been in an area close to Lakeview or Whittier and present-day Kenansville. Another researcher has described it as being on the east shore of Lake Tohopekaliga.[179] That description is consistent with Charles Granville's Railroad & Township Map of Florida, 1886,

South Publishing Company. (Brevard County Historical Commission Archives).[180] In 1865, the Act creating Bassville as the county seat was repealed to allow the county voters to choose the location.[181] Not much is known about what was once the seat of Brevard County. Records indicate that Bassville subsequently had a post office from November 1873 until November 1874.[182]

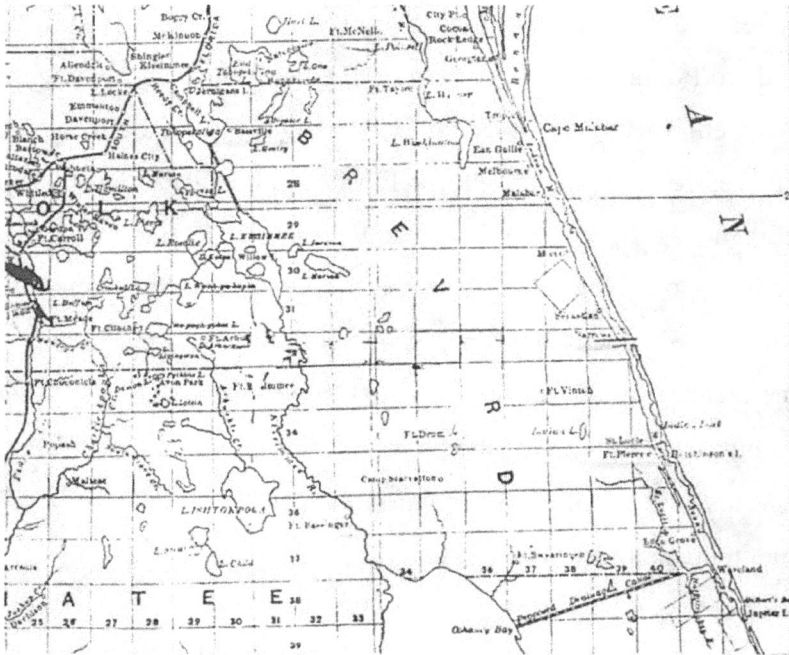

1866 - Charlie Granville's Railroad and
Township Map of Florida
Brevard County Commission Archives
Note: Observe Bassville, The Narrows, and Fort Pierce

C. Reconstruction and Post-Reconstruction (1865-1885)

Following the defeat of the Confederacy, Florida delegates met to formulate a new Florida Constitution in October of 1865. However, the 1865 Florida Constitution never went into effect and was formally rejected by the U.S. Congress, which enacted its own Reconstruction laws over the veto of President Andrew Johnson. The 1865 Constitution provided for the Supreme Court of Florida to be composed of a chief justice and two associate justices appointed by the governor, with Florida Senate confirmation, and for the election of circuit judges. However, the newly proposed constitution did not guarantee the voting rights of freedmen. Florida came under military-imposed martial law from May 1865 to July 1868, at which time it was readmitted to the Union. Thus, with martial law replacing the Florida judicial system in the years immediately following the Civil War, there was a limited number of lawyers in Florida, with none being reported in what is now the Treasure Coast and Brevard County.[183]

In 1868, a new constitution was adopted, which called for a supreme court consisting of three justices appointed for life and seven circuit judges appointed by the governor and confirmed by the senate for a term of eight years. This Constitution of 1868 also provided for seven judicial circuits, the Seventh Judicial Circuit being composed of Volusia, Brevard (which we were at the time), Orange, and Dade counties.[184] The circuit judge was John W. Price, who held court in Enterprise. Judge Price served in the Seventh Circuit during the Reconstruction era from 1867 to 1877.

In March of 1871, James Paine, Sr., and John W. Price joined together for the purposes of writing Governor Harrison Reed with their recommendation of officers for appointment in Brevard County.[185] By May of that same year, Paine was recommending Alexander A. Stewart as Clerk of the Brevard Court and Dr. Charles McLean as county judge.[186] In that same letter, Paine attacked Frank Smith for interfering with Paine's recommendations. In August of 1872, Paine recommended Henry L. Parker as county judge. He described Parker as a native of the state, well qualified by education to fill the office. Paine further noted that correspondence to Henry Parker should be sent to Paine's own address, as Ft. Drum, where Parker lived, had no post office.

In 1874, the seat of Brevard County was Bovine, located on the northwest side of Eau Gallie[187] and on the northeast side of Lake Washington. Records show that Bovine had a post office from 1884 until it was discontinued in favor of Eau Gallie in 1904.[188] The 1914 Atlas of Florida Growers shows Bovine to be located between sections 25 & 26 in Township 28 South, Range 36 East.[189] It was apparently founded by one of Brevard's largest cattlemen, Bethel Stewart. (He was likely a relative of A. A. Stewart of Eau Gallie, whose biography is included in this chapter.) It served a small number of cattlemen, lumbermen, and turpentine operators and had a post office run by Postmistress Belle M. Stewart.[190] There is a reference that court was held under an oak tree.[191] That same year, the county commissioners also authorized the courthouse to be built near Jackson Simons' store near present-day Eau Gallie. However, it was probably not built.[192] (It is ironic that while the official seat of Brevard today is Titusville, the same general area of Bovine is only a little south of the current Harry T. & Harriette V. Moore Judicial Complex[193] for Brevard, in the relatively new community of Viera.)

The county commissioners changed their minds in 1875 and voted for Lake View[194] as the county seat. The seat was changed again to Bassville in April of 1876. In 1879, the seat was Savages' Store at the site of old Fort Taylor on Lake Winder.[195]

The records concerning the courts and county seats for this area until 1879 are confusing due in part to the changes in the county seats and political power bases, shifts in the relatively sparse population, and the broad geographical areas covered. There were also fires affecting court and county commission records.[196]

These problems were compounded by the feud between the Barbers and Mizells. It was a feud between Brevard and Orange County residents, of cracker versus republican carpetbagger. This feud resulted, *inter alia*, in the murder of Orange County Sheriff &

Tax Collector David Mizell on February 21, 1870, in the vicinity of the Orange County/Brevard County line at Bull Creek, south of Deer Park. He was the brother of Judge John Mizell of Orlando. Possibly forty people died as a result of the feud. Other related consequences of the feud included the burning of a courthouse in western Brevard and the loss of land to the west of the Kissimmee River for Brevard County.[197]

With the addition of the lower part of Volusia County to Brevard in 1879, the county seat was moved to Titusville. (Titusville, which was founded in 1867, had been named after Colonel Titus, a Confederate soldier who defeated Captain Clark Rice in a game of dominoes, which resulted in the name in Titus' favor. That location had previously been known as Sand Point.[198]

Titusville was chosen as the county site in a county election held on October 7, 1879. It was initially to be the site or seat for ten years.[199] Colonel Titus worked diligently to have the county seat located in Titusville, and his dream, a political coup, was realized when the vote taken on the above date was as follows:

For Eau Gallie	35
For Rockledge	39
For Titusville	195

The Brevard election districts, at the time, included: (1) LaGrange; (2) Titusville; (3) City Point; (4) Eau Gallie; (5) Taylor Creek; (6) Merritt Island; (7) Capt. Burnham's Grove, and districts west of the St. Johns River; (8) Yates; (9) Bassville; (10) Lakeview; and (11)Ft. Drum.[200] (As a reference, the City of Melbourne, which annexed the City of Eau Gallie in the 1960s, and today equals the size of the county seat of Titusville, was not incorporated until December 22, 1888, and then it was as the "Village of Melbourne.") Melbourne did have a post office as early as 1880.

The Brevard County Commissioners originally authorized Col. Titus to obtain "the church" for county purposes until they could build a courthouse.[201] Colonel Titus gave the land on which the county court building stands today in Titusville, but it was given with the restriction on use only for county or public purposes. On March 5, 1880, the Board of County Commissioners for Brevard County awarded a contract to F. B. Sackett to build a jail for Brevard County at a price of $565.00. The jail was a wooden structure about 8' x 10' and 8' high. Andrew Gibson was the first jailer.

On October 19, 1880, F. B. Sackett was employed to draw working plans and specifications for the courthouse to be built at Titusville, in accord with the general election.[202] In the December 15, 1880, issue of The Star, notice was given by the Board of County Commissioners for bids to erect a county courthouse on the corner of

~133~

Palm and Pine Streets. The courthouse was started in 1881 and completed in approximately 1883.[203]

On November 8, 1887, the Brevard County Commissioners appointed the sheriff as "janitor" of the courthouse. It is assumed that the term meant more of a custodial or trusted capacity than a personal service.

There was great population growth in Brevard County following the Civil War. The county census for 1860 was 260 persons, which grew to 1,216 by 1870, a growth of almost 500%. Most of this growth occurred between 1865 and 1870.[204]

Occasional amendments were made to the judicial system in Florida until an overhaul in 1885. This new constitution, considered Florida's fifth, replaced the "Carpetbag" Constitution of 1868. The Constitution of 1885 was adopted at a convention on June 9, 1885, and became effective on January 1, 1887. It continued in basic form until 1968, except for Article V, the judicial department, which was substantially revised in 1956.

Article V of the Constitution of 1885 continued to provide that there shall be seven circuit judges, who shall be appointed by the governor and be confirmed by the senate. The term, however, was reduced to six years compared to the eight years provided under the previous Constitution of 1868.

By way of contrast, circuit judges were originally elected by the legislature. In 1852, however, circuit judges were elected by the qualified electorate. The practice of appointment by the governor started with the Constitution of 1861 and continued until 1942, when circuit judges were elected by the populace, which elections became non-partisan in 1971.

The Seventh Judicial Circuit, originally created under the Constitution of 1868, continued in existence in 1885 and consisted of the counties of Volusia, Brevard, Orange, and Dade.

The Constitution of 1885 provided that the legislature may establish not more than 20 Judicial Circuits.[205] It was not, however, until approximately 1903 that an Eighth Circuit was created, and this area (then Brevard County) was still in the Seventh Circuit.[206]

By 1887, a new precinct was created in Brevard County known as the "Narrows."[207] This area was in the vicinity of the future Vero Beach. As a reference, the Narrows post office was established on April 2, 1884, and discontinued on May 15, 1913, in favor of Quay, now the Winter Beach area of Indian River County.[208] The Narrows Post Office was on Gem Island,[209] which is now part of John's Island. (There was a prior post office in that approximate location called Reams, established on 25 Sep 1892 (and discontinued in favor of the Narrows 20 Jul 1896).

On May 12, 1887, Osceola County, Florida's 40th county, was established by the Florida legislature. It was taken in part from the western part of Brevard County. It was named after the Seminole Chief, Osceola, and its seat was Kissimmee.

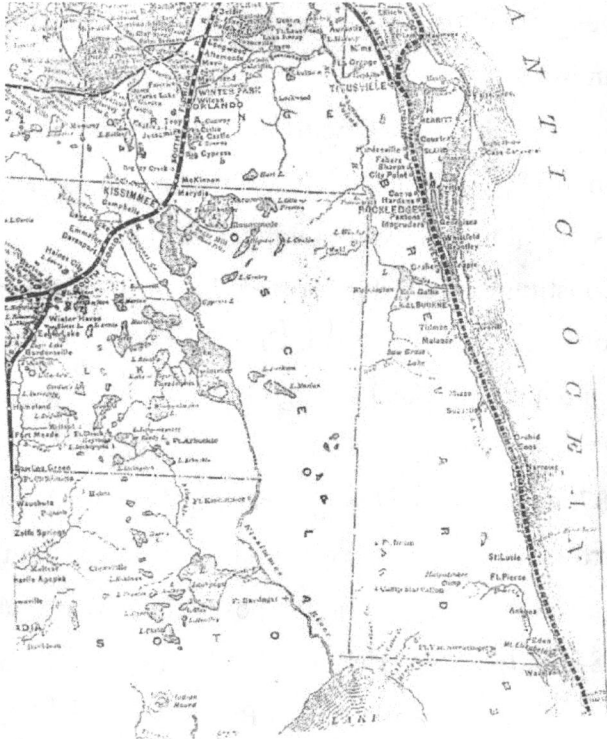

1891 Map of Jacksonville, Tampa, and Key West Rail System Map
Courtesy of Brevard County Historical Commission Archives
Note the new Osceola Co, the Narrows, and Hardees & Magruders
by Rockledge.

Some improper acts are recognized as crimes only with the passage of time. For years, flying feathered creatures were fair game and in great demand because of their plumage. On March 14, 1903, President Theodore Roosevelt established Pelican Island in the Indian River as the first federal bird reservation, giving birth to the National Wildlife Refuge System. The President later followed that executive order by making it a crime to hunt any bird or take or harm any bird's egg on any unreserved mangrove or island in Sections 9 & 10.[210]

The Circuit Court docket book for Brevard County commencing in 1897 survives. It includes both the criminal and civil docket. Crimes tried then included assault with intent to rape (which resulted in a not guilty finding) and fraudulent alteration of brands on an animal (which case was continued). Civil actions included trespass and assumpsit, a common law action for breach of promise. Attorneys appearing to argue cases before Circuit Judge John D. Broome included Minor S. Jones and Robbins Graham, who handled the defense of most cases. A typical disposition of a County Court appeal to the Circuit Court reads as follows: "This case is affirmed at cost of the Plaintiff in Error. Mandate is ordered to be sent down to County Court of Brevard County. In Open Court, this 25th day of November 1897. John D. Broome, Judge."[211]

At the turn of the century, circuit court sessions generally averaged two weeks. Occasionally, there would be four weeks of circuit court during the two annual sessions, which would be indicative of a large amount of crime for that year.[212]

By 1900, the population around Ft. Pierce had increased due in large part to crop freezes in the late 1890s in northern Brevard County. Ft. Pierce was incorporated in 1901. The people of lower Brevard wanted county government closer to home and lobbied the legislature to that effect. In 1905, what is now St. Lucie and Indian River Counties were taken from Brevard County to form St. Lucie County, the same name and a portion of the same land area which had been St. Lucia County from 1844 to 1855.

A list of the Circuit Judges with jurisdiction over what is now Indian River County, including the then particular circuit, dating back to the creation of the State of Florida, until St. Lucie County was created, is as follows:

Years	Judge	Circuit
1845	Open	Southern
1845-1853	Thomas Douglas	Eastern
1853-1857	William A. Forward	Eastern
1858-1867	B. A. Putnam	Eastern
1868-1877	John W. Price	Seventh
1877-1885	William Archer Cocke	Seventh
1885-1887	Eleazer K. Foster	Seventh
1887-1898	John D. Broome	Seventh
1898-1911	Minor S. Jones	Seventh

A partial list of the Probate and County judges from statehood to the creation of St. Lucie County, with approximate years of service, is as follows:

JUDGES OF PROBATE

1845-1851	John S. Hermans
1851-1853	D. H. Gettis
1853-1855	John S. Hermans

COUNTY JUDGES

1855-1860	Oliver H. Perry
1860-1865	James G. Benton
1865	John Barber
	James Paine, Sr.
1870s	Charles McLane
1872	Henry L. Parker
	Charles B. Magruder
1870s	Abner D. Johnston
1880	A. J. Whitlock

1881-1887	James A. McCrory
1887-1898	Minor S. Jones[213]
1898-1905	D. L. Gaulden

The next paragraph contains a partial offering of the Clerks of Court and their approximate time frame of service from the time of statehood for this area through the creation of St. Lucie County in 1905.

In 1845, the Clerk was Joseph S. Osborne. He was succeeded by J.C. Hemming and possibly D.H. Gettis. From 1850 to 1855, Henry A. Crane served as the Clerk. There was likely no Clerk for the next five years until William Cook took over and was succeeded by James Padgett. In 1871, A.A. Stewart was installed and served as Clerk in Brevard County until 1912, which was seven years after St. Lucie County was carved from Brevard County. There may have been a hiatus in his service as John M. Lee was the Clerk in approximately 1875 when the county seat seemed to move back and forth from the coast to the Lakeview area.

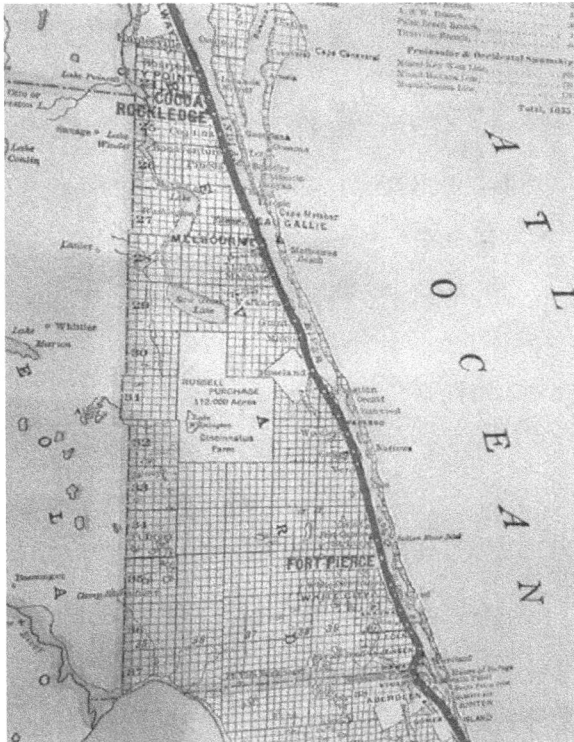

A portion of the peninsula of Florida…
published by Florida East Coast Railway, Ca. 1914.
Note the large Russell Purchase - Cincinnatus Farms in what is now
Fellsmere. Also notice Woodley, the Narrows, and Hardeeville at the
top of St. Lucie County and Eldred and Ankona to the south.
Whittier to the Northwest is now in Osceola County.

Besides Circuit Judges, County Judges, and Clerks of Court, Brevard County had numerous Justices of the Peace for the then very large county. In the 1870s, Brevard County included an area from

Mims to St. Lucie and west to Kissimmee and Orlando. Prior to the re-creation of St. Lucie County in 1905, Justices of the Peace for our area included; Frank C. Smith, 1875, St. Lucie, A.A. Stewart, 1872, Indian River, John Houston 1872, Indian River, A.D. Johnston, 1872, 1875 Indian River, Arch Henry, 1875, 1878, St. Lucie, J Padgett, Bassville, 1875, John M. Swain, St. Lucie, 1879, 1882, & Ft. Drum 1903, Walter Kitching, New Haven (Sebastian), 1883, James F. Bell, St. Lucie, 1883, 1887, 1889, 1892, George V. Barker, Eden, 1885, A. J. Whitlock, City Point, 1881, 1885, James T. Gray, Narrows (Gem Island), 1887, William J. McMillan Ft. Pierce 1889, J. D. Vann, Sebastian 1891, W. Omar* Jacobs, Roseland, 1893, John C. Hoyles, Roseland 1893, J. T. Gray, Narrows, 1889. B. F. Beal, Narrows, 1889, A. C. Dittman, Ft. Pierce, 1891, Robert Hardee, Sebastian 1895, L.S. Eldred, Ankona, 1895, A. L. Lowder*, Sebastian, 1897, J. Lee, Ft. Drum, 1897, W. L. Keefer, Woodley (Winter Beach), 1897 & Quay 1903, Horatio G. Bronson, Ft. Pierce, 1900, 1901, B.F. Hardesty, Sebastian, 1901. The records of Officials from the State Archives for Brevard County start in 1872, and I have looked at them through 1905. I provide some biographical information for many of them further below.

* State records are written in cursive and are a little unclear.

D. Biographical Information on Circuit Judges for this area, 1845-1905, in the order of their service.

<u>Douglas, Thomas, Eastern Judicial Circuit Judge 1845-1853</u>

In July of 1845, the initial Florida Constitution provided that circuit judges would be elected by the general assembly. William Marvin was elected to the circuit judgeship for the southern circuit. However, he declined to serve, and George W. McCray was then appointed by Governor Moseley in his place. Similar to the election of Marvin, the legislature in 1845 actually elected another person to be the initial circuit judge for the Eastern District of Florida, namely Isaac H. Bronson.[214] Bronson, who had served as a Federal Territorial Judge and hoped to serve again (which he subsequently did in a federal district court), declined to serve as Circuit Judge. Thomas Douglas was then appointed. In addition to being our Eastern Circuit Judge after the State of Florida was created, he was, at the same time, the first Chief Justice of the Supreme Court of Florida.

Douglas was born on April 27, 1790, in Wallingford, Connecticut. Douglas' father, John Ballard Douglass or Douglas, was a shoemaker and bought a farm located between Hartford and New Haven, Connecticut, when Thomas Douglas was age ten. Thomas Douglas, as a young man, tried to find a better life for himself and his wife, Hannah Sanford. He moved his family to Indiana in 1815, but his efforts to start his own business there soon failed. Douglas then began "reading law" to earn his license to practice. It has been reported that he read two hundred pages of legal text and two hundred pages of history daily, in addition to reading the Bible and newspapers.[215] Oddly enough, Douglas succeeded in being elected a judge in Jefferson County, Indiana, before he was even licensed to practice law.

During a trip along Florida's Gulf Coast in 1824, Douglas visited Pensacola and decided to apply for the position of District Attorney for the Western District of Florida. His application was denied, but in 1826 his friends in Congress were influential in having him appointed by President John Quincy Adams as District Attorney for the Eastern District of Florida. The opening came about as a result of Territorial Judge Joseph Smith being accused of battery and the prosecutor, District Attorney Edgar Macon, being held by Smith in contempt.

Douglas then moved to St. Augustine, where he was greeted by Judge Joseph Smith. Smith was a mentor to Douglas, but they also had a hostile relationship because of Douglas's moralistic and anti-alcohol sentiments. Douglas boarded in the house that used to belong to British Chief Justice William Drayton. As District Attorney, his duties brought him to court in Jacksonville and St. Augustine. There were three attempts to assassinate Douglas while he was the district attorney.

In 1828, Congress created a third superior court district in Florida. Instead of making life easier for District Attorney Douglas, however, the same act unsettled private land claims, which were then to be adjudicated in the superior court. Douglas became renowned for his tremendous knowledge concerning Spanish land claims.[216]

Douglas opposed General Jackson's quest for the Presidency, and upon Jackson's election, Douglas expected to be removed from office. However, Jackson acknowledged that Douglas knew "more about Spanish land grants than any other man in the United States." Douglas held that position until he resigned on October 8, 1845, when he received notification of his appointment as a circuit judge for the Eastern District of Florida. He also served on the Supreme Court of Florida starting in 1845, at the same time as a circuit judge. He became the first chief justice of the Supreme Court of Florida and served in that capacity until 1851. He continued, however, as a circuit judge, defeating William Forward (who later defeated him in the legislature) for circuit judge in 1853. Douglas had a prior stint as a representative to the Legislative Council from St. Johns County in 1838.

In 1853, the Florida State Constitution was amended so that the election of supreme court justices was made by the general electorate rather than the legislature. That amendment provided for the election of judges to a six-year term. Thomas Douglas was one of the first justices chosen by popular election held in 1853. He resumed serving on the Supreme Court on January 2, 1854. At that time, the Supreme Court met in Marianna, Jacksonville, and Tampa. Douglas, however, did not complete his term. While returning home to Jacksonville from Tallahassee in May 1855, he became seriously ill and died four months later on September 11, 1855, at the age of 65.

Bird M. Pearson, a descendant of William Penn and the Byrds of Virginia, was elected to fill Justice Douglas's unexpired term on the Supreme Court.

William A. Forward, Eastern Judicial Circuit Judge 1853-1857

Justice William Augustus Forward was born in New York in approximately 1812. He moved to Canada in 1816 and subsequently studied law. Forward fought in the Canadian Rebellions of 1837 - 1838, during which he was taken prisoner and deported from Canada. Thereafter, he returned to New York, where he was mentored by former Congressman Issac Bronson. When Bronson accepted the Eastern Florida Superior Court Judge's position, Forward followed to St. Augustine, Florida. Forward soon became involved in state politics, serving as Speaker of the last territorial House of Representatives (Legislative Council) in 1845, state senator (1845, 1848 & 1850), state rep (1847), and circuit judge.

William A. Forward was also an attorney in St. Augustine and was elected its mayor in 1843. In 1845, he was considered for the circuit judgeship for the southern circuit, being promoted by the democratic senators in the Florida Legislature. However, that was the year that the legislature could not agree upon a judge for a long time, and when Samual W. Carmack was finally elected, Carmack declined to serve.

In 1850, Forward lived in St. Augustine with his second wife, Mary Hutchinson, who was born in New Hampshire in approximately 1813. Her father was a New York lawyer, and her grandfather was one of the Presidents of Dartmouth College. (Forward's first wife, Almira, died in November 1841. Their daughter also died that same month.) The United States Census shows that the Forwards in 1850 had four children, plus a law student, Charles Broward, living with them. The oldest child, Lydia J., was born in Canada, and the rest of the children were born in Florida.

As an attorney, William A. Forward handled a very interesting case, which highlighted a portion of the history of this area. More particularly, he represented the widow of John Barker, one of the early settlers of Indian River County under the Armed Occupation Act of 1842.

Barker had obtained a permit under the Act in 1843, and in 1848, he applied for a land patent. His application was signed by John S.

Hermans, who we know to be a probate judge in the late 1840s and early 1850s in Fort Pierce. The treasury agent, apparently on December 18, 1848, approved the claim. However, shortly thereafter, Indians attacked the settlement and particularly Barker and his brother-in-law, William F. Russell, whose sister Martha was John's wife. John Barker was killed by the Indians on or about July 13, 1849.

Prior history had the Barker premises and the attack, occurring near the Sebastian River. Today, that property is thought to be near the St. Lucie Village, the Fort Capron area, across from the former St. Lucie Inlet. Years later, in the lawsuit, Mrs. Barker, in claiming the property, had to explain, with William A. Forward arguing for her, why she failed to apply for letters of administration on account of her husband John, who died intestate (without a will). The explanation was that after the Indian attack at the Indian River, there was no judge of probate or clerk, or other officers left in the county by whom administration could have been granted. There was a dispute, however, on the actual land owned by Barker on his application and the map from the St. Augustine land office. The case even involved the work of Surveyor General B. A. Putnam, who, like Forward, would be a circuit judge for the Eastern District of Florida. (See Putnam's Biographical information below.) It took seven years to resolve the dispute over the permit.[217]

In 1851, Forward was once again considered for a circuit judgeship, the eastern circuit this time. However, the incumbent, Thomas Douglas, who was also the Chief Justice of the Supreme Court of Florida, won the circuit court election. Nevertheless, Forward was elected as circuit judge by the legislature over Douglas in 1853, and Douglas went back to the Supreme Court in 1854.

The circuit judgeship to which William A. Forward was appointed was for the Eastern Judicial Circuit of Florida, which would include the area of what is now known as Indian River County. He served as circuit judge from January 1853 until his resignation in July 1857. While Forward was replaced in 1857 as circuit judge by B. F. Putnam, Forward went on to be a justice of the Supreme Court of Florida, being elected by popular vote in 1859.

Forward served on the Supreme Court of Florida during the Civil War and through the 1865 term. When the Civil War broke out after his election to the Supreme Court, Justice Forward volunteered to serve as a private in the Second Regiment of the Florida Infantry, but the "earnest entreaties" of his friends persuaded him to remain on the bench.

During the Civil War, Justice Forward authored an opinion that is noteworthy, Yulee v. Canova, 11 Fla. 9 (Fla. 1865). That case involved the issues of whether A. A. Canova, a Major and Chief of Subsistence and Commissary in the Confederate Army, acting under the Confederate Congress Impressment Act, could seize sugar owned by one of Florida's first two senators, Senator David Levy Yulee (otherwise a confederate supporter), without just compensation and what was just compensation and whether a confederate impressment schedule of sugar prices would govern. It has been reported that the case generated interest throughout the southeastern Confederacy.[218]

Forward's son, William F. Forward, married Annie J. Reid, a granddaughter of Governor and Superior Court Justice Robert Raymond Reid. (See Chapter 2). They had six children.

Forward was living in Palatka in July 1865 when he fell ill. He died on October 19, 1865, in Savannah, Georgia, while heading north for medical treatment.

B. A. Putnam, Eastern Judicial Circuit Judge, 1858-1867

Benjamin Alexander Putnam was probably born on December 16, 1801, on the Putnam Plantation near Savannah, Georgia. (Other references show 1803 as the year of birth and Charleston, South Carolina, as the place). He was the son of Benjamin and Anne Sophia Putnam. Benjamin's father was an Army surgeon during the Revolutionary War. His uncle was General Israel Putnam, who fought in the Revolutionary War.

In 1816, Benjamin A. Putnam went to New York City, where he attended a private school for one year. Then he attended Phillips

Andover Academy in Andover, Massachusetts, for a part of a year, and in 1819 he entered Harvard and was a member of the class of 1823. (In 1852, he was granted his Bachelor of Arts degree and a Master of Arts Degree after a petition from his classmates, from Harvard.) Putnam left Harvard for St. Augustine, where he studied law privately and in March 1824 was admitted to the Bar.

While practicing in St. Augustine, he soon became affiliated with Judge Joseph L. Smith, U.S. Territorial Judge of East Florida. Smith recommended Putnam for district attorney in 1826, which opening arguably came about by Smith's treatment of the previous district attorney, Edgar Macon. However, Thomas Douglas was commissioned by President John Quincy Adams for the job.

On March 26, 1830, in Charleston, Mr. Putnam married Helen Kirby, the daughter of Ephraim Kirby of Litchfield, Connecticut. Helen was also Judge Joseph Smith's sister-in-law. The couple had a daughter, Catherine, born in 1831. Putnam was appointed Justice of the Peace for St. Johns County in 1833.

In the Seminole Indian War, 1835-1842, Putnam served as major, colonel, and adjutant general. He organized the Second Regiment under Brigadier General Joseph Hernandez, who formed the Florida Militia. (It is after Joseph Hernandez that the Hernandez Trail from Haulover at Fort Ann (east of Titusville between the Indian River and

Mosquito Lagoon) to Fort Capron (north of Fort Pierce) became known.)

In the battle of Dunlawton, Putnam was wounded, fighting alongside several other judicial figures such as Douglas Dummett and James Ormond. Putnam carried a bullet in his leg for the rest of his life. Major Putnam's men, who protected settlers south of St. Augustine, were known as the "Mosquito Roarers."

From 1835 to 1840, Putnam was a representative in the (Territorial) Legislature of Florida. In 1844, Putnam was a member of the Senate, and in 1848 served as Speaker of the Florida House of Representatives. Putnam, an East Coast Whig, was defeated for Congress in the first state election in Florida in 1845 by East Florida Democrat David Levy, soon to be known as David Levy Yulee.

Putnam County, Florida, formed January 13, 1849, was named for Benjamin Putnam. (This is to be contrasted with the many Putnam Counties throughout the country named after Putnam's uncle, General Putnam.)

On May 14, 1849, President Zachary Taylor appointed Putnam Surveyor General of Florida, a post he occupied until 1854. In October 1857, Putnam was appointed judge of the Eastern Circuit to fill the unexpired term of Judge William A. Forward. Thereafter, in 1860, Putnam was elected to an eight-year term and held office until

1868. He was known from that time forward as Judge Putnam rather than Major Putnam.

Judge Putnam sat on the Supreme Court on occasion when a justice had to recuse himself. One of Putnam's Supreme Court opinions, as previously alluded to, was near and dear to lawyers. He ruled that lawyers can be compensated on the basis of quantum meruit and that they had a lien for their services, second to none, on a judgment which they might obtain for a client.[219] Judge Putnam was also the first President of the Florida Historical Society in 1856.

In a Reconstruction period case, a fellow named James Denton had shot an African American in that man's own yard in Micanopy. The civilian authorities didn't apprehend Denton. The federal soldiers stepped in, but a mob in Gainesville set the prisoner free. He eluded arrest for about a year. Finally, he was tried before Judge Putnam and was convicted of manslaughter, fined $225.00, and sentenced to one day in jail.[220]

Judge Putnam died at his home in Palatka on January 25, 1869. He was survived by his wife, Helen, who died in 1888. Daughter, Catherine, had married John C. Calhoun, M.D., the eldest son of John C. Calhoun, Statesman and Parliamentarian of South Carolina. When Dr. Calhoun died soon after that marriage, Catherine married the doctor's brother, Loundes. When Loundes passed away, she returned to Palatka with her three sons: Benjamin Putnam Calhoun, John

Caldwell Calhoun, and William Loundes Calhoun. Judge Putnam, his wife, children, and grandchildren are buried in the Westview Cemetery in Palatka with prominent grave monuments. One of the inscriptions on Putman's grave reads:

A GRADUATE OF HARVARD COLLEGE, HONORED & ESTEEMED FOR THE INTEGRITY OF HIS CHARACTER, THE PURITY OF HIS LIFE & THE VIGOR OF HIS INTELLECT.

John Price, Seventh Judicial Circuit Judge, 1868-1877

John W. Price was born in 1827 in Georgia. His parents were also born in Georgia. It was reported that John W. Price, one of the substantial and long-time Jacksonville residents, was part of a meeting on March 20, 1862, of the Loyal Citizens and remained in Jacksonville welcoming the Union troops. He was a representative to the Florida House from Alachua County in 1862 and 1863.

On May 17, 1864, a convention of "Union Men of Florida" was held in Jacksonville. The purpose of the convention was to elect delegates to the Republican National Convention in Baltimore on June 7, 1864. One of the delegates was John W. Price.[221]

Price was part of another delegation the next year. He and several East Florida Unionists journeyed to Washington to meet with President Andrew Johnson to discuss the candidates for a military governor for Florida.[222]

In 1868, John W. Price was appointed as the first judge of the newly created Seventh Judicial Circuit, which was established as a result of the Constitution of 1868.[223] His term commenced in August of that year. One of his terms expired on July 9, 1876; he was reappointed on August 26, 1876, but his interim appointment expired in January 1877.

The 1870 federal census shows John W. Price of the County of Volusia in the municipality of Enterprise as being the judge of the circuit court. He was forty-three years old at the time. He lived at that location with his wife, Elizabeth, who was born in Alabama in approximately 1831. There were two children: a son, age sixteen, and a daughter, two months, each of whom had been born in Florida.

Circuit Judge John W. Price is not to be confused with John W. Price, who, the same census shows, is living in Live Oak in Suwannee County and is a judge of the county court. The latter was then thirty-seven and also came from Georgia. He was married to Harriet and had five children. The circuit judge probably should also not be confused with Captain John Price, a sheriff of Duval County, who was born near Jacksonville in 1839.

John W. Price practiced law in Enterprise and Deland and Volusia County and was a landowner in Enterprise during the 1880s and 1890s. John W. Price was a delegate to the Liberal Republican State Convention held in Jacksonville in 1872. He was nominated for

Sheriff of Duval County when Napoleon Bonaparte Broward announced that he would not accept the nomination for sheriff.

In 1883, Price was reported as practicing law in Orlando. The 1885 state census shows him as a lawyer and living with his wife, M. E. Price and daughter, M. E. Price, age sixteen. They are likely the same wife, Elizabeth, and daughter, Mary, mentioned in the earlier census. (The ages are within a year, and the birthplaces are the same.)

William Archer Cocke, Seventh Judicial Circuit Judge, 1877-1885

William Archer Cocke is a descendant of Richard Cocke, who emigrated from Leeds, Yorkshire, England, sometime prior to 1636 and settled in Henrico County, Virginia. Richard Cocke was a member of the House of Burgesses from 1644 to 1654. William Archer Cocke's father was William Archer Cocke, who was born on May 20, 1796, and died on August 29, 1821. William Archer Cocke's mother was Catherine Murray, who was born on November 10, 1798, married Mr. William Archer Cocke on December 1, 1819, and passed away on October 25, 1878.

The Judge's grandfather was William Archer Cocke, born on December 22, 1771, and who died on January 13, 1844. His wife was Catherine Murray Winston (Ronald), who was born on October 18, 1771, and died on March 2, 1840. The Cockes were descendants of James Howell Cocke and Mary Magdeline Chastain of Virginia.

William Archer Cocke (the judge) was born on May 10, 1822, in Virginia. He married Kate Parkhill on April 5, 1853. Kate Parkhill was born on August 26, 1826, in Virginia. The Cockes had no children. Cocke's occupation was a lawyer.

Judge William Archer Cocke graduated from the College of William & Mary. He was a former Whig who became a Democrat before the Civil War. William Archer Cocke served in an important civil position under the government at Richmond during the Civil War. He was an ex-slave holder.

Cocke moved to Monticello, Florida, to practice his profession in 1863. He was known as a lawyer of some repute, an author, and a historian. He authored "A Treatise on the Common and Civil Law, as embraced in the Jurisprudence of the United States," New York, 1871, which has been quoted as authority in the highest courts of England and America.[224]

He was a Vice Chairman of the Constitutional Union Party Convention held in Tallahassee on September 25, 1867. He was a southern Democrat during the carpetbag rule in Florida. He may have been appointed circuit judge, along with several other Democrats, by Governor Harrison Reed in 1868. There is information that the appointment was to the Second Circuit, but that is not supported, and it was really the First Judicial Circuit.[225]During Governor Reed's administration, Judge Cocke had reason to issue a warrant for the arrest of Reed's Lieutenant Governor, W. H. Gleason of Eau Gallie.[226]

The 1870 census shows William A. Cocke as a lawyer living in Monticello in Jefferson County with his wife, Kate Parkhill, and a Julia C. Cocke, age 72, who was also from Virginia.

Cocke was appointed attorney general by Governor Ossian Hart, a Republican, taking office on January 16, 1873, and serving until 1877. The appointment came apparently after Judge Cocke had supported Grant for President among "disaffected democrats." Cocke had abandoned his party in 1872 because of his opposition to the Greeley-Brown ticket.[227]

In 1874, Governor Hart asked Attorney General Cocke to resign over the Attorney General's response, or lack thereof, to the claim of F. Vose against the Board of Trustees of the Internal Improvement Fund. (Vose had obtained an injunction and placed the Internal Improvement Fund in receivership.) Cocke did not resign.

When Governor Hart died and the governor's office was taken over by Governor Stearns, who had been referred to as "the most rotten piece of gubernatorial timber that was ever placed at the helm of government,"[228] Stearns asked his cabinet to resign out of courtesy to him. The governor intended to reappoint the cabinet, except for Attorney General Cocke. Cocke did not fall into that trap, however, by missing the meeting when the resignations of the cabinet were to have occurred, and the Governor had to decline to accept the resignations of those given. (This was the second governor to seek Cocke's resignation as Attorney General.)

William Archer Cocke was noted for his efforts in trying to convince the Florida Legislature, although unsuccessfully, to better protect the state from fraudulent schemes, such as in the J. P. & M. Railroad four-million-dollar bond issuance.[229]

Cocke, as attorney general, was active in voter recounts. He was on the Board of State Canvassers (of elections) during the controversial recounting of ballots over the Tilden-Hayes presidential vote and the Florida statewide elections. Litigation followed those efforts and resulted in the election of Governor Drew in 1876. It has been written that "Cocke's legal training and his Democratic predilections often contradicted during board canvassing proceedings; he tended to overemphasize ethical compliance with the law while dismissing more material irregularities with little examination."[230]

Cocke served as circuit judge of the Seventh Judicial Circuit, which included the area now a part of Indian River County, from January 10, 1877, until January 18, 1885.

The 1885 state census, and particularly the agricultural records, show that William Archer Cocke was the owner of twenty acres, which had a farm value of $12,000.00. Implements and equipment were valued at $50.00, livestock at $50.00, and the cost of fertilizer purchased in 1884 was $300.00. He paid wages in that year of $400.00 and had one horse.

Judge Cocke died on October 17, 1887, and is buried in Lakeview Cemetery, Sanford, FL. His spouse died in December 1906.

Eleazer K. Foster, Seventh Judicial Circuit Judge, 1885-1887

Eleazer Kingsbury Foster was born in New Haven, Connecticut, on October 31, 1841, and graduated with distinction from Yale University in 1863. He studied at Yale Law School and, in 1865, was admitted to the Bar. He came to Florida in 1866 for health reasons. He was Collector of Customs at St. Augustine in 1867 and State Attorney for the Fourth Judicial Circuit in 1868. In 1872, he moved to Orange County, where he established a fine reputation for his legal work.

In 1874, he married Mary G. Benedict, daughter of Dr. Nathan and Emma Benedict of St. Augustine. In 1880, he was Chairman of the Orange County Delegation to the State Convention, and on January 31, 1881, he assumed the office of Superintendent of Public Instruction in Governor Wm. D. Bloxham's Cabinet. He held this position until February 1884, when he resigned and became General Attorney for the Florida Southern Railway Company. In January

1885, Governor Edward A. Perry appointed him as Circuit Judge of the Seventh Judicial Circuit. Eleazer K. Foster commenced serving as circuit judge on January 24, 1885. (William Archer Cocke's term expired on January 18, 1885). Foster served until he resigned on May 5, 1887. He died on December 8, 1899, in New Haven, Connecticut, and was survived by his wife, a son, and two daughters.

John D. Broome, Seventh Judicial Circuit Judge, 1887-1898

John D. Broome was born May 6, 1835, in Hamburg, South Carolina. He was the son of James E. Broome, whose parents were John and Jeanette (Witherspoon) Broome, also from Hamburg, South Carolina. As a child, John D. Broome was brought to this state by his father, who became the third governor of Florida on October 3, 1853, and served until October 5, 1857. This was at the same time Democrat Franklin Pierce was elected President. With Broome's election as governor, the so-called "South Carolina School" held a dominant role in the Democratic Party in the state.[231]

John D. Broome was educated at Mercer University and practiced law in Fernandina until 1866. During the Civil War, he served on the staff of General Finley. He was also a surveyor of Volusia County for eight years. In 1866, he moved to New York and lived there for eight years. In 1874, he returned to Florida and resumed the practice of law in DeLand, Volusia County. There, he became prominent and was a member of the Constitutional Convention of 1885. He served as Circuit Court Judge for the Seventh Judicial Circuit, including Brevard County, from 1887 to 1898. Incidentally, C. C. Chillingworth, the father of the future Circuit Judge C. E. Chillingworth, was admitted to the Bar by Judge Broome in Titusville in 1892. The oldest circuit court docket available for Brevard shows Judge Broome's docket for 1897.

John Broome had a younger brother, James Emilius Broome, who was born in Tallahassee, Florida, on March 26, 1846. The brother was likely not the probate court judge for Leon County in the 1840s, despite references to the contrary, but rather it was his father of the same name, the future Governor.[232] The brother served as a state senator from Gadsden County from 1890 to 1902.

Florida Governor James Broome, father of Judge John Broome

Minor S. Jones
Courtesy of St. Lucie County History Museum

Minor S. Jones, Seventh Judicial Circuit Judge, 1898-1911

Minor Stanfield Jones was born in Lake City, Florida, on December 19, 1849. He was the son of James Stanfield Jones, who was born in Virginia in 1817. His mother's name was Mary Elizabeth Partridge Summerlin Jones, who was born on October 12, 1817, and died on November 17, 1888.

The parents of Minor's father, James Stanfield Jones, were James Jones and Narcissa Burdett. James Stanfield Jones went to Texas as a boy and was associated with Sam Houston, who was also from Virginia. James Stanfield Jones allegedly wrote the original Declaration of Independence of Texas in his own handwriting. This same gentleman came to Florida wanting to return to a more conservative southern-style community close to the East Coast. He had been called "The Professor" and wrote for several newspapers, including those in Madison and Tallahassee, Florida, as well as being the editor of The Morning News in Savannah, Georgia. "The Professor" was the secretary to President Jefferson Davis during the Civil War.

Minor S. Jones served as a midshipman in the Confederate Navy as a teenager. He moved to Indian River after the war. On July 9, 1872, he married Gertrude Elizabeth Paine, the daughter of Judge James Paine, who started St. Lucie Village in 1857. Gertrude was born on January 1, 1855, and died on June 14, 1939, in Titusville.

Minor, at one point, was a Deputy U.S. Marshal for the Indian River area, which probably exposed him to law enforcement. Judge Jones studied law the old-fashioned way. When once asked about his alma mater, he said it was "Blackstone[233] and light wood knot (fat pinewood) fire." Mr. Jones was admitted to the bar in 1878, and he and his family moved to Titusville in 1884. The 1885 census shows Minor as a lawyer living with his wife, his four children, and his father.

Titusville was incorporated in 1886, and Mr. Jones became the city's first mayor. Minor S. Jones was appointed county judge in 1887 and served until 1898, when he was elevated to the circuit bench. (He once had a house in Quay–Winter Beach in this county, which he sold to Ely Walker on Feb. 2, 1902). He served as circuit judge on the Seventh Circuit from 1898 to 1911. His circuit encompassed one-third of the counties in Florida and reached far into the frontier section of the state. In the early days, there was a crude courthouse building to which Judge Jones came by horseback twice a year to hold court. This was likely in Whittier, near present-day Kenansville, the latter of which was named after Henry Flagler's third wife, Mary Kenan. Jones camped along the way and carried his food and supplies in his saddlebags.

One of the more famous tales associated with Judge Jones is the "mullet" story, originating around 1894-95 when a freeze destroyed the citrus crop. It took three to four years for citrus production to recover, and during that time, a ban on seine nets had closed the mullet season. Many residents complained that their livelihood was being taken away. First, a freeze destroyed the citrus, and now the government was preventing them from fishing.

It was not generally well known at the time that mullet were vegetarians that fed on seaweed and grasses, and that they had a gizzard to help digest that food. Judge Jones had been contemplating how to declare the law invalid and arranged for the sheriff to arrest someone for fishing for mullet with a seine net. Before all onlookers in the courtroom, he reportedly dissected a mullet, claiming that it differed from all other fish in that it had a gizzard. The accused had not, therefore, violated the law because he had caught mullet that resembled chickens more than fish. The case was dismissed and helped reopen the fishing industry throughout the state. This is the reason that mullet are sometimes referred to as "Indian River Chicken."[234]

A somewhat renowned Tampa lawyer, Patrick Crisp Whitaker, must have picked up on Judge Jones' ruling. Whitaker successfully argued in 1919 that his clients could not be guilty of fishing out of season "because the mullet caught had gizzards, and while they may have lived in the water like fish, whales live in the water and aren't fish, beavers live in the water and are not fish, and that mullet with the gizzard must be some kind of aquatic foul." [235]

Another prominent case handled by Judge Jones was a case involving Seminole leader, Captain Tom Tiger, who was probably the first Florida Indian to take the stand in a Florida Court. Tom Tiger had been bilked on a horse lease by a white man. While historically out of luck because of a lack of access to the courts by the Indians, Tom's white friend, the author of The Seminoles of Florida, pressed criminal charges, i.e., obtaining goods under false pretenses. Because of proof problems, i.e., the written promise on a cartridge box which had been lost during a rainstorm, Jones directed a verdict for the defendant. However, it is believed that Jones was a part of a group of court officials who contributed to buy a new horse for Tom Tiger.[236]

Judge Minor S. Jones edited the Titusville News along with James A. McCrory, which began publishing in 1882, competing with the Titusville Star. That paper was sold and moved to Cocoa, and by 1888, Judge Jones was suing it for libel!

Judge Minor S. Jones handled the first trial of D. J. Disney, who was charged with the murder of Sheriff Dan S. Carlton in Fort Pierce. The trial occurred in the fall of 1915, and it lasted two days. The jury was unable to reach a verdict, which resulted in a re-trial and a change in venue to Orlando in May of 1916. This time, the circuit judge was James W. Perkins. The verdict was a conviction for manslaughter and was upheld by the Supreme Court later that year.[237]

Judge Jones died in Titusville on July 20, 1922. He was survived by his wife, Gertrude, and their four children: John C., Minor S., Jr., Wade H. (b 11/13/1878 - d 1/18/1924), and Annie C. (Wright). Great tributes to Judge Jones were carried in the Star Advocate of July 28, 1922, the Gainesville Sun, the Ft. Pierce newspaper, and the Miami Metropolis.

Minor's son, Minor S. Jones, II (or Jr), a one-time Brevard Co. Sheriff,[238] was a nephew of Thomas Paine, a descendant of the Judge James Paine, Sr. family. Minor S. Jones, II, a/k/a "Stanley," followed in his Uncle Tom's footsteps in the cattle business, following the 1894-1895 freeze. Stanley had as his location the area north and west of Quay (Winter Beach) to the St. Johns River, then south to his Uncle

Tom's operation. Between them both they had about 250 square miles of range with varying habitats.[239] Stanley was born on July 16, 1873, in St. Lucie County, Florida, and died on May 26, 1960, in Kissimmee Hospital, not too far from where he was living in Kenansville.

On Veterans Day 1955, portraits of Minor S. Jones and Charles O. Andrews (the father of Judge Andrews, discussed in the chapter on the Fourth District Court of Appeal) were unveiled at the Lake County Courthouse in Tavares, Florida.

E. Biographical Information on Judicial Figures, other than circuit judges, 1845-1905, in alphabetical order:

John Barber, Brevard County Judge, 1865

John Barber, to be distinguished from John Barker below, was likely an Armed Occupation Act settler, obtaining permit number 530. In 1864, he is shown as a voter in Precinct Number 2, North Yates, (western) Brevard County. He was a Brevard County commissioner during the Civil War. His years likely included 1860-1865. Following the Civil War, Barber served as an interim judge for Brevard County and represented Brevard County at the Florida Constitutional Convention of 1865. He was also known as a cattle herder.

There is a John Barber who served in the military for Florida in the Seminole War in the late 1850s. This might have been him. He may have also been the John Barber who lived with his wife, Margaret, and family in Brevard County, according to the 1870 federal census. At that time, he was 38 years old, and his wife was 31. His occupation was listed as a farmer, and his wife was a housekeeper. He had five children, ranging from John, Jr., age 11, to Ellen, age 3. Mr. and Mrs. Barber and their children were all born in Florida. Mr. Barber's personal estate at the time amounted to $250.00.

John Barker, St. Lucia County Justice of the Peace, 1845

John Barker was appointed St. Lucia County Justice of the Peace on March 7, 1845. He was an Armed Occupation Act settler, receiving permit number 69 for property on the Indian River Lagoon. He lived near his brother-in-law, William F. Russell, the Inspector of Customs at the Indian River Inlet. He was a member, with William B. Davis and Ossian B. Hart, of the first St. Lucia County Commission in 1844. His home was synonymous with Precinct Number 2 for St. Lucie County during that period. Barker also owned a store, which sometimes traded with the Indians, at what was called Barker's Bluff.

Barker has the dubious distinction of being murdered by several Seminole Indians near Ft. Pierce on July 12, 1849, which helped to give rise to the Third Seminole War (1855-1858). A detailed account of this event was recorded by Caleb Brayton, whose biographical information is set forth in the preceding chapter.

Barker's widow, Martha Russell Barker, subsequently maintained a claim for Barker's land, which is referenced in her attorney, William Forward's, biographical information in this chapter.

F. B. Beal, Narrows (Gem Island) Justice of the Peace, 1889

Frank B. Beal was born in Florida about 1862. His parents had each come from Georgia. As indicated, he was the Justice of the Peace in 1889 for the Narrows, then in Brevard County, now known as Gem Island within John's Island.

By 1900 and 1910, the U.S. Census reveals that he was living at City Point in the same Brevard County, with his wife, Ella, and numerous children. He was described as a fruit farmer and orange grower in the respective censuses. In 1923, he is shown as being present for a Cocoa Civic League meeting.[240]

J. F. Bell, St. Lucie Justice of the Peace, 1883, 1887, 1889, 1892

James Frank "J. F." Bell was born in Florida on Sept. 19, 1856. His parents were Alexander Cone Bell (1827-1898) and Susan Amanda Stewart Bell (1834-1913). J. F. married Eloise C. Hendry Bell (1861-1946) in 1878. They had four children. J. F. also had five siblings.

In 1887, Bell acquired 80 acres from the Florida Internal Improvement Fund along the north fork of the St. Lucie River, north of present-day White City. Besides being the Justice of the Peace for the years mentioned above, he was on the initial St. Lucie County Commission from 1905 to 1908.

There is a story about J. F. Bell, as Justice of the Peace and possibly "town marshal" (a/k/a constable) in 1886. It involved tracking down an alleged rapist for a rape that occurred by the Sebastian River. The suspect's name was Gore, and Bell and his posse tracked the suspect to the Fort Basinger area. When Gore refused to surrender and threatened to shoot, he was killed by a shotgun.[241]

Bell died April 2, 1921, and is buried in Riverview Memorial Park, Ft. Pierce.

Benton, James G., Brevard County Judge, 1855-1865

James G. Benton was likely the Brevard County Judge for the five years after the county was formed in 1855 and for the five years surrounding the Civil War.[242]

John Cleland, St. Lucia County Judge and Justice of the Peace, 1844-1845

John C. Cleland, a/k/a Clelland, a/k/a Clealand, was likely Colonel John C. Cleland, an adjutant of the Second Brigade of the

Florida Militia during the Second Seminole War. He participated in the Battle of Dunlawton in January 1836. During the war, he had a home in St. Augustine and held a ball, which Army Surgeon Dr. Motte noted in his diary, Journey into the Wilderness, as having attended. After the Seminole War, Cleland likely moved to Charleston, South Carolina. He was also very helpful in preserving the history of the battle of Dunlawton and of General Hernandez's movements.[243]

Cleland was an Armed Occupation Act Settler along the Indian River by 1843. His homestead was in Ankona on the west bank of the Indian River, south of Ft. Pierce. He had a family at the time of his application. The application (permit number 84) also indicates that Cleland has been a resident of Florida since April 1828. His name appears as a resident of St. Augustine on both the 1830 and 1840 U.S. censuses.

Cleland's name is permanently affixed in the Legislative Territorial Acts of Florida, as his home was named as the initial seat of St. Lucia County in 1844. He also may have been the first county court judge of St. Lucia County, being appointed on March 15, 1844.

Cleland was also a justice of the peace, serving in that capacity by March 15, 1845, as evidenced by the Armed Occupation Act application of Nathaniel C. Scobie. State Archives records show that Cleland was also a notary public and justice of the peace in St. Johns County, being commissioned for each on April 6, 1842.

Henry A. Crane, St. Lucia County Clerk, 1850-1855

This is a continuation from his bio in Chapter 2, as his clerk service straddled the time of statehood in 1845.

Crane was appointed Captain of Company A, Second Florida Cavalry (Union side) in 1864. Following the Civil War, Crane, joined by his wife and 6 daughters, went on to be a keeper of the lighthouse in Key West from March 2, 1867, to September 15, 1868. He was also a clerk of courts there and a state senator from District 24 in 1869 and 1870, and a State House of Representatives member from Monroe County in 1871 and 1872.

He died in Key West on June 18, 1888.

William B. Davis, St. Lucia County Justice of the Peace

William B. Davis was born around the turn of the century in Connecticut. He was an Armed Occupation Act Settler, having application number 128. Voting records show that he voted in Precinct Number 1, St. Lucie County, in 1844 and 1849, and in Precinct Number 2, a/k/a John Barker, St. Lucie County, in 1845. He was a justice of the peace somewhere between 1845 and 1854 in St. Lucie County.[244] Davis also served on the last County Commission for old St. Lucie County in approximately 1854, until Brevard County was organized in 1855. He was the second sheriff for Brevard County in 1858.[245]

William Davis' homestead was located approximately eight miles south of Fort Capron, which today is the 4100 block of South Indian River Drive, Ft. Pierce. On this location, 4111 South Indian River Drive is the only remaining landmark of the settlers of the Armed Occupation Act. At this site, a coquina rock fireplace, with the date of 1844 carved into a lower rock, still exists.

William B. Davis is also mentioned as being part of the meeting at Captain James Paine, Sr.'s house in 1861 when the safety of the residents in connection with the Civil War was discussed and resulted in a resolution sent to Governor Madison S. Perry, requesting assistance for the protection of their homes with a 100-mile coast line and their young men now being in Virginia. However, the Governor couldn't oblige. Local residents had to be satisfied with a home guard company commanded by Captain James A. Paine.[246]

Davis was a keeper of the Jupiter Light House from July 10, 1866, to December 16, 1869.

A. C. Dittman, aka Dittmar, Ft. Pierce Justice of the Peace 1891

Albert C. Dittman was likely born in Wisconsin around 1856. Both his parents were born in Germany. As mentioned, he was the Justice of the Peace in Ft. Pierce, when it was a part of Brevard County, in 1891. By 1910 an Albert C. Dittman was age 54 and living in Ft. Pierce with his wife, Cora Irene Hood (50), 3 daughters, a son, and a sister-in-law. He was described as an Agent & Real Estate & Homes. In 1912, he was appointed Postmaster of Ft. Pierce. Daughter, Irene Blanch Dittman, was born Aug 18, 1896, and married Aaron Knight Roberts and had three children. Irene died in 1972 in Jacksonville.

D. L. Gaulden, Brevard County Judge, 1900-1905

D. L. Gaulden was born in approximately 1855. By 1885, he was living on Merritt Island, according to the Florida State Census of that year. He was living with his wife, H. E. Gaulden, age 28, and his father-in-law, M. E. Stephens, age 56, who was listed as a Capitalist. Mr. Stephens was born in New York, and his daughter, Mrs. Gaulden, was born in Michigan. D. L. Gaulden's occupation at the time was listed as a lawyer. His front-page advertisements as a lawyer in The Florida Star can be found in such editions as that of February 10, 1886.

D. L. Gaulden served as county prosecutor and became a county judge in 1898 after Minor Jones stepped down to become circuit judge. Judge Gaulden served until 1905, when he resumed his old position as county prosecutor.

D. L. Gaulden was an active entrepreneur. His first venture was selling Georgia yellow pine in the late 1880s. He also chartered the

Eureka Fish Company with a capitalization of $10,000 to engage in general fishing in 1905.

D. H. Gettis, St. Lucia County Probate Judge, 1851-1853

D. H. Gettis, a/k/a Captain Gattis, was likely born in Alabama in approximately 1818. According to census information, he was a farmer in St. Lucie County by 1850. He probably lived near Mills Burnham. He was elected as St. Lucie or St. Lucia County Commissioner in 1850. He also served as Judge of Probate from 1851 to 1853.

The St. Lucie County records were kept in the Gettis home by 1849. They were destroyed during an Indian attack in July 1849 when the home was burned to the ground.

The Indian affair began when four outlaw Seminoles attacked and killed an Indian River man (John Barker). The Indians purportedly pillaged homes, burned fields, and killed cattle. Secretary of War Millard Fillmore sent troops to the Indian River. Ft. Capron was then built near the homes where the attack had begun.

James T. Gray, Narrows Justice of the Peace, 1887, 1889

There were two James T. Grays prominent in this area, known as the Narrows, around the 1890s. One was black, and the other was white. James T. Gray, an African American, was from Marlboro,

South Carolina, born about 1846. His father was Alix Gray, and his mother, Purline. James T. married Drucilla, who was also born in South Carolina. By 1870, they were living in Lake City with 3 children. The 1900 Census shows James T. Gray, a black man, living in Woodley, on the west side of the Indian River, in what is now Winter Beach. He was aged 54 and widowed. He was described then as a merchant. He filed for Homestead in Brevard County in 1900, asserting he was from Toledo (that same Winter Beach area), for land that was in Gifford. That same year, he was the Postmaster for Gifford. He served in that capacity for at least 1900 – 1905. He married Anna (1899-1968) in 1906. By 1910, they were living in Gifford with their 5-year-old daughter, Sadie. He is then described as a farmer.

This James T. Gray was prominent in the Winter Beach and Gifford communities. He created a subdivision in Gifford, called J. T. Grays Town of Gifford Subdivision, which was recorded January 16, 1904, in Plat Book 1, page 69 of the Public Records of Brevard County, Florida. He sold a number of lots in the next couple of years. He was also likely involved in another subdivision in Gifford, bearing his former wife's remarried last name, Battle. It was the Battle Ave. of Spruce Park Addition to Gifford Subdivision.

In J. Noble Richards' book, there is a J. T. Gray described as an aristocrat from Georgia, who is credited as having established a plantation which he named Woodley.[247] This is not the same Gray as the above-referenced. This was another Gray family, a white family, emanating from Columbia, Muscogee County, Georgia, who apparently had land in Woodley and on the Gem Island side of the Indian River. There was an E. L. Gray who married into the very prominent Michael family. He and James T. Gray were brothers. James T. Gray was the youngest of his seven siblings, being born in 1830. Their parents were Richard Gray (1781-1851) and Margaret A. "Peggy" Beavers Gray (1790-1863). James married Elvira King on Oct. 6, 1869, in Georgia. They had one daughter, Margaret Emma Gray Michael, on June 12, 1872, who was born in Georgia. E. L. Gray and James T. Gray apparently arrived in the Narrows area in the early 1880s, and by 1883, James T. Gray was shipping vegetables from the Narrows. See this endnote for more background.[248]

Eagle Company Fish Dock
Hardee Service Station
Main Street and Indian River Drive
Courtesy of Sebastian Area Historical Museum

R. A. Hardee, Sebastian Justice of the Peace 1895

Captain Robert Augustus Hardee was born in Bulloch County, Ga., on May 27, 1833. He was married for the first time on May 29, 1860, in Brooks, Ga., to Melissa V. Williams. He was a captain of Company H, 9th Ga. Vol. Infantry from Brooks and fought at

Gettysburg. He served with great heroism. Following the war, he and his brothers, who had lost their land in Georgia, engaged in the cotton business. Mrs. R. A. Hardee passed away in 1866 in Brooks County. R. A. Hardee and his brothers settled on the Indian River in about 1868. His settlement, near Cocoa, was called Hardees or Hardeeville on maps. R. A. Hardee would marry Emma Provida Willard (1850-1924) in about 1871.

Hardee served in the Florida House of Representatives for our then Brevard County in 1873-1874 and 1879. He is one of the fishermen credited with establishing the settlement we now know as Cocoa, Florida, in 1881 or 1882, but it was under the name of Indian River City. However, the U. S. postal authorities wouldn't accept that name, as it was too long, and ultimately Cocoa was used for the town name. Hardee moved to Sebastian, then called New Haven, in 1889. He was also a Brevard County Commissioner.

Capt. Hardee died Nov 29, 1909, in St. Lucie County, and is buried in the Sebastian Cemetery.

It is interesting to note that his son, of the same title and similar name, and also a state representative, from our then St. Lucie County, in 1909, Capt. Robert G. Hardee (1872-1947) is not only buried close by to R. A. Hardee's grave, but the nearby Main Street Boat Ramp in Sebastian is named after Capt. Robert Hardee, the son. The Capt. title for him likely came from growing up with boats on the river.

The Hardees were quite prominent in Sebastian, with their beautiful house and Hardee Service Station located on the northeast end of Main Street and Indian River Drive, and having a dock there for their Eagle (Fish) Company. Their now very large "Hardee Oak" is still standing by the end of Main Street and Indian River Drive.

Sgt. B.F. Hardesty, Sebastian Justice of the Peace, 1901

Benjamin Franklin Hardesty was born April 15, 1842, in Washington, St. Landry, Louisiana. His father, Robert Bryant Hardesty (1806-1881), was from Virginia, and his mother, Mary Ann Rideout (1813-1845), was from Maine. B. F. spent part of his childhood in Indianapolis, but after his mother died, he returned to Louisiana with his father. B. F. Hardesty's ancestry was interesting. His mother's family descended from Sir Nicholas Rideout, who amassed a fortune in New York shipbuilding, and his father was a descendant of the Bryants, a pioneer family from New Jersey, which included William Cullen Bryant.

B. F. served in the Confederacy and became a Sergeant in the 1st Special Louisiana Battalion, serving from 1861 to 1865, and was wounded in action at Paynes Farm, Va., on November 29, 1863. He married Gabriella "Ella" Cozine of St. Mary Parish, La., on May 19, 1864.

The Hardestys came to Sebastian in 1894. They were early members of the Sebastian Methodist Church. He was a carpenter and helped to build the Ercildoune Hotel in 1889[249] and the refurbishment of the Methodist Church in 1901. He was a teacher in Brevard County and subsequently served on the St. Lucie County School Board (1905-1908) and was a Justice of the Peace in Sebastian in 1901. The 1910 Census shows him in Saint Lucie, Florida, as a fruit grower, but likely in Sebastian. He was then 68, and his wife, Ella, was 67. They seemed to live next door to the future Sebastian mayor, T. B. Hicks. Hardesty and his wife celebrated their 50th wedding anniversary in Sebastian on May 19, 1914.

Hardesty died on July 6, 1917, in Sebastian at age 75. He was considered one of St. Lucie County's best-known residents. He was survived by his wife and three daughters who were with him at his passing: Mrs. Ernest (Louella) Foster of Sebastian, Mrs. Otto (Annie) Praeger of Washington, D.C., wife of the Second Assistant Postmaster-General of the United States, and Mrs. Lamar C (Gertrude) Stewart of Sebastian. He also may have had a son, Levi Hardesty (1866-1918). B. F. Hardesty is buried in the Sebastian Cemetery.

Ossian Hart, St. Lucia County Commissioner, lawyer, and Supreme Court Justice

It would be remiss not to mention Ossian Hart under this heading of Judicial Figures other than circuit Judges, while St. Lucia County was in existence. See his biography in Chapter 2.

J.C. Hemming, St. Lucia County Clerk of Court, 1847-1850

J.C. Hemming became a resident of Florida in August 1832. He was living in St. Augustine in St. Johns County in 1840. Hemming was an Armed Occupation Act settler, applying for land in the North East Quarter of Section 21, Township 15 South, Range 22 East (SE of Ocala) on August 22, 1843, as permit number 820. He was a justice of the peace of St. Johns County as of March 5, 1844.

Hemming was the second Clerk of Court for St. Lucia County. He succeeded Joseph S. Osborne in approximately 1847 when the legislature combined the office of the clerks of St. Lucia and Orange Counties and served until 1850. As indicated in the 1860 census, Hemming was living in Jacksonville by that time.

The 1840 census shows a J.E. Hemmings in St. Augustine, St. Johns County, living with another male, and they each are between 20 and 30 years old.

There is a record of a June 22, 1841, marriage of John C. Hemming and Maria O. Dupont in St. Johns Co. Also, the 1850

Census for Jacksonville, Duval County, shows John C. Hemming as owning 16 slaves.

The 1860 Census for Jacksonville describes John C. Hemming as a "Gentleman," from England, and there seems to be 6 children living with him, two of whom are named below, and a 17-year-old Jane V. Dupont, with her own personal estate of $2,000.00. His was $40,000.00, not including land valued at $2,200.00.

The 1870 Census for Jacksonville shows John C. Hemming as being born in England about 1815 and that his wife is Mary E. Hemming, 22 years his junior, and children Marietta and Frederick, who were mentioned in the 1860 Census. This is consistent with the 1880 Census, although his wife is Mary C., and John's birth in England is shown as about 1819. The marital age gap narrowed to 16 years. He is listed as a real estate broker. The 1871 Jacksonville City Directory shows J.C. Hemming as a real estate agent and commission merchant. For information on Hemmings' extraordinary service during the Civil War, and particularly with a famous boat, please go to this endnote.[250]

Archibald Henry, St. Lucie (Brevard County) Justice of the Peace 1875,1878

As indicated in the heading, Henry was a Justice of the Peace for that place and time. Research reveals that he served as a Keeper of the First House of Refuge, which was in Brevard County, but is now known as Jaycee Park in Vero Beach. He served there from April 3, 1888, to July 9, 1890, when he was discharged. The Houses of Refuge in Florida are the subject of various books.

Archibald Henry was born in Ireland.

John S. Hermans, St. Lucia County Probate Judge, 1848-1851 and 1853-1855

John S. Hermans, a/k/a Heermans, was born in New York in approximately 1792. He had two children, Philip and Joseph, who were born in Canada. John may also have been called "Old Phil," and his son, "Young Phil," Herman."[251]

Hermans was a settler under the Armed Occupation Act on the west side of the Indian River, 12 miles south of Fort Capron, or approximately eight to ten miles South of Fort Pierce. J. M. Hawkes writes in his "East Coast of Florida" that, "the landmarks by which the Herman Place had been described were two tall coconut trees standing near each other, and the hedges of lime bushes."

Hermans served as Judge of Probate from the late 1840s until 1851 and again from 1853 to 1855. In 1852, Judge Hermans was appointed County Commissioner. He also served as justice of the peace in the late 1850s.

In 1855 and again in 1856, Judge Hermans encouraged the government to drain submerged land in the interior of Brevard. Hermans also served in the Florida House of Representatives from St. Lucie County in 1852 and Brevard County from 1856 to 1859.

On March 17, 1854, Judge Hermans had the occasion to write to the Florida Secretary of State and complain that his commission as a Judge of Probate, dated December 13, 1853, was delivered via Miami mail on March 1. He respectfully suggested scrutiny of the management of the post office. He indicated that it frequently occurred that papers from Tallahassee came by way of Key West, perhaps going to Savannah from there, and back to Miami for a three-month process. He suggested that it would only take three weeks via the St. Johns River, which would be bad enough. He then concluded:

> "After due consideration, notwithstanding the solicitations of his excellency and flattering his high opinion of my qualifications, I have come to the conclusion to abide by my former resolve not to accept the commission. It is unnecessary for me to give all my reasons. They are well known here and known before they elected me, and that I have been anxious those six years to be relieved from the duties of the office. Yet it was believed that I would accept. I have thus far kept the county together, and as it is increasing and there are those better qualified than myself and younger men that don't live so far from the place of business, I must be allowed to decline accepting." [252]

The 1870 U.S. Census for Brevard County shows John S. Hermans, age seventy, living alone with an occupation of fruit farmer.

<u>John C. Houston, Brevard County Justice of the Peace, 1872[253]</u>

<u>Abner D. Johnston, a/k/a Johnson, Brevard County Judge, mid-1870s</u>

A. D. Johnston, Sr. and Jr., were living in Brevard County at the time of the 1880 United States Census. They were registered for the district west of the St. Johns River, which included Brevard County at that time. They were likely cattlemen. Their occupation listed on the census was "stock raising farm."

A. D. Johnston, Sr. was born in South Carolina, as were his parents. A. D. Johnston, Sr. was born in 1809. His wife, Frances Raines Pickett, was born in 1814 in South Carolina. They had eight children, including James Francis Pickett Johnston, who was born in South Carolina in 1835. James Francis Pickett Johnston was a Brevard County cattleman, state representative, and constitutional convention delegate. A. D. Johnston, Jr., the youngest of the family, was born in Florida in 1848.

A. D. Johnston, Sr., and his son James served with the Florida Mounted Volunteers, each as Captains, during the Seminole War in the 1850s.

The 1870 census shows Abner Johnston, Sr., and Abner Johnston, Jr. with a Sumterville post office address in Sumter County, Florida. Sr. was purportedly 63, a farmer, and born in South Carolina. Abner, Jr., was listed as 22 years old and also born in South Carolina (birthplace conflicts with the above) and was an overseer of the farm. Sr. owned real estate valued at $5,000.00 and $4,000.00 in personal property.

More than likely, because of their respective ages, the senior Johnston was the county judge in the 1870s. Johnston likely sat in the western part of Brevard County, where the county court was held for a number of years in the 1870s. In fact, the Florida Archives shows him in Bassville in 1875, and as County Judge.[254] It also shows him as County Treasurer in 1877. His wife Frances passed away on January 15, 1880, in Sumter, Florida. She is buried in Ocala, Marion County, FL.

The 1885 Florida Census shows the two Abner Johnstons as producers of agriculture in the Kissimmee River area of the County of Brevard. A. D. Johnston, Jr. owned 40 acres of improved and 120 acres of unimproved land, with $31,000.00 in livestock. A. D. Johnston, Sr. owned 20 acres of improved and 60 acres of unimproved farmland.

It is unclear when Abner D. Johnston, Sr., passed away, but he is buried with his wife in Ocala. Abner D. Johnston, Jr. died on October 12, 1886, in Orlando, Fla., and was survived by his wife, Lula, and daughter, Queen. James F. P. Johnston died on February 12, 1906.

W. L. Keefer, Woodley (Winter Beach), Brevard Co., Justice of the Peace, 1897 & Quay 1903

William L. Keefer was born on Feb. 10, 1860, in Pennsylvania. He was the son of Joseph Adam Keefer and Christina Keefer. He was the youngest of four children. By the time he was 20 and still living at home in Pa., he was an apprentice in the wool industry. In the late 1880s, early 1890s, Keefer lived in the Woodley-Quay area, where he was Justice of the Peace in 1897 and 1903. On August 31, 1905, he married Annie M. King in St. Lucie County, Florida. By 1910, the couple was living with their adopted 6-year-old daughter Lucile in Ft. Pierce, FL. He was the Postmaster.

The Keefers later moved to Arizona, where W. L. died on March 7, 1956. He was interred there in Glendale, at Glendale Memorial Park.

Walter Kitching, New Haven (Sebastian) Justice of the Peace, 1883

Kitching was born in Leeds, West Yorkshire, England, and immigrated to the United States in 1867 at age 21. He made a great deal of money as a merchant, particularly selling to the Native Americans in several southern states.

In 1883, he purchased land in Wabasso reportedly for $1.25 an acre. That same year, he was made Justice of the Peace for New Haven, now known as Sebastian. Being an enterprising merchant and located by the river, it was natural that he developed a river trade, acquiring three vessels to transport goods for merchants from Cocoa to Jupiter. He went on to be quite a merchant in Stuart, Florida, having multiple stores, with one located between the river and the relatively new East Coast Railroad. The 1885 Florida State Census shows Walter as single, age 39, and living in the Sebastian area, but next door to 8 other Kitchings. He also acquired from the U. S. government property on May 25, 1885, that was in the Cape Canaveral area.

He married Emma Michael in 1894, and they built a home at 210 Atlanta Ave., Stuart. It consisted of 20 acres, and he raised Pineapples and had a couple of exotic trees, which are still there. Kitching donated the land for the Methodist Church in Stuart. Kitching also started and served as president of the first bank in Stuart, the Bank of Stuart.

A Walter Kitching is shown as a Keeper of the House of Refuge in the future Vero Beach in 1914. This is likely a different person. They apparently were not directly related, except that the Keeper's grandparents also came from England.

Kitching died on August 20, 1932, at 86 years old and is interred at Fernhill Memorial Gardens and Mausoleum, Stuart, Fla., where there is a monument to his and his wife's honor. A friend of Kitching's is quoted as saying about him: "He was one of the best men who ever lived in this world, …his gentle and courteous manner, purity of thought, and manifold kindness to everyone, rich and poor alike, were among his chief virtues; he was a pious man and loved his God and his Church and never was there a more loyal member."

John M. Lee, Brevard County Clerk, 1875, and possible JP, 1897

Lee was born about 1854 in Ga. Both his parents were from Georgia as well. Lee, a twenty-five-year-old resident of Lake View, was Clerk of the Circuit Court, taking that position in 1875. He was also a Florida state senator in 1879, although "unseated."

In a Congressional investigation of the contest between Republican Horatio Bisbee, Jr., and Democrat Noble A. Hull, it was made clear that the 1878 election had been quite "informal." Votes had been cast by persons whose names were not on registration lists and who had not taken oaths of qualification. Furthermore, no poll lists had been kept.

As Clerk, Lee's assistant was Eugene Gaulden. Mr. Gaulden had purported altered the tabulation of the votes from the precinct, and the United States Marshall alleged that the crime had been committed with Mr. Lee's knowledge. Mr. Lee, Sheriff Abner Wright, and Justice of the Peace Johns were charged with violations of federal election laws, and Mr. Lee and Sheriff Wright were convicted. Mr. Wright escaped from the authorities in Jacksonville and fled. Eugene

Gaulden was also charged, but he escaped prosecution by fleeing the country.[255] Mr. Lee was sent to prison in Albany, New York, served his sentence, and returned to the county to hold public office again.

John M. Lee continued to serve as county judge, sheriff, clerk, and school superintendent, although Alexander Tindall replaced Mr. Lee as Superintendent of Schools.

The 1880 Census shows Lee as the Clerk of Court in Brevard County, in the District West of the St. Johns River. It shows him as age 26 and married, but his wife is not shown. As noted earlier, there was also a J. Lee shown as Justice of the Peace at Ft. Drum in 1897. That could be the same person. There is a James Milton Lee buried in the Ft. Drum Cemetery, who died Dec 11, 1938, but he was born on Feb. 1, 1869. That would make him too young to be the clerk described above, but he could have been the Justice of the Peace.

James P. Lightburn, St. Lucia County Justice of the Peace, 1840s

James P. Lightburn was a Justice of the Peace in St. Lucie County in the 1840s. He is shown as a voter in Precinct #1 for St. Lucie County in the years 1844 and 1849, and at Precinct #2, a/k/a John Barker, in St. Lucie County in 1845. Lightburn is shown on the 1850 Census as living in St. Lucie County and as being born in the West Indies in approximately 1815. He went on to become Keeper of the

Lighthouse at Loggerhead Key, Dry Tortugas, from June of 1861 until at least July of 1862.

C. B. Magruder, Brevard County Judge, 1870s

C. B. Magruder, a/k/a Charles Magruder, a/k/a Cephus Bailey Magruder, a/k/a Major C.B. Magruder, was born near Augusta, Georgia, on March 26, 1828, the son of George Magruder (1772-1836) and Susannah C Williams Magruder (1782-1867). He is shown as owning 12 slaves in Monroe County, Georgia, in 1850. He was a captain of his company for the Confederacy in the Civil War. As a result of the war and Emancipation, he lost his slaves and plantation near Thomasville, Georgia.

Magruder then moved to Jefferson County, Florida. His first wife, Sarah Frances Smith Magruder (1838-1865), died, and he remarried on June 28, 1868. He is listed in the 1870 U.S. Census in Jefferson County, where he resided with his second wife, Cornelia Brown Smith Magruder (1844-1925), age 26, and five children: Charles, George, James, Sarah, and Albert.

In the early 1870s, Magruder explored most of central Florida and settled on an area south of Sand Point (now known as Titusville). The particular area he developed along the Indian River had a great deal of coquina rock, and so he named the location Rockledge. He cultivated citrus and became prominent. The earliest records of the

Florida State Archives show him as being the interim county judge in 1874, as well as being the interim sheriff, each for Brevard County. He was also the County Surveyor by 1878.

The steamboat was introduced along the Indian River in approximately 1877 and thrived until the advent of the railroad. A list of the Indian River Steamboat Landings showed "Magruders" on the west side of the Indian River. It was noted as 25 miles south of Titusville, 3 miles south of Rockledge, and 114 miles north of Jupiter.[256]

In 1876, Magruder displayed citrus at the Philadelphia Exposition, which commemorated the one hundredth anniversary of the birth of the nation. He also had comparable displays at the early southern fairs in Atlanta, Louisville, and New Orleans in the early 1880s. He was also a government surveyor on the east coast of Florida, going as far south as what is now Miami. Magruder's wife, Cornelia B. Magruder, was a college graduate who had taught school before marriage. The Magruders provided the first schoolhouse in Rockledge on their property and provided a paid teacher at that location.

Magruder is shown via the federal census in 1880 with his wife and now seven children in Rockledge, and via the Florida state census of 1885, as living in Brevard County in the Rockledge District, but the oldest son, Charles, had left the roost. C. B. Magruder apparently lived near to future Clerk of Court of St. Lucie County, J. E. Fultz. Magruder was the first mayor of the town of Rockledge, which was created in 1887.

The 1885 Florida State Census shows C. B. Magruder with farm property in Rockledge and Charles Magruder with farm property in Merritt Island. That same census shows C. B. Magruder as age 57, a fruit grower, and born in Georgia. His wife was Cornelia, age 40, and they had six children living with them. The youngest was eight months, and the second youngest, Lawson, age 7, was born in Florida. This was unlike their other siblings' origin, who were likely from Magruder's first marriage, and which children were born in Georgia. The youngest daughter, Cornelia (1884-1972), who became Mrs. W. C. Sessions, wrote about C.B. Magruder's settling of Rockledge, whose articles appeared in the January 3 and January 10, 1954, Tampa Tribune.

C.B. Magruder was not only a farmer; he ran a sawmill. He also helped to incorporate the Titusville and Rockledge Railway Company in 1882. However, that planned railroad to the county seat (Titusville) was not built. Magruder also raised pineapples on Merritt Island and was the president of the first growers' association, the Indian River Pineapple and Coconut Grove Association, in 1886. Also, when trade name infringement was a problem with "Indian River" fruit, the

Indian River Growers Association was formed in 1892, with C. B. Magruder as its president.

C. B. Magruder died on Oct. 31, 1910, in Rockledge and is buried in the Cocoa City Cemetery.

James A. McCrory, Brevard County Judge, 1881-1887

James A. McCrory was born in approximately 1854 in Georgia. Each of his parents was born in South Carolina. By the time he was twenty-six years old, he was a resident of Titusville. He acted as justice of the peace in 1880, holding court on the first and third Monday of each month.[257] By 1881, he was serving as both the deputy clerk of court and the county judge, the latter term being from 1881 until 1887, when he was succeeded by his friend, Minor S. Jones, as county judge. The county seat had just been moved to Titusville at that time.

The year 1880 marked the third successive biennial congressional investigation into congressional elections in Florida. McCrory was a leading witness in the investigation involving the vote counting complaint by Horatio Bisbee, who was beaten in the election by Jesse J. Finley. McCrory's testimony made it clear that there were again irregularities in the precincts in the northern part of the county.

McCrory edited, with Judge Minor S. Jones, the Titusville News, which began publishing in 1882, competing with the Titusville Star.

The purpose of Jones and McCrory in creating this newspaper was to urge a constitutional convention to encourage a more democratic constitution, to allow people to elect their local officials. Such a convention was approved by the voters in 1884, and it met in 1885. It cut back on the state government. It also ushered in the era of Democratic County leaders.

McCrory was also a partner with Minor S. Jones and A.A. Stewart (whose biographies appear in this chapter) in trying to create the Indian River and Northern Transportation Company to run a railroad between Rockledge and Lake Poinsett, which did not happen.

The Florida State Census shows J.A. McCrory's occupation in 1885 as the probate judge. McCrory appeared to be living in the household of A. A. Stewart, who was the clerk of the court at that time.

Judge James A. McCrory is not to be confused with J. Lee McCrory, who was a county judge in Volusia County and who served at least four terms in the early 1900s.

Charles McLane, Brevard County Court Judge, 1870s

Charles McLane, aka McLean, was another protégé of James Paine, Sr. Paine recommended McLane as county judge to Governor Reed by letter dated July 22, 1871. McLane served as county judge of Brevard during the Republican hegemony.[258] McLane was a doctor.

James Padgett, Brevard County Court Clerk, circa 1865

James Tippen Padgett was born on November 4, 1837, in Ware County, Georgia. He was the oldest son of Elijah Padgett, who moved to southern Brevard County, near the Okeechobee area, by 1860. Elijah was one of six children of Hopkins and Mary Padgett, who were each born in South Carolina around 1770.

James T. Padgett married Louisa Alvarez, daughter of Joseph and Nancy Alvarez. She was born on February 13, 1844, in Alachua County. James T. and Louisa Padgett had eleven children between 1860 and 1885.

Immediately following the Civil War, in which he was a Confederate soldier, James Padgett was the Clerk of the Brevard County Court, serving on an interim basis. He is also listed as a voter in 1860 in Precinct Number 2 in Brevard County. He again shows up in Precinct No. 2, then known as North Yates, in Brevard County in 1864. He was a Justice of the Peace for Brevard County by 1875.

James T. Padgett married a second time, in 1900 in Olney (Fort Drum), Okeechobee County, Florida, to Vandalia "Vannie" Ella Willis, daughter of John and Frances (Vann) Willis. Vandalia was born July 29, 1877, at Lokosee, Florida (southeast of present-day Kenansville), her parents having come from Early County, Georgia, and via the Kissimmee River valley. The couple added seven more children to the Padgett household between 1900 and 1917.

James T. Padgett died May 14, 1917, and was purportedly buried in a cemetery located in the southeast corner of Indian River County. His widow, Vandalia, subsequently married a Mr. Boatwright, and she died on January 20, 1961. She is buried at Ft. Drum Cemetery, where there is also a nearby monument to James T. Padgett and others.

James Paine, Sr., Brevard County Court Judge and Justice of the Peace

Captain or Major James E. Paine, a/k/a James Paine, Sr., or Judge Paine, was born in Virginia in approximately 1811. With the rank of major, James Paine, Sr., completed his tour of duty in the United States Army at Fort Capron. He resigned to settle on 40 acres along the Indian River about one mile south of the Fort. James Paine, Sr., is credited with having founded the village of St. Lucie in 1856. His family joined him in 1857 and consisted of his wife, Johanna; three sons, John, James, Jr., and Thomas; and one daughter, Gertrude Elizabeth, all of whom were born in South Carolina. The family thereafter had another son, Trueman, born in Florida in 1861.

In 1861, when the State of Florida and the infant Confederate States were preparing for war, Brevard County residents followed suit, cooperating when they could. On August 21, 1861, a letter was written from Indian River by James Paine, A. Oswald Lang,[259] and Francis A. Ivey to Governor Madison S. Perry. They felt "it is a solemn duty of every citizen to try and serve his state and county in whatever capacity he may be most able." Thus, they justified "putting out the Lights at both Jupiter Inlet and Cape Florida."

One week later, the townspeople met at the home of James Paine and made plans for their protection. James Paine was named to a committee to draft resolutions advising Governor Madison S. Perry to send soldiers to Indian River for the protection of its people. Governor Perry was unable to send the troops, and local residents had to be satisfied with a home guard company commanded by Captain James Paine. Paine was the Jupiter Inlet Keeper (for the Confederate States of America) from January 11, 1862, to June 17, 1863.

At the time of the Civil War, his oldest son, John, joined the Confederate Army and was killed in Virginia. James, Jr., a teenager at that time, joined the forces of General Beauregard and took part in the one major battle fought in Florida at Olustee. He survived the War and returned home.

After the Civil War, Captain Paine was appointed justice of the peace for his district. He was also a postmaster and was a political advisor for the county, recommending numerous appointments for county offices to Governors Reed and Hart. James Paine, Sr., served as county judge and as collector of revenue. He was a state representative for Brevard County in 1871 and 1872. He also served as superintendent of schools until 1874.

James, Jr., born April 28, 1845, delivered the mail along the Indian River, including delivering the mail to a man in Jupiter known as the "Barefoot Mailman," who carried the mail as he walked along the beach to Miami. James later became postmaster at St. Lucie and served continuously for 37 years. He was also the deputy collector.

Judge Paine's daughter, Gertrude Elizabeth, married Minor S. Jones. (See his biography in this chapter.) Judge Paine's son, Thomas Paine, born May 25, 1850, established a cattle operation around 1870 west of St. Lucie, back to the St. Johns River.

James Paine, Sr., still lived in St. Lucie and served as Collector of the Port in the early 1880s. He died on November 15, 1882. He is buried adjacent to the Old Dixie Highway between Vero Beach and Fort Pierce inside "Jas. Paine Circle" on a plot that Paine acquired in 1857. His wife, Johanna, who died on October 28, 1895, is also buried there with him, inside the iron fence located on the property. In 1910, James Paine, Jr., sold the west half of the property to the St. Lucie School Board for $50.00. In 1935, Gertrude Paine Jones (Mrs. Minor S. Jones - wife of Judge Minor S. Jones - first Circuit Judge of St. Lucie County) deeded the east half of the property to the school board for $1.00. Son, Thomas Paine, died on October 11, 1918, and is buried in Titusville at the La Grange Cemetery. Son, James, Jr., died on October 30, 1922, and is also buried there.

Henry L. Parker, Brevard County Court Judge, 1872

Henry L. Parker was born in Columbia County, Florida, on April 15, 1832. He was a brother of John and Streaty Parker, and all three are considered pioneer cattlemen in the lower Kissimmee River valley in the 1870s. (For additional information on Streaty Parker, see the biographical information under circuit judge James Alderman, *infra.*)

Henry L. Parker was Sheriff of Hillsborough County in 1855. He then returned to Columbia County and married Elizabeth Matilda (Brinkley) Holmes, a widow with one child. He appears in the 1860 census in Columbia County. The family then moved to Brevard County, where Parker built and operated a ferry at Bluff Hammock. They later moved to the Basinger area but sold their premises to Noel Raulerson, Sr., in 1874.

Henry L. Parker was appointed county judge in 1872. He lived at Fort Drum, but his post office address was St. Lucie (St. Lucie Village), approximately forty miles east of his residence. He was recommended for that post by James Paine, Sr., in a letter to Governor Harrison Reed on August 29, 1872. Parker soon moved to Lake View, the Brevard County Seat, in 1874.

On August 24, 1876, Elizabeth Parker died, and the next year, Parker married Ruth Ann Richards. A few years later, the Parkers were back in the Ft. Drum area, where Parker opened up a general store and trading post with his stepson, Henry Holmes. They also worked cattle.[260]

Parker also served as a County Commissioner for Brevard County during the Republican hegemony, including in 1879 and 1880. He was a state representative from Brevard County in 1881. Parker was the Postmaster for Fort Drum in 1888. Henry L. Parker & Son was the major merchandising firm for that area. They did a great deal of business with the Cow Creek Seminole Indians and shipped a large number of pelts through Fort Pierce. Henry L. Parker represented Brevard County, along with Alexander Bell of St. Lucie, at the Constitutional Convention of 1885. By 1893, Henry Parker was the state representative again for Brevard County, and again in 1899.

Henry Parker died at Ft. Drum on March 3, 1908. His widow, Ruth, died on July 11, 1911, and is buried with Henry and Elizabeth Parker in the Ft. Drum cemetery. Parker had only one natural child, Florah (with his wife Elizabeth), who was born on December 1, 1872, and died on March 6, 1887, and is buried at the Parker gravesite as well.

Samuel Peck, St. Lucia County Court Judge and Justice of the Peace, 1844-1845

Samuel Peck is covered in the prior chapter. He is in here twice, as his judicial roles straddled statehood, and for a couple of additional facts. His Armed Occupation Act Settler permit was number 63. His property was located on the west bank of St. Lucie Sound, three miles south of Gilbert's Bar. Peck shows up as a voter in St. Lucia County in 1844 but does not appear on the census in St. Lucie County in 1850 or on the census for Brevard County in 1860. He left the area in 1845.

Oliver H. Perry, Brevard County Court Judge, 1855-1860

Oliver H. Perry was likely born in New York in approximately 1815. This information is gleaned from the 1860 census for Volusia County. He was listed next to two prominent lighthouse keepers of Cape Canaveral, Mills O. Burnham and his son-in-law assistant, Henry Wilson. The district in Volusia was then called Sand Point, which today we know as Titusville, the seat of Brevard County since 1879. Perry's occupation was shown as a farmer with $400.00 worth of personal property.

Shofner, in his book on Brevard County, shows Oliver H. Perry to be the Brevard County Judge, probably from its inception, 1855-1860.[261]

Ruben H. Pinkham, St. Lucia County Justice of the Peace, 1850

Ruben H. Pinkham was born in New York in approximately 1796. He was known as Captain Pinkham. Robert Ranson, in his East Coast Florida Memoirs, 1837 to 1886, describes Pinkham as an English pilot (sea captain) who had settled in St. Augustine, married there, and then became an Armed Occupation Act settler. The reference to "English" may be incorrect.

Niles Register, March 24, 1827, Appointments, shows Reuben R. Pinkham as being appointed a lieutenant in the U.S. Navy. Reuben Pinkham obtained permit number 19 for land within a quarter mile of the Indian River Inlet. The property was by Blue Hole Creek, which is north of Jack Island. (The previous inlet was farther north than the Ft. Pierce Inlet is today.) At one time, he owned the only schooner in the Indian River Colony and was the chief source of transportation and supplies from St. Augustine.

An advertisement in the Florida Herald on January 10, 1835, indicates that Pinkham was trying to sell his lot and house on the east side of Charlotte Street in St. Augustine. Nevertheless, he is shown as living in St. Augustine during the 1840 census. He is also shown as a registered voter for the John Barker Precinct in St. Lucie County in 1844.

Pinkham, together with John S. Hermans, a fellow homesteader, was an affiant on the Armed Occupation Act application of John

Barker on November 30, 1848. Pinkham was also commissioned as Port Warden for St. Lucie County on March 7, 1845.

It was Captain Pinkham's schooner to which fellow colonists, William Russell, Caleb Brayton, and D. H. Gettis, escaped in 1849 when the Indians killed Russell's brother-in-law, John Barker, and wounded Russell as he stood on the deck of that boat. They escaped to St. Augustine.

The 1850 Census shows "Ruben" H. Pinkham as living in St. Augustine. He was 54 years old then, suggesting he was born in 1796. His occupation was listed as a "mariner," and he was shown to be born in New York.[262] His wife apparently was Aghata, who was born in Florida. The census showed the couple then having six children, varying in age from 1 to 16, all born in Florida. Records also indicate that Pinkham was a Justice of the Peace for St. Lucie County circa 1850. The 1830 census for New York shows a Reuben Pinkham or Pinkman in Hudson, Columbia County. Lighthouse keeper records show that Pinkham was Second Assistant Keeper at the St. Augustine Lighthouse from October 8, 1878, to January 18, 1879.

William F. Russell, St. Lucia County Justice of the Peace, about 1850

William Russell was born in North Carolina in about 1805. He likely served in the Seminole War and had the rank of Major. He was an Armed Occupational Act settler in the Ft. Pierce area in the 1840s.

His wife was Susan. His brother-in-law, via Russell's sister, Martha, was John Barker, who the Indians killed in 1849 near the St. Lucie Inlet. Russell was shot in the same fray and escaped, as did his family members before him, to New Smyrna and St. Augustine. In the escape, Russell self-treated his wound in the dark. Unfortunately, what Russell thought to be salve was ink, and after his arm turned black by the next morning, he purportedly had to have Dr. Peck amputate his arm.[263]

He returned to this area and continued to be a county commissioner for St. Lucia County, from 1847 to 1855, when St Lucie County became Brevard County. He was a Justice of the Peace around 1850. He was also an inspector of customs at this time. The 1850 census for St. Lucie County shows him as age 45 and as "Inspt. Customs" and living with his wife, Susan, age 40, and 6 children, including likely twins, Amelia and Susan, each age 14. They were the oldest, and the first 4 children were born in North Carolina, and the last two, in Florida. That particular census page is a virtual who's who in St. Lucia County Judicial circles, including Douglas Dummett, N. C. Scobie, John S. Hermans, Mills O. Burnham, James Lightburn, and Caleb Brayton.

Russell was a member of the Florida House of Representatives and Speaker in 1854, being preceded as representative from St. Lucia County by John S. Hermans. Russell is credited with naming Brevard

County after his friend Theodorus W. Brevard. As mentioned before, the first site of the Brevard County seat, Susannah, could have been named for his wife or their location. Russell resigned prior to adjournment in the 1855 term of the legislature.

On May 1, 1855, Russell acquired land just south of present-day Ft. Pierce. In 1860, Russell was still living in Brevard County, with an Indian River post office as the location, and with his wife and 4 children. Twin, Amelia, is now called Mildred, and son James is living in a nearby household at age 22. James is described as a Mail Carrier, and his father is described as a Farmer.

In 1870, the U. S. Census shows Russell as living with his wife in Sand Point (the future Titusville) in then Volusia County. He is still described as a Farmer. Son, James, again appears to be nearby and is described as a Farm Laborer. James is also shown as being born in Florida, which conflicts with the 1850 census.

Around 1875, Russell returned to the Ft. Pierce area and built a two-story house in the St. Lucie Village area, now called the Russell-Padrick House at 2817 North Indian River Drive, and it is considered the oldest standing house in St. Lucie County.

Russell appears to have moved to the Orlando, Orange County area by 1880, and he likely passed away there.

<u>N. C. Scobie, St. Lucia County Justice of the Peace, 1843</u>

Nathaniel C. Scobie, or Scobia, or Scoby, or Scobin, was an Armed Occupation Act settler in the Ft. Pierce area and served as a justice of the peace. He was likely born in 1805 in Nova Scotia, according to the 1850 census of St. Lucie County. His Armed Occupation Act permit was number 4 at the Land Office at St. Augustine. The application indicates that Scobie became a resident of Florida in October 1829. Census records show that he lived in St. Augustine in 1830, likely with his wife, and also in 1840. He likely arrived via Boston from Nova Scotia in 1820.

As of August 4, 1842, he occupied land on the barrier island near Ft. Pierce. His Armed Occupation Act permit was filed on March 15, 1843. He was married at the time of his application. Incidentally, the justice of the peace on his Armed Occupation Act application was John C. Cleland. Almost three months later, Scobie was commissioned as a justice of the peace for the then Mosquito County.

Scobie fought and served with his friends, Dummett and Cleland, in the Second Seminole War. Scobie was wounded at the Battle of Dunlawton (judicial figure, George Anderson's, plantation), and fought alongside judicial figures Dummett, Putnam, and Ormond. This was reported by Cleland.[264]

Scobie was the first operator of the Cape Canaveral lighthouse in about 1847. He was a relative of Capt. Douglas Dummett,

Collector of the Port of New Smyrna. The 1850 Census for St. Lucie County shows that Scobie was back in the Ft. Pierce area, living next to Dummett. Scobie was then living with his wife, Margaret Westroy, who was born on March 25, 1810, and their three children, all of whom were born in Florida.

Scobie was one of the St. Lucie County Commissioners elected in 1852, serving in that capacity with C.L. Brayton and John S. Hermans, whose brief biographies are set forth in this book. A voter registration list shows Scobie as being a voter in Precinct 1 or "Indian River" for St. Lucia County in 1852.

Land records showed that Nathaniel C. Scobie acquired property near the present-day Cape Canaveral on December 15, 1871.

Scobie and his wife were buried near Dummett's father in the Protestant Cemetery just outside the city gates in St. Augustine.

Frank C. Smith, Clerk of Court 1868, and Justice of the Peace 1879-1880s

Captain Frank C. Smith was born in Georgia in about 1824. His parents were also from Ga. He married Katie Furay (born in 1855) of New York. They had a son, Frank E. Smith, born about 1880. Frank C. Smith also had a brother, John.

Smith owned a store – a trading post in Ft. Pierce, and would ship Indian goods north. He was also a postmaster there. He was also a Florida State Representative for Brevard County from 1868 to 1870. This was the time he was also the Clerk of Court for Brevard Co. (Apparently, there was no state representative from Brevard in 1866-1867). He was succeeded by James Paine, Sr. Smith was a Republican and seemed to be at odds with Paine.

Smith is considered to be the first settler in the Micco Grant area in 1877 and acquired several properties on each side of Grant Road, extending to the river. He was a postmaster for Chipco, on the Indian River north of Sebastian in 1880, and then in Micco, which replaced the Chipco Post Office in 1884. Both Frank and his brother John were Justices of the Peace in the 1870s and 1880s. Frank's Captain title likely came from the Civil War.

Alexander A. Stewart
Courtesy of Jim Ball

A. A. Stewart, Brevard County Circuit Court Clerk, 1871-1912

Alexander Asa Stewart was born in 1840 in Jasper, Florida. His parents, Israel M. and Annie Stewart, came from Georgia. His family moved to Hamilton County, Florida, and both A. A. Stewart's father and grandfather served in Florida's volunteer militia during the Second Seminole War. Both Israel (the father) and A. A.'s brother, John Quincy Stewart, served in the Florida Legislature, Israel being in the first legislature when Florida was admitted as a state.

A. A. Stewart was a medical student at the Savannah Medical College in 1860 but left in order to serve in various capacities in the Confederate Army. In 1864, he was captured by Union soldiers and was imprisoned for over a year at various locations, including Governor's Island, New York. He was paroled at Madison, Florida, in 1865.

Stewart married Maria Elizabeth Robinson (May 21, 1846 - September 7, 1925) of South Carolina on December 12, 1867, in Hamilton County, Florida. Her parents were from Ireland and South Carolina, respectively. Maria was one of 8 daughters of the twice-widowed Mary Ann Robinson. A. A. Stewart and his wife moved to Brevard County in 1868. They had nine children, all of whom were born in Florida. Mrs. Stewart was a homemaker and teacher.

Stewart was appointed the first full-time Clerk of the Circuit Court for Brevard County in 1871 and served in that capacity until

1912. There was a hiatus in his service, however, due to the fraudulent ballot counting by John M. Lee (see his bio in this chapter), who briefly took A. A. Stewart's position as Clerk of Court.

Teacher Certificate of Maria Stewart
Courtesy of Jim Ball

A.A. Stewart at brick courthouse storage, 1903
Courtesy of Jim Ball

A. A. Stewart's appointments to the clerk of the circuit court in
Brevard County, 1872 and 1873
by Governors Reed and Stearns – Courtesy of Jim Ball

Stewart's initial appointment came upon the recommendation of
James Paine, Sr. of St. Lucie Village. Stewart was initially appointed
clerk by Governor Reed and reappointed by Governors Hart, Stearns,
and nine other governors. In 1874, the earliest date of certain records
at the Florida State Archives, he is shown to be not only the Clerk of
the Circuit Court, but the Assessor of Taxes and Collector of Taxes.[265]

Brevard County Courthouse Circa 1880s with Clerk A. A. Stewart
and Judge J. A. McCrory
Courtesy of Jim Ball

Alexander A. Stewart was active with Judge J. A. McCrory and Minor S. Jones in the formation of a rail line to compete with the Titusville and Rockledge Railroad Company. Stewart's line, to be known as the Indian River and Northern Transportation Company, and intended to run between Rockledge and Lake Poinsettia, was not built. A. A. Stewart also ran a sawmill and was a permittee to plant and harvest artificial oyster beds in the Indian River. The sawmill was later sold to Hardee and Roberts. (See Hardee bio in this chapter). A. A. Stewart was also a partner with Minor S. Jones in the Brevard Abstract of Title Company.

While Stewart and his family had homesteaded on Merritt Island, they moved to Titusville in 1883, which brought him much closer to the relatively new county seat and new courthouse, from which he would administer his duties. They also had a home in Bonaventure, in Brevard County, along the river south of Rockledge.

When Stewart retired in January 1913, the East Coast Advocate, on Jan. 10, 1913, noted that "He goes out of office with the best and kindest feelings from everyone. Mr. Stewart retires from office with the knowledge and satisfaction that he has done his best for the good of Brevard County."

At the time of Stewart's death on March 9, 1922, he was a member of Indian River Lodge, No. 90, Free and Accepted Masons, of which organization he was a charter member and the first Worshipful Master. He held that honor for eight different years. He is buried in Oaklawn Cemetery in Titusville.

John M. Swain, St. Lucie Justice of the Peace, 1879, 1882

John Morgan Swain or Swaine was born December 20, 1855, in Georgia. His father was Rev. Joel Wooten Swain (1836-1900), and his mother was Martha Ellen Smith Swain (1829-1895). As mentioned, he was the Justice of the Peace for St. Lucie, in Brevard County, for the years indicated. He was married to Sarah Ellen "Ella" Anderson Swain, and they had ten children. He was granted a Homestead by the land office in Gainesville in 1897 for property in St. Lucie County, which today is west of the Turnpike and south of Yeehaw Junction.

He may have been the J. M. Swaine who attended a drainage district organizational meeting for western St. Lucie County on August 13. 1915, where he is described as a long-time resident and surveyor. See the next chapter.

In 1917, he was a state representative from St. Lucie County and is known for introducing the bill that year that was to create Okeechobee County from St. Lucie, Osceola, and DeSoto Counties, which passed. The Ft. Pierce City Directory for 1920 shows him living with Ella, and he is a "far" (likely farmer).

Swain died in Ft. Pierce on March 11, 1925, at age 69, and he is buried in the Ft. Drum Cemetery in Okeechobee County.

Henry Titus – Brevard County Justice of the Peace

Henry Titus is mentioned in this chapter as the one for whom the Brevard County Seat was named in 1879, and Titusville has remained the seat to this day. Here is a summary of his biography, as it is both interesting and he was also a Justice of the Peace.

Titus was born in Trenton, New Jersey, on February 13, 1823, the first of nine children of Theodore Titus and Catherine Flick Howell. He was raised in Wilkes-Barre, Pennsylvania, and attended West Point, but did not graduate. He seemed to have been a soldier of fortune and was involved in an unauthorized 1850 invasion of Cuba. He was shipwrecked in 1852 and later was a part of Bleeding Kansas in 1856, where, under attack by John Brown's raiders, he was wounded and captured in the Battle of Fort Titus. (Yes, named after him.) Thereafter, he was involved in an authorized military excursion in Nicaragua.

Titus next lived in New York City, but then went to Arizona, where he and his brother had ore mines. Thereafter, he returned to Jacksonville, Florida, where he had once been a grocer and mill operator in the early 1850s. During the Civil War, he was a quartermaster in the Florida Militia. (His Colonel title was honorary.) He transported Confederate draft dodgers to Nassau but subsequently lost his steamer to a Northern Blockade and was captured on the Indian River.

Following the war, Titus, who was referred to as an uninhibited proslavery filibusterer, wounded a former Union soldier quite seriously on a Jacksonville street. Tried in the Mayor's Court, he testified, "I had a political discussion with this fellow... he used some language that did not suit me, and I knocked him in the head with my stick." He was fined $5.00 but appealed to the county court, where a jury found him not guilty![266]

After again moving to New York City in 1865, with his family, he returned to Florida in 1867 and ran businesses in Sandpoint – now Titusville, as mentioned above on the creation of the county seat.

Besides being a Justice of the Peace and a notary for Volusia County, his son, Theodore Titus, Sr., went on to be a distinguished jurist in Georgia, and his great-grandson, Theodore Titus, III, served five terms in the Georgia House of Representatives. Titus had another great-grandson, John D. Ensey, who was called the Mango Man of Merritt Island for his raising and selling mangoes there.[267]

Henry Titus died in Titusville on August 7, 1881. Titus is buried in LaGrange Cemetery in Titusville.

J. D. Vann, Sebastian Justice of the Peace, 1891

John D. Vann became a homesteader in Florida when his land grant was approved by President Chester A. Arthur at the U. S. General Land Office in Gainesville on June 13, 1883. The property was in Section 19 of Township 20 S and Range 36 East. That is located between the Indian River and the Mosquito Lagoon, northeast of Titusville. In 1885, he was running a store and restaurant by the Haulover Canal on Merritt Island. He was also a Brevard County Commissioner after the 1885 Florida Constitution was created. On January 29, 1890, he may have been appointed Postmaster of Clifton, in Brevard County, which was around Merritt Island. (There is a discrepancy in the Vann first name.)

A Florida death index has a John D. Vann passing away in Volusia County in 1914.

W. D. Ward, Justice of the Peace, St. Lucia County

William D. Ward was likely born in approximately 1812 in Maine. His occupation was a blacksmith. Ward was a justice of the peace during the first St. Lucie or St. Lucia County period. Ward was an Armed Occupation Act settler, becoming a resident along the Indian River in February 1842 as part of the Indian River Colony. His homestead was likely three miles north of Fort Pierce. His Armed Occupation Act Permit was number 57; he applied in April 1843.

Ward was a member of the second group of St. Lucie County Commissioners in 1847. He succeeded board members who included William B. Davis, John Barker, and Ossian Hart and served with, among others, William F. Russell. Voter records show that Ward voted in precinct number 2, a/k/a the John Barker precinct, in St. Lucie County in 1844 and 1845.

A copy of a letter Mr. Ward wrote the President of the United States on September 3, 1849, survives. It addressed the investment that Ward had made in tropical fruits along the Indian River, which was thwarted by the Indian expeditions, including the attack upon Russell and Barker, and the burning of Captain Gattis' home in July of 1848. (Ward was living at the time the letter was authored in New Smyrna.)

Ward moved to Jacksonville, Duval County, and shows up in the 1850 census in that county. He was living in St. Johns County in 1860.

A. J. Whitlock, Brevard County Court Judge, 1881

A. J. Whitlock was born in Georgia in 1827. His parents were also born in Georgia. A. J. Whitlock was a county judge in Brevard County in 1881.[268]

In 1878, Whitlock became a Justice of the Peace for Brevard County, where his address was City Point. (City Point was 16 miles south of Titusville). He was a Justice of the Peace for at least 10 years.[269] Whitlock was also active in 1880 in the Indian River Fruit and Vegetable Growers Protective Association, one of the earliest associations to address problems of growers. He was specifically in charge of complaints about freight rates and reporting them to the Railroad Commission. In 1881, he was the first postmaster of the newly established City Point Post Office.

By 1885, he was still the postmaster, living in City Point. He lived with his thirteen-year-old son and six-year-old daughter, both of whom were born in Florida. The agricultural schedule for the 1885 census showed that he owned three acres of permanent meadow and two acres of woodland forest. His farm was valued at $8,000.00, and the value of his farm production was $50.00.

Whitlock died in 1901.

Chapter 4 - St. Lucie County Through the Creation of Indian River County

A. Creation of St. Lucie County - 1905

In the early 1900s, sentiment had been growing among the people of lower Brevard County for the legislature to create a new county in order that the government might be closer to home.[270]The population of lower Brevard had been increasing due to the terrible winter freeze of 1894-1895, which moved planters of pineapples, particularly, to the southern part of Brevard County.[271]

On May 24, 1905, the state responded by creating St. Lucie County, the state's forty-sixth county. This was the second county to bear that name because the original St. Lucie or St. Lucia County was created as Florida's 25th county on March 14, 1844, and was renamed as Brevard County on January 6, 1855. The county was named for St. Lucie of Syracuse. The boundaries of the new county were Sebastian River on the north, St. Lucie River on the south, and Osceola County on the west.

The seat of St. Lucie County was Ft. Pierce, a city which was incorporated on February 2, 1901. Ft. Pierce had once existed, however, when Lt. Col. Benjamin K. Pierce, later known as General Pierce, established the blockhouse on the west side of the Indian

River on January 2, 1838, during the Second Seminole War. Pierce was the brother of President Franklin Pierce.

The creation of St. Lucie County came into effect on July 1, 1905, and was celebrated with a Fourth of July parade with speeches by C. T. McCarty, Esq., and Claude Homestead.

The first grand jury for the newly-created St. Lucie County in 1905 consisted of the following: T. J. O'Brien, Pete Robinson, A. Y. W. Hogg, Lee Faber, A. M. Sample, William Fee, W. P. Lassiter, David Lee Alderman, H. E. Crooks, William E. Tylander, A. B. Lowery, John C. Jones, State Attorney J. G. Coats, Gosper Tucker, K. B. Raulerson, E. C. Summerlin, Henry A. Holmes, Harry Jennings, E. T. Traynor, and W. S. Musgrove. The first Clerk of the Circuit Court of St. Lucie County in 1905 was J. E. Fultz. The sheriff at that time was Bob Lennard. The sole county commissioner to come from the area of what would become Indian River County was Paul Kroegel of Sebastian, who had recently been named our nation's first game warden by President Theodore Roosevelt in 1903.

As explained in the next chapter, Indian River County was created in 1925. While the land in what is Indian River County was a part of St. Lucie County, the circuit judge when St. Lucie County was [re]-created in 1905 was Minor Jones. That judge is still known for his ruling that a mullet is not a fish because of the fact that it has a gizzard like a chicken, unlike other species of fish. (See his biographical information in Chapter 3).

1907 Rand McNally Map

Note Orchard, Enos, Woodley, and Toledo

all between Sebastian and Gifford

After St. Lucie County was created in 1905, court was held shortly thereafter in the new Improvement Club Hall on the east side of North Second Street, for which construction was started on September 17, 1905.[272] Another landmark from approximately 1905, which still exists, was more recently called the Court Reporters, Inc.

building, but once contained the law office of Hemmings and Andrews, which is located immediately north of the St. Lucie County Courthouse parking garage at 211 S. Second Street. See page 246.

St. Lucie County Courthouse
Courtesy of St. Lucie County History Museum

In 1909, a two-story brick courthouse was constructed in Fort Pierce. The site of this imposing structure was almost identical to where the present courthouse sits. It was the future venue for the famous trial of Judge Peel in 1961, which is discussed under the biography of D.C. Smith in Chapter 7.

It is interesting that in George M. Chapin's book on Florida in 1914,[273] he referenced Ft. Pierce as the principal city and county seat of St. Lucie County with a population of 2,000. He goes on to note, "Other important points as centers of population are… Sebastian,…(and) Gifford." Still further, he discloses where one of the most important land developments in the state was going on – Fellsmere. There is no mention of Vero. It does not even appear on the 1913 map Chapin included in his book.[274]

I found a front-page story about the creation of a drainage district for St. Lucie County that appeared on August 13, 1915, of interest, as it mentions at least 4 judges, whose names appear below, at the same organizational meeting.[275] The meeting occurred at the courthouse and had over 150 people in attendance. Those who went by the title of judge in the article included John R. Johnson, J. E. Andrews, F. L. Hemmings, and Judge Otis R. Parker. The last name surprised me because his son of the same name (Jr.) went on to be a St. Lucie County Judge, and Otis Sr. was Judge John R. Johnson's brother-in-law (see below under Johnson), but I learned that Otis Parker Sr. was a mayor/municipal judge. (I have only covered municipal judges, as you read further, for the municipalities in present-day Indian River County.) The article also refers to J. M. Swaine, described as an old resident and surveyor for many years. Could that be the Justice of the Peace referred to in the prior chapter?

On May 8, 1917, Okeechobee County was created by the Florida Legislature, which was taken in part from our then St. Lucie County.

The City of Okeechobee was the seat of the new county. The name comes from the Hitchiti Creek words for "big water." Okeechobee County would stay connected to St. Lucie County and subsequently Indian River County and Martin County (each subsequently created in part from St. Lucie County) and would continue to be in the same judicial circuit, even when those circuit numbers and other counties in the circuit changed. See the next chapter for more on those circuits.

In 1917, the salary of the County Judge for St. Lucie County was set by the legislature at $1,200.00 per annum.[276] The act also transferred any suit within the jurisdiction of the county court (i.e., less than $500.00) then pending before the Justices of the Peace for St. Lucie County, to the County Court.

By 1920, the first bridge across the Indian River in St. Lucie County was completed.[277] This horizontal draw-span bridge was in Vero, as it was then known. Shortly thereafter, the Sheriff of St. Lucie County would be arresting the movie theater operator in Vero for Sunday showings, which would give rise to the creation of a new county, Indian River County, which is discussed in the next chapter.

The circuit court judges for St. Lucie County, prior to Indian River County's creation, were as follows:

1898-1911	Minor S. Jones	Seventh
1911-1917[278]	James W. Perkins	Seventh
1917-1920	E. B. Donnell	Fifteenth

1921-1923	E. C. Davis	Fifteenth
1923-1925+[279]	C. E. Chillingworth	Fifteenth
1925-1938	Elwyn Thomas	Twenty-First

The county court judges of St. Lucie County, prior to Indian River County's creation, were as follows:

James E. Andrews	July 1, 1905 - December 31, 1906
Fred Fee	January 8, 1907 - January 4, 1909
F. L. Hemmings	January 5, 1909 - January 20, 1914
J. R. Johnson	June 30, 1914 - September 23, 1922
Angus Sumner	September 29, 1922 - January 14, 1926

From the time that St. Lucie was [re]created in 1905 until well past the creation of Indian River County in 1925, there were two Clerks of the Court. They were:

J.E. Fultz	1905 - 1916
P.C. Eldred	1916 - 1925+

We also know that Sebastian, Fellsmere, Quay, and Vero, while a part of St. Lucie County, had justices of the peace. See chapters on most of those municipalities, *infra*.

B. Biographies of Circuit Judges in St. Lucie County – 1905 to 1925

Minor S. Jones, Seventh Judicial Circuit Judge, 1898-1911

See biographical information set forth under Chapter 3 for Minor S. Jones.

James W. Perkins
Photo from the Florida Department of Transportation

James W. Perkins, Seventh Judicial Circuit Judge, 1911-1917[280]

James W. Perkins was born in Rome, Floyd County, Georgia, on December 7, 1862. His father was James P. Perkins, who came to Sumter County, Florida, in approximately 1869 as one of its early settlers. James P. Perkins then moved to Monroe County in 1871 and became prominent in public affairs, representing that county in the legislature for two years. Later, James P. Perkins moved his family to Fort Myers and was active in the development of that part of the state where he resided until 1885. In 1885, President Grover Cleveland appointed him as Clerk of the Indian Agency in Arizona. James P. Perkins moved to Arizona and died there in 1896.

James W. Perkins was educated in public schools in Monroe County, although one author said he had no common school education.[281] When he was thirteen years old, he became a sailor, but after five years of life at sea, he secured a clerkship in a store in Fort Myers. He attended Eastman Business College, where he graduated in 1884, and then spent time in Arizona and other locations in the West.

In 1897, the future Judge Perkins returned to Florida at Leesburg for two years. In 1889, he came to DeLand and worked as an assistant bookkeeper in the large mercantile house of Dreka & Coe. He resigned that position to accept the appointment as First Deputy Sheriff of Volusia County. At approximately that time, he commenced the study of law and, in 1892, resigned his office to enter the Cumberland School of Law in Lebanon, Tennessee. In June 1893, he graduated from that institution and returned to DeLand to practice. He was appointed by Governor H.L. Mitchell as prosecuting attorney for the Criminal Court of Volusia County and, through reappointment, served continuously until 1904. He also served as a judge of the criminal court for two years. In 1899, he was elected mayor of DeLand. For eight years, he was the secretary and treasurer of the County Executive Committee. In 1897, he married the former Mary Smith of Pomeroy, Ohio.

He was elected to the state senate and served in the session of 1911, when he was appointed judge of the Seventh Judicial Circuit by Governor Gilchrist. He was reappointed in 1917 by Governor Catts. James W. Perkins was circuit court judge of our then Seventh Circuit from 1911 through 1917, when the Fifteenth Circuit was created. While the land, which is now located in Indian River County, then became a part of the newly created Fifteenth Circuit, James W. Perkins continued as a circuit judge of the Seventh Circuit until 1923.

When the legislature in 1917 created the Fifteenth Judicial Circuit by Chapter 7351, that act provided that a judge should be appointed, confirmed, and hold office for the term provided by the Constitution. After the legislature adjourned, Governor Catts appointed E. B. Donnell. His appointment was confirmed at a special session of the legislature in November of 1918.

In 1921, Judge Perkins and his wife, May S. Perkins, designed and had built a beautiful brick home in Deland, which Mrs. Perkins bequeathed to her niece, Helen Louise Stoudenmire, in 1950. Mrs. Stoudenmire's husband, C. Aubry Stoudenmire, was a 1939 graduate of the Stetson College of Law and a prominent DeLand attorney. They, in turn, gifted the home to Stetson University in 1964, where the building subsequently became known as the "Brick Palace," and was repurposed a number of times by and for the University.

It has been reported that Judge Perkins was one of the best storytellers. He reportedly understood how to awaken the keen interest of listeners and knew how to make them laugh. In his later years, he was the Chairman of the Florida State Road Dept., being appointed by Governor Cone in 1940-1941.

E. B. Donnell, Fifteenth Judicial Circuit Judge, 1917-1920

E. B. Donnell is not to be confused with J. B. Donnelly, who was a municipal magistrate of the Town of Palm Beach in 1925. Ezra Ballard Donnell was born near Lebanon in Wilson County, Tennessee, on March 11, 1880. He was the son of a Tennessee farmer, James Peter Donnell, and his wife, Mary Frances Bass.

At age seventeen, he served his country in the Spanish-American War from 1898 to 1900 and was discharged as a corporal. He graduated from Peabody College, Nashville, Tennessee, in 1904 with a bachelor's degree in education. He played football in college. From 1905 to 1911, he taught school in Louisiana and was Superintendent of Schools in Baton Rouge from 1908 to 1911.

Donnell came to Florida in 1911 and studied law at the University of Florida, where he received his bachelor's degree in law in 1912. He was admitted to practice law that same year. He practiced law in Jacksonville and was Attorney for Duval County from 1916 to June 14, 1917, when he was appointed Judge of the Fifteenth Judicial Circuit. There was apparently a battle between two candidates for the judgeship, and E. B. Donnell, the County Attorney for Duval County, was suggested as a compromise candidate and was appointed by Governor Sidney J. Catts. The Fifteenth Judicial Circuit was then comprised of St. Lucie, Okeechobee, Palm Beach, and Brevard Counties. Shortly thereafter, in the primary of 1917, Donnell was nominated for a full six-year term without opposition. Donnell's original appointment by Governor Catts occurred after the Legislature in 1917 adjourned. The confirmation of his first commission was not made by the Florida Senate until November 1918, which created a commencement-of-term issue. (See In Re Advising Opinion to Governor, 80 So. 519 (Fla. 1919) and State v. Gibler, 124 So. 375 (Fla. 1929).

In 1920, Judge Donnell had been criticized by some, and the Palm Beach Post noted on May 20, 1920, that Judge Donnell answered his "traducers" in a dignified speech in the city park.

In December of 1920, a Palm Beach headline noted that E. B. Donnell refused to gratify Governor Catts by resigning as judge of the Fifteenth Circuit. The judge had just returned from a term held in Fort Pierce. The possible resignation had something to do with the reinstatement of Edgar C. Thompson as state attorney, which it was felt might tempt Judge Donnell to resign. Thompson purportedly enjoyed his cocktails, and E. B. Donnell was a prohibitionist. Donnell indicated that if he resigned, he would leave the selection to incoming Governor Kerry A. Hardee. Four years into Judge Donnell's term, he resigned, and Judge E. C. Davis was appointed to complete that term in 1921.

After resigning from the circuit court, Judge Donnell practiced with the firm Blackwell, Donnell & McCracken. He was also a member and former lieutenant/governor of Kiwanis International, and he was President of the West Palm Beach Shrine Club. He served as Chairman of the State Democratic Committee from 1952 to 1956. Judge Donnell was a city commissioner from 1932 to 1937 for West Palm Beach and Mayor from 1937 to 1939. A headline of the Palm Beach Post on March 20, 1928, noted that Judge E. B. Donnell and a Mrs. Selby opened a cooking school sponsored by the Palm Beach Post.

Judge Donnell was married to Rena Roberts of Nashville, Tennessee, in July 1909 in Nashville. She was an alumna of Peabody College and an artist. Her parents were Martin S. and Fedonia (Kirby) Roberts. The Judge and his wife had four children - Rena, Freda,

Elizabeth, and Ballard - and nine grandchildren. E. B. Donnell died on July 12, 1964.

Donnell's son, Ballard, was active as an attorney in Palm Beach County, serving as Town Attorney for Jupiter in 1957 (replacing his father in that position) and being the sole Legal Aid attorney for sixteen years. It was noted that Ballard devoted his life to helping those less fortunate. On December 11, 1995, the Palm Beach County Bar Association passed a memorial resolution in memory of Ballard R. Donnell, who died on June 28, 1995.

E. C. Davis, Fifteenth Judicial Circuit Judge, 1921-1923

E. C. Davis was born on a farm near Marion, Indiana, on September 14, 1867. He was the son of Elwood and Rachel (Shugart) Davis. Judge Davis' father was a Quaker minister.

Judge Davis graduated from the high school at Fairmount, Grant County, Indiana, and also attended Spiceland Academy, a Quaker school where his uncle, Clarkson Davis, was then principal. As a young man, Judge Davis served in the United States Indian Service, clerking in Haskell Institute in Lawrence, Kansas, and subsequently, he was an agent for a tribe of Apache Indians in Dulce, New Mexico. Thereafter, he studied law at the office of his cousin, Foster Davis, a lawyer in Fairmount, Indiana. E. C. Davis was admitted to the Bar in Indiana in 1895, practicing in Fairmount and subsequently Madison,

Indiana. He also became a prominent attorney in Crown Point, the county seat of Lake County, Indiana. There, he served several terms as a representative in the Indiana Legislature. He also acted as Special Judge on the Circuit bench in important trials. He was a member of the County Republican Executive Committee and a member of the State Executive Committee.

In 1916, Judge Davis came to South Florida to benefit his son's health. In 1917, he made Lake Worth his permanent home and practiced law in West Palm Beach. He was the right-of-way attorney for the Lake Worth Drainage District, and subsequently the general attorney for the district. He organized the People's Bank of Lake Worth and served as its president until its merger with First National Bank in 1922. In February of 1921, Governor Hardee appointed Davis to the Circuit Judgeship. The Florida Senate confirmed his appointment in June 1921.[282] He served the balance of Judge Donnell's term, that is, until June of 1923, and then returned to private practice.

In West Palm Beach, Judge Davis was a member of the Lions Club and affiliated with the Knights of Pythias and the Modern Woodmen of the World. He was Chairman of the Palm Beach County Republican organization. He was married to the former Anna D. Perkins of Madison, Indiana. The couple had one son, Leslie.

C. E. Chillingworth, Fifteenth Judicial Circuit Judge, 1923-1925+[283]

Charles E. Chillingworth was born in West Palm Beach on October 24, 1896. He was one of three children born to Charles Curtis Chillingworth and Jennie Dietz Chillingworth. C. E. Chillingworth was the great-grandson of Charles G. and Ann Jolley Chillingworth, who came to the United States from Staffordshire, England, in 1835, moving initially to New York City and then settling in the town of Clay, Onondaga County, New York. C. E. Chillingworth's mother, Jennie Dietz, was born in Syracuse, New York, on May 26, 1868.

C. E. Chillingworth is one of the most famous circuit judges in the history of Florida, due in large part to his being murdered by a West Palm Beach municipal judge, Joseph Peel. However, Judge Chillingworth came from a prominent family, and he was an outstanding jurist through many years of service.

Charles' father, Charles Curtis Chillingworth, was a well-respected Florida lawyer. He was born in Liverpool, New York, on May 12, 1868. In 1891, Charles C. Chillingworth graduated from Cornell University and then studied law in Atlanta, Ga. He then moved to the east coast of Florida, where he taught school in an orange grove near Haulover, just north of Titusville. He was admitted to the Florida Bar by Circuit Judge John D. Broome in Titusville on February 9, 1892, after an examination in open court. Charles Curtis Chillingworth then joined the law firm of Robbins & Graham, at one time the oldest and leading law firm on the east coast of Florida, at Titusville. Chillingworth then opened an office for that firm in Juno, the seat of Dade County at that time.

Charles C. Chillingworth later practiced in Palm Beach and was instrumental in developing Palm City. He was also the first municipal attorney for West Palm Beach and Lantana. Besides C. E. Chillingworth, C. C. Chillingworth had another son, who was a prominent lawyer in West Palm Beach, Richard Chillingworth.

Charles. C. Chillingworth died in West Palm Beach on October 25, 1936. He prepared a family history, which was published posthumously by his children in December 1936. Further details of this family are available at the Palm Beach Historical Society.

C. E. Chillingworth's grandfather, Richard Chillingworth, was an early mayor of West Palm Beach in 1901, where he served until 1914. Richard was also elected Sheriff of Dade County, following his initial appointment in 1896 as replacement Sheriff for Sam Lewis, who had been lynched in 1895. (At that time, West Palm Beach was a part of Dade County.) Richard Chillingworth served as sheriff until 1901.

C. E. Chillingworth grew up in West Palm Beach. He graduated from Palm Beach High School on June 13, 1913. He graduated from the University of Florida College of Law on June 5, 1917.

That same year, at 21 years of age, he was admitted to the Florida Bar as well as the United States District Court for the Northern and Southern Districts of Florida. He also became a member of the U.S. Naval Reserve and thereafter attended the U.S. Naval Academy. He was ordered to sea aboard the U.S.S. Minneapolis and was later stationed in various bases across the country. He resigned from the Navy in July 1919 to practice law. At age 24, he was admitted to practice before the Supreme Court of the United States.

On November 5, 1920, C. E. Chillingworth married Marjorie Crouse McKinley. They had three children: Nevea, born December 5, 1922; Ann, born December 31, 1924; and Marie, born September 17, 1928. Two became lawyers.

In November 1920, C. E. Chillingworth was elected county judge and served from January 1921 to June 12, 1923, when he resigned to become the state's youngest circuit judge (at age 26) the next day. Judge Chillingworth was appointed to the circuit court for the Fifteenth Judicial Circuit. One of his early cases involved an arrest in Vero (soon to be known as Vero Beach), which was part of the catalyst (the movie theater operator arrests) that created Indian River County.

Shortly after Judge Chillingworth became a circuit judge of the Fifteenth Judicial Circuit, the Twenty-First Judicial Circuit was created for St. Lucie County, Martin County, Okeechobee County, and Indian River County. While Judge Chillingworth was then no longer the circuit judge for this area because of the creation of the Twenty-First Circuit, he served with distinction in the Fifteenth Judicial Circuit until his disappearance on June 16, 1955.[284] For more information on the murder, see "The Murder Trial of Judge Peel" by Jim Bishop, which was presided over by then Circuit Judge D. C. Smith (See chapter 7) in 1961.[285]

Elwyn Thomas, Twenty-First Circuit Judge, 1925-1938[286]

See biographical information set forth under Chapter 7 for Elwyn Thomas.

C. Biographies of St. Lucie County Judges - 1905 to 1925

James E. Andrews, St. Lucie County Court Judge, 1905-1906

James E. Andrews was born in Painesville, Ohio, on October 12, 1869. He was the son of Edward Oliver Andrews and Martha M. Palmer. Judge Andrews came to Eden, St. Lucie County, from Painesville, Ohio, in the early 1890s. His first wife was named Emmergine. She was born in Colorado.

J. E. Andrews was one of the incorporators for the creation of the City of Fort Pierce on February 2, 1901, in Brevard County, Florida. When St. Lucie County was organized in 1905, Judge Andrews was appointed its first county judge. He was also a promoter of the establishment of the Fort Pierce Board of Trade, which was created to enhance the chances of Fort Pierce keeping the county seat, which initially was only temporarily located in Fort Pierce.

Andrews served as county judge through December 1906. Prior to that time, he practiced law in Fort Pierce, was a grower of citrus and pineapples, and was a prominent developer throughout St. Lucie County. Judge Andrews, who advertised his services as a real estate agent, had his "Office over the Bank." He also had a law office with F.L. Hemmings, as mentioned above, which building stands to this day on the north side of the new courthouse parking garage. (P 246).

In 1914, Judge Andrews was divorced. In that same year, he built as his home what for many years was a Vero Beach landmark. It was a beautiful wood structure on the southeast corner of Kings Highway (58th Ave) and State Road 60. It became the home of a variety of restaurants in the 1980s and 1990s. In 1998, portions of the structure were stored on site for subsequent relocation to Harbor Branch Oceanographic Institution in St. Lucie County,[287] as the former Andrews' real property became a Walgreens Drug Store. I watched that house being moved along the side of the main relief canal in Vero Beach and then being barged down the Indian River, which I viewed from on top of the 17th St. Bridge, now known as the Alma Lee Loy Bridge.

Judge Andrews is credited with being the realtor who was instrumental in having Herman Zeuch purchase fifty thousand acres for the Indian River Farms Company, which is greatly responsible for the growth of Vero Beach.

Between 1912 and 1914, Judge Andrews, with William Atkin, organized the Farmers Bank of Vero. Judge Andrews served as its President for several years. Prior to that, he had been President of the St. Lucie County Bank. In 1915, he became the Manager of the Indian River Farms Company. In 1916, he relocated from Vero back to Fort Pierce.

Judge Andrews died in Jacksonville on December 5, 1922. He was survived by his second wife, Selma, and three daughters, Mrs. C. C. Halliday, Mrs. Leslie Crunch, and Miss Mary Andrews.

Fred Fee, St. Lucie County Court Judge, 1907-1909

Fred Fee was born in Lindsborg, Kansas, on February 15, 1880. His father was Frank H. Fee, who became a prominent merchant and banker in Fort Pierce. Fred's mother was Margaret Irwin Fee.

Frank H. Fee (Fred's father) was born in Niles, Ohio, on March 9, 1850. He was the son of Dr. William Miller Fee, who was married to Mary M. Barnshire. Dr. Fee, who was a neighbor of President William McKinley's parents in Ohio, delivered all the McKinley children, including the future President of the United States. The doctor's father, John Fee, came with his brothers and sisters to Canada from Ireland about 1813, and later, some of the family moved to Pittsburgh, Pennsylvania, and others to Ohio.

Frank H. Fee was educated in the common schools and attended courses at Franklin Academy in Pennsylvania and State Normal College in Edinburg, Pennsylvania. In 1871, he entered the hardware and oil business in Franklin, Pennsylvania. In 1887, he moved to Florida, following his father, Dr. Fee, who had moved to Florida in 1884. Dr. Fee was the first doctor to practice in Melbourne. Dr. Fee was also a founder of Melbourne's First Methodist Church, and Fee Avenue in Melbourne was named for him.

Frank H. Fee continued his hardware business in Melbourne under the name of Fee & Stewart. He also established an undertaking business. The businesses prospered, and Mr. Fee became active in the Melbourne State Bank, which subsequently became the Bank of Fort Pierce after the branch in Fort Pierce prospered. He was the bank's initial president and served for many years. Mr. Fee also moved his undertaking and hardware businesses to Fort Pierce. The hardware company was known as Fee & Stewart Hardware Company. Frank Fee was a member of the Fort Pierce City Council and served as mayor for two years as well.

Frank H. Fee and Margaret Irwin had six children, two of whom survived, William Irwin and Fred.

Fred Fee grew up in Melbourne, Florida, after accompanying his father and grandfather (the doctor) to Melbourne. Mr. Fred Fee went to school in Melbourne and subsequently attended Allegheny College in Meadville, Pennsylvania, and later Stetson University in DeLand, Florida, where he received an A.B. degree in 1904 and an LL.B. in 1905.

Fred started his law practice in Fort Pierce in 1905. He was nominated at the Democratic Primary for county judge in 1906 and elected to that position in November of that year. The fact that he was a young man and had practiced law for only one year at the time is evidence of the high regard in which he was held by the community he served. He served as county judge from January 8, 1907, until January 4, 1909. He was elected to the legislature for the State of Florida in 1911, serving until 1912. Mr. Fee was active in the Southern Methodist Church and a member of the Woodmen of the World.

On September 3, 1907, Fred Fee married Miss Emma Morgan, the daughter of Colonel Eli O. and Leasy (Geiger) Morgan. His wife's father, Colonel Morgan, was one of the prominent cattlemen of the state.

Fred Fee followed his father's tradition and went into banking in 1934, obtaining the charter for First Federal Savings and Loan of Fort Pierce. His son, Frank, subsequently replaced him as general counsel and a board member. Frank Fee started practicing law in Fort Pierce in 1935. First Federal Savings and Loan of Fort Pierce, which became Harbor Federal Savings Bank, had another generation of Fees. Frank H. "Speedy" Fee III served as a board member and general counsel. Speedy, incidentally, was married to former Circuit Judge Nourse's daughter, LeVan. (See Ch. 7). Speedy's son, Frank H. Fee, IV, born August 11, 1975, in Ft. Pierce, also practices law in Ft. Pierce with his father.

Fred Fee died on May 4, 1939.

Hemmings and Andrews Law Office
Courtesy of St. Lucie County History Museum

F. L. Hemmings, St. Lucie County Court Judge, 1909-1914

Fred Leith Hemmings was born January 31, 1872, in Kingsbridge, England, the son of James and Harriet Leith Hemmings. He came to the United States with his parents as an infant, and the family settled in Chicago. Fred attended George Washington University Law School, Washington, D.C., receiving the degree of LL.B. in 1898, LL.M. in 1899, and a D.C.L. in 1900.

He began his practice of law in Chicago following his graduation, but shortly thereafter moved to Shawnee, Oklahoma. In 1903, he went to Lake City, Florida, and engaged in the practice of law in partnership with Otis R. Parker and Congressman Frank Clark. That firm moved to Jacksonville in 1904 and in the following year moved to Ft. Pierce when St. Lucie County was created from a portion of Brevard County. On December 24, 1907, he married Sydnor Davenport, who was from Atlanta, Georgia.

It has been written that Judge Hemmings was considered one of the finest civil lawyers in the state. He served as St. Lucie County Judge from 1909 to 1914 and was attorney for the Board of County Commissioners for many years. He was also attorney for the St. Lucie River and Ft. Pierce Farms Drainage Districts, as well as the Ft. Pierce Port District, all of which he was instrumental in forming. He was also an attorney for the County School Board, the Fellsmere Drainage District, and the Indian River Farms Drainage District. He was a member of the Episcopal Church, the Elks, Oddfellows, Masons (32nd degree), Knights Templar, and Almas Temple Shrine of Washington, D.C.

Judge Hemmings passed away on September 26, 1939, in Ft. Pierce. He was survived by his wife, Sydnor, as well as a daughter, Mrs. L. A. Peacock, of Albany, Georgia, a son, Harold Kinsey, of New York, and a granddaughter, Sydnor Hemmings Peacock. The Judge was buried in Palm Cemetery at Ankona, Florida.

J. R. Johnson, St. Lucie County Court Judge, 1914-1922

J. R. Johnson was born in Alabama. He was County Judge for St. Lucie County from July 7, 1914, until September 1922.

Judge Johnson was the brother of Mrs. Otis R. Parker. Otis R. Parker was a prominent lawyer who practiced in Fort Pierce. Parker's son, Otis R. Parker, Jr., went on to be a county judge.

Judge Johnson and his sister were the children of Captain William B. Johnson. Captain Johnson was born in Roanoke, Alabama, in November 1841. Besides being a farmer, William B. Johnson fought in the Confederate Army under Stonewall Jackson and was later captured at Gettysburg. Captain Johnson died on October 17, 1914, in Montgomery, Alabama, approximately one year after the captain's visit to Fort Pierce.

J. R. Johnson was initially unopposed for county judge. His "political announcement," which was published along with those of a number of other candidates for public office in the *Fort Pierce News* for a cost of $5.00, payable in advance, read as follows: "I respectfully announce myself as a candidate for election to the office of County Judge of Saint Lucie County, Florida, in the approaching Democratic primary election. If elected, I pledge myself to efficiently and impartially discharge the duties of this office. I solicit your support. John R. Johnson." While Judge Johnson was re-elected without opposition for a number of years, he also started running for Mayor of Fort Pierce shortly after he was elected county judge. He was defeated in those elections. He ran again in 1915. In connection with that campaign, he indicated that not having lived here very long and not being known were the reasons he was defeated for mayor in his previous try. He indicated that he had a good record as county judge for the preceding two years.

On May 28, 1915, Judge J. R. Johnson had the occasion to swear in a number of special deputies as a result of the murder that evening of Sheriff Dan S. Carlton in downtown Fort Pierce. (Johnson did not preside over the subsequent murder trial where D. J. Disney was charged with the murder, but rather that was handled by Circuit Judge Minor S. Jones in October of that year.)

In the democratic primary election of June 1916, J. R. Johnson was re-elected by a vote of 643 over C. W. Talmadge (See Chapter 14), who had 485 votes. In the primary of June 1920, he defeated his opponent, H.E. Crooks, 702-279. This was reported in both the Miami News and the Miami Daily Metropolis. The latter was interesting in that besides the front-page article on the elections, there was a page 1 story of the sustaining on appeal to the circuit court (Judge E. B. Donnell discussed elsewhere in this book) the criminal fraud case against the Coe-Mortimer Fertilizer Company of Jacksonville (and New York), which Judge J. R. Johnson handled as the trial judge in the lower court.

Judge Johnson had a beautiful home on Orange Avenue and owned other property in the City of Ft. Pierce and property on Five Mile Creek.

Judge Johnson's role as county judge ended in controversy in 1922. There were reportedly over a thousand signatures of area residents submitted to Governor Hardee seeking the removal of Judge Johnson. The vague grounds of misfeasance, malfeasance, and irregularities of office carried the day. More particularly, a delegation presented a petition to Governor Hardee to remove Judge Johnson. (One of the delegates was Everett Vickers, who is discussed under Sebastian Mayor Judges, infra.) On September 22, 1922, the Judge appeared before the Governor to argue his position, and on or about

September 26, the Governor suspended Judge Johnson. Judge Johnson was replaced by Angus Sumner.

The controversy probably surrounded prohibition issues and not guilty findings. Judge Johnson's brother-in-law, Otis Parker, practiced before him, and that may have inflamed the situation.

Angus Sumner, St. Lucie County Court Judge, 1922-1926

Angus Sumner was born in Dade City, Florida, in 1895. He was the son of Jesse and Annie Sumner. He moved to Fort Pierce in 1921 following a tour of duty in World War I.

Mr. Sumner was a graduate of Florida Southern College and received his law degree from Stetson University Law School in DeLand. He was appointed St. Lucie County Judge on September 29, 1922, and served until January 14, 1926.

Judge Sumner served as state attorney for 18 years and was the past president of the St. Lucie County Bar Association.

He was a member of the First United Methodist Church and was one of its organizers. He was a member of the American Legion for 52 years and a charter member of the Veterans of World War I. Judge Sumner was also one of the organizers of the Veterans of Foreign Wars Post No. 3064 and a member of the Woodmen of the World. He served as president of the Florida Southern College Alumni Association and was a trustee of the college for 30 years.

Judge Angus Sumner died on May 30, 1970, in Fort Pierce. He was survived by his wife, Sarah E. Sumner; a son, Angus J.; and a daughter, Sarah.

D. Biographies St. Lucie County Clerks, 1905-1925

J. E. Fultz, First clerk of St. Lucie County Courts
Courtesy of the St. Lucie County History Museum

John E. Fultz, St. Lucie County Clerk, 1905-1916

John Enos Fultz was born in South Carolina on November 12, 1844. He was the son of John E. and Rulany Fultz, who were each born in South Carolina. John Enos Futz (the future clerk of courts) served with distinction in the Confederate Army.

John Enos Fultz had lived in Rockledge, but when his wife, Elizabeth, died, he moved to and developed what is presently Port St.

Lucie. More particularly, in 1889, Fultz sailed seven miles up the north fork of the St. Lucie River and established a home for his family, which area was called Spruce Bluff, on the west bank, and is now called Blakeslee Creek, where he lived with his second wife, Annie Winters, and family.

A post office was established there on March 12, 1892, for which Fultz was postmaster, and he delivered the mail by boat from the Stuart depot of the Florida East Coast Railway for ten dollars per month. Fultz also raised pineapples and was a member of the school board of the then Brevard County until St. Lucie County was created in 1905.

John Enos Fultz was the first clerk of the re-created St. Lucie County in July of 1905. He was elected in every succeeding election until 1916, when he was beaten in a close contest by P.C. Eldred. Eldred received 575 votes to Fultz's 554 during what must have been a heated election campaign. Fultz's campaign ad suggested that the public not take a chance of electing a "misfit."

Fultz moved from Spruce Bluff to Ft. Pierce and subsequently to Vero in approximately 1916, where he cultivated a grove. Fultz had eight children - George, Viola Gertrude Winters, Pearl, Charles, Herbert, Ethel, and twin boys Oscar and Clarence. Oscar was the father of Peggy Brinson. Mrs. Brinson resided on the property J. E.

Fultz owned in Vero Beach. She was employed by the Council on Aging in Vero Beach.

John E. Fultz died on December 7, 1921, and is buried in Oslo Cemetery, which is located on the SE corner of South Old Dixie Hwy and 3rd St. S.W. On his headstone is engraved, "How desolate our home bereft of thee." Fultz is also mentioned on a separate monument there, recognizing the three Confederate Soldiers buried in that cemetery. Fultz's spouse and other family members are buried there as well. Two of John's children, by his first wife, are buried in the Spruce Bluff Cemetery in Port St. Lucie. There are no longer any grave markers there per se, as the headstones were vandalized, removed, and replaced by a common monument.[288]

Oslo Cemetery – John E. Fultz and Wiley T. Laine

Philo C. Eldred, St. Lucie County Clerk, 1916-1925+

Philo Curtis Eldred was born in Carrollton, Illinois, on August 31, 1873. He was the son of Lucius and Nellie (Cavanaugh) Eldred. P.C. Eldred was a prominent figure in St. Lucie County, having been a justice of the peace (1895), a mayor of Ft. Pierce, and a long-time clerk of the circuit court. In 1916, he defeated the incumbent county clerk for St. Lucie County, John E. Fultz, in a very close election and continued to serve St. Lucie County well after Indian River County was carved from St. Lucie County in 1925.

Mr. Eldred was a charter member of the First Presbyterian Church of Ft. Pierce. Eldred may have been a relative of L.S. Eldred, who was a prominent grower in the Ft. Pierce area in the 1890s. In fact, a village in St. Lucie County in the early 1900s was called "Eldred."

Mr. Eldred died on October 18, 1947, in Jacksonville, Florida, and was survived by his wife, Lenette; a son, Edward, and a daughter, Mrs. Otto Thomas of Atlanta, Georgia.

Chapter 5 - Indian River County Courthouses

A. The County's Creation

The history of the county and circuit courts in Indian River County begins with the county's creation on June 29, 1925.[289] The residents of Indian River County had good luck in their attempt to secede from St. Lucie County, in that the then-Governor, John Wellborn Martin, was interested in having a county named after him. As a result, both Martin Co. and Indian River Co. were formed from parts of St. Lucie Co. by the Florida Legislature on May 30, 1925.

Prior to this point, the City of Vero,[290] which was created in 1919,[291] and the rest of the land that now comprises Indian River County was a part of St. Lucie County. The county seat for St. Lucie County, since it was created in 1905, has been the City of Fort Pierce. The county seat for the newly created Indian River County was the City of Vero.[292]

Prior to 1905, however, this same area was a part of Brevard County and had been since 1855. Before that, the area was a part of Santa Lucia or St. Lucie County, the first time, dating back to 1844. Prior to that, this area was in Mosquito County (since 1824), and before that, the area was initially a part of St. Johns County, which was created in 1821.[293]

Prior to June of 1925, this area, as St. Lucie County, was a part of the Twenty-First Judicial Circuit, which circuit had been formed only a few days earlier.[294] The Twenty-First Judicial Circuit then consisted of the circuit courts of Okeechobee and St. Lucie Counties. St. Lucie had previously been a part of the Fifteenth Judicial Circuit, which had included Broward, Palm Beach, St. Lucie, and Okeechobee.[295] Since June of 1925, the Twenty-First Judicial Circuit had included Indian River County and Martin County as well.[296]

In 1935, the legislature, during difficult economic times, consolidated certain judicial circuits. The circuits were reduced to fifteen. The Ninth Judicial Circuit was formed with the four counties above-referenced, together with Brevard, Orange, Osceola, and Seminole counties, which were to have three circuit judges in its entirety. One judge had to reside in either Seminole or Brevard County, one judge had to reside in Orange or Osceola County, and one judge had to reside in Indian River, Okeechobee, St. Lucie, or Martin County.[297]

The large Ninth Judicial Circuit was broken into three divisions: Division "A," which consisted of Orange and Osceola counties, Division "B," which consisted of Brevard and Seminole counties, and Division "C," comprising Indian River, Martin, Okeechobee, and St. Lucie counties.

Judge D. C. Smith has described that the depression-economy of the 1930s required a scaling back in the circuit. By the creation of the divisions, Judge Elwyn Thomas was able to maintain his circuit judgeship (Division C), and Judge Millard Smith of Brevard and Seminole Counties could maintain his judgeship division (Division B), and Judge Frank A. Smith from the Orlando area could maintain his judgeship for Orange and Seminole Counties (Division A). Judge D. C. Smith also noted that Division C for the Ninth Judicial Circuit continued through the time he became a circuit judge of our Ninth Judicial Circuit in 1957. However, Judge Smith was joining Judge Kanner at that time on Division C, or at least until Judge Kanner was appointed shortly thereafter to the newly created Second District Court of Appeal. Division C of the Ninth Judicial Circuit continued until 1967, when the Nineteenth Judicial Circuit was created, which was and is still comprised of Indian River, Martin, Okeechobee, and St. Lucie counties.[298]

Prior to Indian River County's creation, the circuit judge of the newly created Twenty-First Judicial Circuit was the newly appointed Judge Elwyn Thomas, who began serving on June 6, 1925. Prior to that time, the circuit judge was C. E. Chillingworth[299] of Palm Beach of the Fifteenth Judicial Circuit. Interestingly, Judge Chillingworth took over for St. Lucie County Judge Angus Sumner on the Vero

Theatre case by special appointment of the governor.[300] The facts of the case were a catalyst in the formation of the county.

Governor John W. Martin, who signed the bill creating Indian River County on May 30, 1925, which came into existence on June 29, 1925, immediately appointed five county commissioners: G.A. Braddock, J.W. LaBruce, Donald Forbes, John H. Atkins, and O.O. Helseth. At the first meeting of county commissioners on that same date, by secret ballot, John H. Atkins became the first permanent chairman, and James T. Vocelle was appointed county attorney.

Backing up for just a moment, James T. Vocelle was the attorney who obtained an injunction from Judge Chillingworth in February of 1925, which, for a time, prevented the Sheriff of St. Lucie County from interfering with the shows and making arrests at the Vero Theatre on Sundays.

On July 6, 1925, Governor John W. Martin appointed the following first officials for Indian River County:

County Judge:	Ben W. Ketchum
Clerk of Circuit Court:	Miles Warren
Supervisor of Registration:	Charles D. Toole
County Assessor:	George T. Tippin
Sheriff:	Joel W. Knight

Vero Beach was designated as the temporary seat of the county government until an election could be held. The principal contenders for the county seat were Vero Beach and Quay[301] (now known as Winter Beach), south of Wabasso around the Old Dixie Highway, and North of Gifford and Toledo, the latter of which no longer exists. Allegedly, someone offered a gift of $100,000.00 for a courthouse if the decision was in favor of Quay. It is reported that Vero's business and professional men went to great efforts to turn out the vote, going door to door. All but two Vero registered voters voted, and allegedly, not one citizen from outside of the city voted in favor of Vero.

It is also interesting to note that the small monument across from the 14th Avenue courthouse with the William Jennings Bryan name was not associated with that courthouse, which was built later, but rather by virtue of the celebration of the formation of Indian River County in 1925. It was through the influence of George Tippin that the county was able to have Mr. Bryan speak on the occasion of the county's creation. This speech occurred just before the famous Scopes evolution trial in 1925 and is considered Mr. Bryan's last public address. Mr. Bryan died shortly after doing battle with Clarence Darrow in Tennessee in the Scopes trial.

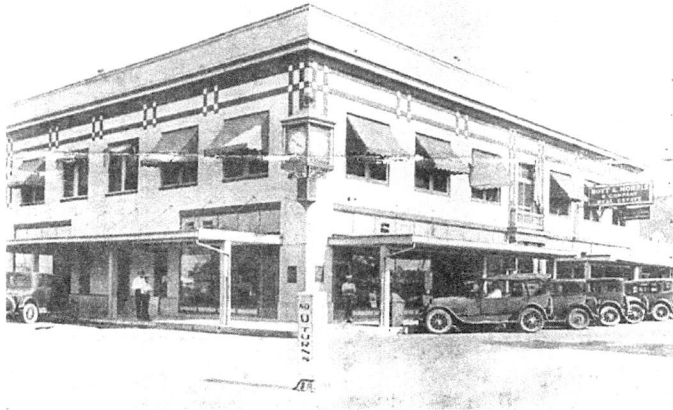

Seminole Building
Courtesy of the Byron T. Cooksey, Esquire Collection

B. The Seminole Building Court

When the county was formed, the first courthouse occupied the second floor of the Seminole Building. The Seminole Building was located at the southeast corner of what is now known as 14th Avenue and 21st Street. At the time, 14th Avenue was known as Seminole Avenue, and 21st Street was First Street. The Seminole building was built by James Hudson Baker, the father of James Douglas Baker, who went on to be the clerk of the circuit court. (See Clerks of the Circuit Court).

The Seminole Building was popular at the time because it was "strongly constructed, adequately protected from fire and by reason of its location...(was considered)... well protected by the city police force...."[302]

In 1925, the Seminole Building was occupied by the Vero Bank and Trust Company. (This bank and the three other banks in Indian River County all closed following the crash in 1929.) The building also contained a title company, East Coast Title and Guarantee Co., Beachland Development Company, and the office of Attorney C. P. Diamond.[303] The building also had the law offices of Nisle & Vocelle, the law offices of Cobb & McCorkle,[304] and a dentist's office. By 1928, the first floor was occupied by the Piggly Wiggly grocery store.

The first rent on the courtroom in the Seminole Building was apparently $400.00 per month, but this was reduced over time, particularly during the economic conditions that existed in the late 1920s. (See the next section on The Palmetto Hotel).

It is also interesting to note that the Seminole Building was just north of the Vero Theater, as it was known in the 1920s, and subsequently the Florida Theatre, as it was known in the 1930s. The theatre building still exists in partially refurbished form today. It was that theatre which was the catalyst for the formation of the county in 1925. That was brought about by the related troublesome civil and criminal issues being decided in Fort Pierce arising from the opening of this new theater in 1924, and particularly its Sunday openings.

Vero Theater, 1926 - Courtesy of the Byron T. Cooksey, Esq. Collection

In 1929, the county received a proposal from Vero Arcade Investment Co. to sell its Campbell Arcade Building to the county for a courthouse. It had some features that were attractive, but the county did not act favorably on the proposal.[305]

Court at the Seminole Building was held in the evening on occasion. In fact, the Spring term of 1931 of the circuit court, the last spring term in the Seminole Building, terminated sessions on Saturday evening.

By 1968, that building housed the Graves-Hardee Real Estate and Insurance Agency. (Pictures exist of this building as it appeared in 1920, 1923, 1926, as well as 1968). A short time later, the building was demolished to make way for a one-story building featuring Anthony's Clothing Store. Later, the building was the site of what was known as Bob Brackett's Credit Data Services, Inc. and MCB Collection Services, Inc. Mr. Brackett is retired County Court Judge Joe Wild's father-in-law. The building inscription read "New Seminole Building, Erected 1968, Renovated 1984. Art Brackett, Architect."

Palmetto Hotel
Courtesy of the Indian River County Historical Society, Archive Center, Indian River County Main Library.

C. The Palmetto Hotel Courthouse

On May 1, 1931, the courtroom moved to what was known as the Palmetto Hotel. This is the site located at Old Dixie Highway and 19th Street, which later became known as Regent Court. The first county commission meeting was held in the new hotel on Tuesday, May 5, 1931, in what was formerly the reception room of the hotel on the first floor.

The move seemed to have been prompted by economics, and particularly the difficult times following the "crash." However, the move was controversial.

On April 13, 1931, by a three-to-two vote, the commissioners voted to move the county offices and court to the Palmetto Hotel. However, the minutes of the county commission meeting for April 24, 1931, reflect that Commissioner LaBruce had offered a resolution detailing the attributes of the Seminole Building and that the apparent lower rate of rent for the Palmetto Hotel was realistically not that much of an improvement. His resolution, however, was not seconded, and the county opted to pay a monthly rent of $125.00 plus city, state, and county taxes at the Palmetto Hotel. This was in contrast to the $400.00 a month it was paying on the Seminole Building prior to October 1, 1929, although there had been credits for rent paid by others to the county on that second floor. That rent, however, seemed to have dried up since October of 1929, which made matters difficult notwithstanding a reduction in rent for the county to $225.00 per month. The Seminole Building apparently had just recently gone into receivership, and its receiver, Luster M. Merriman, was then proposing a rent of $150.00 per month if the county did not opt to go to the Palmetto Hotel.

By a 3 to 2 vote, the Palmetto Hotel was "selected, named, and designated as the official courthouse building for Indian River County, Florida" as of May 1, 1931. It passed with Commissioners Walker, Hamilton, and Yongue in favor and Commissioners LaBruce and Helseth voting no.

The Palmetto Hotel was owned at the time by Mr. and Mrs. George W. Gray, who had operated it as a hotel since it was built in 1919. Two additions had been made to the building by 1931, one to the west in 1921 and one to the south in 1925. The Palmetto Hotel was a frame and stucco building containing 53 rooms. The dining room was 70' x 40' and was regarded as suitable for a courtroom. The kitchen and butler's pantry served as jury rooms.

Initially, Judge Otis M. Cobb selected a suite of four rooms on the second floor in the northeast corner of the building. Clerk Miles A. Warren chose a suite of four rooms on the north side of the hall on the first floor. County Assessor W. R. Duncan selected a suite of rooms on the south side of the hall on the first floor. Sheriff Clark S. Rice selected a suite of three rooms on the second floor over the dining room. Tax Collector Gordon Olmsted selected a suite of five rooms on the second floor over the dining room.

The first term of the county court, the May or spring term, opened on May 5, 1931. The criminal docket contained 35 cases to be disposed of during that term. There were no civil cases entered. The first jury trials began Tuesday morning, May 12, 1931.

One of the first trials scheduled in the circuit court in the new Palmetto Hotel courthouse was scheduled for Monday, May 25th. In that case, State v. J.C. Crosby, the Defendant was charged with murder in the first degree for allegedly killing James Howard. Also on that docket was the trial of L. J. Holland, who was charged with assault to commit murder on his son, William Holland. Judge Elwyn Thomas presided. Mr. Crosby was found guilty of manslaughter, and Mr. Holland was found guilty of assault to commit murder in the first degree in the shooting/wounding of his son. The latter case required the jury to deliberate for ten hours.

It was reported in the Press Journal of May 29, 1931, that the new courtroom of the circuit court was highly commended by Judge Elwyn Thomas and then State Attorney Angus Sumner. The large number of citizens in attendance at the trials was afforded an opportunity to visit the new offices of the various county officials. This was apparently in striking contrast with courthouses in other counties. "An atmosphere of comfort and ease prevails throughout the building that is not found in the former courthouse building," noted the front-page article.

Sherman N. Smith, Jr., whose father was also a lawyer in this county, remembered the transition from the Seminole Building to the Palmetto Hotel. He described the court in the Seminole Building as occupying only a part of the second floor, and that with the move to the Palmetto Hotel, the court quarters and related county offices occupied the entire first floor. Sherman practiced briefly in the Palmetto Hotel Court while waiting for the new courthouse construction in 1935 and 1936.

D. C. Smith related to me that as a lawyer, he tried a few cases in the Palmetto Hotel in the 1930s. Smith was practicing at Fort Pierce at that time but had a large following of clients from the Wabasso area. Judge Smith remembers the courtroom as being adjacent to Old Dixie Highway on the north side of the Hotel (by 19th Street) and being located in what was once probably the dining room of the Hotel. The courtroom had benches for the public. The courthouse in the Palmetto Hotel also had offices for the tax collector, the judge, and the clerk. There was a hallway running east to west. The county judge's office was located a few doors down the hall, adjacent to 19th Street.

Judge Smith related that it was at this location that he applied for his marriage license in 1933, when he married Lide Turner, who passed away in 1962.

Douglas Baker, Judge D. C. Smith's brother-in-law, started in this building as the Clerk of the Circuit (and County) Court in 1937. (See the information under Douglas Baker's name in the chapter on the Clerk of Circuit and County Courts).

Circuit Judge Rupert Smith's aunt, Beatrice Knight, lived next door to the Palmetto Hotel, and Judge Rupert Smith remembers the court being conducted when he would visit his aunt during his childhood.

The Palmetto Hotel later became known as the Charlton Apartments, well before the refurbishments to become the Regent Court. Today, there are two plaques on the old Palmetto Hotel at 1889 Old Dixie Hwy. One merely says, "Circa 1924." The other reads: "Regent Court, Original County Courthouse, Has Been Placed on the National Register of Historic Places, By the United States Department of the Interior, Renovation by B. Anders Nyquist, 1991." (This does not appear to be entirely correct.) More recently, the apartments there have been called the "Courthouse Lofts."

14th Avenue Courthouse
Courtesy of Indian River County Historical Society, Archive Center,
Indian River County Main Library.

D. The 14th Avenue Courthouse

On August 21, 1933, County Commissioner J. D. Yongue submitted plans for a proposed courthouse at a special meeting of the Board of County Commissioners. Clerk Miles Warren was instructed to write C. B. Treadway, Chairman of the State Advisory Board on

Public Works, Tallahassee, and request a loan of $60,000.00 from the federal government to finance the project. The loan was requested with the understanding that 70% was to be repaid within 40 years. Plans submitted by Commissioner Yongue were prepared by an architect named W. H. Garns of Indianapolis, Indiana. The selection of a proposed site for the courthouse had not yet been discussed.[306]

On September 5, 1933, an architect by the name of F. Earl DeLoe of Melbourne, Florida, presented a plan for a new courthouse to the county commissioners. It was proposed that Mr. DeLoe would not have to be paid for his preliminary work in the event that a loan could not be secured, but if it was, he would receive 6% of the total amount.[307]

At a public hearing on September 12, 1933, many prominent citizens expressed their concern about the construction of the courthouse, which was then thought to possibly be erected near the county jail (then located on what is now known as 17th Avenue between 18th and 19th Street – subsequently the Recreation Department Building and then Sunshine Physical Therapy Clinic). The sentiment was expressed that "borrow" had a sound that would bring about public disapproval. The debt and tax load were thought to be already too great, and that borrowing would be better served for mosquito control. One of the pluses for the courthouse was that approximately $25,000.00 would be expended on the labor, putting men to work.[308]

On October 3, 1933, the county reviewed competing proposals of F. Earl DeLoe and W. H. Garns. Each one appeared before the board and submitted their plans and proposals as to their fee for supervision of construction. "After carefully considering every matter pertaining to this subject, and after full and complete discussion by the Board, it was moved, seconded and carried that W. H. Garns be employed on the basis of $2,320.00 in the event that the loan and grant is secured from the federal government--this figure to be on the basis of $58,000.00 and no more."[309]

Garns' plans have been preserved by the county. They bear a date of September 27, 1933. The plans show the first floor to include the following: clerk's office with vault in the southwest corner, with a commissioner's court to its immediate northeast; tax assessor in the southeast corner; county judge's office and vault, and tax collector's office in the north corners. The second floor had a large courtroom extending from the east side to the west side of the building, with a circuit judge's office and law library in the southeast corner and the jury room in the southwest corner. The north end showed the prosecutor's office on the west and the superintendent of schools on the east.

At the same October 3, 1933 meeting, a letter was read from Vero Beach City Clerk, A.C. MacConnell, which offered Lots 1 through 9, Block 35, Original Town, "just North of the Pocahontas Building" and "because of the position facing the railroad, highway and city park are considered ideal for public buildings such as the proposed courthouse." However, no decision was made on a site at that time.[310]

At a meeting of the County Commissioners the next day, October 4, 1933, it was noted that the terms of the architectural contract with Garns were a 4% fee on the $58,000.00 estimate, with the understanding that $1,000.00 would be paid to him when the loan was secured and if it was not that there would be no obligation to the architect.[311] Years later, rumor had it that Mr. Garns had never built a courthouse or any building in Florida. The commission may have decided on Mr. Garns because of price constraints.

Notwithstanding some of the accolades pertaining to the site selection for the then-new courthouse, Sherman N. Smith, Jr. has described the location as a former "swamp or gator hole." This view is supported by others. See Charlotte Lockwood's history of Indian River County, where she writes, "The old-timers' sons, Ralph Harris, Homer Fletcher, and Ed Carter, all remember the frog pond and 'gator holes where the courthouse now stands." A sump pump at the north end of the courthouse has had much use over the years.

The above background helps to explain why the basement of the courthouse was wet since the time of the courthouse's opening and remained that way for years, notwithstanding an approximately two-foot-thick foundation slab.

On October 11, 1933, the Commission, consisting of J. J. P. Hamilton, Chairman, J. D. Yongue, R. E. Mudge, John K. Knight and Edwin A. Helseth, with the Clerk Miles Warren and Sheriff William Frick present, shared a report that a few of the commissioners had met with the City Council and that the city agreed to give authority to the County to construct a courthouse in Vero Beach. The county voted to apply for a $70,000.00 federal loan, and that it would build the courthouse if the loan was granted. At the same meeting, a motion was passed that the Chairman, J. J. P. Hamilton, Commissioner Helseth, Architect Garns, and the Clerk take the application to Tallahassee as soon as possible to present the same to the proper authorities.[312]

On October 18, 1933, Chairman J. J. P. Hamilton, County Commissioner Edwin A. Helseth, Architect Garns, and Clerk Miles Warren went to Tallahassee, taking with them the completed application for the federal loan. Two forms of application were presented, one setting forth the time warrant plan of payment and the other the lease plan. The Board sought to obtain the loan under either plan, which might prove satisfactory.[313]

In November of 1933, Mr. Garns' plans and specifications were accepted by the Board of County Commissioners, subject to government loan approval. The building was to be 116' x 70' and two stories high. It was to be fireproof throughout with two large reinforced concrete fireproof vaults. The floors were to be concrete laid over steel joists. There were to be steel stairs, steel sash, mastic floors, and marble wainscoting for the corridors. The Press Journal of November 10, 1933, showed a rendering of the proposed courthouse, which turned out to be very accurate.

The application for monies from the Public Works Administration seemed to have been held up for some time. County Attorney James T. Vocelle had a longtime friend, Congressman Mark Wilcox, in Washington, so Mr. Vocelle was chosen to do something to try to speed up the process. He went to Washington and is reported as saying with a grin, "Well, you might as well order a bed. I'm going to camp on your doorstep until our application is processed." Congressman Wilcox was reported to have taken Mr. Vocelle to the young lawyer who was in charge of applications, whose desk was piled high with papers. They informed the young man that they would stay until there was action on the application of Indian River County for funds to build a courthouse. They sat, and the young man began shuffling. From the bottom of the pile came the application. It was pulled out, and action was promised. Two weeks later, Vero had received word that the application had been approved.[314]

On March 6, 1934, the County Commission unanimously passed a resolution thanking Senators Duncan U. Fletcher and Park Trammell, and Congressmen J. Mark Wilcox and W. J. Sears for their efforts in connection with the Board's application to the Public Works Administration for a loan to build a modern courthouse for Indian River County. The resolution further asked those representatives to push the application vigorously, explaining that Indian River County had no courthouse and that public records were exposed to fire and other hazards.[315]

Looking at this resolution and other minutes of the County Commission, which involved the Seminole and Palmetto Buildings, having a fireproof courthouse and, particularly, a vault for the safekeeping of materials, was a vital concern. At that point in time, the present courthouse in the Palmetto Hotel was considered to be a fire trap, and the county records were in continual danger of being destroyed. The amount of rent being paid justified the county owning its own courthouse.

On July 5, 1934, the Board set aside $5,000.00 from the budget from October 1, 1931, from the racetrack funds to be used solely for the purpose of paying interest and the retirement of principal to the

Public Works Administration in the event that the loan for the construction of the courthouse was approved, as was anticipated.[316]

On January 28, 1935, James T. Vocelle, President of the Chamber of Commerce, received notice from Congressman W. J. Sears that approval of the Public Works Administration for a loan of $75,000.00 was recommended.[317]

On February 5, 1935, the county commissioners passed a resolution in keeping with a requirement of the Federal Emergency Administration of Public Works, amending its application for a loan by setting forth that Vero Beach had been established as the permanent county seat of the county and that the courthouse would be constructed at the permanent county seat.[318]

It has also been reported that in February of 1935, James T. Vocelle, then President of the Chamber of Commerce, had received notice from the Public Works Administration (PWA) that a supplemental report of the finance division was completed on the project, in which approval for a loan of $75,000.00 was recommended. The notice was sent to Mr. Vocelle from Congressman W. J. Sears and Congressman Mark Wilcox, who continued to be active in securing favorable action. (The original application was disapproved because it offered as security a lease, payable over 30 years.) In the supplemental application, the county offered general obligation bonds as security for the loan from the government in lieu of a leasing arrangement. One-third of the loan was to be a gift from the federal government, and only two-thirds was to be repaid.

On July 12, 1935, the City of Vero Beach gave to Indian River County the site of the courthouse on 14th Avenue, just north of the Pocahontas Building. A cash consideration of $10.00 was arranged.[319] Fast forward to the 1990s - someone had suggested that, in connection with the controversy over trying to save the courthouse, the deed, which was recorded on August 31, 1935, contained a "reverter" clause (to the city). However, the condition seemed to be a conveyance for the purpose of erecting a courthouse, rather than maintaining one. More specifically, the deed, recorded on August 31, 1935, had the following language:

> It is understood by and between the parties hereto that the property hereinabove described and hereby conveyed is to be used as a site for the erection of a Courthouse for Indian River County, Florida, thereon, and should said property not be used for the construction and erection of a courthouse building thereon, the title to said land shall revert to the grantor herein, and this provision is included herein as a condition subsequent.

On September 3, 1935, the county passed a resolution accepting the loan of the United States of America for the construction of the courthouse.[320]

The bid opening for the new 14th Avenue courthouse occurred on Saturday, December 7, 1935. The following is the bid tabulation:

Contractor	Bid with Heating System	Bid Omitting Steam Heating System
Gunn and Goll, Inc.	$76,960	$74,960
Wm. Hensick	69,400	65,150
Watt & Sinclair	74,370	69,795
C. J. Trevail	67,826	63,826
Geo. B. Wills	69,333	67,333
L. M. Newman	67,095	62,845
C. E. Cahow Co.	84,129	79,779

It was noted that L. M. Newman did not file a bid bond or a certified check payable to the county commissioners in the amount equal to five percent (5%) of the bid or in any sum whatsoever, and the bid of C. J. Travail contained a condition that the source of financing be "satisfactory to the contractor." Thereafter, the contract was voted to be awarded to Hensick by the following Commissioners: Helseth, Poole, Vickers, Mudge, and Hamilton, Chairman.[321]

An election, pursuant to the resolution on the issuance of $45,500.00 of bonds for financing and construction of the courthouse, was held on December 16, 1935. The bond issue was overwhelmingly approved, 422 to 14 of the freeholders voting. At that point in time, the Public Works Administration had approved a grant of $31,500.00 for the project, contingent upon the county's financing the balance of the cost of construction of the building. One-half of the racetrack funds received by the county from the state had been set aside in the budget by the County Commission for the purpose of retiring the proposed bond issue. The bonds to be dated September 1, 1935, were to mature serially over a period of 19 years and to bear interest at the rate of 4% per annum, payable semi-annually.[322]

On March 31, 1936, the City of Vero Beach issued a building permit for the new courthouse. Construction was supposed to start on the courthouse in April 1936 and was to cost approximately $70,000.00. At a commission meeting of April 7, 1936, the county employed an inspector, W. H. Garns, at the rate of $35.00 per week.[323]

In July of 1936, the courthouse loan was received, and airmail played an important part in that reception. To expedite the loan, Joe S. Earman, President of Indian River Citrus Bank, and Miles Warren, Clerk of the Board of County Commissioners, went to Atlanta to secure the $38,500.00 from the Federal Reserve Bank. However, due to new regulations that had been put into effect on the validation of papers, changes had to be made before the funds could be forthcoming. The gentlemen had the papers changed immediately and dispatched the corrected papers to Vero Beach by plane that same day. The papers left Atlanta at 5:30 p.m., arriving in Vero Beach at 8:50 p.m. J. J. P. Hamilton, Chairman of the Board of County Commissioners, Charles A. Mitchell, Attorney for the Board, and Postmaster J.J. Schumann were at the local airport to receive the papers. County seals and other necessary legal matters were taken to the airport, the papers were signed, placed in an envelope, postmarked from the post office, and placed on a northbound plane leaving Vero Beach at 9:25 p.m. The letter arrived in Atlanta around midnight and was delivered to Mr. Earman at 6:00 a.m. Friday, Messrs. Earman and Warren were at the Federal Reserve when it opened. The papers were then accepted, and a cashier's check for $38,500.00 was delivered to Mr. Warren. Officials of the Federal Reserve described the fast service as unbelievable.[324]

By late July of 1936, it was clear (before the courthouse was opened) that there was a problem with water in the basement. The county voted to install a drainage system under the separate bid of William Hensick for $140.00.[325]

On March 12, 1937, the move began into the new courthouse. At a county commission meeting on March 12, 1937, the county reviewed an extension of time requested for William Hensick. The request indicated that the time for completion of work had expired on February 1, 1937, and that the courthouse would open on March 12. The request asserted that the delays were excusable because of local weather, flooding in the North that affected the delivery of materials, and change orders. The Commission voted that no penalties or liquidated damages would be assessed against the contractor, William Hensick.[326]

On March 19, 1937, the courthouse was in full operation, including the offices of the tax assessor and collector, county judge, and clerk of the circuit court on the first floor, with the superintendent of public instruction and the sheriff on the second floor. The courtroom on the second floor of the new structure was, at that time, one of the largest and most attractive to be found anywhere.[327]

On March 19, 1937, Commissioner E. P. Poole moved for the modification of the acceptance of the bid from a Palm Beach typewriter company for the furnishing of pews for the courthouse. The motion resulted in changing the composition of the pews from birch wood to one-quarter solid gum wood and that the same be fitted with brass or bronze shoes for the ends of such pews, and that the pews be fitted with one division support, with the understanding that the county would receive from the makers of such pews an unqualified guarantee against sagging of the pews. The motion was unanimously carried. The board also authorized the construction of sidewalks around the courthouse at that time.[328]

Judge Graham W. Stikelether once indicated that he found and saved some of the original pews, which, while cut down, were refitted as the rear pews in one of the new courtrooms when the 14th Avenue Courthouse was expanded in 1981.

The second-floor courtroom of the original courthouse on 14th Avenue extended from the east wall to the west wall and occupied most of the second floor except for small offices at the north and south ends. One difficulty with the courtroom was that you could only get from one side of the building to the other on the second floor by going through the courtroom. This anomaly was carried forward in subsequent redesigns through the final use of the 14th Avenue courthouse. The original large courtroom on the second floor had a great seating capacity.

The initial courtroom permanently displayed a 48-star flag, which took up most of the wall from floor to ceiling behind the judge's bench. The courtroom had a great deal of woodwork.

1. Additions

The courthouse was expanded with additional wings in 1956, 1961, and a new annex building in 1967. The south wing was built first, and then the north wing. The courthouse and annex were remodeled in 1981 and 1982, respectively.

2. The South Wing

In 1956, the Commission consisted of W. C. Graves, Jr., Chairman, H. C. Watts, J. J. P. Hamilton, Aubrey L. Waddell, and Allison Warren. At a meeting on April 20, 1956, with Mr. Warren absent, the Board agreed to employ Robert Frazier to supervise construction of the addition, with the plans and specifications to be prepared by William G. Taylor, Architect. The action was taken with the understanding that work was to be done by the county, and that the county would advertise for bids and purchase all materials needed to receive the benefit of discounts on materials.

On February 17, 1959, the board requested the county engineer to contact a consulting firm and get an estimate of the cost of a survey of the future courthouse extensions and/or buildings, and to report back.

Indian River County Historical Society Collection, Archive Center, Indian River County Main Library
New North Wing
Courtesy of Indian River County Historical Society, Archive Center, Indian River County Main Library.

3. The North Wing

The north wing was constructed in 1961 and resulted in the large county courtroom, which continued, pretty much intact, for the next 33 years. The dedication plaque indicates that the contractor for the North wing was E.M. Netto and the architect was David V. Robison. The county engineer was E.S. Schmucker, Jr. The chairman of the Indian River County Commission was Robert W. Graves,[329] and the other commissioners were Dr. B.Q. Waddell, D. MacDonald, D.B., McCullers, and J. J. P. Hamilton.[330] J.D. Baker, Sr., was the Clerk of the Court, and the county attorney was Sherman N. Smith, Jr.

4. Annex

A two-story annex, much larger than the original courthouse, was built in 1967 to the southwest. The dedication plaque indicated that the architect was William G. Taylor and the contractor was E.M. Netto. The county commission consisted of Robert W. Graves as Chairman, D.B. McCullers, Jr. as Vice Chairman, Jack V. Dritenbas, Richard B. Bogosian, and Donald MacDonald. The county attorney was Sherman N. Smith, Jr., and Ralph Harris was the clerk. Jack Jennings was the county administrator.

Leading up to the 1967 annex were a number of meetings of the County Commissioners in 1966, including reviews of various sketches presented by William G. Taylor, Architect, and John Schlitt,

Jr., his associate. When the plans were finally approved on September 7, 1966, they were advertised for bids on October 5, 1966. The base bid and their prices were as follows:

John C. Abbott	$120,380.00
William Hensick & Sons	$115,560.00
John D. Kroule	$121,691.00
Netto Construction, Inc.	$113,427.00

The contract was awarded to Netto Construction, Inc. on October 19, 1966.

5. Judge Sharp's Courtroom

When Judge Sharp took office in 1978, there was insufficient space at the courthouse. Judge Sharp held court in a temporary modular structure that had been on the lawn of the old hospital, which subsequently became the County Administration Building at 1840 25th Street, just south of the present-day County Administration Complex. Judge Sharp held court in that structure for several years until the remodeling of the 14th Avenue courthouse was completed.

5. 1979 Landscaping

In 1979, considerable landscaping improvements were made to the courthouse. This was performed by the Garden Club of Indian River County. The plans were prepared by Mrs. J. Hubert (Beverly) Graves.[331] The improvements included all of the plantings, hedges, and the Bird of Paradise at the entrance, as well as the Phoenix Reclinata.

Mrs. Graves believes that the Garden Club, whose existence dates back to the original building of this courthouse, was probably involved with the original courthouse landscaping. The Garden Club also sponsored the flower show in the inaugural year of the new 20th Street/16th Avenue Courthouse.

6. 1981 Remodeling

The courthouse and the annex were significantly modified in 1980. This was done in connection with the vacation by the county commission of the administration offices. Until then, the county commission had always held its meetings in the courthouse. (That would seem to have included the Seminole Building and the Palmetto Hotel as well.) The administration offices were then moved to the renovated former Indian River Memorial Hospital, previously located at 1840 25th Street.

On February 27, 1980, the county accepted the bid of Reinhold Construction for the renovation of the courthouse and the county administration complex. Essentially, two controversies arose over the remodeling, namely the litigation between the county and Reinhold Construction, which was Case No. 81-788 of the Circuit Court, In and For Indian River County, Florida, which pertained to the construction problems. In addition, there were related problems associated with what is now called "sick building syndrome."[332]

During the remodeling, both county and circuit court proceedings were held in temporary courtrooms in the 2001 Building at 2001 9th Avenue. Judge Stikelether handled county court trials there. Judges Charles E. Smith and Dwight Geiger handled circuit trials, including twelve-person jury cases.[333] Following the completion of the remodeling, in addition to there being litigation over the work, there was a period of time where County Court Judge Graham W. Stikelether, Jr. held sessions back in the 2001 Building, the Community Church, and the American Legion B.O.Q. This was because of the environmental conditions existing in the newly remodeled courthouse.

In 1982, the fourth courtroom, or Courtroom "D" as it was known, was added on the second floor of the annex building. At the time, it was the most modern and largest of the courtrooms.

Courtroom "D" was the courtroom for the last jury trial[334] to take place in the 14th Avenue Courthouse. The case was <u>Richardson v. Strang</u>, Case No: 94-332-CA-10, and involved a soft tissue injury as a result of an automobile accident. Judge Charles E. Smith presided. The plaintiff's attorneys were David M. Carter and Eugene J. O'Neill. The defendant was represented by Gregory J. Donoghue. The jury awarded $21,200.00 in damages.

E. The 16th Avenue Courthouse/L.B. Vocelle Court

On January 11, 1990, Indian River County Commissioners, consisting of Carolyn Eggert, Chairman, Richard Bird, Vice Chairman, Gary Wheeler, Doug Scurlock, Jr., and Margaret Bowman, chose a $16 million plan for a new judicial complex, which was to have been located one block (south)west of the former courthouse on 14th Avenue. It was noted that the land cost alone for the county would be $3.4 million or about $1 million per acre. The cost included the purchase and relocation of 16 commercial and residential buildings that had to be bought and demolished. The site was attractive because the building would stay in the downtown, and the downtown Vero Beach zoning allowed buildings of up to 50' in height.

In choosing the courthouse plan, the commissioners reviewed 11 different schemes presented by the consultants for Halback, Inc. of

Orlando. The most expensive project was chosen, but the commissioners did express concern about the cost. On December 18, 1990, the county approved a $19 million plan for the courthouse at its present site on 20th Street, with a three-story courthouse to go on the 1500 block and what was reported as a five-story parking garage on the 1600 block. This followed several years of debate and planning on possible courthouse sites and plans. [335] The commissioners at the time the courthouse was approved consisted of the following: Carolyn Eggert, Chairman; Richard Bird, Vice Chairman; Gary Wheeler; Doug Scurlock, Jr.; and Margaret Bowman.

In early 1992, certain members of the Indian River County Bar Association and a civic activist, Frank L. Zorc, raised a concern that the new courthouse may be facing the wrong way because of the imminent relocation of SR 60 to one-way "twin pairs." However, their suggestions were not accepted by the County Commission.[336]

On November 5, 1992, the groundbreaking was held for the new courthouse complex on 20th Street. The design by Pierce, Goodwin, Alexander & Linville of Tampa had a "brand new old building" theme.[337] The G.C. was James A. Cummings Inc. of Ft. Lauderdale.

In August of 1993, it was reported that the county had been taking steps to prevent the sick building syndrome, which had become a significant problem in Florida, and particularly in courthouses. With the courthouse then scheduled to open in May of

1994, innovative steps to "off-gas" the carpet and furniture before employees arrived and to establish a one-year monitoring program for air quality were implemented. The county had hired Gee Jensen for their air quality expertise at a cost of $9,390.00. The building's air system was to bring pre-treated air throughout the building. Centex Rooney, the project manager, was to be on guard to prevent sick building mistakes during construction. (Ironically, Centex Rooney would be on trial in this new courthouse a couple of years later for the alleged sick building that the Martin County Courthouse had become, where Centex Rooney was the contractor.)

A June 29, 1994, article in The Press Journal indicated that a chagrined Indian River County Commission reluctantly approved a $44,120.00 change order, the tenth change order since the project started. The newest change order had 27 construction changes for construction on the new $21 million county courthouse. The article noted that the project was originally scheduled to open in January of 1994, and prior to this week, completion had been set for mid-August. It now looked like it would be October 15, 1994.

On October 8, 1994, the cornerstone was dedicated by Masonic Lodge #250 of Vero Beach.[338] A time capsule was placed behind the cornerstone, containing a Saturday newspaper and the names of the county commissioners and city councilmen.[339] The cornerstone reads:

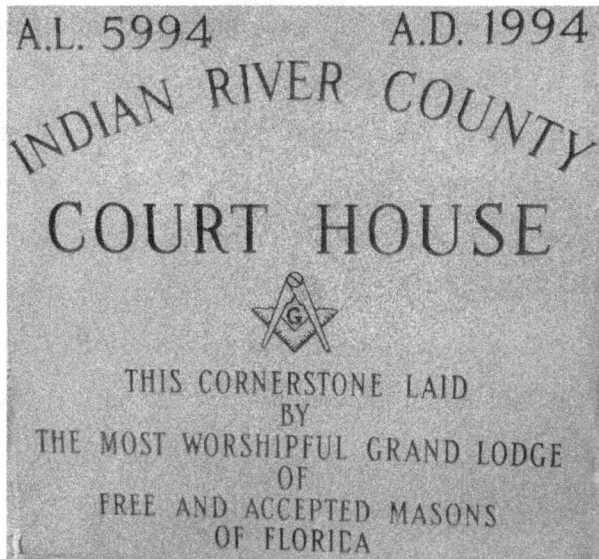

A.L. 5994   A.D. 1994

INDIAN RIVER COUNTY

COURT HOUSE

THIS CORNERSTONE LAID
BY
THE MOST WORSHIPFUL GRAND LODGE
OF
FREE AND ACCEPTED MASONS
OF FLORIDA

The Bar Association and the County Commission had contemplated a state or nationally known speaker connected with the judiciary for a Veterans Day dedication. However, this became controversial.[340] The way it worked out, the dedication speech was written by L. B. Vocelle, Chief Judge of the Nineteenth Judicial Circuit, who was to deliver the speech. The speech, however, was read by Sherman N. Smith, Jr., the former Chief Judge of both the Second District Court of Appeal and Fourth District Court of Appeal, due to Judge Vocelle's recuperation from heart surgery.[341] Each judge is the second of several generations of lawyers who date back to the creation of the county in 1925. Excerpts of the speech were published in the Guest Column of the Press Journal on November 19, 1994.

Indian River County Historical Society Collection, Archive Center, Indian River County Main Library

Sherman N. Smith, Jr.
At the Courthouse dedication
Courtesy of the Indian River County Historical Society, Archive
Center, Indian River County Main Library.

The dedication of the new courthouse occurred on Veterans Day, November 11, 1994, following a parade. The Indian River County Commission consisted of: John Tippin, Chairman; Ken Macht, Vice Chairman; Fran Adams; Carolyn Eggert; and Richard Bird. A copy of the program follows the Conclusion of this book.

F. Saving the 14th Avenue Courthouse

The commissioners were undecided about what to do with the old courthouse. Millie Bunnell of the County Historical Society stated that it needed to be saved for its historical significance. She was quoted as saying, "Later on, people might say, too bad they didn't save that 1935 building...I'd like to think government protects our heritage and is not its enemy."[342] Incidentally, Mrs. Bunnell was the daughter of Ed Carter, who is mentioned earlier in this chapter and who had described the courthouse location as being on a swamp. She was also the aunt of David Carter, mentioned above.

Circuit Judge L. B. Vocelle, local Bar President Robert Nall, and State Attorney Bruce Colton said the old courthouse was not worth saving. They cited dampness in the basement and poor circulation in the building. "I don't want to have a confrontation with the Historical Society, but I think it would be a terrible mistake to retain the structure," said Vocelle, who was representing Circuit Judges Charles Smith and Paul Kanarek, as well.[343] "The less we have to use the old courthouse, the better off we are," said Nall.[344]

For the years 1995 and most of 1996, the old courthouse on 14th Avenue stood vacant while the county commission decided what to do. It entertained efforts by the Indian River County Historical Society to obtain a Florida Historic Preservation Grant and save the courthouse. Ultimately, the commission decided to auction the courthouse and its contents.

On November 22, 1996, the courthouse was purchased at auction by Vero Beach resident Bill Willis, on behalf of The Real Estate and

Management Group, Inc. The old courthouse and annex building, without contents, sold for $412,500.00. The second bidder, however, Bob Brackett, subsequently purchased the courthouse building (without the annex) on December 31, 1996, from The Real Estate Management Group. Brackett completed a renovation of the courthouse and has preserved some of the early courthouse history, as well as providing offices and a place for cultural functions. The building is renamed the Courthouse Executive Center. Mr. Brackett, County Judge Joe Wild's father-in-law, is the same gentleman who was mentioned previously under the Seminole Building portion of this chapter. He owned the building that presently sits where the first courthouse in Indian River County was once located. He also owns the Florida Theater building mentioned previously.

In January of 1997, 16th Avenue in front of the new courthouse was given a dual name with "L.B. Vocelle Court," in honor of former Nineteenth Judicial Circuit Chief Judge L.B. Vocelle, who died on November 30, 1996. The action was taken by the Vero Beach City Council. L. B. Vocelle Ct. is to be distinguished from the (James T). Vocelle Library, which was in the new courthouse. This library, which existed in the Courthouse annex described in a preceding subchapter, was dedicated to Attorney James T. Vocelle, L.B. Vocelle's father.

Chapter 6 – Florida Courts in General in the 20th Century

Since the mid to late 1970s, incidentally, when I started to practice law in Florida, the Judicial system has been straightforward. There were only four levels of courts.

The so-called lowest court was the county court, where there was original jurisdiction on civil cases for claims less than a certain amount. It evolved from $2,500.00 in the 1970s and reached $15,000.00 by July 1992. That court also had original jurisdiction in criminal cases, but was limited to misdemeanors. (Sometimes, County Court Judges were temporarily assigned to the circuit court to help with felony cases, a controversy mentioned in the Indian River County Court Chapter.) Appeals were generally made to the circuit court.

The circuit court had not only appellate jurisdiction of county court appeals, but it also had original jurisdiction in equity cases and jurisdiction in all law (civil) cases, except where the inferior court had it. Generally, circuit courts had original jurisdiction in civil cases in excess of $15,000.00 by July 1992. The circuit court also has had original jurisdiction of probate and guardianship matters and certain types of civil cases, like foreclosures or injunctions, and concurrent jurisdiction with the county court on certain matters, including landlord-tenant matters. The circuit court had original jurisdiction of criminal felony matters. (A felony is a crime punishable by death or a sentence to state prison.)

Circuit Court appeals were to the District Court of Appeal for the applicable circuit. Some appeals went directly to the Supreme Court of Florida, both in the old days, i.e., before the courts of appeal, with the first one, actually three, being created in 1957, and sometimes, notwithstanding there being a District Court of Appeal, a direct appeal from Circuit Court, such as on a conviction involving the death sentence. Art. V, sect 3(b)(1), Fla. Const.

Appeals from the District Court of Appeal were to the Supreme Court.

A diagram illustrating this somewhat straightforward system, the result of Florida Constitutional Amendments in 1972, is illustrated in the 1975-1976 Florida Handbook, by Allen Morris,[345] and particularly the chapter on Courts. It would have to be updated only to show additional courts of appeal and the complete removal of the municipal courts, which were then on their way out. The court tiers in Florida since the mid-1970s are as follows:

Supreme Court of Florida

District Court of Appeal (5 by 1997)

Circuit Courts (20)

County Court

However, the above was not always the case. The court system was very complex. Besides the courts described in Chapters 2 & 3, numerous other courts existed prior to the mid-1970s in Florida. It was written that "Until 1973, Florida had more different kinds of trial courts than any state except New York."[346]

Since the mid-1970s there were no longer municipal courts, a separate (from county court) Small Claims Court or a County Judges Court (for criminal and civil), a County Judges Court for (Probate and Guardianship Matters) or a Justice of the Peace Court, or even a separate Criminal Court (Felonies), Criminal Court (Misdemeanors), or Civil Court of Record or a separate Juvenile Court, all as further explained as this book continues. On the opposite page is an illustration of those courts and levels that preceded the 1970s, including where there was appellate jurisdiction, in that same Florida Handbook series, but for the year 1965-1966, and written by Supreme Court Justice B.K. Roberts.

THE JUDICIAL SYSTEM OF FLORIDA

SUPREME COURT*

DISTRICT COURT OF APPEAL

FINAL APPELLATE JURISDICTION OF DISTRICT COURT OF APPEAL **

CIRCUIT COURT | COUNTY JUDGE'S COURT (Probate & Guardianship Matters) | CRIMINAL COURT (Felonies) | CIVIL COURT OF RECORD

FINAL APPELLATE JURISDICTION OF CIRCUIT COURT

COUNTY COURT | COUNTY JUDGE'S COURT (Civil and Criminal Cases) | CRIMINAL COURT (Misdemeanor)

MUNICIPAL | JUVENILE

JUSTICE OF THE PEACE | SMALL CLAIMS

* Appeal may be taken directly to Supreme Court from trial courts in capital cases, cases involving constitutional questions and bond validation cases.

** Appellate decisions of Circuit Court are reviewable by Supreme Court under certain circumstances. See Article V of Constitution.

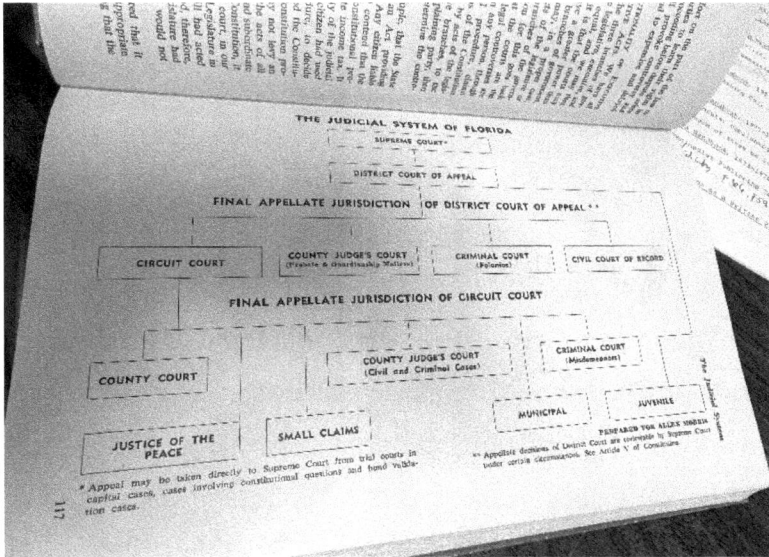

Some, if not most, of the Courts that have vanished, as alluded to, were all the municipal courts – discussed in Chapters 12-15, and a separate small claims court discussed in Chapter 10, and the Justice of the Peace Courts mentioned somewhat in Chapters 2 & 3 and particularly in Chapter 13. Also, as noted in the Indian River County Court chapter, estate administration and juvenile case jurisdiction existed with the County Court since the county's inception in 1925, but that changed to the circuit court by 1973.

The courts that no longer exist, with the judicial system being simplified in the 1970s, could be summarized as follows:

Juvenile Courts, which existed separately, particularly in some locales, were absorbed into the circuit court. Justice of the Peace matters were taken over by the county court. The County Judge's Courts, separate and distinct from the County Court, were absorbed into the County Court. The Criminal Court existed in only certain counties, not Indian River. Small Claims, once a separate court, was absorbed into the county court. The same can be said for the Municipal Courts. A Civil Court of Record existed in some counties. They are no longer there. There was also a Small Claims Magistrate Court and a Magistrate Court that had existed in Florida but were done away with by the Constitutional Amendments in 1968 and 1972.

While the names of those defunct courts largely describe what they did, a few words about the now-defunct Justice of the Peace Courts are in order. These courts existed in England prior to the United States and, as alluded to in the second and third chapters, existed in British Florida and the Florida Territory timeframe. Justices of the Peace were considered to be both judges and administrators.[347] Justices of the Peace were appointed by the Governor prior to 1844 and then were elected. However, the Governor filled vacancies during an incomplete term.

Justice of the Peace Courts had both criminal and civil jurisdiction. However, the limit in a civil matter was $100.00, dating back to the 1885 Florida Constitution,[348] and because of that monetary limitation, they were practically obsolete in the second half of the 20th Century. I have given some names of Justices of the Peace that were located in our predecessor counties, and will provide more in subsequent chapters.

In criminal matters, Justices of the Peace generally dealt with misdemeanors, but a Justice of the Peace could commit an alleged felon to the sheriff of the county. The Justices of the Peace also handled death inquests, as will be noted more specifically in Chapter 13 - Fellsmere.

At one time, there were likely 5 Justice of the Peace Districts in Indian River County. The Districts were numbered 1 for Sebastian, 3 for Fellsmere, and 5 for Vero Beach. (See more of those details in their respective chapters.) I only saw one reference to a District 4 for a Justice of the Peace, for a J. W. Andrews, elected unopposed, in 1926.[349]However, there is apparently the same nomenclature for Constable Districts, and number 4 equates to Quay or Winter Beach.[350] I also saw where H.C. Roland was listed as a Justice of the Peace from Gifford, for 12/7/1914, elected Oct 3, when we were still St. Lucie County. H. C. Roland is also on the Registered Voters list from St. Lucie County in 1914, and his precinct is shown as Quay.[351] In the 1916 Ft. Pierce Directory, Roland is shown as living with his wife in Gifford and working as a teacher.

The Justice of the Peace Courts were abolished in Indian River County by an act of the Florida Legislature in 1953, but it had to be approved by a referendum of the voters,[352] which was in a general election on November 2, 1954.[353] All Justice of the Peace Courts throughout the State of Florida (if not previously abolished) were abolished by an amendment to the Florida Constitution in 1968.

Justice Elwyn Thomas, Wikipedia

Chapter 7 - Circuit Court In and For Indian River County

A. Jurisdiction

The circuit court is the highest trial court in the State of Florida. It is also the court of the most general jurisdiction. The State of Florida is divided into judicial circuits defined by the Legislature. Circuit judges are elected for a term of six years.

Section 5 of Article V of the Constitution of the State of Florida, Subpart B, provides, "That circuit courts shall have jurisdiction of appeals as provided by general law and all original jurisdiction not vested in county courts."

The jurisdiction of the circuit court in 1997 was found in Chapter 26.012 of the Florida Statutes (1995). It included all actions at law not cognizable by the county courts. The jurisdiction in 1925 was not too different.

In 1925, when Indian River County was created, there were twenty-eight judicial circuits. The Twenty-First Judicial Circuit was composed of St. Lucie, Okeechobee, Indian River, and Martin Counties.[354]

In 1925, there was chancery jurisdiction as well as special statutory jurisdiction in the circuit court for actions sounding in ejectment, reestablishment of lost papers and records, adoption of children, declaring tax assessments invalid, changing the name of a person, exercising the right of having eminent domain, and validating bonds.[355] That is largely still the case today.

B. Introduction and Summary of the Circuit Court Judges In and For Indian River County

The Honorable Elwyn Thomas of Ft. Pierce, who was already a circuit judge, was the first circuit judge to preside in Indian River County when the county was formed. Elwyn Thomas was appointed a circuit judge of the Twenty-First Judicial Circuit (which included St. Lucie County) just 23 days before Indian River County was created. He served as judge of the circuit court for the Twenty-First Judicial Circuit (which was subsequently known as the Ninth Judicial Circuit) from 1925 until his election to the Supreme Court in 1938.

In 1935, the legislature consolidated the courts because of the difficult economic times. The Twenty-First Judicial Circuit became Division "C" of the Ninth Judicial Circuit. That circuit was formed with the consolidation of the Twenty-First Judicial Circuit and the counties of Brevard, Osceola, Orange, and Seminole.[356]

In July 1967, the Nineteenth Judicial Circuit was created. It consisted of the counties comprising the old Twenty-First Judicial Circuit, to wit: Indian River, St. Lucie, Okeechobee, and Martin.[357] In 1971, the legislature changed the election of circuit judges to nonpartisan.[358] As of 1973, via a new Article V to the Constitution of 1968, vacancies for judges were filled by a quasi-merit selection process, with the governor appointing one of up to three finalists selected by a judicial nominating commission.[359]

The circuit judges of what is now the Nineteenth Judicial Circuit and its predecessor circuits, either as the Twenty-First Judicial Circuit or Division "C" of the Ninth Judicial Circuit, commencing in 1935, and the years in which they served are set forth below:

Elwyn Thomas	1925 - 1938
Alto Adams	1938 - 1940
Thad H. Carlton	1940 - 1941
A.O. Kanner	1941 - 1957
D.C. Smith	1957 - 1977
John McCarty	1957 - 1960
Wallace Sample	1959 - 1979
C. Pfeiffer Trowbridge	1961 - 1987
James E. Alderman	1973 - 1976
Royce R. Lewis	1974 - 1984
Philip G. Nourse	1977 - 1987
Dwight L. Geiger	1976 - 2005 & 2008-2014
Charles E. Smith	1978 - 1999
G. Kendall Sharp	1979 - 1983

L.B. Vocelle	1979 - 1996
Rupert J. Smith	1983 - 1994
William L. Hendry	1984 - 1995
Martha C. Warner	1986 - 1989
John E. Fennelly	1985 - 2004
Scott M. Kenney	1987 - 2007
Marc A. Cianca	1987 - 2004
Paul B. Kanarek	1988 – 2018
Robert R. Makemson	1989 - 2014
Larry Schack	1991 - 2015
Cynthia G. Angelos	1994 - 2004
Robert Hawley	1995 - 2015
Benjamin L. Bryan, Jr.	1995 - 2009
Cynthia L. Cox	1997 - Present
Burton C. Conner	1997 - 2011

C. Biographies of the Circuit Court Judges Since Indian River County's Creation

Elwyn Thomas, Twenty-First and Ninth Judicial Circuit Court Judge, 1925-1938

Justice Elwyn Thomas was born on July 5, 1894, in Ankona or Eldred,[360] Florida (south of Fort Pierce). Eldred was named after his mother's family. He received his pre-college training at Stetson University Academy and graduated from Stetson University in the School of Liberal Arts in 1913. He later received a Bachelor of Laws Degree in 1915 from that institution. He was also a member of Sigma Nu, Phi Alpha Delta, and Phi Beta Kappa. He was also awarded the Degree of Doctor of Laws by that college in 1951. He was unanimously elected Supreme Justice of Phi Alpha Delta Legal Fraternity in 1956.

He began his law practice while in DeLand, Florida, where he practiced for one year, moving to Fort Pierce in 1916. There he practiced for nine years. He served in the U.S. Army - Coast Artillery Branch in World War I. He was City Attorney for Fort Pierce from 1918 to 1925 and City Attorney for Vero from 1919 to 1923. From 1917 to 1919, he was the Prosecuting Attorney for St. Lucie County. His office was located at 16-20 St. Lucie County Bank Building, Fort Pierce, immediately prior to his being commissioned to the circuit bench of the Twenty-First Judicial Circuit on June 6, 1925. He served in that capacity until 1935, when he was named a judge of the Ninth Judicial Circuit. That change was brought about merely because the circuit number changed, and Thomas continued to serve as a circuit judge and as chief judge of the Ninth Judicial Circuit until 1938.

He was elected, in a special election, to the Supreme Court of Florida in 1938 and commenced serving his term on November 1,

1938. He was Chief Justice of the Supreme Court of Florida from 1947 until 1949, succeeding Justice William H. Ellis, who had retired.

In 1954, Governor Dan McCarty, a Ft. Pierce native, appointed Thomas as Presiding Officer of the newly created judicial council, which came about by a legislative enactment. Justice Thomas continued as a justice on the Supreme Court until his retirement on January 7, 1969.

Thomas was a charter member of the Vero Beach Yacht Club, which commenced in 1926. Justice Thomas died on February 15, 1971. A Resolution in Memory of Justice Thomas was made by the Supreme Court of Florida on May 10, 1971, and is found in Volume 246-247 of the Southern Reporter 2nd Series.

A copy of some of Justice Thomas' campaign materials for the Supreme Court in 1938, including his radio speech given on May 25, 1938, can be found at the Florida State Archives. His speech was quite professional.

Alto Lee Adams, Ninth Judicial Circuit Court Judge, 1938-1940

Alto Lee Adams was born on January 31, 1899, in the village of DeFuniak Springs, Walton County, Florida. Judge Adams graduated from Walton High School in DeFuniak Springs and then attended the University of Florida. His schooling was interrupted by his service in the Navy during World War I. He then returned to the University of

Florida and received his law degree in 1921. It was in summer school at Florida State College for Women that he renewed an acquaintance with his future wife, Carra Williams, who had been a high school classmate of his. (They were engaged in 1925).

Adams started practicing law in Pensacola in 1921 and, in 1924, moved to Fort Pierce, Florida, where he continued his practice for many years. In the 1930s, Alto Adams bought a tract of land for less than $2.00 per acre from a man named Averill from Ohio. This was the beginning of the Adams' Ranch, which is considered to be the home of the Braford bull.[361]

His first judgeship was that of Circuit Judge of the Ninth Judicial Circuit. He was appointed to that position by the late Governor Fred P. Cone in 1938, following the same path as Justice Thomas. Two years later, Governor Cone appointed Judge Adams to the Supreme Court of Florida, where he served from November 25, 1940, to October 22, 1951. He resigned to devote his full time to his business and to seek the office of the governor in the 1952 Democratic primary. He was not successful in the latter, however.

Governor Claude Kirk appointed him again to the Supreme Court of Florida, where he served from November 13, 1967, until August 1, 1968. It caused a furor in some circles because he was appointed by the Republican Governor, as a Republican, while he had previously been a Democrat and was appointed by a Democratic

Governor. Justice Adams retired in 1968; however, he continued to serve in various trial courts through 1972 to relieve crowded dockets.

Justice Adams served on the Supreme Court for a third time in late 1974 and early 1975 to consider two justices of the Florida Supreme Court who had been recommended for removal from office after investigation and trial by the Judicial Qualifications Commission. In the end, the court reprimanded Justices Joseph Boyd and Hal Dekle. The decisions, which included the dissents of Justice Adams, are found at In Re: Dekle, 308 So. 2d. 5 and In Re: Boyd, 308 So. 2d. 13.

Justice Adams had a library at his ranch in St. Lucie County, which still exists. Engraved on the front door is the legend, "Learning is the Most Noble and Worthwhile Endeavor of Man." He also published two books, The Fourth Quarter, an autobiographical book, and The Law of the Land.[362]

Justice Adams died in 1989 and was survived by two children, Alto "Bud" Adams, Jr., and Elaine Adams, seven grandsons, and three great-grandchildren.

Thad H. Carlton, Ninth Judicial Circuit Court Judge, 1940-1941

Thaddeus Hudson Carlton was born in St. Lucie County on February 28, 1906. He was the son of Charles and Rhoda (Vickers) Carlton. Judge Carlton's father was born on March 16, 1878, in

Brevard County, now Okeechobee County, and died in Ft. Pierce on October 31, 1930. Thad's father was a cattleman and citrus grower in St. Lucie County. Thad's mother, Rhoda, was born in DeSoto County, Florida, on August 19, 1886, and died in Ft. Pierce on October 17, 1959.

The Carlton family is a well-known Florida pioneer family. Thad's great-great-grandfather, Alderman Carlton, came from Virginia via the Carolinas and Georgia and ultimately to Florida in the late 1830s. He served as a lieutenant in the Seminole War and was killed in a battle with the Seminole Indians on the Peace River in 1856. Many members of the Carlton family served in the Civil War, some for the Confederate side and some for the Union. Thad's grandfather, Rubin Carlton, served in the Union forces, while two of Thad's grandfathers' younger brothers served in the Confederate Army. They fought on opposite sides in Gettysburg. Thad's maternal grandfather, Richard Vickers, also served in the Confederate Army.

Thad Carlton was educated in the public schools of St. Lucie County, graduating from high school in 1925. He graduated from the University of Florida in 1930 with an LL.B. degree. Upon graduating from law school, Thad opened an office in the Raulerson Building on Second Street and Avenue A in Ft. Pierce.

From 1938 to 1940, Carlton was associated with Wallace Sample and subsequently had associations with T. B. Ellis, Jr., and Ralph

Wilson. In 1950, Carlton practiced by himself, and in 1958, Thad Carlton founded what became known as the firm of Brennan, Hayskar, Jefferson, Walker & Schwerer. It was initially called Carlton and McCain and then Carlton, McCain, Carlton & Vernon. Judge Carlton was also a business partner of Justice Adams before they each became judges.

Thaddeus Carlton married Alka June Pinson on April 19, 1932, in Ft. Pierce. His wife was the daughter of Dr. Van Buren and Virginia (Hackney) Pinson, both of Kentucky. June Pinson was born in Elkhorn City, Kentucky, on March 25, 1910, and graduated from Cumberland High School of that city and from Morehead State College, Morehead, Kentucky. She taught elementary school in Elkhorn City for two years. Her grandparents, Mr. and Mrs. George W. Hackney, moved to Ft. Pierce in 1913. June arrived in 1930 and was secretary to the president of the Ft. Pierce Bank.

Thad Carlton developed a ranch in St. Lucie County called Little Cane Slough. That property is now a large part of Port St. Lucie. Thad Carlton, together with Alto Adams and Ed Belcher, formed ABC Company to remove flood water by digging canals to drain pastures. From 1939 to 1940, Thad Carlton was a member of the Board of Commissioners of the Everglades Drainage District.

Judge Carlton was appointed to the Circuit Court (of the Ninth Circuit) by Governor Frederick Preston Cone in 1940. Justice Adams said the appointment came at his suggestion and recommendation. Justice Adams also explained that Judge Carlton sacrificed his law practice to take the judgeship, but that he knew Carlton would make a good judge.

While Judge Carlton served briefly as a circuit judge, at that time a circuit court appointment had to be approved by the Senate. In 1941, Governor Spessard Holland, who had succeeded Governor Cone, did not send Carlton's name to the Florida Senate for consideration but instead sent the name of A. O. Kanner. Kanner, who had been a state senator, was then appointed to the circuit court.

During Judge Carlton's tenure, at least seven of his cases from the circuit court found their way to the Supreme Court of Florida in the years 1941 and 1942, and all but one were affirmed.[363] Thad H. Carlton also served in the Florida House of Representatives for Ft. Pierce in 1943. He was also an Assistant State Attorney for 11 years, 1943-1953.

Judge Thad Carlton is not to be confused with his son and former law partner, Charlie Carlton, who practiced law in Ft. Pierce until he was appointed to a circuit court judgeship by Governor Kirk. Just before the end of his term, Governor Kirk appointed Charlie Carlton as circuit judge for the Twentieth Circuit (on the west coast of Florida). Judge Carlton's son, Charles Thaddeus Carlton, was born on November 7, 1935, in Ft. Pierce.

Judge Thad Carlton was past president of Ft. Pierce Kiwanis Club; past Exalted Ruler of Ft. Pierce Elks Lodge #1520; a member of Ft. Pierce Woodmen of the World; and a member of the Indian Hills Country Club and Pelican Yacht Club.

Thaddeus Carlton passed away on September 2, 1965, at age 59. He was survived by his wife, June, and son, Charles, three brothers, Ruben, Charles, and Carl, and two sisters, Mrs. Melvin A. Hayes and Miss Mary Carlton, all of Ft. Pierce.

A. O. Kanner, Ninth Judicial Circuit Court Judge, 1941-1957

Judge A. O. (Abram Otto) Kanner was a native of Sanford, Florida, being born on November 2, 1893. His parents were Romanian Jews who settled in Sanford. He was the eldest of the five children of Charles and Pauline Abram Kanner. A. O. Kanner graduated from high school in Sanford and attended the University of North Carolina for two years, then Stetson College of Law, where he received his degree and was admitted to the Florida Bar in 1915.

Kanner commenced the practice of law in the Jacksonville firm of Alexander and Martin. This started his longstanding friendship with the future Governor John W. Martin, for whom Martin County is named.

After serving in the Army, from which he was honorably discharged for medical reasons, Kanner practiced in Jacksonville with Edward Joseph Smith. Both helped elect Martin as Mayor of Jacksonville and then as Governor. Smith was appointed the first County Court judge for Martin County, and Kanner was at the same time appointed State Attorney for the 21st Judicial Circuit. Kanner won six terms in the Florida House for Martin County (1927-1935) and two in the Senate for the 33rd District (1937-1941). In 1941, he was appointed by Governor Spessard L. Holland as one of three Circuit Judges for the then Ninth Judicial Circuit, which consisted of seven counties, including Martin and Indian River. Judge Kanner took Thad Carlton's place. Kanner never had opposition for reelection as a circuit judge.

As a result of constitutional changes in 1956, three courts of appeal were created by the legislature in 1957. In June of 1957, Governor Leroy Collins appointed Circuit Court Judge A. O. Kanner of Stuart as the first appointee to the newly-created "Mid-Florida District" (or Second District Court of Appeal), with headquarters at Lakeland. The two other judges appointed to this district were Robert J. Pleus, an Orlando attorney, and Circuit Judge William A. Allen of Sebring. Judge Kanner was named Senior and Presiding Judge for a six-year term. Kanner was then age 61. After a time, Judge Kanner served under Sherman N. Smith, Jr., who joined the Second District Court of Appeal in 1961 and became chief judge in 1963, before

Sherman became Chief Judge of the newly created Fourth District Court of Appeal in 1965.

Kanner was Chairman of the Board of Trustees of Martin Memorial Hospital, the first Exalted Ruler of the Stuart-Jensen BPOE, a 32nd degree Mason, Scottish Rite, a Shriner, and Worshipful Master of the Stuart Lodge. He was also instrumental in organizing the Citizens Bank of Stuart during the depression, which later became First National Bank and Trust Company and subsequently Seacoast National Bank.

Kanner was a prominent legislator. State Road 76, from the Federal Highway to Lake Okeechobee, which he helped bring about, is named after him.[364] There is also the "Kanner Act," dealing with counties being able to use gas tax revenues to buy bonds, which was helpful during the depression, and the "Kanner Amendment," which constitutionally abolished personal property taxes on motor vehicles.

Kanner died in 1967. He was survived at the time by his wife, Mary Alice (Linch), who helped to construct the Martin County Library. They are buried in Beth El Memorial Park in Ft. Pierce, FL.

D.C. Smith, Ninth and Nineteenth Judicial Circuit Court Judge, 1957-1977

On June 6, 1957, David Clair "Bo" Smith became a Circuit Judge of the Ninth Judicial Circuit. He was sworn in by Circuit Judge A.O.

Kanner. Judge Smith had been appointed the preceding week to the newly created circuit court judgeship for Division C of the Ninth Judicial Circuit of Florida by Governor Leroy Collins. Division C encompassed Indian River, St. Lucie, Martin, and Okeechobee Counties.

Judge Smith was one of three additional judges named to the Ninth Circuit. This came about as a result of a population count and enabling legislation that doubled the number of judges in the circuit, which also included Brevard, Orange, Osceola, and Seminole counties. It was contemplated, at that point, that Judge Smith would have his offices in Vero Beach and that Judge A.O. Kanner would maintain his offices in Fort Pierce. Judge Smith is considered to be the first resident circuit judge for Indian River County.

Judge Smith had been serving his second term as Prosecuting Attorney for Indian River County. After his appointment to the circuit court, Governor Collins appointed John R. Gould, then Vero Beach Municipal Judge, as the Prosecuting Attorney for Indian River County.

When Judge Smith was sworn in, his brother-in-law, W. A. Pattishall, a circuit judge from Orlando, was present along with his brother-in-law, Douglas Baker, the Clerk of the Circuit Court in Indian River County. Doug was married to D.C.'s sister, Marion Smith Baker.

D. C. Smith was born in 1906[365] and resided in Wabasso with his parents and five sisters until 1918, when his father, E. E. Smith, who held many positions during his life on the Treasure Coast, became St. Lucie County School Superintendent. While E.E. Smith was the school superintendent, the family lived in Viking, which is presently known as Indrio, between Vero Beach and Fort Pierce. While I digress, the cornerstone of City Hall in Fellsmere, the former Fellsmere School built in 1915, has E. E. Smith's name is engraved as a member of the St. Lucie County Board of Public Instruction.

Judge Smith graduated from Fort Pierce High School in 1924 and studied law at the University of Florida, where he received an LL.B. Degree in 1929 and later a J.D. Degree. While at the university, he served on the student body Executive Council; was a member of Blue Key, a student honor society; a member of Phi Delta Phi, an honorary legal fraternity; and was president of the student Y.M.C.A. After graduation, Judge Smith practiced law in Orlando for two years at his brother-in-law, William Pattishall's law office. In 1931, he opened his office in Fort Pierce, where he practiced until 1950, under Smith McCarty Brown, when he moved his practice to Vero Beach. He practiced in Vero Beach until he became a judge in 1957.

He married Miss Lide Jane Turner of Crystal River, Florida, in 1933. They had two daughters, and Lide passed away in 1942. In

1943, he married Juanita Ayers McElhannon of Lakeland, Florida. Smith said, "Each was a very happy marriage."

Judge Smith is well known for being the trial judge in the murder trial of Judge Peel in 1961. Judge Peel was a municipal judge in West Palm Beach who was accused of killing West Palm Beach Circuit Judge C. E. Chillingworth (see Chapter 4) and his wife, who had disappeared five years earlier. The trial was held in Fort Pierce and resulted in a book by Jim Bishop. Jim Bishop wrote the following of Judge Smith: "Moment by moment, day by day, his stature was growing with the press and their spectators. He was fair without being grim; he could smile without losing dignity; he sensed that the defense was in difficulty and in his rulings, he tossed doubtful decisions to Welsh (Peel's attorney); he commanded respect without demanding it ...."[366]

Judge Smith served as the circuit court judge for twenty years. Following his retirement in 1977, he participated in special judicial assignments for another ten years. (On a personal note, Judge Smith swore me into the bar a few weeks before he retired. That allowed me to attend as a Florida lawyer the investiture of his replacement, Judge Charles E. Smith (see his bio below), on the first business day in January 1978.)

D.C. Smith died May 10, 2003. He was survived by his wife, Juanita McElhannon Smith, and his (and Lide's) two daughters,

Claire Lewis of Hampton, Virginia, and Kay Langford of Newport News, Virginia.

John McCarty, Ninth and Nineteenth Judicial Court Judge, 1957-1960

John Moore McCarty was born in Fort Pierce, Florida, on November 23, 1915. He was the youngest son of Daniel James McCarty and Frances Lardner Moore. John's brother, Dan McCarty, was Governor of Florida from January to September 28, 1953, when he died while serving as governor.

John McCarty's grandfather was C. T. McCarty, who came to Florida in 1884 and was a lawyer and the first president of the Board of Trade (now the Chamber of Commerce) in Fort Pierce. John's father, Daniel, was a businessman and citrus grower in Fort Pierce who died when John was six years old. John's mother was a native of North Carolina who was left with five children during the height of the depression, and yet she saw them educated on the way to the governorship, the senate, the judicial office, and other public offices.

John McCarty served three times as president of his high school class, was active in athletics, and was a winner of the Balfour Award for scholarship. At the University of Florida in Gainesville, he played football, was the student chaplain of Weed Hall, the Episcopal Youth Center secretary, and later president of the student body. He received his undergraduate and law degrees from the University of Florida in 1941.

He entered law practice in Fort Pierce after graduation but was interrupted by Army duty. McCarty served as a major in the U.S. Army Field Artillery and led assaults against the Japanese on the islands of the Pacific Theater. He was awarded a Bronze Star Medal.

John returned to Fort Pierce in 1946, where he organized a law firm with Charles R. P. Brown called McCarty and Brown. The firm subsequently became Smith, McCarty and Brown, then McCarty & Brown, when D. C. Smith moved his practice to Vero Beach, and then Brown & Cooksey in 1957, when John was appointed circuit judge (discussed below).

John served as Municipal Judge of Fort Pierce for several years in the late 1940s. In 1953, he went to Tallahassee to serve as administrative assistant to his brother, Governor Daniel Thomas McCarty, the state's thirty-first governor. John McCarty was one of those who helped to continue the functions of government during the illness of his brother, who died in office.

John McCarty was sworn in as a Ninth Judicial Circuit Judge on September 20, 1957, in the St. Lucie County Courthouse in Fort Pierce. John was appointed circuit judge by Governor Leroy Collins. He succeeded Judge A.O. Kanner of Stuart, who was named to the Mid-Florida, also known as Central Florida, Court of Appeals and subsequently known as the Second District Court of Appeal. Judge McCarty joined Judge D.C. Smith of Vero Beach to run that part of the circuit consisting of Indian River, St. Lucie, Martin, and Okeechobee counties.

John resigned as circuit judge at the end of 1959 in order to run for governor. There was a large field of contenders for the office that year. McCarty came out fourth among ten candidates.

John then went back into private practice. The firm was known as McCarty, Brown, Cooksey & Alderman in 1962. In that same year, McCarty was elected to the Florida Senate and served through 1967. McCarty served as Florida Bar President from 1971 to 1972 and was a member of the Board of Governors of that body for six years. He was also the president of the St. Lucie County Bar Association.

On July 16, 1941, John married Martha Louise Fosgate of Orlando. John's wife was born in Arlington, Massachusetts, the daughter of Chester C. and Margaret Cowell Fosgate. Her father was originally from Massachusetts and was subsequently a citrus grower in Orange County, Florida. Her mother was from Pennsylvania. The McCartys had three children: John Moore McCarty, Jr., Margaret Evelyn, and Thomas Chester.

Judge McCarty died on May 19, 1995, being predeceased by his wife in 1979 and their son John in 1994. A Resolution in Memoriam of John M. McCarty by the Florida Bar was published in The Florida

Bar Journal/October 1995, and there is also a tribute published in the Southern Reporter 2nd Series.

While the intent of this book is to only cover the judges for this county and its predecessor courts through 1999, I should add that Judge McCarty's granddaughter, Lillian B. Ewen, became a circuit court judge for the 19th Judicial Circuit in 2025.

<u>Wallace Sample, Ninth and Nineteenth Judicial Circuit Court Judge, 1959-1979</u>

Judge John Wallace Sample was born in Fort Pierce, Florida, on May 30, 1912, the son of Adrian M. and Annie Moore Sample. Adrian Sample was born near Charlotte, North Carolina, on September 4, 1869, and died in Fort Pierce on December 31, 1931. Mrs. Adrian Sample was born near Charlotte, North Carolina, on April 30, 1876, and died in Fort Pierce on May 21, 1921.

Judge Sample's father, Adrian, came to Florida in 1893, settling first in Eau Gallie, where he built an ice plant and was in the fish business. He owned and operated the Indian River and Lake Worth Fish Company, which, in approximately 1915, became the Sample Fish Company with fish houses in Eau Gallie, Fort Pierce, Salerno, and West Palm Beach. Adrian's brother, D.H., later took over the business, and Adrian went into the pineapple and citrus growing business. Adrian was a member of the school board and, for several years, was the Superintendent of Public Instruction for St. Lucie County.

Judge Sample was educated in local schools in Fort Pierce, graduating from Fort Pierce High School and later from the University of Florida Law School, Class of 1937. In 1935, while attending the University of Florida, Sample was editor of the "Seminole," the annual of the University.

Judge Sample practiced law in Fort Pierce from 1937 to 1959. He was first associated with Alto Adams, Sr., as well as with Thad Carlton, Frank Fee, and Otis R. Parker, Jr. He was a Municipal Court Judge for the City of Fort Pierce (1944-1945) as well as its city attorney (1946 to 1951). Sample also served his country in the military in 1945, completing basic training in Camp Robinson, Arkansas, and serving in the Judge Advocate's Office at Fort Ord, California. He was also Mayor of the City of Fort Pierce from 1953 to 1954.

In 1959, Sample was appointed circuit judge by Governor Leroy Collins after John McCarty had resigned to run for governor. Judge Sample retired as a circuit judge in 1979. As a circuit judge, he authored Florida Grand Jury Instructions, which are in general use throughout Florida. Sample had temporary assignments serving on the Court of Appeal for both the Second and Fourth Districts. He served for fifteen years on the Florida Supreme Court Committee on Standard Jury Instructions in criminal cases.

Judge Sample was the President of the St. Lucie County Bar Association, the Fort Pierce Kiwanis Club, and the Fort Pierce Junior Chamber of Commerce. He was a member of the Pelican Yacht Club and a faithful member of the First Presbyterian Church of Fort Pierce.

Judge Sample was married to Helen Young Sample in Fort Pierce on May 31, 1941. Mrs. Sample is the daughter of John and Christine Jensen Young of Homer, New York. She was born on October 22, 1914, in Glyndon, Minnesota. The Samples had a son, John Adrian Sample, and daughters, Christine Sample Forney and Linda Sample Kyser. Judge Sample died on June 14, 1991. He was predeceased by his wife.

It has been said that Judge Sample's biggest contribution as mayor was the Indian River Memorial Park. However, this park was also responsible for his defeat in the reelection campaign after his single two-year term.

"Sample steered the city through the process of getting riparian rights along the river (it probably would be impossible today), found a dredge owner desperate for work, pumped up the till for what the city could pay, which was very little. But when Sample was running for reelection, the future park was still a barren stretch of sand. His political opponent convinced citizens that it had been a waste of city money and spoke of Wallace Sample's sandbox. So, the park, now one of Fort Pierce's jewels, defeated Sample."[367]

It is interesting to note that the St. Lucie County Law Library, when it was located in the new courthouse, had a picture on the wall of Judge Sample's cousin, J. M. "Jack" Sample who was a county judge from January 3, 1961, to July 29, 1967, and of Judge Sample's father, A. M. Sample, who appeared as a juror in the first grand jury in the (re)creation of St. Lucie County in 1905. Those photos continue to exist in the Rupert J. Smith Law Library, relocated nearby.

C. Pfeiffer Trowbridge, Ninth and Nineteenth Judicial Circuit Court Judge, 1961-1987

Judge C. Pfeiffer Trowbridge was born in Ottawa, Illinois, on August 24, 1928, and grew up in Illinois. He received his Bachelor of Arts degree from Denison University in 1950 and his Juris Doctorate degree from the University of Virginia in 1953, where he graduated first in his class and was editor of the Law Review. He served in the United States Army for three years as a judge advocate and practiced law for four years after that in Stuart, Florida.

Judge Trowbridge was appointed by Governor Leroy Collins on December 29, 1960, as a circuit judge of the then Ninth Judicial

Circuit. Judge Trowbridge was one of twenty-one circuit judges appointed by Governor Leroy Collins in the last few days of his term as governor. This was due to the 1960 census, upon which circuit court judgeships were based at that time, rather than the action of the legislature. Incoming Governor Farris Bryant tried to stop those appointments with a lawsuit, but was unsuccessful. (For additional facts on Judge Trowbridge… see this endnote.[368])

Judge Trowbridge retired in 1987 and subsequently sat as a senior circuit judge on special assignments. He died in Stuart, Florida, on May 21, 2017, and was survived by his children, Teri Egan, Leslie Trowbridge, David "Dutch" Radabaugh, Ashley Lounge, Allison Trowbridge, and Christian Trowbridge.

James E. Alderman, Nineteenth Judicial Circuit Court Judge, 1973-1976

Justice James E. Alderman was born on November 1, 1936, in Fort Pierce, Florida. He was a sixth-generation Floridian.

Justice Alderman's great-great-great-grandfather was Captain William Brinton Hooker, who moved from Ware County, Georgia, to Hamilton County, Florida, in 1830. Hooker, who was accompanied by his parents, Mr. & Mrs. Stephen Hooker, and several of his younger siblings, married and established a plantation near present-day White Springs, Florida, along the Suwannee River. In 1838, he represented Hamilton County at the Constitutional Convention held at St. Joseph and signed Florida's First Constitution in 1839.

With the passage of the Armed Occupational Act, Hooker settled in Hillsborough County in the 1840s and was the largest cattleman in the state by 1860. He owned over 10,000 head of cattle on the open range.

Another ancestor of Justice Alderman was Stephen Hollingsworth, who moved to Hillsborough County in 1843. His son, John Henry, married Captain Hooker's daughter in 1845.

Justice Alderman's great-great-grandfather, James Alderman, moved from Thomas County, Georgia, to Hillsborough County, Florida, in approximately 1848. Alderman's Ford on the Big Alafia River in Hillsborough County was named for James Alderman, who first established the ford at that location. He was one of the early cattlemen in Hillsborough County and was said to have had thousands of head of cattle on the open range.

The Alderman family had originally settled in New England in the 1600s and had several prominent politicians in the family. Descendants subsequently moved to North Carolina and then Georgia.

Justice Alderman's great-grandfather, William Alderman, was born in Thomas County, Georgia, in 1838 and died at Micco Bluff on the Kissimmee River in 1893. William Alderman was a cattleman in the Alafia River section of Hillsborough County. William Alderman's wife was Martha Jane Hollingsworth, the granddaughter of Captain Hooker. She died in Basinger, Florida, on December 23, 1929.

B.E. (Burgess Elliott) Alderman, Justice Alderman's grandfather, was the son of William and Martha Jane Alderman. B. E. "Teet" Alderman was also a cattleman who, in the early 1900s, ran cattle on the open range west of Fort Pierce and east of the Kissimmee River. In the late 1930s, he purchased land in Okeechobee and St. Lucie Counties, part of which is now known as the Alderman Ranch. In the 1950s, the ranch was divided between his three surviving children, B.E. Alderman Jr., Thekla A. Sauls, and Ernestine Van Landingham.

Readding Blount (Jas. Alderman's great-great-grandfather) came to Florida with his family in approximately 1850 and settled on the Peace River. He is reputed to be the first settler of Bartow. His son-in-law was Streaty Parker, a hero of the Third Seminole War. Parker married Mary Blount, and they had a son, Readding Blount Parker, Sr., who was born in Columbia County, Florida, on February 28, 1849, and died in Osceola County on February 18, 1891.

Readding Blount Parker, Sr. (Jas. Alderman's great-grandfather) married Ellen Willingham. Ellen was born at Ft. Meade, May 14, 1851, and died in Ft. Pierce on March 8, 1933. Readding Blount Parker, Sr., like his father, Streaty Parker, was a cattleman who grazed his cattle on the open range. In 1879, he established his permanent residence at Lake Marian in Osceola County. His home became known as the "Parker Place." According to legend, he buried the gold from the sale of his cattle around the house, and for years after his death, his spirit purportedly haunted the place, guarding the gold.

Parker was also appointed to the original County Commission of Osceola County when it was created in 1887. In fact, he was a member of the Board of County Commissioners when plans were approved for the construction of the red brick courthouse in Kissimmee. Today, that building is the oldest courthouse in Florida that is still being used as a courthouse.

The Parkers had five children. Their second daughter was named Dollie Lee. She was born on May 19, 1882, in Whittier, Florida. Whittier was approximately where Kenansville in Osceola County is today, and as mentioned in Chapter 3, it was a seat of our then Brevard County circa that time.

Burgess Elliott Alderman married Dollie Lee Parker on March 24, 1901. Mr. and Mrs. B. E. Alderman had four children, the oldest of whom, Burgess Elliott, Jr., was born at Basinger on March 22, 1903, and married Frances Allen, the daughter of Dr. James Allen of Jacksonville. They had two children, James E. Alderman and Linda Joyce Alderman DeLoney.

Justice James E. Alderman attended Fort Pierce High School and graduated in 1954. He attended the University of Florida, receiving his B.A. degree in 1958 and his law degree in 1961. At the University, he was a member of Sigma Phi Epsilon Social Fraternity, Phi Alpha Delta Legal Fraternity, and Florida Blue Key.

Following graduation, he returned to Fort Pierce, where he began practice with Charles R. P. Brown, John McCarty, and B.T. Cooksey. He later formed a partnership with Charles R. P. Brown, which was known as Brown & Alderman. He was engaged in the private practice of law with Mr. Brown until 1971. During this time, he also served as a part-time U.S. Commissioner and part-time U.S. Magistrate for the Southern District of Florida. He was also involved in civic affairs, serving as President of the Fort Pierce - St. Lucie County Chamber of Commerce and the St. Lucie County Fair Association.

In 1971, he was appointed County Judge of St. Lucie County by Governor Reubin O'D. Askew to fill the unexpired term of Judge Jack Rogers, who retired. In 1972, he ran for and was elected Circuit Judge of the Nineteenth Judicial Circuit for a term beginning January 1973. In 1976, he was appointed by Governor Askew to fill a vacancy on the Fourth District Court of Appeal. In 1977, he was selected Chief Judge of the District Court. In 1978, he was appointed by Governor Askew to fill a vacancy on the Florida Supreme Court. While a member of that court, he was selected and served as Chief Justice from 1983 to 1984.

In 1985, he retired from the court and returned to Fort Pierce to assume the active management of the family cattle ranch. Until 1990, he also practiced law in Fort Pierce. He subsequently sat as a Senior Justice in the circuit and appellate courts by special assignment. Justice Alderman is known as the only supreme court justice in Florida who has served at every level of the judiciary, having been a county and circuit judge, a district court of appeals judge, and a justice of the supreme court.[369]

Justice Alderman died in Vero Beach on June 10, 2021. He was predeceased by his wife, Jennie.

Royce R. Lewis, Nineteenth Judicial Circuit Court Judge, 1974-1984

Judge Royce Lewis was born May 2, 1926, in Jacksonville, Florida. He was a U.S. Navy Veteran of World War II, having served in the submarine service and being awarded both a Purple Heart and a Silver Star for saving an injured man from the top of a submarine.

He did his undergraduate work at Stetson University and graduated from Stetson University School of Law in 1950, and began practicing law thereafter in Fort Pierce. In 1959, he became a municipal judge for the City of Fort Pierce, where he served until 1973, when the court was abolished. That same year, Governor Reubin O'D. Askew appointed Judge Lewis to the circuit court. He was successful in a subsequent election to the circuit court and served until his retirement in 1985 for health reasons. He handled numerous criminal and civil cases.

Judge Lewis passed away on April 16, 1994. He was survived by his wife, Louise, and his four daughters, Theresa, Jeanine, Linda, and Cindy.

Philip G. Nourse, Nineteenth Judicial Circuit Court Judge, 1977-1987

Judge Philip G. Nourse was born on February 15, 1923, in Cleveland, Ohio. His father, Guy Oliver Nourse, was born in Texas in 1898 and graduated from Western Reserve Law School in Ohio in 1922. Judge Nourse's mother died of pneumonia when he was two weeks old, and he was raised by an aunt until the age of seven.

Judge Nourse's grandfather was likely Corydon Elliott "C. E." Nourse, mentioned in Chapter 13. C. E. was Vice Commissioner of Fellsmere when Chief Commissioner Charles Piffard disappeared in 1922. C. E. Nourse was an interesting man. He designed and built, including the carpentry work on, the Methodist Episcopal Church in Fellsmere. He was born about 1873 in Ohio. His wife was Bertha, and they were living in Fellsmere by 1910 with 4 children, including Guy, then 11, who was Judge Nourse's father. A fifth child was added by 1920. C.E. Nourse appears within the 1930 census, and C. E. subsequently married Edna LaBruce in 1933, in St. Lucie County.

They had been neighbors in Fellsmere. C. E. Nourse died in Stuart in 1952.

In the early 1930s, Philip Nourse moved to Fellsmere, Florida. The future Judge Nourse set a record as a Boy Scout and as an Eagle Scout with over 60 merit badges. He graduated from Ft. Pierce High School in 1941. From 1942 to 1945, he served in the infantry division of the U.S. Army in World War II and, at the same time, took correspondence courses from Johns Hopkins.

Philip Nourse received both his undergraduate and law degrees from the University of Florida, the law degree being conferred in 1947. He later founded the St. Lucie Abstract Title and Insurance Co., which he owned with his father and his daughter, LeVan Fee, for over 50 years.

Judge Nourse was the assistant state attorney from 1976 to 1979. He served the four county areas of Indian River, Okeechobee, Martin, and St. Lucie counties. He was also a past president of the St. Lucie County Bar Association. In 1979, Judge Nourse was elected circuit court judge and held that office until May 1, 1986, when he retired. He tried cases that ranged from probate to murder. As a prosecutor and judge, he sent four people to the electric chair.

Following retirement, Judge Nourse taught at Indian River Community College. He also held a record for the longest-standing member of the Ft. Pierce Rotary Club, of over 50 years. He died on

August 17, 2010, at his home of 59 years in Ft. Pierce and was survived by his wife of 63 years, Jimmie, and their two children, Levan and Jimmie Anne. LeVan was married to Frank H. "Speedy" Fee, III, and Jimmie Anne Haisley worked at Indian River Community College.[370]

Dwight L. Geiger, Nineteenth Judicial Court Judge, 1976-2005 & 2008-2014

Judge Dwight L. Geiger was born in New Kensington, Pennsylvania, on May 24, 1943. He attended public schools and graduated from Pompano Beach High School. He is a graduate of Stetson University in DeLand, Florida, and the University of Florida, College of Law in Gainesville.

Judge Geiger was elected Martin County Judge in 1972 and was appointed by Governor Reubin O'D. Askew as a Circuit Judge of the Nineteenth Judicial Circuit in 1976. At the time of Judge Geiger's investiture at age 33, he was the youngest circuit court judge in the State of Florida. Judge Geiger was chief judge for the judicial circuit from 1987 to 1990, when, as an officer in the U.S. Army Reserve, he was activated in connection with Operation Desert Storm. He retired from the Army with the grade of colonel in 1994.

Judge Geiger retired to pursue other goals in 2006. However, he returned to the bench in 2008 after winning a contested election and served until his second retirement at the end of 2014. He had four children: Dwight II (deceased), Jaime, Jonathan, and Gabrielle.

Charles E. Smith, Nineteenth Judicial Circuit Court Judge, 1978-1999

Charles E. Smith was born in Vero Beach on December 13, 1929, the son of Sherman N. Smith, Sr., who then practiced law here, and Birdie Lenon Bandy Smith. They each came from Crossville, TN. Judge Smith graduated from Vero Beach High School in 1948 and received a bachelor's degree in 1952 from Florida State University. In 1954, Smith received a Juris Doctor degree from the University of Florida. Judge Smith married the former Dorothy C. Brookwelch in Tallahassee in 1953. They had four children: Alison Lee Seabrook, Reynolds W., Scott Charles, and Lynn Seabrook Smith.

Charles Smith followed in the footsteps of his father and his brother, Sherman N. Smith, Jr., as a prominent attorney. Those brothers practiced together in the late 1960s and 1970s as part of the firms Mitchell, Smith and Mitchell, and Smith, Heath, Smith & O'Haire, whose named partners were all related. Charles Smith was the President of the Indian River County Bar Association from 1962 through 1963 and was a member of the association for over 60 years.

Judge Smith was appointed circuit judge by Governor Reubin O'D. Askew 1977 and sworn in as a circuit court judge in January of

1978. He was reelected to successive terms until his retirement in December 1999. He thereafter served as a senior judge, arbitrator, and mediator until his subsequent retirement in 2016.

As a senior judge, he tried a landmark case in Stuart, Florida, in 2005, involving the auto fatality of two teens who were struck by another teen who had previously attended a party. The issue was whether the parents who hosted a party, for which they arguably allowed alcohol to be brought in, were at least partially responsible for the accident. It was filmed by Court TV. (The jury did not find liability.)[371]

Judge Smith passed away on January 2, 2019, and was survived by his wife and children mentioned above.

G. Kendall Sharp, Nineteenth Judicial Circuit Court Judge, 1979-1983

Judge G. Kendall Sharp was born in Chicago, Illinois, on December 30, 1934, the son of Ed and Florrie Sharp. Growing up, he was an Eagle Scout and attended South Side High School. He attended Phillips Academy in Andover, Massachusetts, from 1950 to 1953 and Yale University from 1953 to 1957, where he received his B.A. degree. In 1954, his parents moved to Vero Beach. In 1960, he was admitted to the University of Virginia Law School and received his degree from that institution in 1963. Between college and law school, he served an active term with the United States Navy, where he was Assistant Navigator aboard the U.S.S. Ranger and on the staff of "Commander," Oceanographic Assistant with the Atlantic Fleet.

After graduating from law school, Ken Sharp joined the law firm of Mitchell & Mitchell in the 1960s and served as a Public Defender of the Nineteenth Judicial Circuit and Municipal Judge for the Town of Indian River Shores. In November of 1978, he was elected as Judge to the Circuit Court in and for the 19th Judicial Circuit, where he served from 1979 until 1983, when he was appointed by President Ronald Reagan as a Judge of the United States District Court for the Middle District of Florida. Judge Sharp served as a United States District Court Judge through 1999, taking senior status on January 1, 2000.

Judge Sharp had two daughters, Kendall Sharp and Julia Carter, the latter of whom is married to Vero Beach attorney David M. Carter.

Judge Sharp passed away at age 87 on March 24, 2022.

L. B. Vocelle, Nineteenth Judicial Circuit Court Judge, 1979-1996

Judge Louis Basil Vocelle was born in Vero Beach on August 4, 1926. He was the son of Mary and Attorney James T. Vocelle, the latter being one of the prominent lawyers and pioneers in the Indian River County Community. As a teenager, L. B. Vocelle served his country in the 28th Marines, Fifth Marine Division in 1944 and 1945 in the South Pacific. He served two terms as State Representative for this area from 1956 to 1962.

He was a graduate of Leon High School, Tallahassee, and of Florida State University in 1949, where he received an undergraduate degree in Political Science. He received his LL.B. law degree from the University of Florida in 1952. (See his photograph on p 355.)

Vocelle was a practicing attorney from 1952 until 1979. He received the Jaycee Distinguished Service Award in 1955 for Outstanding Young Man of Indian River County. He was also active in the Democratic Party. Vocelle was a city attorney for the cities of Vero Beach, Fellsmere, and Sebastian. In October of 1979, he was appointed to the circuit court by Governor Bob Graham.

As a circuit judge, Vocelle was Chairman of the Courthouse Committee and was instrumental in the design of the 16th Avenue Courthouse. He was also chief judge of the Nineteenth Judicial Circuit, being elected by his fellow judges in 1993.

Judge Vocelle had four children. His son, known as Louis B. "Buck" Vocelle, is a third-generation lawyer from Indian River County. Judge Vocelle, who was married to Kathleen "Kay" Vocelle for over 41 years, died on November 30, 1996. The street in front of the 16th Avenue Courthouse was given a double-meaning name with "L.B. Vocelle Court" by the Vero Beach City Council in January 1997 in Vocelle's honor. (The courthouse law library had previously been named in honor of the judge's father, James T. Vocelle.)

Judge Vocelle's wake and funeral were held at St. Helen Church, and he was eulogized by Attorney Charles A. Sullivan, who is mentioned elsewhere in this manuscript.

Rupert J. Smith, Nineteenth Judicial Circuit Court Judge, 1983-1994

Rupert Jasen Smith was born on January 10, 1924, in Fort Pierce, Florida. His father was Charles Lawrence Smith, who was born in White City (outside of Fort Pierce), which was then in Brevard County, on October 12, 1895. Rupert's mother was Alice Marie Boyd, who was born in Eustis, Florida, on March 12, 1900. The Smith family moved to Vero Beach in 1900, where Mr. Charles Smith was a past master of the Masonic Lodge. Mr. and Mrs. Charles Smith later returned to Fort Pierce, where Mr. Smith was a principal in the firm of Freshwater Smith Machine Company, which was organized in 1945. The Smiths had two other children besides Rupert, Lawrence B. Smith and Ronald H. Smith.

Judge Smith grew up in Vero Beach and graduated from Vero Beach Senior High School in 1942. He then served in the U.S. Navy as an Operations Officer with a commission as ensign and served overseas in the Pacific theatre for two years.

Following the war, Rupert Smith attended the American University in Washington, D.C. for a year and then attended the University of Florida, where he received his B.A. on June 6, 1949. He obtained his law degree from that same institution in September of 1950. Smith then opened a law office in Fort Lauderdale, but only practiced for six weeks before he was called back to the service in December of 1950. During the Korean War, he served his country again for two years, primarily in Japan.

In January of 1953, he joined John McCarty in the practice of law (when the firm was known as McCarty and Brown) and, after one year, opened his own practice. He became a member of the House of Representatives for the State of Florida when he was elected in November 1956. He was reelected in 1958 and served until 1960. Judge Smith continued in private practice until his appointment by Governor Bob Graham to the circuit court of the Nineteenth Judicial Circuit. He served as circuit court judge from 1983 until his mandatory retirement age of 70, on December 31, 1994.

Judge Smith died on May 5, 2009, and was survived by three children: Mark Smith of Miami, James Smith of Ft. Pierce, and his daughter, Cynthia Zacharakis of Port. St. Lucie. Judge Smith was preceded in death by his wife, Portia, on June 29, 2006, and also his son, Rupert J. Smith, Jr. The law library adjacent to the courthouse in Fort Pierce is named after Judge Smith.

William L. Hendry, Nineteenth Judicial Circuit Court Judge, 1984-1995

Judge William L. Hendry was born on July 29, 1929, in Okeechobee, Florida. He was the son of William J. Hendry, a state representative from Okeechobee from 1941 to 1951, and Hope Hendry, who was born in Massachusetts. William L. Hendry married the former Etta Merle Sullivan, formerly of White City (south of Ft. Pierce), on May 5, 1951, and they had three children.

Hendry graduated from Okeechobee High School in 1947 and received his B.S. in Agriculture from the University of Florida in 1952. Judge Hendry served in the United States Air Force from 1950 to 1954, where he was Chief Clerk of the Legal Department of Base Staff Judge Advocate. He received his law degree from the University of Florida in 1957. Hendry was admitted to the Florida Bar that same year.

Judge Hendry practiced law in Okeechobee from 1957 to 1981 with an emphasis on real property and government law. He was elected Okeechobee County Judge and took office on January 6, 1981, and served until 1984. He was appointed circuit judge in January 1984 and ran unopposed in 1984 and 1990. He was elected Chief Judge for the Nineteenth Judicial Circuit in November of 1990 (when he took over for Judge Geiger, who was activated in connection with Operation Desert Storm) and served in that capacity until June of 1993. Judge Hendry has been a trustee of the Indian River Community College for over 13 years and was honored by the Okeechobee Campus building being named the Dixon-Hendry Center.

Judge Hendry retired on September 30, 1995. He lost his wife, Etta, on September 2, 2023.

Martha C. Warner, Nineteenth Judicial Circuit Court Judge, 1986-1989

Judge Martha C. Warner was born in St. Louis, Missouri, on October 10, 1950. She married Thomas E. Warner in 1972 and moved to Stuart in 1993. She is a graduate of The Colorado College, receiving a B.A., Magna Cum Laude, in 1971, where she was a member of Phi Beta Kappa. She attended the University of Chicago School of Law from 1971 to 1972 and received her J.D. Degree from the University of Florida with high honors in 1974. There, she was a member of the Order of the Coif and a member of the Editorial Board of the Law Review. In 1995, the Judge obtained a Master of Laws (LL.M.) in Judicial Process from the University of Virginia.

Judge Warner was in private practice from 1974 to 1985 and in 1986 became a circuit judge for the Nineteenth Judicial Circuit. She served in that capacity until 1988. In 1989, she became a Judge for the Fourth District Court of Appeal, where she presently serves.[372]

Her husband is a former Florida State Representative. The Warners have three children: Susan, Patricia, and Edward.

John E. Fennelly, Nineteenth Judicial Circuit Court Judge, 1985-2004

Judge John E. Fennelly was born on August 14, 1943, in Chicago, Illinois. He was the son of Irish Immigrants and took his Catholic faith, education, and service to the country quite seriously. He graduated from St. Rita of Cascia High School, an Augustinian Catholic boys' school on the South Side of Chicago, and then entered the United States Marine Corps.

Judge Fennelly, known as "Jack," had an extensive background in the military. He was a corporal in the United States Marine Corps, a lieutenant in the United States Navy, and a military judge in the Judge Advocate General Corps in the United States Army Reserve.

Upon completion of that service, he became a Chicago Police Officer, rising to the rank of Sergeant, and while working full time, attended Loyola University, where he received his A.B. degree in 1970, and his Juris Doctorate from the Kent College of Law at the Illinois Institute of Technology in 1975. He was also a special agent for the U. S. Treasury Department. He later would obtain an M.J.S. (Master's in Judicial Studies) from the University of Nevada - Reno in 1992.

He was admitted to the Illinois Bar in 1975 and the Florida Bar in 1977, when he became an assistant state attorney for the Nineteenth Judicial Circuit. He was appointed Circuit Judge for the Nineteenth Judicial Circuit in July of 1985.

Judge Fennelly was a lecturer and prolific writer on legal issues, particularly criminal law matters. He retired from the bench at the end of the year 2004.

Judge Fennelly passed away on May 15, 2019. He was predeceased by his wife, Sheila, a longtime chief legal assistant to State Rep. Ken Pruitt, and he was survived by three children, Sean, Kerry, and Padraic, and their spouses, and numerous grandchildren.

Scott M. Kenney, Nineteenth Judicial Circuit Court Judge, 1987-2007

Scott M. Kenney was born in Paterson, New Jersey, on January 21, 1949. He was the son of Capt. Howard M. and Imajean Kenney. He received his B.S. from the American University in 1971 and his Juris Doctorate from the American University Washington College of Law in 1974. Judge Kenney was in private practice from 1974 to 1986 and was a partner in the firm of Fee, Bryan, Koblegard & Kenney. Judge Kenney practiced law in the areas of Real Property, Tax, Subrogation Claims, and Bankruptcy, and worked out of his firm's law offices in both Fort Pierce and Port St. Lucie.

Kenney was appointed circuit judge by Governor Bob Graham and was sworn in on June 30, 1986. He was re-elected from then until his retirement in 2007. In 1999, he was involved in a controversy concerning his ability to serve. This resulted in a stipulation with the Florida Judicial Qualifications Commission dated July 3, 2002.

Judge Kenney died on October 31, 2010, in West Palm Beach. He was survived by his three daughters, Cara L. Kenney of Nashville, TN, Colleen M. King and her husband, Michael, of Ft. Pierce, and Suzanne M. Kenney of Jensen Beach, FL. He was predeceased by his sister, Judith Reissing.

Marc A. Cianca, Nineteenth Judicial Circuit Court Judge, 1987-2004.

Marc A. Cianca was born in McKees, Pennsylvania, on October 3, 1937, and was raised in Hillsborough and Pasco counties. He played center in football for Hillsborough High School. After high school, he served in the U.S. Navy and subsequently attended the University of South Florida, where he was part of the first graduating class, earning a B.A. in History in 1963. At that time, he worked for the Tampa Fire Department and met his love, Inez, and her three children. He then worked as a claims adjustor before going back to school and graduating from the University of Florida College of Law in 1969. He served as Claims Counsel for Baldwin, Lyon, Self

Insurance Claim Programs and moved to Stuart, Florida, where he became an assistant state attorney.

Cianca was elected a county court judge for Martin County in 1976 and graduated from the Florida "New Judges" College in 1976. He served as county judge until 1986, when he was elected to the circuit court. Judge Cianca served on the circuit court, being the Chief Judge in 2001-2003, serving until 2004, and then went on senior judge status until fully retiring to take care of his wife in 2016.

Judge Cianca loved history as well as taking long walks in Stuart. He was predeceased by his wife of 60 years, Inez Weeks Cianca, who died on January 1, 2022. He passed away on June 29, 2024.

Paul B. Kanarek, Nineteenth Judicial Circuit Court Judge, 1988-2018

Judge Paul B. Kanarek was born in Stuart, Florida, in 1950. He received his undergraduate degree from the University of Florida in 1972 and his Juris Doctorate from the University of Florida in 1975. He became a resident of Indian River County that same year and commenced serving as an Assistant Public Defender. After serving from 1978 to 1980 as Chief Assistant Public Defender in the Public Defender's Office of the Nineteenth Judicial Circuit, he began a private practice in Vero Beach.

After an unsuccessful attempt to be elected to the newly created second county court judge position for Indian River County, Kanarek was appointed circuit judge by Governor Bob Martinez in 1988. Judge Kanarek was elected chief judge of the circuit in 1997. Judge Kanarek served as a circuit judge continuously until his retirement in 2018 and then commenced a mediation practice.

Judge Kanarek and his wife, Carol, have two children: Lisa and David.

Robert R. Makemson, Nineteenth Judicial Circuit Court Judge, 1989-2014

Judge Robert R. Makemson was born on December 12, 1947, in Fort Lauderdale, Florida. He graduated from the University of Florida in 1970 with a bachelor's degree in business administration. In 1973, he received his Juris Doctor from Stetson College of Law and was admitted to the Florida Bar that same year. He served as an assistant public defender in Broward County from 1973 to 1976. Judge Makemson was in private practice in Fort Lauderdale, Florida, from 1977 until he became assistant county attorney for Martin County in 1978. He served as assistant county attorney until 1981, when he again went into private practice (in Stuart, Florida).

He was appointed by Governor Bob Martinez as Circuit Court Judge, in and for the Nineteenth Judicial Circuit in 1989, where he served for 25 years, opting to retire at the end of the year 2014. He was a mediator thereafter and sometimes served as a senior judge.

Judge Makemson is married to Marsha Makemson, a former Martin County school teacher who is retired from Indian River State College, and they have a daughter, Katie.

Larry Schack, Nineteenth Judicial Circuit Court Judge, 1991-2015

Judge Larry Schack was born in Brooklyn, New York, in 1953. He graduated from Case Western Reserve University in Cleveland, Ohio, with a B.A. in Biology, cum laude, in 1976. He received his law degree from Boston University School of Law in Boston, Massachusetts, in 1980.

Judge Schack served as the Eleventh Circuit Assistant State Attorney from 1980 to 1981. From 1981 to 1984, he was the Assistant State Attorney and Felony Division Chief in the Fifteenth Circuit. He was in private practice from 1984 to 1988, when he became the Assistant State Attorney Felony Division Supervisor of the Nineteenth Judicial Circuit.

In 1990, Judge Schack was elected circuit judge and took office in January of 1991, serving for 24 years, completing his term on Jan. 5, 2015. In 2014, he was reluctant to stand on street corners to seek re-election after such a length of time on the bench and withdrew from the re-election race. He was known for his fine work with children while serving in the Dependency Division. Following retirement, Judge Schack served as both a mediator and a senior judge.

Cynthia G. Angelos, Nineteenth Judicial Circuit Court Judge, 1994-2004

Judge Cynthia G. Angelos received her Bachelor of Science Degree from James Madison University in 1978 and Juris Doctor from George Mason University School of Law in 1982, where the judge graduated in the top ten percent of her class. After being appointed circuit judge in 1994, Judge Angelos has served in the felony division and was a member of the Appellate Panel for the Nineteenth Judicial Circuit. The judge was also the Chairperson of the Domestic Violence Task Force of the Nineteenth Judicial Circuit. She was Chief Judge of the 19th Judicial Circuit in 2003. Judge Angelos returned to private practice in 2005.

Robert Hawley, Nineteenth Judicial Circuit Court Judge, 1995-2015

Robert Hawley was born on June 30, 1951, in Sioux City, Iowa. He graduated from Forest Hill High School in West Palm Beach in 1969 and graduated from Palm Beach Community College in 1973. Robert received his bachelor's degree from Florida Atlantic University in 1975 and his Juris Doctor from Nova University Law Center in 1987. Prior to Robert Hawley's election to a circuit judgeship on Sept. 8, 1994, he was a shareholder in the Paxton, Crow, Bragg, Smith & Keyser, P.A. in Vero Beach. Judge Hawley was sworn in as circuit judge on January 6, 1995.

Judge Hawley retired from the bench on January 8, 2015, and in retirement served as a mediator. He is married to Pamela Dvorak.

Benjamin "Buck" L. Bryan, Jr., Nineteenth Judicial Circuit Court Judge, 1995-2009

Benjamin L. Bryan, Jr. was born in Lake City, Florida, on November 6, 1937. He moved to Fort Pierce when he was three years old. He graduated from Dan McCarty High School in 1955. "Buck" was educated at Florida State University and received his B.A. in 1959 and his LL.B. from Yale Law School in 1962. He was a member of Phi Alpha Delta and Omicron Delta Kappa. He was admitted to the Florida Bar in 1962. He served in the U.S. Air Force from 1962 to 1965 and was in the active reserve from 1965 to 1987.

Prior to becoming a judge, Bryan was a partner in the Fort Pierce firm of Fee, Bryan & Koblegard. He was President of the St. Lucie County Bar Association from 1971 to 1972. He served as Mayor of Fort Pierce from 1974 to 1976, and prior to becoming a judge, was the attorney for the Fort Pierce Utilities Authority and St. Lucie County School Board. He was a Governor of the Florida Bar from 1981 to 1987. He was a past president of the Fort Pierce Jaycees,

YMCA, and the Fort Pierce/St. Lucie County Chamber of Commerce. He is an elder and deacon of the First Presbyterian Church and was also a trial attorney, having an AV rating from Martindale-Hubbell.

Judge Bryan served until completing his term because of age 70 mandatory retirement, on January 5, 2009. He subsequently served as a mediator in connection with both federal and state court cases and performed "pro bono" legal services as well.

Judge Bryan is married to Mary Ann Bryan. They have four children: Mary Elizabeth "Mimi" Bryan Hoffman, Benjamin L. "Beau" Bryan IV, John Thomas "Tom" Bryan, and David Koblegard Bryan.

Cynthia L. Cox, Nineteenth Judicial Circuit Court Judge, 1997-Present

Cynthia L. Cox was born in Vero Beach, Florida, on December 13, 1960. She is the daughter of Cynthia Peterson and Harry Cox. She graduated from Vero Beach High School in 1978 and attended Indian River Community College from 1978 to 1979. Cox received her Bachelor of Science Degree in Finance and Management in 1982 from Florida State University. She also studied law at Oxford University, St. Edmund Hall, in 1984. In 1986, she received her Juris Doctorate from Florida State University College of Law, where she was in "Who's Who Among American Law Students" and was an editorial assistant for the FSU Law Review. She also studied accounting at the University of South Florida and the University of Tampa in 1987.

Cynthia was first exposed to the practice of law from 1978 to 1979, when she was a legal secretary for the law firm of Smith, O'Haire, Thatcher & Quinn, and subsequently served in various capacities for several other firms. She was also a law clerk at the First District Court of Appeal in 1985 and a Legislative Analyst for the Florida House of Representatives from 1985 to 1986. Cox, who was admitted to the Florida Bar in 1986 and the United States District Court for the Middle District of Florida in 1987, practiced initially with Isphording, Korp, Muirhead, Haworth, and White, Chartered, from 1986 to 1988 in Sarasota and Venice. In 1988, she opened her own practice in Vero Beach, where she remained a sole practitioner until being elected as circuit judge, defeating four other candidates in the Fall of 1996.

Cox was also an Adjunct Professor for Legal Research at Indian River Community College in 1990. She has been active in the Attorney Ad Litem and Guardian Ad Litem programs for the Nineteenth Judicial Circuit, as well as active in pro bono legal services in conjunction with Florida Rural Legal Services. She has also been both a Supreme Court-certified family mediator and arbitrator.

As a practicing lawyer, Cynthia was a member of the Academy of Florida Trial Lawyers, the American Bar Association, the Association of Trial Lawyers of America, and the Florida Association of Women Lawyers. Cynthia was also a director of the Indian River County Bar Association and a member of several committees of the Florida Bar Association. In 1995, she received the Florida Bar President's Pro Bono Award for the Nineteenth Judicial Circuit. Cynthia is married to Thomas Mark Dellerman.

Burton C. Conner, Nineteenth Judicial Circuit Court Judge, 1997-2011

Burton C. Conner was born in Opelika, Alabama, on December 9, 1952. He received his B.A., with honors, from Duke University in 1975 and received his J.D. from the University of Florida, with honors, in 1977. He was admitted to the Florida Bar in 1978. In 1979, Conner opened a private practice in Okeechobee.

Conner was an assistant public defender from 1978 to 1979 and was president of the Okeechobee County Bar Association from 1982 to 1983. He received the Florida Bar President's Pro Bono Service Award in 1984. He served as county judge and acting circuit judge from 1984 to 1988.

In February 1997, Governor Lawton Chiles appointed Conner as a circuit judge to serve the remainder of Judge Vocelle's term through 1998. Prior to being appointed as circuit judge, Conner was a partner in the firm of Conner and Hooker, P.A. Judge Connor was reelected, over opposition, in 1998.

On February 14, 2011, Governor Scott appointed Judge Connor to the Fourth District Court of Appeal in West Palm Beach, where he continues to preside. His appointment was the first judge from the 19th Judicial Circuit in over 20 years, and then, for the first time, there were two judges from that circuit on the Fourth District, where Judge Connor joined Judge Warner.

Connor's wife is Deborah, and they have four children.

L.B. Vocelle – Florida State Archives

Chapter 8 - Clerks of the Circuit and County Courts for Indian River County

A. The Clerk of the Circuit and County Court, in general

The Clerk of the Circuit Court is a constitutional officer. Article V, Section 16 of the Florida Constitution provides as follows:

Clerks of the Circuit Court--"There shall be in each county a Clerk of the Circuit Court who shall be selected pursuant to the provisions of Article VIII, Section 1. Notwithstanding any other provision of the constitution, the duties of the Clerk of the Circuit Court may be divided by special or general law between two officers, one serving as Clerk of Court and one serving as Ex officio Clerk of the Board of County Commissioners, Auditor, Recorder, and Custodian of all county funds. There may be a Clerk of the County Court if authorized by general or special law."

Article VIII, Section 1, "Counties" provides in Subpart (d):

County Officers--"There shall be elected by the electors of each county, for a term of four years, a ... clerk of the circuit court; ... When not otherwise provided by county charter or special law approved by a vote of the electors, the clerk of the circuit court shall be ex officio clerk of the board of county commissioners, auditor, recorder and custodian of all county funds."

More specific duties of the Clerk of the Circuit Court are found in Chapter 28 of the Florida Statutes. The Clerk of the Circuit Court is the clerk and accountant for the Board of County Commissioners. He or she is the Ex officio Auditor of the county. The Clerk is the Recorder of the county. The Clerk invests county funds and records, and maintains all dockets and minute books relating to court cases filed in the circuit and county courts.

The office of the Clerk of the Circuit Court dates to the 1838 Florida Constitution. The Clerk is considered a public trustee and performs checks and balances for the public at the county level.

The Clerk deals with the county government as its accountant and auditor, collector and distributor of statutory assessments, and guardian of public records, public funds, and public property. The Clerk also maintains the court records, ensures that the court's orders, judgments, or directives are carried out within the parameters allowed by law, collects and disburses court fines, fees, and assessments, and collects and disburses court-ordered child support and alimony payments.[373] The Clerk's office also assists the state government with the handling of documentary stamps, intangible tax collection, and disbursements for the Department of Revenue and certain fees and assessments for the benefit of the state trust funds. The office also provides statistical information to the state.

One study has concluded that the Clerk's office performs 926 different constitutional and statutory functions or duties.

Clerks of the Circuit and County Courts in Indian River County through 1999, have consisted of the following:

Miles Warren	July 1925 - January 1937
Douglas Baker	January 1937 - January 1965
Ralph Harris	January 1965 - January 1977
Freda Wright	January 1977- December 1988
Jeffrey Barton	December 1988 - June 2012

B. Biographical information of Clerks of the Circuit and County Courts of Indian River County

Freda Wright   Jeffrey Barton

Miles Adlai Warren, Courtesy of Eugene O'Neill Collection

Miles Adlai Warren, Clerk of the Circuit and County Court of Indian River County, 1925-1937

Miles Adlai Warren, Sr., was the first Clerk of the Circuit and County Courts for Indian River County. He was born on October 10, 1892, in DeFuniak Springs, Florida, one of 8 children of Miles Abraham Warren (1861- 1924) and Caroline Mary Thomas Warren (1864 – 1939). He was appointed Clerk by Governor John Martin in 1925. He was the clerk of the court when it was located at both the Seminole Building and the Palmetto Hotel, and was a key figure in obtaining the approvals and the federal loan for the next courthouse.

Miles Adlai Warren was a deputy clerk of court in Fort Pierce before Indian River County was created. As alluded to, he came from a large family in Walton County. His sisters each completed their educations and contributed much to the teaching profession in many areas of Florida.

Warren and his wife, Maud E. Hart Warren, lived for years just west of the present-day St. Francis Manor. He always walked to work, wearing a hat and a suit, and was described as a typical Cracker politician.

Miles Adlai Warren died at age 94 in Vero Beach on March 29, 1986, and is buried in Crestlawn Cemetery. Mr. and Mrs. Warren had one son, Miles Allison Warren, a highly decorated war hero who served in the 4th Infantry on D-Day and was promoted to colonel. Miles Allison Warren married Brig. General S. A. Woods' daughter, Catherine "Rickey" Woods Warren Kirby. "Al" Warren ran a feed and seed store called Hackney and Warren located on 20th Street in Vero Beach. He later ran Susie Q Ranch in Brevard County and was killed at age 38, on June 21, 1956, in a plane crash in Micco, Florida. Surviving spouse Rickey Warren later married Tom Kirby of Ft. Pierce and moved to Colombia, South America. She and Warren had a daughter, Rebel Warren, and a son, Miles Alexander Warren. Rebel Rd., n/k/a 5th St. S.W., was named after the daughter.

Douglas Baker, Clerk of the Circuit and County Court of Indian River County, 1937-1965

James Douglas (Doug or Douglas) Baker was born on November 14, 1901, at Jensen, now Jensen Beach, Florida. He was one of four children born to James Hudson Baker and Ida Baker. Douglas' father maintained a livery stable in Jensen until 1914. Then, with the advent of the horseless carriage, Mr. James Baker became a carpenter and a general contractor and came to Vero to build the home of Judge Andrews, formerly located on the southeast corner of Kings Highway and State Road 60.[374] Doug's father built the original Seminole Building that housed the county's first courthouse. James Hudson Baker was nominated in 1998 by the City of Vero Beach for the Great Floridians 2000.

Douglas Baker was one of five members of the first senior class of Vero High School, graduating in 1920. In 11th grade, he started dating Sara Marion Smith, an 11th grader at Fort Pierce High School whose father was then the superintendent of public instruction in St. Lucie County. He was also the father of D. C. Smith, Marion's brother. (D. C. Smith is discussed in the preceding chapter).

Douglas Baker and Marion Smith were married on September 6, 1923. Prior to their wedding, Doug had attended the University of Florida, and Marion, known as "Mane," attended Stetson University in DeLand.

Baker had left the University of Florida because of a job offer from Freeman Knight, president of the Farmers Bank. After the crash, Doug worked for McFarlane Furniture Company, where, while driving trucks, he would be able to solicit votes. In 1932, he attempted to win public office, challenging the incumbent, Miles Warren. Mr. Baker lost in a close election and continued his work for McFarlane Furniture. Baker ran again in 1936, again opposing Miles Warren. This time, he defeated Warren 1,101 votes to 962.

When Baker took office, the court was located on Dixie Highway and 19th Street at the site of the Palmetto Hotel. There were two deputy clerks, each of whom had worked for Miles Warren, viz, Ralph Harris and Leila Gray. A 1932 political leaflet, which was reportedly prepared by Doug Baker and Joe Earman, was interesting and amusing! It was in the format of the front page of a newspaper and headlined, "Clerk of Court House Kidnapped. $1.98 Cash Reward Demanded by Gang or They Will Return Him."

Around 1946, Baker, as Clerk of the Court, purchased a Rectigraph, which was a photo recording machine for making permanent records of documents. The machine did away with the need for a darkroom or darkroom equipment. It recorded documents directly to both sides of a sheet of paper with 100 percent white rag content. That was considered the most permanent record science could provide at the time. Because of Baker's ringing endorsement of the machine, photos of the Indian River County Courthouse, as well as Baker and his clerks, Jean Frost and Ruth Glover, were permanently displayed on an advertising brochure by the Rectigraph Division of the Haloid Co., Rochester, New York (a predecessor company to Xerox). The brochure pictured the original 14th Ave. courthouse, surrounded by attractive palm trees.

Douglas Baker was the second Clerk of the Circuit and County Courts and the first clerk in the "new" courthouse on 14th Avenue. He was also the last clerk, for a couple of months, when the court was located at the Palmetto Hotel, when Baker took office in 1937. Baker was the clerk during the construction of both the north and south wings of the 14th Avenue courthouse, some 20 and 25 years, respectively, after he took office.

It was during his clerkship that significant new laws went into effect as of January 1, 1957, for Clerks of the Circuit Court. The new law eliminated approximately 15 sets of record books, such as mortgage books, deed books, and satisfaction of mortgage books. All instruments were thenceforth recorded in one official records book, with one master index being kept rather than three. Section 228.221, Fla. Stat. (1955).

On February 28, 1957, the Vero Beach Press Journal published a letter to the editor as well as a letter to the County Commission by Clerk Baker justifying an increase in salaries for the county officers, notwithstanding some apparent criticism by the Indian River County Taxpayers Association. He wrote:

> The County Commission of Indian River County received the same salary as Okeechobee but less than Martin, St. Lucie, and Brevard, and (he) suggests the annual salary should be at least $1,800.00. (It currently was $1,200.00).
> Our County Attorney receives the same as Brevard, but less than Okeechobee, Martin and St. Lucie and (he) suggests that it should be at least $3,600.00. (It currently was $2,400.00).
> Your Clerk receives less than Okeechobee, Martin, St. Lucie and Brevard and therefore should be $4,200.00 (It had been $3,300.00).

After being re-elected for six successive terms, Baker retired on January 5, 1965.

Other than his campaigns against Miles Warren, Baker was unopposed except in 1948 when O. P. Ward announced his candidacy. Baker was re-elected by a vote of 2,608 to 647. Ward apparently did not harbor animosity towards the Bakers, as sixteen years later, he made a substantial contribution to the campaign fund of G. E. "Buddy" Baker (Doug's son) for tax assessor.

Baker, who had four children, James Douglas Baker, Jr., Don Smith Baker, Linda Lou Metz, and George Edward "Buddy" Baker, passed away on October 31, 1975. His wife Marion, who was D.C. Smith's (Chapter 7) sister, died on December 6, 1995.

Ralph Harris, Clerk of the Circuit and County Court of Indian River County, 1965-1977

Ralph Harris was born on September 28, 1911, in Vero Beach, Florida, the son of Charles and Belle Harris. Ralph's father was one of the early settlers of the original John's Island, coming here from Alachua County in 1895. His mother's family, the Becks, moved here shortly after 1900.

Ralph Harris graduated from Vero Beach High School and attended Massey Business College in Montgomery, Alabama, where he studied business law and government and graduated in 1934. He returned that year to join the staff of Miles Warren and continued in that employment when Doug Baker took over as Clerk. He served as Deputy Clerk of the Circuit Court until he entered the armed forces in 1943. He served in the United States Navy and the Hospital Corps at San Diego and San Francisco. In 1945, he was discharged and returned to the Clerk's Office. He was Chief Deputy Clerk from June 1949 until August 1, 1957. On that date, he had completed 20 years of service in the office where he was first employed as a deputy in August of 1934 (with the hiatus for his World War II service).

Eleven years after his resignation as deputy clerk, he was elected to the office of the Clerk of Circuit Court. He was reelected with opposition in 1968 and continued as clerk until retiring in 1977.

Harris married Bessie Dean Steele in 1935 and had three children: Norman Harris, a former teacher in the Florida school system and then Assistant Superintendent of Schools in Statesville, North Carolina; Mrs. Nina Ettinger, who retired as a teacher and who lived in Brunswick, Georgia; and another daughter, Karen Harris Wise, who was a nurse at Lee Memorial Hospital in Fort Myers.

Harris was a member of the Elks, the American Legion, and Kiwanis. He was the president of the Vero Beach Volunteer Firemen's Association and was noted for his work in the creation of the beach fire station.

Harris died on April 4, 1986, in Lake County, Florida, where he had been a resident. He was buried in Crestlawn Cemetery, Vero Beach, and was survived by his wife and children at that time.

Freda Wright, Clerk of the Circuit and County Court of Indian River County, 1977-1988

Freda was born in Vero Beach in 1922. She graduated from Vero Beach High School. Freda Wright joined Doug Baker's growing staff in 1942. She was elected Clerk of the Circuit Court in 1976 following Harris's retirement and took office in 1977. She enjoyed three terms and retired in 1988.

Freda worked with the "rectigraph" described under the heading of Douglas Baker, above. When Freda joined the office, there was no air conditioning in the building, and there wasn't any for many years. Freda recalls the large courtroom taking up the entire width of the second floor, and that the judge's offices were at the south end of the second floor, with the north end being occupied by the superintendent of schools and civil service. She remembers the expansion of the original courthouse with the south wing, which was constructed under the supervision of E. E. Carter, the superintendent of public works. That wing was used to expand the clerk's office on the west and the property appraiser, Homer Fletcher's office, to the east side of that expansion.

Freda died on December 31, 2012. This lifelong resident of Vero Beach was survived by her daughters, Pamela Ollis of St. Cloud, Brenda Corbin of Marion, N. C., and Kim Norcia of Jensen Beach, numerous siblings, as well as granddaughters and a great-granddaughter.

Jeffrey Barton, Clerk of the Circuit and County Court of Indian River County, 1988-2012

Jeff Barton was born on June 7, 1943, in Monongahela, Pennsylvania. He received his bachelor's degree in finance, insurance, real estate, and accounting from Florida State University in 1965. In 1967, he received an M.B.A. degree in Finance from the University of Florida.

Barton was a councilman for the City of Vero Beach from 1980 to 1984. He was the Assistant Director of Utility Services for Indian River County and the Director of the Office of Management and Budget for Indian River County. He was a former officer of the Bryn Mawr Corporation as well as an officer of the former Security Federal Savings & Loan Association and Indian River Federal Savings & Loan Association.

From April 1978 through July 1983, Barton served as Finance Director for the Clerk of the Circuit Court. One of the first major projects he was involved in was the consolidation of over four dozen checking and savings accounts into a single account, providing better control and a greater pool of investment money. The acquisition of a utility system by Indian River County necessitated upgrading the county's computer capabilities to handle billing and collecting responsibilities; he was instrumental in completing this task.

During Barton's tenure as Finance Director, a new state requirement called for governing bodies to have an outside audit. He was responsible for coordinating the process, from the selection of a firm to its final presentation to the Board of County Commissioners. He also secured a commitment from the board to provide the Clerk's office with the resources necessary to meet the requirements for applying for an award given for excellence in governmental financial accounting reporting.

Barton was elected and commenced serving as Clerk of Court in 1988 and was re-elected as Clerk of the Court continuously until his retirement in June 2012. After a long illness, he passed away on October 18. 2014. He was survived by his wife, Kathryn F. Barton, and son, Andrew Barton, both local Certified Public Accountants, and daughter, Sheila Barton of Bethesda, Md.

Chapter 9 - County Court in and for Indian River County

A. County Court Jurisdiction:

Chapter 10072 of the Laws of Florida (1925) organized and established a County Court in and for Indian River County. The term of the Indian River County Court was first established by another special act, Chapter 11361 of the Laws of Florida (1925).

Section 3 of Chapter 10072 reads in part, "The County Judge of said County shall be the Judge of said Court...." While that seems to be redundant, especially today, the county judge or judges of each county were then established under Section 7 of Article V of the Florida Constitution, and "in such number as the Legislature shall provide, who shall be elected by the qualified voters of the county." Subsequently, the particular act of the Legislature (Chapter 10072 of the Laws of Florida, 1925) creating the County Court in Indian River County was in addition to the County Judge's Court, which came earlier, which continued until 1973, but with the same judge.

If that is still confusing, consider that prior to 1973, there was both a County Court whose jurisdiction in 1925 "shall not exceed $500.00," and there was also a County Judge's Court where the original jurisdiction did not exceed $100.00. As Judge Mank said in 1968, "The County Judge is also Judge of the Indian River County

Court."[375] The County Judge's Court was absorbed into the County Court by 1973. In addition to the civil jurisdictional differences, there were other courts below the circuit court level that are discussed in Chapter 6. The diagrams illustrated in The Florida Handbook publications of 1967 -1968[376] and 1977-1978[377] show the numerous obsolete courts and how they were subsumed into the county and circuit courts, the only remaining trial courts. All of the changes occurred by way of the statewide voters of Florida on March 14, 1972, approving the revisions to the judicial article of the Florida Constitution.

Today, the county court's jurisdiction includes what the County Judge's Court could do, except for probate, guardianship, and juvenile cases, which were essentially transferred to the circuit court in 1973, where they remain today. That subject, however, brings up a controversy arising in Indian River County over whether county court judges may act indefinitely as circuit judges in certain areas.[378] The Supreme Court of Florida held that an assignment of a county court judge to act as a circuit judge, made by a chief judge of a circuit court, was not reviewable in a district court of appeal, but rather, exclusive jurisdiction was with the Supreme Court. The Supreme Court upheld Judge L. B. Vocelle's assignment of Judge Joe Wild to acting circuit judge, but limited the assignment of another county judge.

By 1999, the civil jurisdictional limit of the county court was $15,000.00. The county court then included a small claims court, which had once been a separate court and is covered elsewhere in this history. (Chapter 10.)

It is interesting to note that the county judge's salary in 1925 was $1,200.00 per year, paid quarterly by the county, and a fee of $1.00 for each civil case docketed.[379] (On January 1, 1997, the county judges' salary went to $95,765.00, paid by the state.) Also worth noting is that the prosecuting attorney's salary under the 1925 act was $400.00 per year with a "fee" of $5.00 for each conviction, to be taxed and paid as other costs in criminal cases...." The 1925 Act also provided that the Clerk of the Circuit Court shall be the Clerk of the County Court, which is still the case.

The jurisdiction by 1997 of the county court was found at Chapter 34.01 and 34.011 of the Florida Statutes and included original jurisdiction of all misdemeanors not cognizable by the circuit court, all violations of municipal and county ordinances, and civil actions, if the amount of controversy does not exceed $15,000.00 exclusive of interest, costs and attorney fees, except those within the exclusive jurisdiction of the circuit court. The county court also had concurrent jurisdiction with the circuit court on landlord-tenant matters if the amount in controversy was within the jurisdictional limit of the county court.

Prior to 1978, county judges did not have to be members of The Florida Bar in counties having a population of 40,000 or less.[380] However, a non-Florida Bar member judge elected as a county judge before July 1, 1978, in any county having a population of 40,000 or less, could still stand for election and serve.[381]

Circuit and county judge elections became non-partisan as of 1971.[382]Circuit and county judgeships continued to be elected offices, although the supreme court and district court of appeal judges went to merit selection under an amendment to Article V, Section 10 of the Constitution, 1972, effective January 1, 1973.

B. County Court Judges of Indian River County thru 1999:

B. W. Ketchum	7/25 - 12/26
Otis M. Cobb	12/26 - 5/31
L. M. Merriman	06/31 - 12/32
C. P. Diamond	01/33 - 12/36
Otis M. Cobb	12/36 - 9/10/58
Without Judge	9/10/58 - 9/17/58
G. E. Bryant, Jr.[383]	9/18/58 - 10/18/58
Miles B. Mank, II[384]	10/19/58 - 12/72
Graham W. Stikelether, Jr.	1/73 - 12/84
Daniel M. Kilbride, Jr.	1985 - 1988
James Balsiger	1985 - 1996

| Joe Wild | 1989 - 2018 |
| David Morgan | 1997 - 2020 |

C. Biographical Information of County Court Judges of Indian River County

B. W. Ketchum, Indian River County Court Judge, 1925-1926

Judge B.W. Ketchum served as County Court Judge from July 1925 to December 1926. Governor John W. Martin appointed him as the first County Judge for Indian River County as of July 6, 1925.

Judge Ketchum served in the armed forces in World War II and had been a reporter for the Associated Press in France during World War I. He practiced law after World War II.

He was born in and lived for a number of years in Key West, Florida. He died in 1961 and was survived by his wife, Elma L. Ketchum; his brother, Reverend Charles H. Ketchum; and two sisters, Louise Ketchum and Mrs. Earl S. Yates. More info in this note.[385]

Otis M. Cobb, Indian River County Court Judge, 1926-1931 and 1936-1958

Judge Otis M. Cobb was born in Live Oak, Florida, in 1902. He grew up in Sanford, Florida, and attended the University of Florida around 1924. He then opened one of the first law firms in Vero Beach with Ed McCorkle. Their office was located in the Farmer's Bank, which became the site of Grant Furniture Plaza on the corner of 14th Avenue and State Road 60 (20th Street).

Cobb, who succeeded Ketchum, was the first elected County Court Judge for Indian River County. He served initially from December 1926 until May 1931, when he was replaced by L.M. Merriman, to the chagrin of Judge Cobb. See further details below.

One of Judge Cobb's trials in 1930 was of interest, as he had to declare a mistrial over a man charged with being "drunk" or "intoxicated," as the jury felt that the legislature failed to define those terms, even though it was a violation of the law to be found in that condition.[386]

The Vero Beach Press Journal reported on June 5, 1931, that the Florida Senate had voted for the removal of Judge Cobb. He had been charged with malfeasance, misfeasance, and incompetency, which was denied, and he refused to resign. He believed the charges were politically motivated.

Cobb was re-elected in 1936, although losing in the primary on June 2, 1936, where C.P. Diamond had 353 votes, Cobb had 324, and a Mr. Walters had 111. However, in the second primary of June 23, 1936, Cobb had 977 votes to Diamond's 917, purportedly recovering back pay from the time he was out of office and served until

September 10, 1958. In his 1948 re-election, he defeated R. W. Swing by a vote of 2,782 to 466.

Cobb married Gladys Honeywell, who was then a student at Stetson University, in July 1927. Gladys Honeywell was the sister of Bud Honeywell, the grandfather of Attorney Todd Fennell of Vero Beach. Judge Cobb's mother-in-law, Bessie Honeywell, was appointed probation officer by Governor Martin just before the county's creation.[387]

At one point, Sherman N. Smith, Sr., ran against Cobb, and Cobb was successful. Notwithstanding that, it is reported that Cobb's son, Otis M. "Hank" Cobb, Jr., continued as a close boyhood friend of Sherman's son, Charles E. Smith, who became a circuit judge, as mentioned in a prior chapter. Hank also went on to become a lawyer, practicing in Tampa until he died at the early age of thirty-eight in 1969.

Judge Cobb died September 11, 1958. He was survived by his wife, Gladys, and his son, Otis M. Cobb, Jr., of Vero Beach.

L. M. Merriman, Indian River County Court Judge, 1931-1932

Luster Mason Merriman was born in Bluffton, Indiana, on April 5, 1903, the son of Ingram A. and Ida B. Merriman. He was the descendant of one of this nation's earliest families. His great-great-great-great-grandfather, William Merriman, was one of two brothers who came to this country from England in the late 1600s, and his great-grandfather, William B. Merriman IV, was known to have lived in Baltimore, Maryland, as early as 1756.

L.M. Merriman attended the public schools of Bluffton and attended Franklin College and Marion Business College, both in Indiana. He received his law degree from the Indiana Law School at Indianapolis in 1925 and came to Vero Beach later that year. He was admitted to practice in Florida in 1928, first practicing as an attorney in the booming land sales industry of that time. He served as a county court judge from June 1931 to December 1932, having been appointed by Governor Doyle E. Carlton. That opening for county judge occurred by reason of the action of the Florida State Senate in the executive session on June 3, 1931, which resulted in the removal of Judge Cobb.[388]

In 1932, Merriman became the head of the Indian River County Abstract Company. During World War II, he was a member of the Ration Board and was the County Fuel Administrator. He was the first non-mayor Vero Beach Municipal judge, starting in 1934 and serving for several years in that capacity.

He also practiced law in the firm of Merriman, Boring, and Sutherland; the firm continued until 1963. Judge Merriman was an active practitioner of probate and investment law and was respected for his knowledge of estate and income tax law, as well as corporation and real estate law. He was also an attorney emeritus for the Los Angeles Dodgers, having served the team's interests in this area for many years.

Judge Merriman was a director of the Indian River Citrus Bank and of the Beach Bank of Vero Beach, a member of the Lawyers' Club of Washington, D.C., and of the University Club of New York City. He was a member of Vero Beach Lodge #250, Free and Accepted Masons, and of the Lake Worth, Florida, Consistory of the Scottish Rite. He was the president of the Vero Beach Rotary Club and belonged to the Riomar Country Club, the Riomar Bay Yacht Club, the Vero Beach Country Club, the Dodgertown Golf Club, and the Ponte Vedra Club in Jacksonville.

Merriman was married to the former Jeanette Bazler of Columbus, Ohio, whose father, Bruce Bazler, was active in real estate in Vero Beach. Mrs. Merriman was a member of the Indian River County School Board from 1950 to 1964 and was its chairman for four years.

Judge Merriman died on March 31, 1980, in Clearwater, Florida. The Merrimans were the parents of Mrs. Carol Merriman Billard Osmer of Jupiter, Florida; Richard M. Merriman of Dunedin, Florida, who died on January 24, 1997; and Mrs. Jane Merriman Keltner of Dunedin, Florida.

C. P. Diamond, Indian River County Court Judge, 1933-1936

C. P. Diamond was born on January 1, 1887, in Milton, Florida. He attended Stetson University and graduated from the College of Law at the University of Florida in 1913.

He practiced law in Perry, Florida, until 1925, except during his World War I service. In 1925, Mr. and Mrs. Diamond moved to Vero Beach, where he established his law office. The sign for his solo practice was hung over the sidewalk on what is now 14th Avenue on the then Seminole Building.

C. P. Diamond represented Sheriff J. W. Knight against the Indian River County Commissioners in a case appealed from Circuit Judge Elwyn Thomas to the Supreme Court of Florida, which was decided on March 26, 1928.[389] He served as County Judge of Indian River County from 1932 until 1936. C. P. Diamond defeated Otis M. Cobb and George W. Walters for county judge in the June 2, 1936, election by a vote of 899 to 878 to 287. In 1942, he became associated with the Mitchell, Smith, and Mitchell law firm, which was later changed to Smith, Diamond, and Heath, where he practiced until he died. Diamond was a member of the First Baptist Church, Kiwanis Club, Masonic Lodge, and Veterans of Foreign Wars.

He died in Vero Beach on March 6, 1960. He was survived by his wife, Sarah; a son, James Henry Diamond, a 1948 graduate of Vero Beach High School who attended Mars Hills College; a grandson, David, of St. Paul, Minnesota; and five brothers: John T. Diamond of Jay, Florida; Samuel I. Diamond of Montgomery, Alabama; Emory G. Diamond of Miami, Florida; Earl Diamond of Pensacola; and Walker Diamond of Jacksonville, Florida.

Otis M. Cobb, Indian River County Court Judge, 12/26 – 5/31 and 12/36 – 9/10/58

See Otis M. Cobb above.

G. E. Bryant, Jr., Indian River County Court Judge, 1958

Glover Emerson "Bo" Bryant, Jr. was born in LaGrange, Georgia, on February 8, 1922. He served as a lieutenant in the U.S. Navy in World War II. He received his undergraduate degree from the University of Georgia and his law degree from Stetson Law School. He married his wife, Mary Ann, on September 22, 1945. He was elected to the Okeechobee County Court for six terms, starting in 1956, sometimes opposed and sometimes not. Bryant served as a temporary County Court Judge in Indian River County from September 18, 1958, to October 18, 1958, between Judge Cobb's death and the appointment of Miles Mank. He retired as Okeechobee County Judge on December 31, 1980.

Bryant died on April 28, 1985. He was survived by his wife, Mary Ann Bryant. They had two children: Anne Marie McNair of

Orlando, and a son, G. E. "Skip" Bryant III. Skip Bryant was a deputy sheriff for Okeechobee County who was killed on November 8, 1992, in a plane crash while on duty searching for lost boaters over Lake Okeechobee.

Miles B. Mank, II, Indian River County Court Judge, 1958-1972

Miles Boggs Mank, II, was born in Portland, Maine, on June 2, 1920. He graduated from the University of Maine in 1942. He was one of a small number of graduates because he was active in the Reserves. He went on to serve under General Patton's Third Army in the Fourth Armored Command Division (tanks) and was wounded in the Battle of the Bulge, for which he received one of two Purple Hearts. Mank's tank was lost in that battle, and he spent three years in hospitals thereafter.

Mank attended the University of Florida as part of its "First Veterans Class" and received his LL.B. in 1948 (replaced by a Juris Doctorate in 1967). He was admitted to the Florida Bar on October 5, 1948, and then went on to clerk for a lawyer in Southampton, Long Island, New York, for approximately one year. Mank was an FBI agent in New York for eight years. He then returned to Florida and entered private practice with the late Cornelius Walker in Vero Beach.

In 1957 and 1958, Mank was a Municipal Judge for the City of Vero Beach. When County Judge Otis Cobb died in 1958, Governor

Leroy Collins appointed Mank to replace him. Judge Mank was re-elected for successive terms through 1972. Mank was president of the Indian River County Bar Association from 1961 through 1962.

As a juvenile court judge in 1969, Mank had occasion to hear what he called at the time "the most serious case in the history of this court." It involved a 16-year-old Wabasso girl accused of undergoing an abortion. The judge took the unusual step of opening the proceedings involving the juvenile to the press. She was sent, over the objections of her attorney, to the state correctional school.[390]

In 1972, Mank sought a newly created circuit judgeship, but it was won by James Alderman of Fort Pierce. Mank went on to become an assistant state attorney under Bob Stone for several years and then retired from public service, but continued in private practice until he retired in 2001.

Judge Mank was an adjunct professor of criminal law at Stetson University and taught a similar course at Indian River Community College. He wrote the chapter on the county court in J. Noble Richards' book entitled Hibiscus City.[391]

Mank died on November 12, 2004, and was survived by his wife of 38 years, Shirley, and children, Dr. Carolyn M. Egana, Miles Boggs Mank III, William F. Mank, James Nelson Mank, Donna C. Anderson & Donald R. Carl. His son James Nelson Mank died on November 2, 2013.

Graham W. Stikelether, Jr., Indian River County Judge, 1973-1984

Graham W. "Dick" Stikelether, Jr. was born on April 30, 1930, in Wichita, Kansas, and grew up in Tallahassee, Florida. At one time, in Tallahassee, he was a classmate of the late L. B. "Buck" Vocelle, former circuit judge in Vero Beach. He attended the University of Florida, Tallahassee branch, at Florida State College for Women (now Florida State University). Following service in the Coast Guard, Stikelether returned to F.S.U., where he excelled in debating and public speaking. He then entered law school at the University of Florida. He was a member of the Florida Blue Key (leadership fraternity) and received his LL.B. in 1961 (replaced with a Juris Doctorate in 1967).

Stikelether's first job as a lawyer was as an assistant to Florida Attorney General Richard Ervin, for whom he drafted special legislation. In July 1961, he helped Sherman N. Smith, Jr., open his office at the Second District Court of Appeal in Lakeland. Stikelether was an aide to Sherman N. Smith, Jr., and to Judge A. O. Kanner. (Kanner, who served in both houses of the Legislature, remembered Stikelether as a lad who sold newspapers at the Supreme Court Building in Tallahassee). In 1962, Stikelether worked in private practice with Charles E. Smith and George Heath in Vero Beach, where he was very active in public issues. "Dick," as he was known, was the legal advisor and liaison to State Senator Merrill Barber and State Representative Art Karst in creating the Fourth District Court of Appeal and placing it in Vero Beach. (The court was later moved to West Palm Beach.)

In September 1972, he was elected county court judge in the first primary over two other opponents -- garnering seventy-six percent of the vote -- and was sworn in under the new Article V of the Florida Constitution. Judge Stikelether periodically held county court in the municipalities of Sebastian and Fellsmere in the 1970s.

In 1974, he was put on trial by the Judicial Qualifications Commission for an alleged abuse of judicial discretion and other charges. Judge Stikelether believed the charges emanated from a few local defense attorneys who didn't like him. A three-judge panel held four days of testimony in Vero Beach starting Oct 31, 1974, and 28 days later, a verdict resulted in all charges being dropped.

He was re-elected for additional terms in 1976 and 1980 and was also an acting circuit judge at various times. During his twelve years of service, he received eight Citizen of the Year awards.

Dick was passionate about saving the manatees and was on the board of *Save the Manatees,* and was commended by Jimmy Buffett, who headed that board.

Stikelether died on February 22, 2009, and was survived by his two children: Deborah Marie Kanehl of Vero Beach and Graham W.

Stikelether, III, of Ft. Pierce, and a sister, Sara Lou Smith of Tallahassee, Florida.

Daniel M. Kilbride, Jr., Indian River County Court Judge, 1985-1988

Daniel M. Kilbride, Jr. was born on May 20, 1944, in Brooklyn, New York. As a teenager, he moved to Florida, where he attended Stetson University in DeLand and graduated with a B.A. degree in history in 1965.

From 1966 to 1971, Kilbride was in the U.S. Air Force and served as a criminal investigator and counterintelligence officer. In 1967, he married Claire Suzanne Key, and they have two children, Daniel and Kathleen.

Kilbride attended Stetson University College of Law in St. Petersburg, receiving his law degree in 1974. Shortly thereafter, he moved to Vero Beach, where he was appointed assistant city attorney. He was also the city prosecutor and served in both capacities until 1977. In addition, he served part-time as city attorney in Sebastian from 1977 to 1984 and in Fellsmere from 1979 to 1984.

Kilbride was elected county judge in 1984, taking office in January 1985, and also served as an acting circuit judge. He held these offices until 1989, when he became a hearing officer with the Division of Administrative Hearings in Tallahassee, a position that he held until his retirement on April 29, 2011.

<u>James Balsiger, Indian River County Court Judge, 1985-1996</u>

James Bortree Balsiger was born on June 19, 1935, in Emporium, Pa., to James Wendell Balsiger and Esther Marie Bortree Balsiger. He graduated from Palm Beach Junior College and Florida State University and received his law degree from the Walter F. George School of Law of Mercer University. He also served four (4) years in the U.S. Navy.

Admitted to practice in Florida in 1964, Balsiger served in private practice and was Assistant County Solicitor for Broward County from 1965 until 1969. He worked in both a supervisory capacity and as a felony prosecutor. In 1969, he was appointed Chief Judge of the Fort Lauderdale Municipal Court, where he served until the court's abolition on January 3, 1977, pursuant to Article V of the Florida Constitution. As chief judge, his court received recognition from the American Bar Association, including being named the most outstanding in the United States in 1974. That same year, Balsiger received the Outstanding Court Award from the Florida Municipal Judges Association.

From 1977 to 1980, he was the legal advisor to the Fort Lauderdale Police Department. He was an Assistant State Attorney for the Nineteenth Judicial Circuit from 1980 until 1985, prosecuting major cases in Indian River and Okeechobee counties.

On January 8, 1985, he was sworn in as county judge for Indian River County after being elected to a four-year term and was re-elected every four years thereafter. While serving as a county judge, he was given circuit court jurisdiction by the Supreme Court of Florida. He retired in December 1996. In 2014, he was honored by the Florida Bar Association and the Indian River County Bar Association for his 50 years of being a Florida lawyer.

Judge Balsiger passed away in Ft. Pierce on July 12, 2023, and was survived by his sister, Mrs. Ann Hackett, and four daughters, Wendy Rhodes, Amy Milchin, Carolanne Balsiger, and Jamie Ward, and numerous grandchildren.

Joe Wild

Joe Wild, Indian River County Court Judge, 1989-2018

Judge Wild was born on April 17, 1955, in Ft. Leonard Wood, Missouri, and moved to Vero Beach in 1969. He graduated from Vero Beach High School in 1974 and was awarded his B.A. degree from Catawba College in 1978, where he was valedictorian. He received his Juris Doctorate degree with high honors from the Florida State University College of Law in 1980.

He was an assistant state attorney in Leon County from 1981 to 1982 and then in Indian River County, in both the county court and major felonies division, from 1982 to 1988. He was elected county court judge, where he served from 1989 to 2018. He has also served as an acting circuit judge. Judge Wild's activity as an acting circuit judge received statewide attention after his consecutive assignments as an acting circuit judge were questioned and found their way to the Supreme Court.[392]The Supreme Court quashed the opinion of the Fourth District Court of Appeal and ruled that the assignments were valid.

Wild was active, while serving as county judge, in the Education Foundation of Indian River County, Kiwanis, Character Counts of Indian River County, and as a referee in basketball and football for the Florida High School Athletic Association. He also serves as a deacon at Vero Beach Church of Christ.

Judge Wild served continuously as County Court Judge until his retirement at the end of 2018. Wild is married to the former Glenda Brackett. They have four daughters and a son.

David Morgan

David Morgan, Indian River County Court Judge, 1997-2020

David Morgan was born on April 16, 1957, in Vero Beach, Florida. He graduated from Vero Beach High School in 1974, received a B.A. degree from Mercer University in 1978, and his law degree from the Walter F. George School of Law at Mercer in 1981.

Upon graduation from law school, Morgan worked as an assistant state attorney in Martin County from 1981 to 1984 and in Indian River County from 1984 to 1985. He served as the attorney in charge of the Indian River County State Attorney's Office from 1990 to 1992, and as Chief Assistant State Attorney in the Nineteenth Judicial Circuit from 1992 to 1996. He was the 1994 recipient of the Eugene Berry Award for excellence in prosecution, given by the Florida Prosecuting Attorneys Association.

He was elected county court judge in September 1996 and began serving in that position on January 7, 1997, until he retired at the end of 2020. He is married to Nikki Robinson, a retired assistant state attorney.

Chapter 10 - Small Claims Court

A. History

Small claims courts had been established in many counties prior to 1951 by independent or special acts of the Legislature, which varied slightly in terms but were uniform to the extent of a jurisdictional limit of not more than $100.00.[393] In 1951, the Legislature, by a general act, provided for the establishment in each county of a small claims court when "activated" by the county commissioners. Under the act in 1951, the jurisdictional limit was $250.00, and judges were elected by the voters of the county to serve a four-year term.[394]

The small claims court, which was to be established by the act in each county, had the following method of activation:

> No small claims court shall be activated unless and until the Board of County Commissioners of the respective county shall determine that there is sufficient local need for such court and shall evidence such need by the option to adopt a resolution setting forth such need either 1) on its own motion; or 2) by petition, signed by not less than 25 registered voters of such county requesting such activation....

Section 42.02 of the Florida Statutes (1951).

The compensation set forth in the statute for the judges was interesting. A portion of Section 42.05 of the Florida Statutes (1951) provided as follows:

All fees collected by the judge as authorized by Section 42.11, after deducting costs, shall be retained by him as his sole remuneration, but in no event shall the sum to be retained exceed $7,500.00.

a) All monies collected by the judge in excess of $7,500.00, after deducting costs, shall be paid annually into the general county funds.

In 1955, by a special act of the Legislature,[395] a small claims court was created for any county in the state which had a population of "not less than 11,460 persons and not more than 11,875 persons according to the last federal census" and exempted the county from the provisions of Chapter 42 of the Florida Statutes (the general act pertaining to small claims courts created in 1951) and it fixed the governing provisions for said court. This act was responsible for the creation of the small claims court in Indian River County.

An act such as this is known as a "Population Act." There are three types of laws in Florida: general laws, which apply statewide; special laws, which apply to a specific person, place, or legal entity; and population laws, which apply only to geographic areas with certain population bounds. Such an act is constitutional and may be general or special. It is considered general if the population category is open-ended. General laws do not have the publication or referendum requirements of a special act.[396]

The special act was adjusted in 1961 pertaining to populations with not less than 23,000 and not more than 28,000, according to the last official decennial census, and exempted those counties from the provisions of Chapter 42 of the Florida Statutes. In 1963, the same special act pertaining to the same population and exempting those counties from Chapter 42 of the Florida Statutes was amended again and repealed the prior special acts mentioned above, but then reinstated them in large part. One change was the doing away with a trial de novo opportunity in the circuit court, which sat as the appellate court of small claims under the prior special act.

In 1969, the special act was tailor-made for Indian River County and exempted the county from the provisions of Chapter 42 of the Florida Statutes and repealed the previously cited law from 1963. The act was again amended in 1971, tailor-made for Indian River County, and it increased the jurisdictional limit from $500.00 in 1969 to $750.00 in 1971.

The first judge of the Small Claims Court in Indian River County was J. Pasco Woods. After completing his eighth and final year as small claims judge, Woods said in his final report that he had conscientiously handled claims for the benefit of both the plaintiffs and the defendants and that he had rendered judgments according to law. In Woods' final year (1960), there were a record-breaking 712 claims amounting to a total of $102,881.71 sought. The final report indicated that of the claims, the following occurred: 1) $18,998.96 was paid in cases agreed upon before they reached trial; 2) agreements were made to pay in full in cases amounting to $22,442.34; 3) no service of process in cases amounting to $7,278.16; 4) the total amount on which judgments were attained was $54,161.81, more than half of the amount for which claims were sought. The judge indicated that a good portion of the judgments were satisfied, and that any outstanding judgment was good for twenty years and accrued six percent interest.[397]

In the summer of 1966, a session of the small claims court was held on July 26 with Judge Chester E. Clem presiding. Sixty-six cases were heard.

The following are the small claims court judges who served from the time the court was created in Indian River County in 1955 until the time it was absorbed into the county court by the constitutional amendments approved by the electorate in 1972, effective in 1973:

J. Pasco Woods	1955 - 1961
Charles A. Sullivan	1961 - 1964
Michael O'Haire	1964 - 1965

| Chester E. Clem, Jr. | 1965 - 1971 |
| Bill Cobb | 1972 - 1973 |

The small claims court was initially held in the basement of the Del Mar Hotel. (The Del Mar Hotel, razed in the early 1960s, was located on the southeast corner of 15th Avenue and 21st Street, now the parking lot behind the new courthouse.) Thereafter, the small claims court was moved into the upper middle section of the courthouse on 14th Avenue, which also housed the county court.

Hotel Vero Del Mar
Courtesy of the Byron T. Cooksey, Esq. Collection

14th Avenue Courthouse center, Del Mar Hotel, far left, and an empty lot across, which became the 16th Avenue Courthouse
Courtesy of Indian River County Historical Society, Archive Center, Indian River County Main Library

Hotel Vero Del Mar
Courtesy of Indian River County Historical Society, Archive Center, Indian River County Main Library

As mentioned in the chapter on the courts in general, and like the various municipal courts covered in this manuscript, the small claims court was absorbed into the County Court in 1973.

B. Small Claims Court Judges

<u>J. Pasco Woods, Small Claims Court Judge, 1955-1961</u>

J. Pasco Woods was born in Taylor County, Florida, on July 12, 1908. He was the son of J.P. Woods and Ola (Head) Woods.

J. Pasco Woods attended local public schools in Taylor County and graduated from the University of Florida with a Bachelor of Arts in Education in 1932. He taught in Florida public schools for several years while working on his law degree. Woods taught English and social studies in Vero Beach. He also taught at the Florida School for Boys in Marianna and schools in Williston, West Palm Beach, and Titusville. He received his Bachelor of Laws degree from the University of Florida in 1939.

Woods served in the Navy for twenty-eight months during World War II. Upon his discharge, he returned to Vero Beach.

Woods was active in scouting in Vero Beach and was a member of the First Methodist Church, American Legion, Veterans of Foreign Wars, and the Vero Beach Kiwanis Club.

Woods, who operated a one-person law firm, was the first judge of the small claims court, serving from its inception in 1955 until 1960, just prior to his death in 1961. He held court in the basement of the Del Mar Hotel.

Woods died May 6, 1961, and was survived by his wife, Mildred; one son, James Pasco Woods, Jr., of Vero Beach; two brothers, V. H. Woods of Leesburg and J. I. Woods of Gainesville; and one sister, Mrs. H. G. Blanton of Tallahassee.

Charles A. Sullivan, Small Claims Court Judge, 1961-1964

See bio information under City of Vero Beach - Municipal Court.

Michael O'Haire, Small Claims Court Judge, 1964-1965

Michael O'Haire was born in Buffalo, New York, in 1939 and admitted to the Florida Bar in 1963. He graduated from Kenyon

College in Ohio in 1960, where he was a recipient of the Woodrow Wilson National Fellowship and graduated magna cum laude with a B.A. in English. He received his LL.B. (later replaced with a Juris Doctorate) from Harvard University in 1963.

O'Haire was a Vero Beach High School classmate of Shirley Smith O'Haire (the daughter of Sherman Smith, Jr., discussed in Chapter 11). Mike would marry Shirley, with the couple having a son and two daughters.

O'Haire was appointed by Governor Farris Bryant in 1964 to fill the remaining term of Charles A. Sullivan, who had resigned to seek political office. O'Haire was president of the Indian River County Bar Association in 1968. Mike practiced with his father-in-law, Sherman N. Smith, Jr., and had been a principal in law firms which had various names, including Smith, Heath, Smith, and O'Haire; O'Haire, Quinn, & Candler, Chartered, and O'Haire, Quinn & Casalino, Chartered. Mike's son, Sean, was also a lawyer and lived in Indian River County until his passing in 2024.

Michael O'Haire died on Oct. 3, 2022, at age 83 and was survived by his wife, Shirley, his son, and daughters Meghan Candler, Deidre O'Haire, and daughter-in-law Baerbel O'Haire, son-in-law Rick Candler, and his deceased brother Tom's wife, Gail O'Haire, and five grandchildren.

Chester E. Clem, Jr., Small Claims Court Judge, 1965-1971

Chester Clem was born in Sanford, Florida, on December 28, 1937, and admitted to the Florida Bar in 1963. He is a 1959 graduate of the University of Florida with a Bachelor of Science degree in Business Administration and received his Juris Doctorate in 1967, replacing the LL.B. conferred in 1963.

Clem appears in this history as both a municipal judge for Fellsmere from 1965 to 1971 and as a judge of the small claims court in Indian River County from 1965 to 1971. He wrote the chapter on the Small Claims Court in J. Noble Richards' book, Florida's Hibiscus City, Vero Beach. Chester resigned in 1971 to become an assistant state attorney and to run for state representative. He served as a Florida state representative from 1972 through 1976 and was the attorney for Indian River Shores starting in 1977, for which municipality he served for many years.

Chester's second wife, Debra "Kay" Scott Clem, a long-time Indian River County Supervisor of Elections, died on June 9, 2024. Together, they had twin daughters, Mary Kate (a Vero Beach attorney) and Liz (TJ). Chester had 3 sons by his prior marriage: Zander (an attorney in Orlando), Jeff, and Chester.

Bill Cobb, Small Claims Court Judge, 1972-1972

William Marshall "Bill" Cobb, the last small claims court judge in Indian River County, was born on April 30, 1944, in Lexington, Kentucky. He came to Florida as a boy, growing up in the McAnsh Park area of Vero Beach. He was a 1967 graduate of Florida State University and received his law degree from the University of Florida in 1970. He was admitted to the Florida Bar in 1970 and was appointed small claims court judge by Governor Reubin O'D. Askew.

Cobb practiced for years with Charles Sullivan, whose firm had various names. (See Sullivan's biographical information under Vero Beach Municipal Judges). Cobb was not related to County Court Judge Otis Cobb, although Judge Otis Cobb was Bill's Sunday school teacher.

Bill retired from the Sullivan firm in about 1986 and lived for a time in Cody, Wyoming, pursuing his love of hunting. He returned to Vero Beach in the 1990s to handle his burgeoning citrus business at "20-Mile Bend" by State Road 60.

Bill Cobb passed away on June 26, 1998, and is buried in Crestlawn Cemetery in Vero Beach. He was survived by his wife, Janet Cobb, and sons, Bo and John Cobb, the latter being a local firefighter. Bo died in Pompano Beach on April 18, 2008. Bill also left three daughters, Lucy Cobb Brobst, Shannon Smith, and Cassie Cobb.

Chapter 11 - Fourth District Court of Appeal

A. History of the Fourth District Court of Appeal:

As mentioned in the second chapter, the first appellate court in Florida since statehood in 1845 was the Florida Supreme Court. The first members were circuit court judges, who also sat on the Supreme Court. Later, the Florida Legislature appointed the Supreme Court justices, and then the justices were elected by the people. The selection procedure was subsequently changed again to appointment by the governor.

It was not until 1956 that the need for an intermediate appellate court or courts became authorized, which was made by an amendment to Article V of the Florida Constitution.[398] The intermediate appellate courts began with the First, Second, and Third District Courts of Appeal, with the Second District encompassing all of Central Florida, from the east coast to the west coast.[399]

The Fourth District Court of Appeal was later created out of ten counties on the east side of Central Florida. More specifically, the Fourth District Court of Appeal was created in 1965 by an act of the Legislature.[400] That act, while approved by the governor and filed with the office of Secretary of State each on July, 1, 1965, was to become law "only if Senate Joint Resolution No. 261 proposing an amendment to subsections (1) and (2) of Article V of the Constitution of Florida is agreed to and adopted by the legislature at (that) session and approved by the electors of the State, in which event (the) act was to take effect immediately after such approval."[401] The approval occurred at a special election on November 2, 1965.

Salaries for the three judges for the Fourth District were set initially at $23,000.00 per year. The Fourth Appellate District was first composed of Brevard, Broward, Indian River, Martin, Okeechobee, Orange, Osceola, Palm Beach, St. Lucie, and Seminole counties.[402]The Fourth District now consists of the Fifteenth, Seventeenth, and Nineteenth Judicial Circuits.[403] Thus, the Fourth District Court of Appeal by the year 2000 entertained appeals from Palm Beach, Broward, Martin, St. Lucie, Indian River, and Okeechobee Counties.[404]

The first Chief Judge of the Fourth District Court of Appeal was the Honorable Sherman N. Smith, Jr., who had previously served as the Chief Judge of the Second District Court of Appeal, of which Indian River County had been a part, since it was then in the Ninth Judicial Circuit. It is interesting to note that Smith, when appointed to the Second District Court of Appeal, joined our former Circuit Judge A. O. Kanner. Graham W. Stikelether, Jr., who was an aide to both judges, said that they were rarely reversed by the Supreme Court of Florida.

The other two judges of the newly created Fourth District Court of Appeal were Charles O. Andrews, Jr., of Orange County, who also emanated from the Second District Court of Appeal, and James H. Walden, a circuit judge from Broward County.

The first location of the Fourth District was not set forth in the act passed by the Legislature in 1965, but rather was to have been selected by a fourteen-member commission consisting of seven members of the Supreme Court, the Governor, Secretary of State, Attorney General, Comptroller, Superintendent of Public Instruction, State Treasurer, and Commissioner of Agriculture.[405] The first judges were appointed by the governor. Their successors and additional judges were elected by the voters.

Smith, who was appointed to the Second District Court of Appeal by Governor Farris Bryant, was appointed Chief Judge of the new Fourth District Court of Appeal by Governor Haydon Burns. Stikelether, who went on to become a county judge and was an aide to Smith when Smith was with the Second District Court of Appeal, was active in working with State Senator Merrill Barber and State Representative Art Karst, both of Vero Beach, in placing the appellate court in Vero Beach.

Apparently, representatives from both Orlando and West Palm asserted that the court should be located in their city, that is, near a population center. One legislator suggested a proper site would be a compromise, with the court being placed at the geographic center of the district, namely in Yeehaw Junction in Osceola County near the western end of Indian River County. The suggestion was not taken seriously, but the geographic idea was accepted, and Vero Beach was chosen.[406]

Smith said the first offices of the court were in the Dudley Lock Company building just south of the fire station on Old Dixie Highway. Those offices were used while the second floor of the newly completed City Hall of Vero Beach was being prepared for the court. The architect, incidentally, was William G. Taylor, who was the architect on the 14th Avenue courthouse annex in 1956. Even while the headquarters of the court was located on Old Dixie Highway, oral arguments were heard at City Hall, initially in the City Council chambers.[407] When the second floor was completed, those quarters for the Fourth District were still considered temporary until a permanent site could be found, possibly on the eastern shore of the Indian River. In fact, Indian River County offered three permanent sites, including five acres on A1A in Indian River Shores and land near the planned Vero Beach Cultural Center on the east shore of Indian River, south of Beachland Boulevard.[408]

The first case to emanate from the Fourth District Court of Appeal was Cuyler v. Elliott, 182 So. 2d 55 (Fla. 4th DCA 1965), decided on December 27, 1965. The opinion is interesting in that it was a two-sentence "Per Curiam. Affirmed" decision with Chief Judge Smith and Judge Andrews concurring. However, there was a three-page dissent by Associate Judge Paul D. Barnes. (Judge Barnes was not a permanent member of the Fourth District, but having been a circuit judge in South Florida and a supreme court justice, he sat temporarily on this intermediate appellate court.)

In 1966, Smith was defeated for re-election by Spencer C. Cross, a Republican. This was the election in which Governor Claude Kirk and a myriad of other Republicans were swept into office for the first time since Reconstruction (1877). It had been reported that the Republican victory had a coattail effect on judicial elections. Of the Republican judges originally elected to their seats, 35.7 percent won their seats while Kirk was in office, compared to only 9.6 percent who had obtained their electoral victories prior to the Kirk administration.[409] This event also helped prompt a change in the way judges were selected, making the elections non-partisan.[410]That legislative enactment followed two unsuccessful attempts to change Article V of the Florida Constitution in 1968 and 1970, but was followed by a revised Article V in 1972, which allowed for a merit system for filling interim vacancies by the governor and a judicial nominating commission, and a change to retention of appellate judges for the electorate.[411]

In January of 1967, State Representative Art Karst introduced a bill to expand the number of judges on the Fourth District from three to five. It was filed during a special session of the legislature for possible presentation at the next session.[412]Subsequently, the legislature did increase the number of judges from three to five.[413]

The Legislature moved the Fourth District Court of Appeal to Palm Beach County on May 8, 1967, effective July 1, 1967.[414] Judge Stikelether indicated that, unfortunately, in 1967, because of the efforts of politicians from Fort Pierce and West Palm Beach, the court was moved to Palm Beach County, where it still sits. Others have linked the move to the election.[415] Governor Kirk was from Palm Beach County.

The first Marshall was Sidney R. Johnson from Vero Beach, who accompanied the court when it moved to West Palm Beach. The first clerk while the court was in Vero Beach was Thomas Thatcher, followed by Stephanie Petrulak, Julia Maddox, the daughter of the county court judge from Okeechobee, Stephanie Petrulak (again), and then Evelyn R. Flack.

The last members of the Fourth District Court of Appeal in Vero Beach, which was increased to five members right before the Legislature moved it to Palm Beach County, consisted of the following: Chief Judge James H. Walden, Spencer C. Cross, David L. McCain, John A. Reed, Jr., and William C. Owen, Jr.

Judge Owen said the court, while based in Vero Beach, sat in the population centers of Orlando, West Palm Beach, Fort Lauderdale, and Titusville at least once a term. He also said that in the transition, when the courthouse was being built in West Palm Beach, several of the appellate judges maintained offices in Vero Beach while others, including himself, worked in temporary offices in West Palm Beach.

By January 1995, fifteen judges were serving in the First District Court of Appeal, fourteen in the Second District Court of Appeal, eleven in the Third District Court of Appeal, twelve in the Fourth District Court of Appeal, and nine in the Fifth District Court of Appeal.[416]

B. Biographies of the judges of the Fourth District Court of Appeal while the Court was located in Vero Beach

Sherman N. Smith, Jr., Fourth District Court of Appeal Judge, 1965-1967

Sherman N. Smith, Jr. was born in Crossville, Tennessee, on June 13, 1914, the son of Sherman N. Smith, Sr., who was born in Boatland, Tennessee, on September 15, 1887, and Birdie Bandy Smith, who was born in Crossville, Tennessee, on February 23, 1892.

Sherman's father practiced law in Vero Beach from 1925 until his death on January 22, 1958. Smith, Sr., graduated from Cumberland University Law School in the Class of 1914. He practiced law in

Crossville, Tennessee, where he also served as county judge until 1922, when he moved to Henrietta, Oklahoma. He came to Vero Beach in 1925.

Sherman N. Smith, Jr., graduated from Vero Beach High School in 1932 and attended Tennessee Polytechnic Institute, Cookeville, Tennessee, and Cumberland University Law School in Lebanon, Tennessee, where he received an LL.B. degree in 1935. (This law school has turned out many judges.)

He was admitted to the Florida Bar in 1935 and started practicing in Vero Beach with the law firm of Vocelle & Mitchell. He married Olive Heath in Vero Beach on August 22, 1937. Sherman was arguing before the Supreme Court by the time he was twenty-four. See, for example, Brown v. Indian River Orange Lands, 179 So. 789 (Fla. 1938), a case which Sherman won at the trial level and on appeal. (The following year, he argued another case before the Supreme Court of Florida, where the opposing counsel was his father!)

Soon, Vocelle and Mitchell became Mitchell, Smith & Mitchell. Later, it became Smith, Diamond & Heath when George Heath, Sherman's brother-in-law, joined the firm. Subsequently, it became Smith, Heath, Smith & O'Haire after Sherman was joined by his brother Charles, a future circuit court judge, and Sherman's son-in-law, Michael O'Haire. (See the biographical information on each one under the chapter on circuit judges and small claims court judges, respectively.) In his later years, Sherman N. Smith, Jr. practiced with his son, Sherman N. Smith, III, a third-generation attorney in Indian River County.

Sherman N. Smith, Jr. served as an officer in the United States Navy from September 1942 until January 1946 during World War II. He served in the amphibious forces in invasions of North Africa, southern France, and the Pacific. He received five major engagement stars for engagements in the European Theater and one in the Pacific Theater. He was one of the first Americans sent into Hiroshima following its bombing. He also received the Navy Unit Citation and the Commendation of the Secretary of the Navy. He was also a member of the American Legion and the Veterans of Foreign Wars, serving as one of its commanders.

Sherman N. Smith, Jr. was elected prosecuting attorney of Indian River County in 1940 and held the office for twelve years, including his time in the Navy. He was a member of the House of Representatives of the Florida Legislature from 1952 to 1956 and received the Allen Morris Award for being the most outstanding first-term member of the legislature.

In 1957, Smith led the effort to revitalize the Indian River County Bar Association, which had been dormant for years. He was elected president in that reorganization effort. The new board promised a comprehensive law library for the Indian River County courthouse and, through its effort, succeeded.

Sherman N. Smith, Jr., was attorney for the cities of Sebastian, Fellsmere, and Vero Beach and the Indian River Farms Drainage District. He also served as the president of the Vero Beach Kiwanis Club.

Sherman N. Smith Jr. was appointed to the Second District Court of Appeal in Lakeland in 1961 by Governor Farris Bryant. In 1963, Smith was elected as chief judge, becoming the youngest chief appellate judge in Florida at that time.

In 1965, he was appointed as chief judge of the newly created Fourth District Court of Appeal by Governor Haydon Burns. Smith literally set up the Fourth District Court of Appeal in Vero Beach, first at the Dudley Lock Company on Old Dixie Highway and then on the second floor of the Vero Beach City Hall. Smith served until 1967, when Republicans, led by the first Republican elected governor since Reconstruction, Claude Kirk, swept into office. However, the loss of such an outstanding jurist in a partisan election helped to change the law in order to allow for non-partisan elections at the lower level and judicial retention at the appellate level. Judge Smith is considered to be the only chief judge who served on two different courts of appeal.

Former county judge Graham W. Stikelether, Jr., an aide to Smith while he was on the bench, has noted that at one point, Smith was the

Chairman of the State Milk Commission. This was considered at the time to be one of Florida's most powerful offices.

Smith was married for over fifty years to Olive Heath, who died in 1991. The Smiths raised three children: Shirley Olive O'Haire, Attorney Sherman N. Smith, III, and Roger L. Smith. Shirley was married to Attorney Michael O'Haire, and they were the parents of Sherman's grandson, the first fourth-generation Indian River County lawyer, Sean O'Haire, who died in 2024.

Smith was a 50-year honoree of the Indian River County Bar Association, whose celebration took place in December 1985. The testimonial luncheon featured an address by former Governor Farris Bryant. The seconding remarks were made by James H. Walden, Judge of the Fourth District Court of Appeal, and James T. Vocelle, "Dean" of the Indian River County Bar Association.

Sherman N. Smith, Jr., delivered then Chief Circuit Judge L. B. Vocelle's keynote address for the dedication of the new Indian River County Courthouse. This occurred on Veterans Day, 1994.

Smith practiced law in Florida for 63 years, until shortly before his death on January 7, 1998, in Vero Beach. He was married at the time of his death to the former Joyce Whitfield Salter, who died on Sept 13, 2018. In December 1998, the City of Vero Beach nominated Smith for Great Floridians 2000, which he received, and his plaque is on the wall in the refurbished 14th Avenue Courthouse Executive Center.

Charles O. Andrews, Jr., Fourth District Court of Appeal Judge, 1965 to 1967

Charles O. Andrews, Jr. was the son of Charles O. Andrews, who was a former Walton County Criminal Court Judge and former circuit judge of the Seventeenth Judicial Circuit in the early 1920s, as well as U.S. Senator from Florida from 1935 to 1946. Charles O. Andrews, Jr.'s mother was Margaret Spears of Tallahassee. Her family was one of the first to settle in Florida after the purchase from Spain. Charles O. Andrews, Sr.'s parents were John and Mary Andrews. Charles O. Andrews, Sr.'s grandfather moved to Florida from the Carolinas when Florida was a territory and settled in the portion of Walton County which later became Holmes County. Charles O. Andrews, Sr.'s father was the treasurer of Holmes County and served in Clanton's Cavalry in the Confederate Army.

Judge Charles O. Andrews, Jr., received his undergraduate and law degrees from the University of Florida. He served in the Florida House of Representatives for Orange County in 1949 and 1951. He had been serving on the Second District Court of Appeal under Sherman N. Smith, Jr., when the Fourth District Court of Appeal was created in 1965, and continued to serve under Smith at the newly created Fourth District Court of Appeal in Vero Beach. Andrews returned to private practice on September 26, 1967. Spencer C. Cross (see below) described Judge Andrews as a fine gentleman.

Andrews died in 1969 and was survived by his wife, Mathilde Mizener "Mitzi" Andrews, and two sons, Charles O. Andrews III, of Winter Park, and David Andrews of Concord, Massachusetts.

James H. Walden, Fourth District Court of Appeal Judge, 1965 - 1976 (and 1982-1990).

James H. Walden was born on September 14, 1921, in Pinehurst, Georgia. He received his B.S. and B.A. degrees from the University of Florida and his law degree from that university in 1948. At the University of Florida, he was a member of Phi Delta Phi and was admitted to the Florida Bar in 1948.

Walden was City Attorney for Dania, Florida, from 1950 through 1955. He was a Circuit Judge of the Seventeenth Judicial Circuit (Fort Lauderdale) from 1955 to 1965. He was appointed to the first panel of judges on the Fourth District Court of Appeal when it was created. He was Chief Judge from 1967 to 1969. He resigned in 1976 to return to private practice because he needed a higher income to pay for the education of his five children. He was City Attorney for the City of Fort Lauderdale, Florida, in 1978 and Special Counsel for the City of Fort Lauderdale from 1978 to 1982.

In 1982, Governor Bob Graham reappointed Judge Walden to this same court. That was the first time since the judicial nominating process was instituted in Florida that a judge had been reappointed after resigning. He served again until December 31, 1990.

Judge Walden died on June 25, 1995. He was survived by his brother and law partner, Clarke Walden, and five children: James S. Walden of Montgomery, Alabama; Patricia W. Nader of Flat Rock, North Carolina; Frederick C. Walden of Jensen Beach, Florida; Cynthia W. Lanier of Orlando, Florida; and Robert L. Walden of West Palm Beach, Florida. A fitting Memorial Session for the Honorable James H. Walden held by the Fourth District Court of Appeal is published in the Southern Reporter Second Series, Vol 690-691.

Spencer C. Cross, Fourth District Court of Appeal Judge, 1967-1979

Spencer C. Cross was born on October 21, 1921, in Rutledge, Georgia (near Madison). His father was Cleve, and his mother, Estelle. Judge Cross grew up in Atlanta, Georgia, and attended the Fair Street (Public) School. (Fair Street is now known as Memorial Drive in Atlanta). He moved to Ocoee, Florida, in 1935 and graduated from Ocoee High School in 1941. He attended Rollins College in Winter Park, Florida, and attended summer sessions at Stetson University in DeLand. He received his law degree, a Juris Doctorate, from the University of Miami in May of 1953.

Prior to becoming a judge, Cross practiced in Ocoee and was the city attorney there for thirteen years. Cross, as a Republican, defeated Sherman N. Smith, Jr., for the Fourth District Court of Appeal position in the election of 1966 and became a member of the Fourth District Court of Appeal in January of 1967. Cross was Chief Judge of the Fourth District Court of Appeal from 1972 to 1974, and prior to that, was helpful in setting up the court when it moved from Vero Beach to West Palm Beach.

In 1979, the Fifth District Court of Appeal was created. Cross, who was planning to retire, was asked by Supreme Court Justice Arthur England to help set up the Fifth District Court of Appeal. Cross did this with the assistance of Judge Parker Lee McDonald (who went on to be a justice of the Florida Supreme Court). Cross retired from the Fifth District Court of Appeal on September 1, 1980, and returned to private practice in Ocoee, Florida. He died in Ocoee on March 12, 2008, and was buried in Fairplay, Ga.

John A. Reed, Jr., Fourth District Court of Appeal Judge,1967-1973

John Alton Reed, Jr. was born in Washington, D.C., on June 29, 1931, the son of John Alton and Emma Ball Reed. He was educated at Duke University, where he received his A.B. degree in 1954 and his LL.B. in 1956. There, he was a member of the Order of the Coif as well as the Duke University Law Journal. He was admitted to the Florida Bar in 1956.

Judge Reed initially practiced law in Tampa for a year. He then practiced for 10 years in Orlando, 1958-1967.

Judge Reed replaced Judge Charles O. Andrews, Jr. on the Fourth District Court of Appeal in 1967, taking office on October 2, 1967, where he served until 1973, the last two years of which he was the chief judge of that court. Thereafter, Reed was a United States District Court Judge for the Middle District of Florida from 1973 until 1984. He then practiced commercial law as a partner with the firm of Lowndes, Drosdick, Doster, Kantor and Reed, P.A. in Orlando for about 20 years. He retired to Sapphire, N.C., and died on February 19. 2015. He was survived by his wife of 61 years, Louisa nee Wardman, and three daughters, Donna Reed of Portland, Oregon, Joanne Reed of Fairfield, Iowa, and Debbie Martin of Naples, Florida, as well as grandchildren and great-grandchildren.

David L. McCain, Fourth District Court of Appeal Judge, 1967-1970

David Lucius McCain was born in Sebastian, Florida, on July 23, 1931. His house was located by the Indian River. It was allegedly once the location of some liquor smuggling by his father, R.G. Bob McCain. The same site was also the location of Sebastian Municipal

Court Judge Middleton's home, and subsequently, the McCain garage on the river became the site of Hurricane Harbor Restaurant.

David McCain was president and valedictorian of his class at Vero Beach High School, from which he graduated in 1949. In high school in 1948, his class picked him to attend "Boys State" at Tallahassee, which was sponsored by the local American Legion Post. He subsequently received his LL.B. in 1955 from the University of Florida, where he was a member of the Blue Key leadership fraternity, Hall of Fame, president of Kappa Sigma Social Fraternity, vice-president of Alpha Phi Omega, and a member of the honorary law fraternity, Phi Delta Phi.

From 1955 to 1957, he served as a captain in the U.S. Air Force. He was Assistant Staff Judge Advocate for Headquarters 30th Air Division and was active in court-martials, including the appellate review level. He received a commendation for his services from the Headquarters of the Air Force.

Justice McCain had eight children: Tamara Lee McCain, Cassandra Lynn McCain, Laurette Elaine McCain, Melanie McCain, David T. McCain, Diane Cossin, Karen Cossin, and Lucinda McCain. McCain worked in private practice in Ft. Pierce with retired Circuit Judge Thad Carlton under the name of Carlton and McCain. The firm later became known as Carlton, McCain, Brennan, and McAliley.

David McCain was appointed to the Fourth District Court of Appeal in 1967 and was elevated to the Supreme Court of Florida on December 14, 1970, each appointment being made by Governor Claude Kirk. The Supreme Court appointment followed McCain's unsuccessful candidacy for the Supreme Court in 1968. He was 39 when appointed, then the youngest Supreme Court justice in Florida history. He was elected over the opposition in 1972. On August 31, 1975, he resigned, following a threat of impeachment for improperly influencing decisions of lower courts.[417] McCain was disbarred on June 15, 1978. For additional background on Justice McCain, see The Florida Bar v. McCain, 361 So. 2d 700 (Fla. 1978).

Justice McCain's opinion in Mt. Sinai Hosp. of Greater Miami, Inc. v. Jordan, 290 So. 2d 484 (Fla. 1974), is cited in textbooks on the issue of consideration for a charitable pledge.[418]

McCain died on November 12, 1986, in Jacksonville, Florida, as a fugitive.[419] He was survived by his wife, Joyce, and their children.

William C. Owen, Jr., Fourth District Court of Appeal Judge,1967 - 1976

William C. Owen, Jr. was born on December 24, 1922, in Memphis, Tennessee. His parents were William Cecil Owen and Viola Foerg Owen, pioneer residents of Clewiston, Florida.

Owen's father was born in Brownsville, Tennessee. He graduated from the University of Tennessee in 1918 with a civil engineering degree and served as a Second Lieutenant in the Field Artillery during the First World War. Owen, Sr., came to Florida in 1925 and settled in Clewiston, where he was associated with Elliott and Harmon Engineering Company. Later, he was employed by the United States Sugar Corporation in Clewiston and, in about 1950, was named a vice president of that corporation in charge of engineering, transportation, and real estate. At the time of his death in October 1960, he was president of Clewiston Federal Savings and Loan Association and had been active in civic affairs throughout his many years of residence there.

Owen, Jr. graduated from Clewiston High School in 1939 and Tennessee Military Institute in Sweetwater, Tennessee, in 1940. He graduated from Tulane University in New Orleans, where he received his B.A. degree in 1944. He was also on the golf team. He served in the U.S. Navy from July 1943 to July 1946, where he was commissioned as an ensign and promoted to lieutenant (jg) and subsequently promoted to lieutenant after release from active duty. He received his law degree from the University of Florida in 1948. He was admitted to the Florida Bar in 1948. Owen practiced law in Clewiston for ten years before going to West Palm Beach to become a member of the firm of Miller, Hewitt, Cone, Owen and Wagner, later Miller, Cone, Owen, Wagner and Nugent, and Cone, Owen, Wagner, Nugent, Johnson & McKeown.

Owen was appointed to the Fourth District Court of Appeal in December 1967 by Governor Claude Kirk and served until April 30, 1976. He was Chief Judge from July 1, 1973, to June 30, 1975. After serving on the Fourth District, Owen returned to his old law firm and continued practicing for the next four and one-half years. That firm, which was very prominent, was Cone, Owen, Wagner, Nugent, Johnson & McKeown.

In 1981, Judge Owen retired from practice but, as a retired judge, served periodically on the First, Third, and Fourth District Courts of Appeal. In November 1982, Governor Bob Graham appointed him to the circuit court, where he served from November 1982 until August 1987, doing the reverse of most judges, who generally moved from a so-called lower court to a higher court. Judge Owen subsequently served as a senior judge at the appellate and circuit levels.

Owen married Phyllis Antoinette Eidson, the daughter of Frank Vinton and Phyllis (Murray) Eidson, in Thomasville, Georgia, on March 19, 1949. Mrs. Owen was a graduate of Thomasville High School and of Agnes Scott College at Decatur, Georgia, in the class of 1948. Mrs. Owen was a member of the Daughters of the American Revolution. Her father was a member of the Mayflower Society through the Vintons and John Alden, his New England ancestors.

Owen and his wife had four children: Antoinette, born January 12, 1951, in Pahokee, Florida; Claire, born September 17, 1952, in Clewiston, Florida; William C. Owen, III, born June 6, 1954, in Clewiston, Florida; and Frank Vinton Eidson Owen, born April 14, 1957, in West Palm Beach.

Judge Owen died on January 17, 2017, in West Palm Beach.

Chapter 12 - City of Vero Beach Municipal Court and Justices of the Peace

A. History of the Vero Beach Municipal Court

In addition to the county and circuit courts in Indian River County, which have been continuous since 1925, and the Fourth District Court of Appeal, which sat in Vero Beach from 1966 to 1967, there was a municipal court in the City of Vero Beach. (There were also municipal courts in the City of Sebastian, the Town of Fellsmere, and the Town of Indian River Shores).

Before getting to the Vero Beach Municipal Court, I should note that before Vero Beach was created in 1925 and Vero was created in 1919, there were Justices of the Peace and Justice of the Peace Courts and Dockets. (See Chapter 6, Florida Courts in General and Chapter 13, Fellsmere). Not much is known about the particular cases, but the Justices of the Peace for Vero and Vero Beach were as follows: G. C. Bartlett, 1917; C. G. Redstone, 1921 (resigned 1922). Paul H. Nisle, 1922 (resigned 1924) and Fred E. King, 1925, Alex MacWilliam, 1926, 1929, George W. Walland, 1939 (died in office), C. E. Cox, 1941 (filled a term), and Hamilton Floyd, 1945 -1953.

Municipal courts are not courts of general jurisdiction but are entirely local in nature and deal exclusively with the violation of city ordinances. The Florida Constitution, while generally prohibiting the legislature from passing local laws, allowed the legislature to regulate the practice of municipal courts by special or local laws.[420] Municipal courts were subsequently abolished, however, as set forth near the end of this chapter.

It has been noted that reference must be made to the applicable special or local act, and the municipal ordinances adopted pursuant thereto, for the jurisdiction of any particular municipal court.[421] The special acts creating this municipality and the other municipalities in Indian River County are consistent with the general statute allowing broad mayoral powers to see that city ordinances are enforced, which was first adopted in Section 25 of Chapter 1688 of the Laws of 1869.[422]

The City of Vero was created as a municipality by the Legislature of the State of Florida on June 10, 1919.[423] The Act gave the mayor the role of the judge of the municipal court.[424] In addition, one of the first ordinances of the newly created city prescribed the jurisdiction and procedure of the municipal court. This ordinance was passed on July 17, 1919.[425]

The city in the 1990s still had its Mayor's Docket for the years 1919 through 1940. The first case was a charge of "Fighting, Not in Self Defense." The plea was guilty, and a $10.00 fine was imposed by Mayor A. W. Young. Other typical charges during this period included exceeding the speed limit, drunkenness, and using profane language. The latter charge resulted on one occasion in Young imposing a $1.00 fine on August 30, 1920.

In 1921, S. E. Twitchell served as mayor pro tempore, as well as W. J. Maher, each of whom acted as municipal judge from time to time. From 1921 through 1923, while Fred E. King was mayor and judge of the court, charges often included "drunk and disorderly conduct."

In 1923, when Mayor B. T. Redstone took over, charges included parking overtime, which often resulted in a $2.00 fine, reckless driving, and "bathing in public with no suit." The latter charge resulted on one occasion in a disposition of "discharged with warning."

In September of 1927, "J.C.D.," who had to be J. C. DuBose, a city councilman, would fill in for Redstone. In 1928, Mayor Alex MacWilliam took over as municipal judge, and he continued in that capacity through June of 1931.

Alex MacWilliam, Sr.- Wikipedia

Vero Beach City Hall – Built in 1924
Courtesy of the Byron T. Cooksey, Esq. Collection

The city was reincorporated by the state in 1929.[426]The act provided, inter alia, that although the mayor was the judge of the municipal court, it also "Provided, however, that the City Council, with the written consent of or at the request of the Mayor, shall have the power to elect by a majority vote, a suitable person who shall preferably be a duly licensed and practicing attorney at law of said City and who shall also be a qualified electorate therein, to be a judge of the municipal court of the City of Vero Beach, ..."[427]

In 1931, Councilman L. A. Moeller often acted as mayor and judge for MacWilliam. City Court Clerk A. C. MacConnell often seemingly handled the disposition of cases where no mayor/judge's name appears on the docket. The May 29, 1933, entry for a charge of public drunkenness and fighting not in self-defense resulted in a disposition of "turned over to Judge Diamond," who was the county court judge.

In 1934, a City of Vero Beach ordinance was passed allowing the city council to elect by majority vote a suitable person, who should be a qualified electorate of the city, to be judge of the municipal court whose term shall be coextensive with the term of the office of the mayor, but who shall hold over until his successor shall be elected and qualified. The salary for the municipal judge was set at $35.00 per month.[428] The first non-mayor municipal judge elected by the council was Luster M. Merriman. The docket shows that he handled cases from December 2, 1935, through 1938. In 1938, C. R. McClure, a city councilman, is shown on the docket as the acting mayor. In March of 1939, Mayor W. F. Cox appeared as the mayor judge.

The first docket book ended as of April 15, 1940. There do not seem to be records at the city clerk's office of the charges and disposition of ordinance violations after that date.

In 1941, an ordinance was passed allowing the mayor or mayor pro tempore or another legally appointed person acting as municipal judge of the City of Vero Beach to receive the same compensation provided as was paid to the municipal judge.[429]

When the state reincorporated the city in 1941, the act[430] once again specified the mayor as municipal judge and also gave the council, with the written consent of the mayor, the right to appoint a licensed attorney, who had to be a resident of Vero Beach, as municipal judge. Even then, the mayor had the right to act as judge when the appointed licensed attorney/municipal judge was absent or ill.

The state reincorporated the city in 1943.[431] That act was similar to the 1941 and 1929 acts insofar as the municipal judge was concerned.

After Judge Merriman, the next licensed lawyer/municipal judge appears to be J. W. Boring, who commenced serving in 1947. A report for the first six months of his term of the municipal court for 1947 indicates a total of 82 municipal court cases were recorded. Penalties included over $3,500.00 in fines and forfeited bonds, and 174 days of imprisonment. Thirty-nine cases involved people found intoxicated within the city limits, and twenty-eight cases involved reckless driving. There were three cases of drunken driving, three alleged vagrants, three cases of assault and battery, two people fighting, one case of illegal possession of bolita tickets, and a concealed weapon charge. Another case involved the use of obscene and profane language, which was dismissed. The average intoxicated person was imprisoned for three days and fined $16.00.[432]

Judge Boring called his municipal court sessions to order every Monday morning.[433] He served until January 1948, when he joined

Judge Merriman, who was then the city attorney. They were appointed city attorneys by Mayor Merrill P. Barber and approved by the council. J. Pasco Woods was appointed successor municipal judge at that time.[434]

In 1949, an ordinance was passed fixing the witness fee for those summoned before the municipal court at $2.00 and $.05 per mile for actual distance traveled to and from said court.[435] (As a reference, the mileage rate for witnesses in Florida in the 1990s was $.06).[436]

In 1951, the city's charter was changed by the state to require that the municipal judge "be a practicing attorney-at-law in the City of Vero Beach, duly qualified to practice in the courts of the State of Florida, and a resident of Vero Beach, who shall be appointed by the council for a term of one year or until his successor is appointed and qualifies."[437] "The mayor shall be the acting municipal judge to preside over the municipal court in the absence or disqualification of the municipal judge."[438] In 1955, the salary of the municipal judge was set at $100.00 per month, to be paid semi-monthly.[439]

Another typical example of the municipal court would be the cases summarized in the following article appearing in the January 3, 1957, edition of the Vero Beach Press Journal:

Brief Session of Court Held

The lightest docket in months faced Municipal Court Judge John R. Gould on Monday, the last day of the old year, with but three persons receiving sentences. George A. Dent of Middlesex, Ontario, Canada, was fined $25.00 for reckless driving by failure to yield right-of-way, causing an accident. Albert Kersey of Vero Beach was sentenced to serve two days in jail for public drunkenness. Robert Jordan McLemore of Radford, Virginia, was sentenced to one and one-half days in jail for public drunkenness.

A list of those Mayors acting as Judge and the subsequent non-Mayor Municipal Judges is set forth below:

Municipal Judges	
1919 – 1921	A. W. Young
1921 – 1923	Fred E. King
1923 – 1927	B. T. Redstone
1927 – 1934	Alex MacWilliam
1934 – 1938	Luster Merriman (non-mayor)
1935 – 1937	A. W. Young
1937 – 1939	W. F. Cox
1940 – 1947	Alex MacWilliam

(Not set forth above are acting mayors or mayors pro tempore that acted as municipal judges, which included S. E. Twitchell, W. J. Maher, J. C. DuBose, and L. A. Moeller).

Practicing Attorney Judges	
1947 – 1948	J. W. Boring
1948 – 1950	J. Pasco Woods
1951 – 1952	J. W. Boring
1953	Cornelius Walker
1954	R. S. Swing
1955 – 1956	John R. Gould
1957	Miles B. Mank, II
1958	Charles A. Sullivan
1959 – 1969	Charles E. Smith
1969 - 1977[440]	George G. Collins, Jr.

As noted in the preceding endnote, municipal courts in Florida were abolished in favor of the applicable county court by a change in the Florida Constitution approved by the voters in 1972, effective January 3, 1977, although most municipal courts in major populations were abolished on January 1, 1973.

B. Biographies of Justices of the Peace from Vero Beach

G. C. Bartlett, Vero Justice of the Peace, 1917

G.C. Bartlett was born in Illinois around 1884. In the 1910 Census, he was living in Chicago with his wife, Emma, who was from

Pennsylvania, and his son, Stuart. By the 1920 Census, he was living in Vero, and he had his mother-in-law, Mary Wheaton, living with them as well. They were neighbors of Paul Nisle, discussed below. Bartlett had become a Justice of the Peace for Vero on Sept. 15, 1917, seemingly taking the place of Larry Silas that same month.

A City Directory for Ft. Pierce in 1918 shows the Bartletts living in Vero, and he is the secretary to the St. Lucie Lumber and Supply Co. The 1935 State Census shows G. C. Bartlett and his wife living in Vero Beach, and he is a hardware merchant.

When Bartlett's son, Stuart, registered for the draft for World War II, he indicated that not only was his father, Gordon Cecil Bartlett, his contact, the son's place of employment was Bartlett Lumber and Supply Co., Vero Beach. That business was once located on Dixie Avenue and 19th Place. Its telephone number was 3.

C. G. Redstone, Vero Justice of the Peace, 1921,1922

See B. T. Redstone, Mayor Judge of Vero Beach, biography, as his father, C. G. (Charles Gilbert), is covered quite a bit in it. C. G. was Justice of the Peace for Vero as of Sept 12. 1921, but resigned on June 12, 1922.

Paul H. Nisle, Vero Justice of the Peace, 1922-1924

Nisle was born in Oshkosh, WI, in August of 1875. He married Ida Peters of Sterling, Ill., and lived in Chicago, where his son Paul, Jr. was born Sept 20, 1906. His daughter, Marcia, was born there as well. The family moved to Florida, first to Dunnellon, Marion County, in 1912, where he established the Marion County Advocate. They moved to Vero in 1919, and he founded and was the editor of the Vero Press, which he owned with a few others.

In May of 1922, he sold his interest in the newspaper but purchased the insurance agency of L.A. Moeller. Nisle was appointed Justice of the Peace by Governor Hardee on June 15, 1922. Later that summer, on August 31, tragedy struck as son Paul died while trying to save his 13-year-old sister, Marcia, in the ocean in Vero. She survived.

In November of that year, Paul and his wife built a house where the parking garage is for the present courthouse on 16th Ave. He passed the bar in 1923 and had a law office in the Seminole Building, where the first Indian River County Court would be located. He had numerous ads in the local newspaper and sometimes under the name of Nisle and Vocelle, as in James T. Vocelle, mentioned in other chapters. That firm became the county's first prosecuting law firm in 1925.

On March 11, 1932, his wife died, and later that year, Paul died of a heart attack at age 52, on Nov 26, 1932, in Chicago. His daughter was then living in Chicago. After a service was held there, his body was shipped to Vero Beach for a funeral at the First Baptist Church, and then he was buried with his wife in the Ft. Pierce Cemetery.

Fred E. King, Vero Beach Justice of the Peace, 1925

See his bio under VB Mayor Judges

Alex MacWilliam. Vero Beach Justice of the Peace, 1926,1929

See his bio under VB Mayor Judges.

George W. Walland, Vero Beach Justice of the Peace, 1939

Walland was the Justice of the Peace for Vero Beach, commencing May 1, 1939. He died while in office.

C. E. Cox, Vero Beach Justice of the Peace, 1941

Charles E. "Cephus" Cox was born in Tibbee, Mississippi, in 1897. When his mother passed away, the unpleasant mortuary experience prompted him to take an interest in that business. He first lived in Florida in Lakeland and then in Ft. Pierce, where he worked for a funeral home. In 1930, he started his own funeral home in Vero Beach, apparently Vero's first. He was known for having a funeral license 13, issued by the State of Florida. J. Charles Gifford joined him and was married to Cephus's daughter, Margaret, in 1957. The then Cox Gifford Funeral Home had various additional names over the years, but still exists as Cox Gifford Seawinds.

Cox's term as Justice of the Peace for Vero Beach commenced Jan 7, 1941. Prior to that time, W. F. Cox, Mayor Judge of Vero Beach, described in this chapter, was mayor at the same time that Cephus Cox was on the Vero Beach City Council in 1937, and Cephus was reelected in 1939. However, I don't see where they were related.

Mr. Cephus Cox was very active in his community and, among other things, helped purchase the land to become Crestlawn Cemetery. Mr. Cox died in December 1990 in his early age of 90. He is buried in Crestlawn Cemetery. His wife, Esther, predeceased him in May 1973 and is also buried in Crestlawn.

Hamilton H. Floyd, Vero Beach Justice of the Peace, 1945-1949

Hamilton Hopkins Floyd was born in St. Augustine, Florida, on Jan. 12, 1914. In 1938, he married Lillian Maxine Hicks (1920-1980). In 1995, he married Betty Jo Davenport (1930-2001).

He moved to Vero Beach from Lake Worth and, in 1942, opened Floyd Funeral Home on the corner of 19th Place and 15th Ave. In the late 1940s, he acquired the Cox Funeral Home (Cox would later get back in the business) and continued to operate Floyd Funeral Home on the 1150 block of 20th St. In 1957, the funeral home was located in a new facility at 2405 14th Ave, where it remained for the next 26 years. Glenn Strunk joined Mr. Floyd in 1972. In 1973, Glenn became a part owner, and the name was changed to Floyd Strunk Funeral Home. By 1983, Mr. Floyd had retired, and the funeral home was relocated to 17th St. and as Strunk Funeral Home.

Mr. Floyd was a two-term Justice of the Peace for Vero Beach, with terms from 1945 to 1949. He was likely the last Justice of the Peace from Vero Beach, as the Justices of the Peace were abolished in Florida after that. See Chapter 6.

Mr. Floyd died in Roseland on March 25, 1998, at age 84, and is buried in Crestlawn Cemetery.

C. Biographical Information on Municipal Judges for the City of Vero or Vero Beach

A. W. Young, Vero Municipal Court Judge, 1919-1921 and 1935-1937

State Senator A. W. "Uncle Tony" Young was born on July 27, 1865, in Godfrey, Illinois. He married Irene Daley of Delhi, Illinois, in 1892. He served as Mayor of Alton, Illinois, prior to moving to Vero Beach in 1912. He was associated with H. J. Zeuch in the Indian River Farms Drainage District Development as sales manager after the drainage of much of what is now Indian River County. Mr. Young served several terms in the Florida House and Senate. He planted several hundred acres of citrus and was the first person to grow sea island cotton in this area. He also promoted the growing of sugar cane.

He was active in promoting the City of Vero Beach, serving as its first mayor in 1919 and was reelected for several terms. He served in Army Intelligence during World War I and was a member of the American Legion, Elks, and a 32nd Degree Mason. While in the legislature, he was instrumental in creating Indian River and Martin counties.

After the 1928 hurricane, he was appointed to the Everglades Drainage District to supervise the construction of dikes around Lake Okeechobee. The U.S. Secretary of Agriculture appointed him to represent the Indian River District on the Growers Administrative Commission, where he served for several years. He was also president of the Indian River Citrus League.

When Young was again elected to the office of mayor, succeeding retiring Mayor Alex MacWilliam on December 10, 1935, he defeated W. F. Cox by a vote of 357 to 354. It was and still is the closest election ever held in the county.[441] Young also operated the Vero Del Mar Hotel for four years before selling it in 1947.

Young died on June 12, 1948. He was survived by his wife, Mrs. Irene D. Young, and two adopted children: George Toohey Young, then of Vero Beach; and Mrs. Ada L. Marks, then of Detroit, Michigan; a brother, Charles W. of Vero Beach; two sisters, Mrs. W. P. Didlake of Alton, Illinois, and Mrs. Margaret Kelly of Curlew, Washington.

Fred E. King, Vero Municipal Court Judge, 1921-1923

Fred E. King was born in Stratford, England, in 1869. He came to this country as a child, settling in Detroit with his family.

In 1887, he married Miss Effie E. Perine and moved to Norfolk, Virginia, where he engaged in the manufacturing business as the Fred E. King company, manufacturing blow pipes and sheet metal products. He retired from that business in 1917 and then moved to Vero Beach, where he acquired property and became a U.S. citizen.

King took an active interest in community affairs and served as the first secretary of the Chamber of Commerce. He was elected mayor of Vero, serving from December 15, 1921, to December 15, 1923. During his administration, the foundation was laid for the present municipality of Vero Beach. The first building to house the municipal light plant was built, the city water works system was established, the first storm sewers were laid, Pocahontas Park was acquired, and a park board was created. The fire department was also organized, and the first motor-driven equipment was purchased. The city hall was built, and street paving was carried out in Edgewood Addition and Osceola Park, and other sections of the city.

King was a member of the Masonic order, a member of the Khedive Temple Shriners, the Rotary Club, and the United Commercial Travelers. He was an elder in a Presbyterian church in Norfolk, Virginia. For the two years preceding his death, he was a sales manager for Brook Sheet Metal Works in Norfolk.

King died April 27, 1931. He was survived by his widow, Effie E. King, a cousin, Horace Kindrick of Detroit, a nephew, Fred Bradley of Detroit, and two nieces, Mareita King of Detroit and Mareita Tudor of Vero Beach.

B. T. Redstone, Vero Beach Municipal Court Judge, 1923-1927

Bayard Taylor Redstone was born on March 13, 1879, in Tracy Mills, New Brunswick, Canada. His father was Charles Gilbert "C. G." Redstone, whose family had migrated to New Brunswick from the Isle of Whyte in Great Britain. C. G. Redstone married Alice A. Taylor on February 3, 1878. The Taylor family had originally come from Aberdeen, Scotland. C. G. Redstone and his wife, Alice, had four children, including B.T., by 1885, when they moved to Olean, New York. There, they had two daughters who died during infancy. In 1892, Alice died, and C. G. married her sister, Angelina, "Ann." They had one child, Harold Gilbert Redstone, who was born in 1895.

C. G. Redstone built refineries and tanneries in the Olean area. Son, B.T., was employed at the tannery as a record keeper because of his high school degree. C. G. Redstone also worked with his brother-in-law, B. U. Taylor, who was a general contractor in the Olean area and subsequently in West Virginia, where they built a sawmill. By 1903, C. G. and his wife, Ann, and son, Harold, followed Ann's cousin, Eugene Spiller, to Eau Gallie, Florida. Mr. Spiller had moved there for health reasons. In Eau Gallie, C.G. Redstone built houses. Son, Ray, soon joined his father.

In 1910, Redstone signed a contract to build a bridge over the Sebastian River. The contract was with both St. Lucie and Brevard counties, which were separated by the Sebastian River at that time. B. T. Redstone, who married Anna Marie Jeffries of Brooklyn, New York, in 1911 and honeymooned in Florida, joined his father and brother, Ray, working on the bridge. Earlier, during construction, a hurricane in 1910 scattered the pilings, and the Redstones were left without a lumber source as the Roseland Sawmill Company was destroyed as well. The Redstones improvised and made a sawmill for the project. The sawmill was then moved to Vero.

In 1915, B. T.'s father started the Redstone Lumber & Supply Company, which operated on the east side of the railroad tracks in Vero. Old timers remember "B. T." driving an ox team hauling lumber from west of the city to the Redstone sawmill. At one point, the

Redstones had thirty-six teams of oxen that would haul lumber from the north part of the county back to the railroad tracks in Vero Beach. The store was located just south of 20th Street, with the front door on 14th Avenue and the back door on Old Dixie Highway. The sawmill later burned down, but the family, including B. T., continued to operate the hardware store that went with the sawmill.

C. G. Redstone was president of the first Vero City Council (in conjunction with Mayor Young). His son, Harold Gilbert Redstone, was city clerk from 1923 until 1933. While B. T.'s father was the first president of the <u>Vero</u> City Council when the city was incorporated in 1919, the City of <u>Vero Beach</u> was created in 1925 while B. T. was the mayor. The city name was changed because the city annexed the beach in 1925. B. T. served as mayor from 1923 to 1927.

B. T. Redstone also served as a state representative in 1919, was an organizer and Master of the Masonic Lodge, was a Scottish Rite Mason, and a member of the Woodmen of the World.

As noted above, B. T. was married to Anna Marie Jeffries. She was a philanthropist who had connections, having been married into the politically active Redstone family, which included C. G., B. T., and Harold Redstone. She died in 1926. No children were born of that marriage. A small park across from St. Helen Church on State Road 60, Redstone Park, was dedicated to her memory. The park existed for a long time with a marker and a beautiful Phoenix Reclinata Palm, prior to the creation of the State Road 60 "twin pairs" in approximately 1992.

B. T. remarried in about 1928. He and his wife, the former Alice Weeks Milkins, had no children, although she had a child from a prior marriage, Charlotte Milkins, who married John Adkins of Vero Beach.

B. T. died on September 17, 1969, and was survived by his wife, one brother, Harold G., and two grandchildren.

Alex MacWilliam, Sr., Vero Beach Municipal Court Judge, 1927-1934 and 1940-1947

Alex MacWilliam, Sr., was born in Edinburgh, Scotland, on May 11, 1891. He came to this country and to Cleveland, Ohio, with his parents in 1907.

In World War I, he served as a First Lieutenant of Infantry, with the 316th Machine Gun Battalion in France. He was wounded in both legs and received the Distinguished Service Cross, the Silver Star, the Purple Heart (twice), and the French Croix de Guerre. Sent home to Cleveland to recover from his wounds, he was advised by his doctors to go to the Vero area, which he did in 1919, arriving on a stretcher carried in a rowboat. When he had recuperated, Mr. MacWilliam stayed on to manage and develop Riomar, one of Vero's finest areas, which at that time was called Cleveland Colony. Versed in landscape architecture, he designed and built a golf course for the Riomar Club and built the club building as well. He supervised the construction of many beautiful homes in this area, and from that time on, until his retirement in 1951, he was active in real estate. (At least three more generations of Alex MacWilliams would specialize in real estate in Vero Beach.)

In 1920, he married Jeanette O'Flaherty, an immigrant from Galway, Ireland. They lived in one of the first houses in Riomar and had 8 children: Edgar, Bill, Alex, Jr., Helen MacWilliam, Glenn, Joan MacWilliam Schardt, Peter, Barbara MacWilliam Fultz, and Robert. Alex MacWilliam, Sr., was a member of St. Helen Catholic Church, American Legion, Veterans of Foreign Wars, and the local chapter of Veterans of World War I. He was a past commander of Felix Poppell Post #39.

Alex MacWilliam was eminent in government on various levels. Three times he was mayor of Vero Beach: from 1927 to 1935, from 1939 to 1945, and from 1949 to 1951. He was also one of the founders of Indian River County. In 1925, as a city council member, he was a leader in the fight to create a new county from the northern part of St. Lucie County. He made, with others, the locally famous train trip to Tallahassee to argue for a separate county.

MacWilliam felt that an independent county, with its own Mosquito Control District, was necessary for the development of the

Indian River area as a tourist attraction and for permanent residents. In 1925, he saw his dream come true. Indian River County was established, together with the Indian River County Mosquito Control District, the first such district in the state. It was modeled after a mosquito control district in New Jersey. MacWilliam served as president of the Mosquito Control District on several occasions.

The very name, "Indian River County," so closely associated with the finest citrus in the world, is credited to MacWilliam. It was MacWilliam's thinking that the name, "Indian River County," would be very valuable to the area's citrus industry, because of the already-famous reputation of Indian River fruit. MacWilliam went on to be a member of the Florida House of Representatives, serving in 1933, and then again in 1945 to 1951.

Alex MacWilliam died on August 13, 1966. His son, Alex MacWilliam, Jr., is mentioned in the Chapter on the Town of Indian River Shores.

A monument with a plaque at Memorial Island is dedicated to Alex MacWilliam's memory. There is a profile of MacWilliam and the inscription: "In Memory of Alexander MacWilliam Sr., whose Efforts and Inspiration Founded the Beautiful Memorial Sanctuary - Dedicated to those who paid the Supreme Sacrifice. May he Walk Through These Paths of Beauty Forever. 1967."

<u>Luster M. Merriman, Vero Beach Municipal Court Judge, 1934-1938</u>

See biographical information listed under the chapter on County Judges.

<u>Wiley Festus Cox, Vero Beach Municipal Court Judge, 1937-1939</u>

W. F. Cox was born in Taylor County, Florida, on August 14, 1895. He moved to Vero with his family in 1904. He attended normal school and became a schoolteacher, teaching at Fort Drum and serving as principal of a school in Pasco County. While continuing his education at the University of Florida, he met and married his wife, Fannie.

During World War I, Cox served in France, Germany, and Austria with the U.S. Army. Upon his return, he joined his father in the mercantile business. Eventually, there were Cox Grocery Stores in Vero Beach, Winter Beach, and Wabasso. He sold them about the time World War II started.

Cox was also a citrus grower from about 1928 and was active in politics, serving at one time as chairman of the County Democratic Committee. He was the chairperson of the Indian River County Mosquito Control District. He was mayor of Vero Beach from December 1937, when he was elected without opposition, through December 1939. He was secretary, treasurer, and superintendent of plant and operations for the Indian River Farms Drainage District for about twenty-five years, retiring in 1969. He also served as pastor of the Indian River Church of the Primitive Baptist Faith and Order in Winter Beach until his death. His pastorship lasted about thirty-five years.

Cox died in Vero Beach on January 31, 1978. Survivors included his wife, Fannie, two daughters, Frances Lindsey of Vero Beach and Clemmie Law of Satellite Beach, ten grandchildren, and five great-grandchildren.

Frances Lindsey worked for the Vero Beach law firm of Mitchell, Smith, and Mitchell, and subsequently for Ken Sharp, as a legal assistant. Her three children included Bobby Lindsey, Patricia Hayes, and Jean Lindsey.

J. W. "Bill" Boring, Vero Beach Municipal Court Judge, 1947-1948

Bill Boring was born on May 24, 1912, in Lakeland, Florida. He graduated from the University of Florida, receiving his B.S. in Business Administration in 1935 and an LL.B. in 1936. Boring was a member of the Florida Blue Key leadership fraternity. He served his country during World War II in the Third Corps Artillery of the U.S. Army and received a Bronze Star, American Defense Medal, and the EAMET Service Medal.

Boring came to Vero Beach to practice with Luster M. Merriman. Boring served as a municipal judge for Vero Beach from 1947 to 1949 and again in 1951 and 1952. Boring was president of the Indian River County Bar Association from 1964 to 1965. He was a city attorney for Vero Beach and chairperson of the Uniform Title Standards for the Property, Probate, and Trust sections of The Florida Bar. He was the president of the Kiwanis Club. He was listed in the Bar Registry of Preeminent Counsel from 1965 to 1967. He practiced with the law firm of Merriman, Boring & Sutherland and opened his own office in the early 1960's where he was soon joined by his son, James L. Boring.[442] They practiced under the name of Boring & Boring until 1966.

J. W. Boring died on November 1, 1966, in Vero Beach, Florida. He was survived by his wife, Mary, who died in 1998, his son, and his daughter, Joyce Boring Brown of King George County, Fredericksburg, Virginia.

Boring's widow, Mary, and her sister, Wilma Christianson, are the daughters of Pearl Newman. Pearl Newman is noted for her publication, "Early Life on the Indian River," published in 1953.

J. Pasco Woods, Vero Beach Municipal Court Judge, 1948-1950

See bibliographic information under Small Claim Judges, supra.

<u>Cornelius "Cory" Walker, Vero Beach Municipal Court Judge, 1954</u>

Cornelius Walker was born on July 15, 1921, in Baltimore, Maryland. He was educated at Loyola College in Baltimore, Maryland, graduating in 1942. He then attended officer cadet school, known as the six-week wonder course, at Notre Dame and served in the United States Navy as a lieutenant (jg) in World War II.

Walker received his law degree from the University of Florida in about 1947. He first worked in Tallahassee for James T. Vocelle, then the chairman of the Florida Industrial Commission, and subsequently followed Vocelle to Vero Beach in the early 1950s. Walker practiced briefly with Vocelle and was then in private practice, and practiced with Miles Mank. He was a member of St. Helen Church, the Elks Club, Serra International, Veterans of Foreign Wars, and the American, Florida, and Indian River County Bar Associations. He was the second president of the Indian River County Library Association, taking office in 1959.

Walker died on December 25, 1966, at age 45. He was survived by his wife, Marie J., who died on October 3, 1993. He was also survived by their seven children: Veronica Hackett, Cheryl Ann Walker, Margaret Lupfer, Diane Lembo of Vero Beach, Cornelius Walker, Jr., Denise Heuston, and Clare Walker-Dupree.

R. S. Swing, Vero Beach Municipal Court Judge, 1954

R.S. Swing aka R.S. Swing, Jr., was born in Kansas City, Missouri, on October 4, 1918. He was the son of Roy Swing, Sr., who was born on March 10, 1884, and died in Vero Beach, Florida, on July 2, 1959. R.S. Swing Jr's mother was Elizabeth M. Swing. R. W. Swing, Jr.'s grandfather was Tillford C. Swing, and his grandmother (on his father's side) was Ida Stewart.

Swing was a graduate of the University of Missouri Law School and practiced law in Orlando before the war. He served in the U.S. Army in World War II for three and one-half years, two of which were overseas, including North Africa.

Swing moved to Vero Beach following World War II, locating in the Seminole Building. Swing practiced abstract and title law. Swing worked with O. O. Summer in connection with the East Coast Title Company, as well as in solo private practice. His office was subsequently located in the Pocahontas Building. In 1954, the city council appointed him as municipal judge for Vero Beach. Swing was a bachelor all his life and was active in the Veterans of Foreign Wars.

Swing was an avid golfer and fisherman, essentially achieving his goal of retiring from the practice of law at age forty and spending many years on the golf course (Vero Beach Country Club). His lady friend for the last thirty-five years of his life was Ethel MacIntyre.

Judge Swing died on July 1, 1979, in Miami. He was survived by his brother, David, of Lee's Summit, Missouri.

John R. Gould, Vero Beach Municipal Court Judge, 1955-1956

John Rockwell Gould was born in Chicago, Illinois, on October 15, 1921. He moved to Florida with his family as a teenager and graduated from Stuart High School in 1939. He served on an aircraft carrier in the U.S. Navy during World War II and was honorably discharged in 1945. He was awarded a Purple Heart for injuries suffered when his plane crashed into the North Atlantic on takeoff from a carrier.

Gould completed his undergraduate studies at Stetson University in 1947 and received his Bachelor of Laws at Stetson in 1948. John was admitted to practice in Florida on December 20, 1948, and began his practice at the law firm of Mitchell, Smith, and Mitchell, for which he had clerked during the fall of that year. In 1955, he left that firm and opened his own office at 2908 Ocean Drive (near Corey's Pharmacy), which was the first law firm on Vero's beach (barrier island). In 1960, Gould was President of the Indian River County Bar Association. In 1962, B. T. Cooksey joined Gould and Darrell Fennell to form Gould, Cooksey & Fennell.

Gould was a judge for the Vero Beach Municipal Court from 1955 to 1957 and was a member of the Florida Municipal Judges

Association, an organization now defunct. He was also the attorney for both the Indian River County Commissioners and the City of Vero Beach. He served as county prosecuting attorney from 1957 to 1965 and was a member of the Selective Service Board from 1958 to 1968. Gould was a member of the Board of Governors of the Florida Bar from 1969 to 1974.

Gould was a fellow of the American College of Probate Counsel and a director of the Florida Bar Foundation from 1974 through 1976. He was a director of the Beach Bank of Vero Beach, which became Northern Trust, and a director of The Florida National Bank.

Gould was married to the former Jean Trigg and raised six children: Janie Gould, Susan Gould Price, Stanton Gould, Attorney James Gould, Attorney Margaret Gould Thessin, and Charles Gould, CPA. Mr. Gould died on December 14, 1988. At that time, his firm was known as Gould, Cooksey, Fennell, Appleby, Barkett & O'Neill, P.A.

Miles B. Mank, II, Vero Beach Municipal Judge, 1957

See bibliographical information under County Court Judges, <u>infra</u>.

Charles A. Sullivan is being sworn in by Judge D.C. Smith
Courtesy of Charles A. Sullivan Family

Charles A. Sullivan, Vero Beach Municipal Court Judge, 1958

Charles Anderton Sullivan was born September 19, 1932, at Hastings-On-Hudson, New York, but grew up in Miami, where he graduated from Edison High School. He attended the College of William and Mary, Florida State University, and the University of Miami. He earned his law degree from the University of Miami in 1957 and came to Vero Beach to practice law with the law firm of Vocelle, Vocelle & Sullivan. In 1961, he established his own firm,

Sullivan & Burch. Mr. Sullivan's law firm name has evolved over the years and was known for years as Sullivan & Sullivan, where he practiced with his son, Charles A. "Chuck" Sullivan, Jr.

Sullivan was the city judge of Vero Beach from 1958 to 1960, the youngest at the time in the state. He was also a judge of the small claims court of Indian River County from 1960 to 1964.

Charles was a highly successful attorney and was in great demand from many clients. He also developed a lot of properties, including popular commercial spots throughout the county.

Charles Sullivan passed away on Nov. 8, 2023. He was married to the former Henrietta MacConnell, who predeceased him and whose father, A. C. MacConnell, was Clerk of the City of Vero Beach 1933-1951. The Sullivans had three other children besides Chuck: Michael (1955-2021), Kathleen Sullivan, and Patricia Sullivan Radford.

Charles E. Smith, Vero Beach Municipal Court Judge, 1959-1969

See biographical information under Circuit Judges, supra.

George G. Collins, Jr., Vero Beach Municipal Court Judge, 1969-1977

George G. "Joe" Collins, Jr., was born in Hanover, New Hampshire, on March 18, 1943, and admitted to the Florida Bar in

1968. He graduated from Rollins College with a B.A. in 1965 and received his Juris Doctorate in 1968 from Stetson University. He was a municipal judge for Vero Beach from 1970 to 1977 and county attorney from 1976 to 1981.

He handled the start of the first jury trial in the history of the Vero Beach Municipal Court on January 14, 1971. In December 1970, the Vero Beach City Council authorized jury trials on demand. In this case, two of the three defendants changed their plea midway through the trial, and a third defendant was *nol prossed*.

Collins was president of the Indian River County Bar Association in 1979 and is a board-certified real estate lawyer. He is married to the former Mary Schmidt, who came from Sarasota, Florida. They have two sons: George ("Geoff") G. Collins, III, a local dentist, and R. Scott Collins, an attorney who has an LL.M. from the University of Florida and practices in Sarasota. "Joe" Collins also has a daughter-in-law, Edith E. Collins, wife of Geoff Glover Collins, III, who practices law in Vero Beach.

Joe Collins has been a principal in his law firm for over 50 years, whose firm is currently called Collins Brown Barkett, Chartered.

Chapter 13 - Town of Fellsmere Municipal Court and Justices of the Peace

A. History of Fellsmere Courts

Prior to the development of Fellsmere, the land upon which Fellsmere is situated was known as Cincinnatus Farms. Anthony O. Russell, inventor of Bicycle Playing Cards and owner of Cincinnatus Farms Company, built the Sebastian and Cincinnatus Farms Railroad in 1896 near the headwaters of the St. Johns River. The Cincinnatus Farms Company excavated 34 miles of canals to drain thousands of acres of swampland with the intent of selling five and ten-acre farms with access only by rail.[443]

In the years 1907 and 1908, torrential rains covered Cincinnatus Farms with three feet of water. Drainage was too costly, and the railroad shut down. Shortly thereafter, E. Nelson Fell, a native of New Zealand and a former mining engineer, took on the challenge to reclaim submerged lands. In March 1910, he and his wife, Anne, purchased 118,000 acres of Cincinnatus Farms property, which was then in St. Lucie County. Nelson Fell and colleague, Oscar Crosby, formed the Fellsmere Farms Company on May 23, 1910. The Fellsmere Farms Company excavated, drained, and plotted tracts for three different areas known as Fellsmere, Broadmoor, and Grassland. Grassland was never developed. Broadmoor, located approximately five miles west of Fellsmere, was developed in 1914 but ceased to exist in 1920 as a town. It was officially vacated by the Indian River Board of County Commissioners on December 2, 2008. Despite a devastating flood in 1915 and subsequent years, Fellsmere managed to survive.

The first newspaper for Fellsmere, and for that matter the future Indian River County, The Fellsmere Farmer, came into existence on February 21,1912. It became the Fellsmere Tribune in January 1914. When the town became incorporated on May 12, 1915, it was the first in Florida to permit women to vote in city elections.[444] This predated the Nineteenth Amendment to the U.S. Constitution by five years. The Nineteenth Amendment was known as the "Women's Suffrage" amendment because it gave women the unconditional right to vote in all elections in all States.

Fellsmere City Attorney, Patrick Alexander Vans Agnew, who was also the former City Attorney of Kissimmee, the Fellsmere Farms Company attorney, and principal attorney for Vans Agnew & Crawford in Jacksonville, Florida, drafted the Town of Fellsmere charter.[445]

Mr. Vans Agnew married Marian Fell, who was E. Nelson and Anne Fell's oldest daughter, on June 9, 1914. It was after her that the Marian Fell Library in Fellsmere was named. The library opened its doors on May 1, 1915. In 2014, the library was completely restored by the City of Fellsmere.

While P. A. Vans Agnew is likely more famous in this day and age for being ahead of his time concerning women's suffrage, P. A. Vans Agnew received notoriety at the time for being backwards in his thinking. In 1908, P. A. Vans Agnew was the City Attorney for Kissimmee and helped draft a city ordinance to regulate the speed of airplanes over Kissimmee, which might otherwise scare animals. The ordinance, which was not passed, received international headlines, including "Mayor Takes Time by Forlock."[446]

It is also interesting to note the coincidence that Attorney Vans Agnew had a brother, Frank Vans Agnew, postmaster of Kissimmee, who married Marian Fell's youngest sister, Olivia.[447]

Justice of the Peace Court

Before getting to the Chief Commissioner Courts and the Municipal Courts for Fellsmere described below, it should be noted that, at least by 1914, there was a Justice of the Peace Court. As mentioned in a previous chapter, the Justice of the Peace (JP) was required to keep a docket. While the Fellsmere City Clerk does not seem to have the judicial records of the Commissioner's Court or the Mayor Judge Municipal Court, the Clerk has the docket from the Justice of the Peace Court.

The docket book is pretty interesting. It runs from November 11, 1914, to April 1935 and covers the 14th District of the Justice of the Peace Court when Fellsmere was a part of St. Lucie County, and then it becomes the 3rd District when Fellsmere is in Indian River County in 1925. The first case on Nov. 11 shows the Justice of the Peace as C. W. Talmadge, and that is as Justice of the Peace and not as Chief Commissioner (which he soon would become). He would wear two hats, it seems, although there were limits by the State of Florida to what other offices a JP could hold. The other JPs that appear in the docket book for Fellsmere are Alfred P. Ivory, F. W. Dole, and P. H. McEachron, the latter being after he was a mayor judge, as shown further below.

There were some interesting matters on the docket, which included:

11/11/14 State v A. Jackson, Assault with a Deadly Weapon. Found guilty and fined $5.00 plus costs by Justice of the Peace, C.W. Talmadge.

5/31/20 State of Florida v Ralph Conner, Murder as per finding of Coroner's Jury, (which preceded this arraignment, each handled by Justice of the Peace, Alford L Ivory), and the plea was not guilty and the defendant was "committed in custody of the sheriff to the Jail of St. Lucie County, at Fort Pierce, Florida, there to remain until this case is tried and disposed of by the Court – as provided by Law."

3/3/27   State v Francis Noble. Assault and Battery, for which he pled guilty. This was the first Criminal matter in the new 3rd District of the Justice of the Peace Court, now in Indian River County. The Justice of the Peace was now F. W. Dole.

The Justices of the Peace not only handled criminal cases, but civil cases as well. The first civil case appears to be <u>Harry B. Mace v. Max Mensh</u>, in May 1915. The plaintiff was represented by Penney & Fee, and the defendant had John R. Johnson, likely attorneys from Ft. Pierce. The Justice of the Peace signed those exact words ("Justice of the Peace"), but a separate name does not appear. It was likely C. W. Talmadge. (Mensh opened a store in the Broadmoor section of Fellsmere in 1914. Later on, his son, Sam Mensch, had a dry goods store on North Broadway in Fellsmere.) (See also Joe Bussey bio in this chapter).

Max Mensh was involved in a subsequent lawsuit involving one of his sons, who was allegedly brainwashed away from his Jewish Faith to be sent off to a Christian Theological School in Cleveland by a pastor and another, causing great distress to his family. The jury found one defendant not liable (C. E. Taylor, whose bio is in the next chapter) but awarded damages against the other (pastor) defendant in the amount of $500.00. It was an Indian River County Court case.[448]

Town Commissioner Court

The charter for the <u>Town</u> of Fellsmere, then in St. Lucie County, was created by Chapter 7154 of the Laws of Florida, 1915. The original government was composed of a three-member commission with C. W. Talmadge appointed Chief Commissioner, who served until February of 1916, George F. Green, Vice Commissioner, who served one week before resigning, and Wallace Sherwood, Secretary Commissioner.

George E. King became Chief Commissioner in 1916 and served through 1918. His successor was T. W. McCluer, who served until 1919, when Charles H. Piffard took office as Chief Commissioner. Charles H. Piffard served as Chief Commissioner until March 1922.

Section 30 of that act gave jurisdiction for the trial of all offenses against the town to the Chief Commissioner. The act also stated that until a municipal election has been held, the number of individual registered voters of the town shall be considered to be 150 in order to calculate the votes necessary for the percentages required for commissioner recalls or ordinance repeal.

City Mayor Judge Court

In 1925, the Town of Fellsmere became the <u>City</u> of Fellsmere in the newly created Indian River County. The act designated that the mayor was P. H. McEachron. The mayor was given jurisdiction for the trial of all offenses against the city and was the judge of the municipal court (Section 15). That same section also gave the city council the power to elect a municipal judge.

The Justices of the Peace for Fellsmere included at least these individuals and years:

C. W. Talmadge	1914 -1918
Alfred P. Ivory	1919 -1920
D. H. Saunders	1920 - 1922
F. W. Dole	1927-1931
P. H. McEachron	1934 -1935

The Fellsmere Chief Commissioner Judges were approximately as follows:

C. W. Talmadge	1915 - 1916
George E. King	1916 - 1918
T. W. McCluer	1918-1919
Charles H. Piffard	1919 – 1922[449]
R. L. Kinney	1922 - 1925[450]

The mayor/judges and then non-mayor municipal judges that have served in the City of Fellsmere, as best as can be reconstructed, are as follows:

Mayor/Judges:	
P. H. McEachron	1925 - 1928
G. F. Green	1928 - 1935
S. C. Barnes	1935 – 1936
H. C. Watts	1936 – 1937
J. J. Bustin	1936 - 1937[451]
S. C. Barns	1937 - 1939[452]
R. D. Cunningham	1939 - 1943
G. D. Young	1943 - 1946
E. W. Morris	1946 - 1946
G. T. McCarty	1946 - 1948
M. L. Medlin	1948 - 1950
H. C. Watts	1950 - 1953
Thomas Snell	1953 - 1956
Americus Day	1956 - 1958
Thomas Snell	1958 - 1962
John H. Cann	1962 - 1964
Thomas Snell	1964 – 1965
Joe Bussey	1965 – 1966

John H. Cann	1966 – 1968
Daniel G. Frisby	1968 – 1970
John H. Cann	1970 - 1972
Non-Mayor Municipal Judges:	
Chester Clem	1965 - 1971[453]

Municipal Court was held in the former State Bank of Fellsmere building (now the Fellsmere Community Center at 56 N. Broadway), which was down the street from another longstanding structure, the Fellsmere Estates Corporation building, which former County Commissioner Fran Adams refurbished as the Marsh Landing Restaurant at 44 N. Broadway. The State Bank of Fellsmere building was constructed in 1913 and closed in 1922. It reopened as the Citizens Bank in 1924 but closed again in 1925. The State of Florida subsequently took over and gave the former bank building to Indian River County, which leased it to the City of Fellsmere. It housed the Fellsmere city hall, police department, and municipal court. In 1982, it became the Fellsmere Community Building. From 1985 to 1996, the building was also used by the Fellsmere Volunteer Ambulance Squad. In 1997, the City of Fellsmere applied for a grant and received $300,000 from the Florida Legislature and the Florida Department of Environmental Protection in memory of Harry T. and Harriet V. Moore, after the slain civil rights leaders, and after whom the Brevard

Hall of Justice is also named. (See Chapter 3). The building was completely renovated by Chilberg Construction Company in 2004 and is now known as the Fellsmere Community Center.

Mayor Snell has described Fellsmere as being the first municipality in Indian River County with a bank, an electric light and ice plant, first master planned community, the first with paved sidewalks and roads, the first to allow women the right to vote in Florida and south of the Mason-Dixon Line, the first with a play house/movie theater, library, masonry school building, and public swimming pool. It had the shortest railroad with the longest name at the time. Originally called the Fellsmere Railroad, it was completed in 1910. It became the Trans Florida Central Railroad in 1924 and operated a train from Fellsmere to Sebastian essentially along the westbound lanes of County Road 512, where the railroad owned a right-of-way. The railroad's initial function was to transport materials, equipment, supplies, mail, and passengers to Fellsmere. Later, in the 1930s, it was used to transport sugar for the Fellsmere Sugar Company. The railroad ceased operation on November 30, 1952, and the tracks were removed during 1956-1957.

Judge Stikelether has reported that he held (county) court in the 1970s in Fellsmere on a weekly basis. The 1970s also brought about the end of the Municipal Court. The Constitutional Amendments approved by the voters in 1972 had the courts phased out to termination by January 1, 1977. However, most municipal courts ended sooner. See, for example, the Chapter on Sebastian. In the case of Fellsmere, where the records are sparse, Judge Chester Clem resigned in 1971 to run for State Representative. It is unclear whether the court continued for a couple more years, reverted to a Mayor Judge, or had another lawyer judge. Not seeing anything on this, I suspect it was largely taken over by the Indian River County Court.

B. Biographical Information on Fellsmere Justices of the Peace

C.W. Talmadge, Fellsmere Justice of the Peace 1914-1918

Talmadge served Fellsmere in a couple of judicial capacities. Being the first Chief Commissioner as of May 18, 1915, of the newly created town, his job included being the Commissioner Judge of the town court concerning offenses against the town. He also had been the Justice of the Peace at least as far back as 1914 in what was District 14 of St. Lucie County. His Justice of the Peace role continued until at least May 2, 1918.

The Ft. Pierce City Directories for 1916 and 1918 show Talmadge as being in Fellsmere, with his wife, Rose. He was a sec (secretary commissioner), justice of the peace, and in real estate and insurance businesses.

On March 16, 1918, he was sworn in as Vice Commission for Fellsmere, evidencing his great desire to serve his community and that he was capable of doing so. He was possibly a lawyer, as Richard Votapka refers to a meeting at the law office of Talmadge and Baker in Fellsmere in 1915.[454] However, the Florida Bar has not been able to confirm this. In addition, there is a certain lawsuit that went to the Supreme Court of Kansas, where Talmadge is described as an assignor of a real estate commission, as a real estate agent with one named T. J. Braniff, involving real property in Fellsmere.[455]

Alfred L. Ivory, Fellsmere Justice of the Peace, 1918

Alfred L. Ivory was a Justice of the Peace for Fellsmere District in 1918 and was also a Fellsmere City Clerk. In Ft. Pierce City Directories, he is shown as a civil engineer and a sec commr (secretary commissioner), living in Fellsmere with his wife, Ruth. He passed away at age 70 in Pittsburgh, Pa., on September 8, 1926, while visiting his brother.

D. H Saunders Sebastian Justice of the Peace 1920-1922

David Howard Saunders was born in Sac-Bay, Michigan, on July 16, 1890. He was one of the sons of Captain George and Mrs. Devises or Deaizes Saunders, who brought the family to Ft. Pierce in the early 1900s. His father was from Rhode Island, and his mother from

Canada. He had three brothers. Brother Ray worked for the Ford Dealer in Ft. Pierce, and brother Perry T. Saunders was a prominent engineer with his headquarters in New York City.[456] The oldest brother was George.

Growing up in Ft. Pierce, D. H. Saunders played on Ft. Pierce's first baseball team in 1904, the Rose Budd Baseball Club, coached by J. Frank Budd, whose son was also on the team.[457] Saunders married Emma V. Hall on November 16, 1915, in St. Lucie County. She was one of the first teachers in Fellsmere. A Ft. Pierce City Directory in 1916 shows D. H. as a Notary Public for Fellsmere.

Saunders was a Justice of the Peace when Fellsmere was a part of St. Lucie County. The November 6, 1920, Fellsmere Tribune shows him being elected to the Justice position. Another newspaper reports he was elected on Nov. 2, 1920.[458]State Archives records show he was elected to start serving on Jan 4, 1921, but he resigned on Feb. 18, 1922. That followed an unsuccessful run for Tax Assessor for St. Lucie County, where he was defeated by Felix Poppell, 512 to 480. In his first election for Justice of the Peace, he received 104 uncontested votes in Fellsmere.

When he and his wife lived in Fellsmere until about 1923, they were involved in numerous activities, including his being the Worthy Patron and she the Conductress of the Fellsmere Eastern Star. He was secretary of the Fellsmere Commercial Club and also a Mason,

UDF&AM, Fellsmere Lodge.[459] He was also secretary-treasurer of the Fellsmere Athletic Association, all while being the Manager of East Coast Lumber and Supply Co. in Fellsmere. He also played the saxophone.

By 1925, the directory shows that he and his wife were living on Avenue C in Ft. Pierce and that he was a travelling salesman. They were still living in Ft. Pierce by 1980, and he was known as D. H. "Banty" Saunders, and he had been associated with several lumber companies over the years, and at one time served as the Trustee in Bankruptcy for Winter Beach Lumber Co.[460]

Capt. Murray Howard Voth, who died in 2015, credits Saunders and his wife for raising him. Voth went on to be an Episcopal Minister and military chaplain in the Navy and a Vietnam War hero, receiving two Purple Hearts for his two different combat injuries in his service with the U. S. Marines and Navy.

D. H. Saunders was also a state representative from Ft. Pierce from 1945 to 1951. He was President of the St. Lucie County Historical Society in 1961 and, in 1963, was on the first St. Lucie County Historical Commission.

The North Causeway bridge in Ft. Pierce is the D. H. "Banty" Saunders Bridge, built in 1963. In 2025, it was being replaced with a new high bridge.

Saunders died on March 4, 1980, and is buried in Riverview Memorial Park in Ft. Pierce, Florida.

F. W. Dole, Fellsmere Justice of the Peace, 1928-1931

Dole was born in April 1872 in Fairfield, Jefferson County, Iowa. His parents were Joseph and Mariah, or Marie Ellen Dole. F. W., which stands for Frank Woods, married Leona Pearl Loftiss of Illinois on June 28, 1905, in Washington, Colorado. They had two children, Elizabeth Irene Dole and John Wesley Dole, each born in Iowa. By 1910, they were living in Kansas City, Mo., where he owned a restaurant. The Doles moved to Fellsmere, St. Lucie County, within a few years thereafter.

On June 15, 1916, the town Commissioners appointed Dole, the former town assessor, as the first town manager at a salary of $85.00 per month.[461] He moved, however, for a few years in the early 1920s (1921-1924) to Jacksonville, where he was a shipping clerk for American Bakeries Co. He returned to Fellsmere and was appointed in 1925 as the first City Clerk by Mayor McEachron.[462] In addition, he was the Tax Collector for Fellsmere in 1926.[463] Besides being a Justice of the Peace for Fellsmere (District 3) from at least 1928 - 1931, both Mr. Dole and subsequently Mrs. Dole worked as Postmasters in Fellsmere. He was nominated to that position on January 27, 1934, and was confirmed on February 10, 1934, and served until November 27, 1940, which was shortly before his passing. His position was taken over by his wife, who served until February 1, 1941. Mr. Dole was buried in Crestlawn Cemetery in Vero Beach. Mrs. Dole died in 1963.

P. W. McEachron, Fellsmere Justice of the Peace 1934-1935

See Fellsmere Mayor Judges

C. Biographical Information on Chief Commissioner Judges

C. W. Talmadge, Fellsmere Chief Commissioner Judge, 1915-1916

See bio under Justices of the Peace, above.

George E. King, Fellsmere Chief Commissioner Judge, 1916-1918

George E. King was born on August 13, 1850, in Dorchester, Massachusetts. His father was Edward, and his mother was Susan. George E. King married Florence P. Clough on June 20, 1883, in Ayer, Massachusetts. They had 6 children in 10 years. Florence was originally from Maine, and she and George had all their children born in Maine. They lived in Bethel, Maine, per the 1910 U. S. Census. There, he was a bookkeeper. By 1916, the entire family was living in Fellsmere. He was then a fruit farmer.

King became Chief Commissioner of Fellsmere on February 8, 1916, following Talmadge, and served until being succeeded by T. W. McCluer in 1918. As Chief Commissioner, he had occasion to write to President Woodrow Wilson and volunteer the brand new Fellsmere School Building, now City Hall, for a place of recuperation for soldiers of World War I. The president's secretary gratefully responded and said they would forward the offer to the Secretary of War, but apparently, nothing came of the offer, and the school was never used as a hospital.

George E. King died Jan 11, 1927, in Fellsmere at age 76.

T. W. McCluer, Fellsmere Chief Commissioner Judge 1918-1919

T. W. McCluer succeeded George E. King, being sworn in as Chief Commissioner on March 16, 1918, and serving until 1919. The 1918 Ft. Pierce City Directory shows him working for Saunders & McCluer. That is likely D. H. Saunders discussed in this chapter. The 1920 Census shows him as the head of household at age 59, with his wife Edmona, age 53, a librarian, and daughter Bessie, age 24, and son Hunter, age 22. The whole family was born in Missouri. They lived on Orange St., and their neighbors on that street included Peter McEachron, Herbert C. Watts, and George F. Green. Each served Fellsmere as mayor.

Charles H. Piffard, Fellsmere Chief Commissioner Judge, 1919-1922

Charles H. Piffard succeeded McCluer on February 11, 1919, as Chief Commissioner and served until March 1922.

Piffard was born in New York City on February 18, 1874. He was associated with E. Nelson Fell, first at his development in Narcoossee, near St. Cloud, Florida, which preceded Fell's involvement in the future Fellsmere. Piffard also accompanied Fell to Russia in 1902 in connection with mining activities there for about 8 years. They each made a lot of money there, and Charles returned to NYC and was in banking.[464]

Piffard married Helen Louise Brown of Plainfield, N.J., on Dec 31, 1912. While Piffard was in banking, Mr. Fell acquired the land in what was St. Lucie County. Fell convinced Piffard to come to Fellsmere and start the State Bank of Fellsmere. As an inducement, the Fellsmere Farms Company built the Piffards a house. By 1913, the Piffards had arrived in Fellsmere, and he, as president of the bank, saw his bank being built, as well as his home.

Both buildings are still in existence. The bank is now the Harry T. and Harriet V. Moore Community Center, and the house is historic, located at 79 N. Maple St., Fellsmere.

The Piffards were involved with numerous activities in Fellsmere, and one time, Mr. Piffard helped save the day by using his family connections to get a generator to resume providing electricity for the town in 1917. The Piffards had three children born in Fellsmere. Piffard was the municipal judge for Fellsmere from 1919 to 1922. For more on the Piffards, be sure to see Richard Votapka's article on the Charles and Helen Piffard Home, which is on the internet. I must, however, note that as the article indicates, Mr. Piffard suddenly disappeared in 1922, at around the same time that $30,000.00 or $36,000.00 was missing from the bank. He may have gone to Daytona, and when word leaked via the press,[465] he left the country. He subsequently died in Paris in November 1925.

Roy Kinney, Fellsmere Chief Commissioner Judge, 1925

Roy Kinney replaced Mr. Piffard after his sudden disappearance in 1922. Kinney likely continued in that role until 1925, when the new City Charter was created. After Piffard disappeared, the Vice Commissioner was C.E. Nourse, but there is no evidence that he became Chief Commissioner.

Roy Kinney was likely born in Fairfield, ME, but moved to Fellsmere around 1920 with his infant son, Roy Jr., and wife, Dorothy. They also had a daughter, Linda Gail Kinney Green, and a son, Frank Kimball Kinney. Dorothy Kinney was the president of the Fellsmere Library Association. The Kinneys, father and sons, were directors of a business known as Indian River Nurseries and Development Corporation, which was created in 1927 and existed until 1939. Roy Sr. was also one of the directors of the Fellsmere Truckers Association, which existed from 1928 until 1974.

Roy's daughter, Gail Kinney Griffin, related how Mrs. Piffard told the Kinneys to use the Piffard home as the Piffards were leaving town. The Kinneys enjoyed living in that house.

The Kinneys lived in the former Piffard home until 1945. Roy, Jr. served in the Air Force in World War II. In 1959, he became a resident of Sebastian and was a commander of VFW Post 10210 and was a president of the Sebastian Lions Club, and the 2008 Sebastian Man of the Year. There is a Roy Kinney Hall at the VFW Post in Sebastian. Roy Jr. died in 2011 at about 90 years old.

D. Biographical Information on Fellsmere Municipal Judges

P. H. McEachron, Fellsmere Municipal Court Judge, 1925-1932

Peter Harska McEachron was born in Argyle, New York, on December 30, 1862. He married the former Matilda Kirkham of Argyle, New York. The couple came to this area in approximately 1913. They arrived first in Sebastian, where Mr. McEachron operated a grocery store. Subsequently, they moved to Fellsmere, where he also owned a grocery store.

The McEachrons had four children: Mark H. McEachron, Marjorie, who taught Latin at Miami Edison in Miami, another daughter who died at an early age, and a fourth child, Arthur. The mayor's son, Mark, who died on June 8, 1967, had five children: Frances Mullin of Brooklyn, New York, Doris Smith of Huntsville, Alabama, Peter H. McEachron, Grace Osteen of Micanopy, and the youngest, Matilda Barnes, of Fellsmere.

Grandson, Peter H. McEachron, of Boca Raton, was a principal in James Cummings Construction, which was the contractor on the new 20th Street/16th Avenue Vero Beach courthouse.

Mr. McEachron died on January 9, 1939, in Fellsmere and is buried in the Fellsmere cemetery.

G. F. Green, Fellsmere Municipal Judge, 1932-1935

George Frank Green was born on April 26, 1857, in Missouri, but spent many years working in the cotton fields of Texas and on a cotton gin. He married Annie Wade, of Montague, Texas. The couple came to Fellsmere in December 1912 for health reasons. He was on his way to Palm Beach and stopped by the Fellsmere area, and ended up settling there.

Green became a citrus grower but had business setbacks with the weather problems and the Depression of 1929. Mr. Green's granddaughter, Matilda Barnes, who is also the granddaughter of another Fellsmere mayor (P. H. McEachron), believed that her grandfather arrived in Fellsmere by sailboat from Titusville, as there was no tolerable road at the time. G. F. Green was Mayor of Fellsmere from 1932 to 1935.

Mr. and Mrs. G. F. Green had six children: Ida, Lilly, Lottie, H. Overton, Grace (Peter H. McEachron, Jr. and Matilda Barnes' mother), and Anna. Ida was married to Jesse E. Dixon, the original train engineer who operated the wood-burning steam train running between Fellsmere and Sebastian. Jesse and Ida Dixon had two children: Orville "Dick" Dixon of Daytona Beach and Carol Jennings of Alco, New Jersey.

Mr. Green was predeceased by his first wife, Annie. Mr. Green died on September 16, 1936. He died in Chicago after moving there with his second wife, Margaret. He is buried in the Fellsmere Cemetery, Row 4.

S. C. Barnes, Fellsmere Municipal Court Judge, 1935-1939

Stephen Candary Barnes was born in Robinson County, North Carolina, on April 19, 1859. He was the son of William and Marie Ann Barnes. He moved to Fellsmere in 1915 and was employed for most of his life as a carpenter. He was a member of Local Carpenter Union #1447 of Vero Beach. He was married to the former Sarah Elizabeth Young.

Mr. Barnes died in Sebastian on April 15, 1939. He was survived by his wife, Sarah. At the time of his death, he was the oldest member of the Local Carpenter Union #1447.

J. J. Bustin, Fellsmere Acting Mayor, Municipal Court Judge 1936-1937

Joseph J. Bustin was born in Pueblo, Colorado April 1, 1895. His parents were each from Pennsylvania. By 1910, he was living in Towanda, Pa., where he resided for the next 10 plus years, except for his military service. He served in the U. S. Army during World War I, from January 14, 1918, to January 22, 1919. He worked in the Ordinance Department both at the University of Pennsylvania and the Augusta Arsenal, Augusta, Ga. He married Elizabeth F. Coyne, of Pennsylvania, in Dallas, Texas, where he was then living, on June 21, 1922.

Bustin was on the first City Council, being appointed by Gov. Martin in 1925. He was Treasurer of the State Bank of Fellsmere, notably when it failed in 1926. He was also the new Assistant Manager of the Trans Florida Central Railroad in 1927. In 1935, he became Secretary Treasurer of Fellsmere Sugar Co. and was in charge of the Fellsmere office. He was Treasurer of the Fellsmere Water Control District. On Feb. 5, 1935, the Indian River County Commission approved his surety's bond in the amount of $500.00 for him as a notary public. He was acting Mayor of Fellsmere from December 21, 1936, to June 14, 1937, filling the unexpired term of H. C. Watts, who left during his term.

Bustin was appointed (along with a few others) by Charles A. Mitchell of the Chamber of Commerce to represent Indian River County at the Governor's Day Celebration at the St. Lucie County Fairgrounds on February 25, 1941, and to help escort Governor Spessard Holland from the Ft. Pierce Courthouse to the fairgrounds. Anyone from Vero Beach (and Fellsmere, etc.) was advised to bear on their cars, streamers saying "Indian River County."

Bustin died on May 13, 1941, and is buried in Crestlawn Cemetery, Vero Beach.

R. D. Cunningham, Fellsmere Municipal Court Judge, 1939-1943

Raymond Dillard Cunningham was born in Corydon, Indiana, on February 21. 1878. He came to Fellsmere in the early 1930s. He was a farmer and had five children: The first two sons died young. He had two more sons, Clifford and Albert, and then a daughter, Rachel, who graduated as a member of the four-person class of Fellsmere High School in 1939. Albert married one of Rachel's classmates, Rosella Stallings.

R. D. Cunningham appears in the 1935 state census as living in Fellsmere with his wife, Margaret, and their three children. The R. D.

Cunningham family seemed to have moved to New Jersey in the early 1940s. R. D. Cunningham died in Camden, N. J. on Feb 20. 1950.

The R. D. Cunningham family is to be distinguished from the J. B. (John Benjamin) Cunningham family. John Benjamin was R. D.'s brother. His family included a daughter, Mrs. Franklin (Helen) Green, who passed away in 1996, and a son, J.B., who was a pilot who moved to New Jersey and is now deceased.

G. D. Young, Fellsmere Municipal Judge, 1943-1946

Guilford Dudley Young was born on November 18, 1878, in Connecticut. He was raised in New Haven. His father was Albert Huntington Young, and his mother was Alice Geraldine Barbour, who were also from Connecticut.

Mr. G. D. Young was a civil engineer and may have attended Yale until his father passed away. During World War I, Mr. G. D. Young was employed by the New York, New Haven, and Hartford Railroad. He did not serve in the war because of his essential service with the railroad line. Mr. Young was married while living in Connecticut and had two daughters, one of whom was Alice Williams of Connecticut.

Mr. Young came to the Fellsmere area during the boom years of the 1920s. Shortly after he was situated, he was joined by Gladys Wallis Wahaples, who also worked for the New York, New Haven Hartford Railroad. They were married in Vero Beach and had several children. Mr. Young was initially in a partnership, but the partner absconded with the company's assets, and the crash of 1929 did not help his financial position. His daughter, Eleanor Young Herndon, was born in 1929. She joined her half-sisters, born of the prior marriage with the first Mrs. G. D. Young. Young and his second wife had two sons as well: Albert Huntington Curtis Young, Sr., of Jacksonville, Florida, and Gilford Dudley Young of Macon, Georgia.[466]

G. D. Young began working for the WPA in Fellsmere as a civil engineer. He assisted on a cross-marsh road from Fellsmere to Kenansville, which was discontinued during construction because it was in an inappropriate place. A suitable road base could not be established over the marsh. Mr. Young then went to work for the Fellsmere Sugar Producers Association, where he worked for many years. He was not only the mayor of Fellsmere from 1943 to 1946, but he was also a deputy sheriff for many years. G. D. Young was a correspondent for the Press Journal newspaper.

In 1967, G. D. Young's daughter, Eleanor Young, married Elton Herndon, and between the two of them (as they had each been married before), they had nine children. Mrs. Herndon later lived in Sneedville, Tennessee. One of Mrs. Herndon's stepchildren is Caroline Herndon, who operated Caroline's Corner, a hairdresser's business in Fellsmere.

G. D. Young died on May 11, 1970, in Orlando and is buried in the Fellsmere cemetery.

E. W. Morris, Fellsmere Municipal Court Judge, 1946

Edgar W. Morris was the postmaster in Fellsmere from 1924 until 1934. He also served for a short time as mayor of Fellsmere from February to June 1946. He lived at one time outside the town limits of Fellsmere on County Road 512.

The Morris home was subsequently sold to Mr. and Mrs. Mett, according to Mrs. Johnnie Cann. Mr. Morris then left the area. Dr. Evelyn Mudge, the daughter of Fellsmere pioneer Colonel Mudge, has described Mr. Morris as an austere gentleman.

Little is known about E. W. Morris. However, according to the Register of Voters of Indian River County, it is likely that Edgar W. Morris was born in the United States in approximately 1866. He was probably married to Julia B. Morris, whose chosen work was a housewife. She was the same age as Mr. Morris and was born in Illinois. Mrs. Morris preceded Mr. Morris in death. He was the executor of her estate.

The Records of Appointments of Postmasters 1832 - September 30, 1971, of the National Archives Series M841, Reel 20, indicate that Morris was serving as postmaster of Fellsmere by August 1924 and that he was reappointed until 1934. An interesting letter dated

May 18, 1928, from E. W. Morris as Fellsmere Postmaster survives in federal records. It was written to the Fourth Assistant Postmaster General in Washington, D.C., and answers an important inquiry from the Fourth Assistant Postmaster by filling in the blanks on where the Fellsmere post office was located.

A portion of the questions with inserted answers underlined, follow:

"The name of the nearest river is Sebastian River, and the post office building is at a distance of six miles on the west side of it."

"The name of the nearest creek is I don't know: There is no creek here, except the Sebastian River."

"The post office building is on the South side of the Trans Florida Central Railroad, and at a distance of 325 feet from the track."

In his cover letter, Morris says:

"Fellsmere is located on the Trans Florida Central RR, which is a spur road running from Fellsmere to Sebastian, Florida. – Sebastian is located on the Florida East Coast RR. Fellsmere is the only P.O. on the Trans Cent. RR. Sebastian River is a creek (and not a large creek), but it is called "Sebastian River. There is no other river or creek in this locality. Indian River is 10 miles east of Fellsmere, but Indian River is an arm of the Atlantic Ocean – and is not a 'river.'"

G. T. McCarty, Fellsmere Municipal Court Judge, 1946-1948

George Teeter McCarty was born in Carroll County, Ohio, on March 15, 1872. His parents were Robert McCarty and Elizabeth Teeter. Mr. McCarty was a realtor and the Mayor of Fellsmere from 1946 to 1948. He was married, and his wife predeceased him.

He defeated G. D. Young for mayor in 1948 by 124 to 13 votes. He was also a southpaw who pitched for the Fellsmere softball team, which traveled to nearby cities and towns.

Mr. McCarty died at age 90 on October 18, 1962, in Orlando, Florida. At that time, he had no immediate survivors. He is buried in the Crestlawn Cemetery, Vero Beach, Florida.

M. L. Medlin, Fellsmere Municipal Court Judge, 1948-1950

Merlan LeRoy (M.L). Medlin was born on January 11, 1913, in Durham, North Carolina. He was married to Frances Medlin of High Point, North Carolina, who was born on October 21, 1920, and who died on January 21, 1970. Mr. Medlin worked for the federal government in Harrisonburg (Shenandoah Valley), Virginia, where he worked with apple-picking labor camps. The government transferred him to West Palm Beach, Florida, and shortly thereafter, he went to work for Fellsmere Sugar Company in approximately 1946.

Medlin was a member of the Fellsmere Community Church, a charter member of the Elks Club of Vero Beach, a member of the

Indian River County School Board from 1949 to 1959, Mayor of Fellsmere for two terms (1948-1950), a member of the Fellsmere City Council for six years, and a member of the Indian River County Memorial Hospital for twelve years.

Mr. Medlin died on March 9, 1971, at age 59, in Fort Pierce. He was survived by a son, W. T. Medlin (1944 – 2024) of Fellsmere, and a granddaughter, Candy Lee Medlin of Fellsmere. W. T. Medlin worked in the citrus industry for Jack M. Barry Groves and was the President of the Fellsmere City Council for two years, commencing in 1972. M. L. Medlin was also survived by two sisters: Cathleen Maynor, born March 20, 1930, in Durham, North Carolina; and Virginia "Lillian," born August 5, 1924, in Anaheim, California. M.L. Medlin is buried in Crestlawn Cemetery.

H. C. Watts, Fellsmere Municipal Court Judge, 1950-1953

Herbert Colson Watts was born on December 8, 1887, in Thomaston, Maine. He was a pioneer in this area, arriving from Maine in 1912. Mr. Watts, better known as "Bill," was one of the civil engineers brought to Fellsmere by Nelson Fell (after whom the town was named) to help lay out the town streets and canals.

Mr. Watts was quoted in Nixon's Smiley's book, Florida, Land of Images, in connection with the horrific flood of Fellsmere in 1915. Smiley noted that the rains started in July and there were 16 inches on August 3, and quoting Watts, "But we hadn't seen anything yet. While we were assessing the problem of how to hasten the drainage, a sheet of water was moving into the marshes from the Central Florida highlands, and as it settled down upon us, we were overwhelmed." Smiley noted you could fish in the streets, and drainage canals meant nothing.[467]

Mr. Watts served not only in the National Guard in Maine, he later was a private in the United States Army in World War I. He was married to Kathryne Whipple Watts and had a daughter, Mignon Watts Kostamo of Orlando. Mr. Watts died on December 5, 1979, and was survived by his wife, daughter, and two grandsons. He is buried in the Fellsmere Cemetery. Mrs. Irene Cann, the wife of Mayor John H. Cann, described H. C. Watts as being a well-respected man.[468]

Thomas N. Snell, Jr., Fellsmere Municipal Court Judge, 1953-1956, 1958-1962, and 1964-1966

Thomas N. Snell, Jr., was born in Wrightsville, Georgia. Wrightsville was the county seat of Johnson County. Mr. Snell was born on February 9, 1908. He was the son of Thomas Nathaniel Snell and Willie Hicks Snell, each of Wrightsville, Georgia. Thomas was the youngest of four children. His three older siblings were James Hicks Snell, Ethel Lucille Snell Smith (who was married to Horace Smith), and William Edwards Snell. When Thomas was two or three years old, his family moved to Venus (near Arcadia), Florida, to homestead. The family moved to Arcadia when phosphate was found. Thomas' father died when Thomas was approximately seven. Thomas lived in the Arcadia area during World War I and Prohibition.

In 1919, while Thomas's brothers worked for the railroad, Thomas, his mother, and his sister moved to Atlanta. Thomas graduated from Tech High School in Atlanta, Georgia, in 1926. He also attended Georgia Tech for one year and then worked for the Citizens & Southern Bank for four years until the Depression. Thereafter, he worked for Appleton Electric, which made electrical conduit fittings, and he was transferred to Chicago in 1941. When Pearl Harbor was attacked, Thomas was employed in various merchant marine jobs from approximately 1942 to 1946. He worked out of Alabama, California, and New York, and literally went around the world during his stint in the merchant marines. Following the war, when there was more money than materials, according to him, Snell went to work for the Georgia Ventilated Awning Company as a bookkeeper. This company made a double-layer awning in Thomaston, Georgia.

When Thomas' sister went looking for accounting work for Thomas' brother, and the Fellsmere Sugar Producers' Association had an interest, his brother was unable to go, so Thomas went instead. He went to work as an accountant on February 1, 1947, at which employment he remained for twenty-six years. Fellsmere Sugar Producers' Association was then housed in the Fellsmere Estates Corporation building. That building was auctioned in the late 1990s and purchased by then County Commissioner Fran Adams, who restored that historic building.

When Snell arrived for the interview, he stayed at the Fellsmere Inn. When he began work, he moved into a company "shotgun" house on Cypress Street, then subsequently Elm Street, and later North Pine Street, where he lived until his death. Snell was elected mayor several times, including once by write-in votes, when he was not even on the ballot. He retired from the sugar company in 1973. His wife, Sara Frances Chapman, died of cancer after thirty-nine years of marriage to Snell. (They were married on July 28, 1934.) Snell met a nurse tending to Mrs. Snell, by the name of Shirley N. Dauer Surles Snell. He married her on February 1, 1976.

Snell was a charter member of the B.P.O.E. Elks Lodge #1774 and was a Master Mason and past Worshipful Master of Fellsmere Lodge #232 F. & A. M. While not mentioned in the foregoing, where Mr. Snell served as mayor/municipal judge for three separate stints as mayor, he had occasion to serve a 4th time as mayor, briefly, in 1978, when he resigned amidst some controversy.

Mayor Snell recalls the court being held in the Fellsmere State Bank, the ivy-covered building. At the time Mr. Snell was mayor, the bank, which had not been in operation since the Depression, was the place for the Councilman meetings. This building is on Main Street next to the fire station and is still standing. It had a walk-in vault and a tile lobby.

Judge Snell indicates that, as a municipal judge, while he was not trained in the law, he tried to apply common sense at all times. If someone was in a fight, it was inappropriate, in his opinion, to levy a large fine that the defendant could not pay, and if the culprit was put in jail, that would not help anyone either. His main goal was to make sure the defendant did not fight again.

Former Mayor Snell, who was age 86 when I interviewed him, remembered serving as the municipal judge as mayor. He recalled Circuit Judge L. B. "Buck" Vocelle acting as City Prosecutor for the City of Fellsmere in the 1950s. Mr. Snell said that he felt uncomfortable acting as a judge and that that position would be better filled by a lawyer. However, the mayor must have been capable, in that after he left Fellsmere Farms, where he worked for Gulf and Western, he continued as mayor for several months while still working for Gulf and Western at South Bay, South of Lake Okeechobee.

At age 90, Snell climbed Stone Mountain in Georgia with a nephew, a great-nephew, and a great-great-nephew. Snell died on May 29, 2002, at age 94. He was survived by his wife of 26 years,

Shirley Dauer Snell, and a stepson and daughter-in-law, Mark and Maureen Surles of Red Lion, Pa.

Americus Day, Fellsmere Municipal Court Judge, 1956-58

Americus Day was born in North Florida on December 12, 1903. He grew up in Greenville, Madison County, Florida, east of Tallahassee. He moved to Fellsmere in the early 1920s. He was the son of Ella Goodman Day and John S. Day. John S. Day was from Americus, Georgia, after which Americus was probably named. He was also known as "Mac." Mrs. Ella Goodman Day was from North Florida.

Americus Day married Ivah K. Weaver of Augusta, Maine, in approximately 1925. She would accompany her parents, Fred and Ethel Weaver of Randolph, Maine, to Florida. They permanently settled in the Fellsmere area in the early 1920's where Ivah met Americus Day.

Day was unopposed for mayor of Fellsmere and elected in 1956. He later served again as mayor and resigned in 1973 for health reasons.

Day was a Mason (a past master of Fellsmere Lodge 232) and was a masonic brother with former Mayor Snell. He was also a heavy equipment operator and contractor, as the A. Day Construction Company, and worked in many locations around the state. Mr. and

Mrs. Americus Day raised five children: Freda Peterson of California; Grace E. Steinmetz of California; and three boys, John Day of Fellsmere, Harold Day of Sebastian, and Raymond Day of Fellsmere. All three boys followed in their father's footsteps in the heavy equipment line. Mr. John Day (1931-2025) operated heavy equipment for the Fellsmere Water Control District.

Americus Day died at age 73 on May 5, 1976, in Sebastian, Florida. He was survived by his wife, Mrs. Ivah Day, who died in 2001 at age 98 in Fellsmere. Mr. Day was also survived by his 3 sons, above named, and 3 daughters, Charlotte Weaver (step-daughter) of Fellsmere, Frieda Peterson, and Grace Steinmetz. He is buried in the Winter Beach Cemetery.

John H. Cann, Fellsmere Municipal Court Judge, 1962-1964

John Hamilton Cann, Sr. was born on December 13, 1924, in Laurel, Clermont, Ohio. He was born to Clyde Charles Cann (then age 38) and Myrtie Lou Brooking (then age 24). John arrived in Fellsmere from Cincinnati, Ohio, on Thanksgiving 1948 and was employed by the Fellsmere Sugar Produce Company for many years. He worked for a couple of years at Piper Aircraft. He subsequently owned his own lumber business in Fellsmere, Cann's Lumber and Building Materials Co., but had to retire for health reasons.

Cann married Irene M. Fretwell, the daughter of William F. and Mamie Fretwell of Fellsmere, on July 29, 1949. Mrs. Irene Cann, born in Winter Beach, moved to Fellsmere when she was four years old. She graduated from high school in Fellsmere in 1942. She worked for the various Fellsmere sugar companies from 1946 through 1987, including Fellsmere Sugar Produce, South Puerto Sugar Company, Florida Division, Okeelanta Sugar Refinery, Inc., Gulf and Western, Fellsmere Farms, Fellsmere Management, and Fellsmere Joint Venture. The sugar refinery was torn down in 1967 when government quotas were cut, and alleged union demands didn't justify its continued existence. It was the first refinery in the State of Florida. The refinery division was sold to Okeelanta South Bay, Florida, and the remaining business continued with the citrus and cattle in Fellsmere.

Mr. Cann was mayor of Fellsmere from 1962 to 1964 but was defeated for reelection for mayor by Thomas Snell by 4 votes, 62 – 58. However, Cann also had additional terms in 1966-1967 and 1970-1971. He was also the City of Fellsmere Marshall from 1958 through 1961 and the Fellsmere fire chief for more than 20 years.

The Canns had one son together, John Patrick Cann of Texas. Mrs. Cann had two children from her previous marriage, and Mr. Cann had one son, John H. Cann.

John H. Cann, Sr., died on July 21, 2003, in Fellsmere. He was survived by his wife and children.

Joe Bussey, Sebastian Mayor Judge 1965

Joseph "Joe" Hightower Bussey was born in Lowndes County, Ga., on June 8, 1911. His parents were Joseph Rush Bussey (1884-1963) and Harriett Hattie Gertrude Bussey (1886-1966). At age 19, in 1930, he started working as a butcher for Sam Mensch at the Fellsmere Cash Grocery. On April 1, 1933, he married Dorothy E. Jones. Joe took over management of the store, still owned by the Mensches, in 1944. It was remodeled, but after 6 years, the store burned down on Christmas Eve, 1950. Joe quickly moved to a nearby vacant grocery store, which had a cooler in it, and his wholesalers made special deliveries to keep the restarted business going. In 1951, Joe bought the business from the Mensches, and he continued to be a well-respected businessman. Then he rebuilt the building as a fireproof building in 1952.

Joe and his wife, Dorothy E. Bussey, had two children, James Edward Bussey and Mary Jo.

In 1960, Bussey was appointed a member of the Fellsmere City Council and was subsequently elected to a two-year term on the council in 1962. In July and August 1965, he served as acting mayor and was elected to the Council again in 1966 and served until 1968.

The Busseys' daughter, Mary Jo Bussey Screws, and her husband, Talmadge Grayson Screws, purchased the grocery building and incorporated the business in 1971.

The Screws sold the store in 1973, and Joe Bussey died on January 3, 1974. That store is on the historical tour of Fellsmere that is conducted by Richard Votapka.

Chester Clem, Fellsmere Municipal Court Judge, 1965-1971

See the biographical information under Small Claims Court biographical information.

Chapter 14 - City of Sebastian Municipal Court and Justices of the Peace

A. History of Sebastian Municipal Court

On December 8, 1924, Sebastian was organized as a municipality and called the "Town of Sebastian" in St. Lucie County.[469] At the organizational meeting, 82 of the 105 registered voters of the proposed Sebastian town corporate limits attended. This was just over one month after the shooting of the Ashley Gang on November 1, 1924, at the south end of the Sebastian Bridge.[470] The formal organization of Sebastian was also some 21 years after the Sebastian community received national attention when President Theodore Roosevelt established the first National Wildlife Refuge at Pelican Island in the Indian River at Sebastian.

Sebastian was formerly known as New Haven. Thomas New, who is credited with having cut the first inlet in 1881, named the area New Haven in 1882. As evidenced by the post office permit, New Haven was changed to Sebastian in 1884. The train arrived in 1894.

Prior to Sebastian's incorporation and the creation of Indian River County, Sebastian had been a part of the First District of St. Lucie County, and even was a district in Brevard County. It had as its justices of the peace, A. L. Lowder 1897-1899 (resigned), W. T. Laine 1905-1911, followed by M. M. Miller 1912-1929, and then, post

Indian River County creation, George Badger 1929-1931 (resigned), and Lisbon Futch 1940. Laine was first elected in 1905, and after being reelected in January 1911, he subsequently resigned. Miller was first elected in 1911 or 1912 and served the north county for about fifteen years, much of it preceding the incorporation of Sebastian,[471] and even thereafter, as he was re-elected in November 1926,[472] but died in office.[473]

Court records from the First District of St. Lucie County indicate that from May 1915 to May 1916, there were twenty-seven offenses in the area. Those included disorderly conduct, illegal fishing, petit larceny, carrying a pistol, taking a mule without permission, and selling whiskey without a license. There was reportedly one case of "bastardy" tried as well.[474]

M. M. Miller was elected as one of the first aldermen of the newly created Town of Sebastian in December of 1924. The first Mayor was T. B. Hicks. Incidentally, it was Judge M. M. Miller's son, Ted, who was the Miller who happened to come along and stop in front of the south side of the chained Sebastian Bridge, which caused the Ashley Gang to stop and be shot in the controversial capture.[475]

In May of 1925, the City of Sebastian was created by the Florida Legislature. Prior thereto, the municipality had merely been a town until this point.[476] This act, which abolished the present municipality of the town of Sebastian, St. Lucie County, Florida, and created the

<u>City</u> of Sebastian, was land still in St. Lucie County, Florida. This occurred just days before the creation of Indian River County.

With respect to a municipal court, that act provided for a "police court" under Section 25. It provided that "the Mayor shall be the Judge of the police court and shall have jurisdiction to try all offenders against the city ordinances. He shall have the power to issue his warrant upon an affidavit alleging the violation of any of the ordinances of the city...." Section 26 directed that the city clerk keep a docket upon which shall be entered all causes tried in said court.

Another charter amendment to the City of Sebastian occurred in November 1925. This act seems to erroneously refer to Sebastian as still being a part of St. Lucie County.[477] However, two preceding acts of the legislature that year, confirming and ratifying bonds pertaining to the Sebastian Bridge District and the City of Sebastian, refer to Sebastian as being in Indian River County.[478]

In 1933, the then-present municipal government of the City of Sebastian was abolished, with a new municipality of the City of Sebastian being created. (Essentially, the charter was redone.) That act directed (in Section 18) that the mayor be the judge of the municipal court with the power by his warrant to have brought before him any person or persons charged with the violation of the ordinances, to decide guilt or innocence of the accused and to punish for contempt of municipal court to the extent of a fine not exceeding

$100.00 or imprisonment not exceeding 30 days or both; such penalties at his discretion. Section 74 of the act authorized the clerk of the City of Sebastian to act as the clerk of the municipal court (and of the city council).

The municipal court and the jail for the City of Sebastian were once located on the first floor of the old City Hall, when located on Louisiana Avenue. In 1957, a building at the southeast corner of US # 1 and Main Street was constructed. It began its use as the Sebastian City Hall in 1958, where the municipal court continued.

At a City Council meeting of December 16, 1947, the salary was set for Mayor Earl Roberts for his services as both Mayor and Judge of the Municipal Court of Sebastian. Mr. Roberts is likely better known for his Earl's Hideaway bar.

On June 19, 1959, at a special meeting of the Sebastian City Council, it accepted Robert Jackson's offer to be City Judge, effective immediately, for four nights each month, until the Council sees fit to change it, at $25.00 per session.[479]

Another amendment to the charter for the City of Sebastian occurred in 1965 to provide for a municipal judge.[480] The act required that the municipal court "shall have a judge who shall be a practicing attorney-at-law in Indian River County and qualified to practice law in the courts of the State...." The municipal judge was to be appointed by the city council for a term of one year or until his successor is appointed and qualifies. The mayor shall be the acting municipal judge to preside over the municipal court in the absence or disqualification of the municipal judge.[481]

The municipal courts in Florida were abolished as of January 3, 1977, at the latest. Article V, Section 20(d) 4, Constitution of the State of Florida (1972). When the "Mayor's Court" in Sebastian was essentially abolished, Robert Jackson had been acting as the primary municipal judge. Bob described the court as taking place at the intersection of U.S. 1 and Main Street, where the combined library/fire station/police station was located for the City of Sebastian. Bob said his compensation was $25.00 per week. During Judge Jackson's tenure, the clerk of the court, who was also clerk of the city council, was Colonel A. T. Jordan.

In 1982, the City of Sebastian moved its government facilities to the old Sebastian Elementary School, which was refurbished for governmental offices. The former city hall, which included the municipal court on U.S. Hwy. # 1 and Main Street, has since become a library, a teen center, and, in 1994, the City's Utility Department. In January 1997, the City of Sebastian approved the renting of the building to the Sebastian River Historical Society and the Sebastian River Area Chamber of Commerce for $1.00 per year.

A list of the mayors and the practicing attorneys who acted as municipal judges in Sebastian is as follows:

T. B. Hicks	December 16, 1924 - December 13, 1925
G. T. Badger	December 14, 1925 - January 5,1940[482]
L. O. Baughman	January 17, 1940 - October 20, 1942
E. W. Vickers	October 20, 1942 - December 10, 1945
L. M. Shafor	December 10, 1945 - December 8, 1947
Earl Roberts	December 8, 1947 - December 12, 1949
J. R. Middleton	December 12, 1949 - December 10, 1951
A. G. Shaffer	December 10, 1951 - December 14, 1955
C. E. Taylor	December 14, 1955 - December 9, 1957
Paul Stevenson	December 9, 1957 - December 14, 1959
Fred Rohme	December 14, 1959 - July 8, 1961*
Amos Simmons	July 8, 1961 - December 11, 1961*
Robert Jackson	1959 - 1973 (with assistance from Chester Clem and Bill Cobb, each of whom is listed under Small Claims Court Judges)

* See clarification on page 521, in front of their biographies.

Based upon the constitutional Amendment abolishing the Municipal Court and more particularly in accordance with Chapter 72-403 of the Florida Statutes, the Municipal Court of the City of Sebastian was abolished effective July 1, 1973.[483] There are minutes on April 9, 1973, which show that Judge Graham W. Stikelether, Jr. spoke to the council to discuss procedures and answer questions on the County taking over the Sebastian City Court, in accordance with the Florida Constitution.

Coincidentally, Judge Stikelether told me that he held court (for the County Court of Indian River County) in Sebastian in the 1970s on a weekly basis.

B. Biographical Information on Sebastian Justices of the Peace

W. T. Laine – Sebastian Justice of the Peace 1905-1911

Wiley Tatum Laine was likely born Oct 12, 1835, in Lincoln County, Georgia. He served 4 years in the Confederacy, commencing in 1860. He was hospitalized for a gunshot wound to the leg. He joined the North Georgia Conference of the Methodist Church, where he served for 15 years. He was married on May 31, 1866, to Annie L. Allsbrook in Fulton County, Ga. They had one son, who died when he was 21.

Laine came to Florida in 1884 in connection with the church, and he helped to build the Methodist Church in Ft. Pierce and then in Sebastian. Laine was first elected in 1905, and after being reelected in January 1911, he subsequently resigned. He also gave up church work to care for his invalid wife. Following her death, he was heartbroken and went to the mountains of N. C. to recuperate, and there he met his second wife, whom he married on June 29, 1913, Martha "Mattie" Carolyn Mast.

While Laine lived in the Sebastian area as a justice of the peace for the years indicated above, by 1916, he was living in the Oslo area, where he was both a Reverend and a fruit grower. The 1916 Ft. Pierce City Directory also has the Laines living in Orchid. The 1918 directory shows Oslo again.

Laine died on August 13, 1918, and is buried in the Oslo cemetery and is listed on the monument to the Confederate soldiers.[484] (See p 254.) He is shown to have been with the Hammer Rifles, Mississippi Regiment in the CSA. The birth year on it doesn't jive with the year set forth above.

M. M. Miller - Sebastian Justice of the Peace, 1912-1929

Milo Milton Miller was born at Hadley, Michigan, on June 16, 1856, where he grew up. He then moved to Troy, Missouri, where he married Barbara Kuda on October 6, 1896. Thereafter, he spent some years in Swifton, Arkansas, and then moved his family to Florida in 1910, locating on a twenty-acre tract of land near Sebastian, where he erected a home.

Mr. Miller was interested in horticulture and started developing the "Square Deal Nursery," which proved a successful venture. He then acquired other property and became active in civic affairs.

Judge Miller, as he was known, was first elected justice of the peace for the north district, also known as the First District of St. Lucie County, in 1912. He served the north county for about fifteen years, much of it preceding the incorporation of the City of Sebastian,[485] and even thereafter, as he was re-elected in November 1926,[486] but died in office.[487] His office was in his home on Louisiana Avenue in Sebastian. He also served eight years on the Board of Commissioners for the Sebastian Inlet District. His efforts contributed largely to the Community Hall erected in the City of Sebastian. He was Secretary of the Board of Directors for most of the remainder of his life.

When the City of Sebastian was incorporated, he was elected a member of the city council, resigning when he moved his residence south of the city, which made him ineligible to continue serving. His house, incidentally, was said to be one of the Sears, Roebuck catalog homes.

He was a member of the Episcopal Church for more than eighteen years and was Council Commander of the local camp of Modern Woodmen. He died on May 3, 1929, in Sebastian and was survived by his widow, Barbara K. Miller, and three children: Mrs. Curtis Bobo of Fort Pierce; Ted R. Miller of Fort Pierce; and Mrs. Ruby Miller Anderson of Sebastian.

George T. Badger, Sebastian Justice of the Peace, Nov 24, 1929 – 1/2/31

See the biographical information under Sebastian Mayor Judges.

Lisbon Futch, Sebastian Justice of the Peace, Jan 3, 1939- Nov. 1940

This info appears in the FL. State Archives in cursive. I originally interpreted the name as Fistok. At the last minute, I found Futch. Because of my index being done, his bio continues in this endnote.[488]

C. Biographical Information on Sebastian Mayor Judges

T. B. Hicks, Sebastian Municipal Court Judge, 1924-1925

Thomas Branch Hicks (1872-1945) was the first Mayor of Sebastian. He was born in Gainesville, Florida, in 1872. His parents were Mary Jane Turner Hicks (1842-1880), who was born in Georgia, and John E. Hicks (1842-1872), who was born in Kentucky. T. B. Hicks was in the fish business in Titusville, Florida, in 1900. He employed, among others, Edwin B. "Ned" Sembler (1866-1941), who subsequently became Mr. Hick's partner in the fish business. The 1916 St. Lucie County Directory listed Hicks' occupation as Wholesale Fish Director.[489]

Thomas Hicks served on the school board and was quite active in politics and civic affairs. At one time, he was a part-owner of a sawmill west of Wabasso, along with Ned and Charlie Sembler. Their lumber was used to build houses in the developing Fellsmere, including the hotel. They also cut cross ties for Henry Flagler's railroad, in the 1890s, which was then advancing to the Keys.

Hicks married Mabel Sembler, the sister of Ned Sembler. The Hicks' daughter, Mattie, was born in 1903, and their son, Edwin, was born in 1906. The Hicks lost their infant son, T. B. Hicks, Jr., in July 1916. The Hicks family also suffered great losses in the late 20s. The hurricane of 1928 destroyed Hicks's docks and boats. That disaster, coupled with the total loss of personal assets in Sebastian during the Depression, destroyed his health. Thomas Hicks never recovered completely. He died in 1945. His wife, Mabel, died July 15, 1965, in Fellsmere.

Thomas Branch Hicks and Mabel Sembler Hicks, 4/20/41 M.K.H
Courtesy of Sebastian Area Historical Society

Mayor George T. Badger
Courtesy of Sebastian Area Historical Museum

G. T. Badger, Sebastian Municipal Judge, 1925-1940

George T. Badger was born in Quitman, Georgia, on February 18, 1880. He was the son of George Marcellas and Ida R. Badger. Mr. Badger purchased property in the Sebastian area in 1909. He developed that property into groves and permanently moved to this county (then St. Lucie) from Cincinnati in 1920.

Badger served in an interesting role following the killing of members of the Ashley Gang in Sebastian in November 1924. Badger was one of the initial six members of the coroner's inquest jury. After testimony was elicited that the prisoners were handcuffed before they were shot, attorney Alto Adams (see Chapter 7), representing the Ashley family, moved that the bodies be exhumed to examine the wrists. Some of the jury seemed interested, but Judge Angus Sumner then declared that the panel had become material witnesses and could not serve impartially. (A subsequent panel ruled that the Ashley Gang deaths were justifiable homicide).[490]

During the period of Governor Martin's term, Badger was instrumental in creating the new county of Indian River, making many trips to Tallahassee for that purpose. He worked for many years on the improvement of Sebastian Inlet. He was also a member of the Indian River Mosquito Control District Commission. He was appointed by Governor Martin and served on the Commission until his death. He was a member of the Sebastian Boosters Club, the National Realtors Association, the Methodist Church of Vero Beach, the Sketch Club, Fellsmere Lodge #232 F. & A.M., and was a Master Mason. He was active in the organization of a bank for Sebastian and the formation of the Chamber of Commerce, of which he was made the initial President.

On December 14, 1925, in the general election, George Badger narrowly defeated T. B. Hicks for mayor, 39 to 35. Mr. Badger likely filled the unexpired term of M. M. Miller as Justice of the Peace on November 24, 1929, but resigned that position on January 2, 1931.

After being continuously re-elected, at least one summer term for the mayor was not terribly demanding. The Press Journal reported on September 20, 1935, in its Sebastian social section, that Mayor George T. Badger and his mother, Mrs. Ida Badger, had returned from a three-month visit with relatives in Atlanta and Quitman, Georgia.

Badger served his city the longest of any mayor in Sebastian's history. At the time of Mr. Badger's death, he was Sebastian's only mayor aside from the initial mayor, Mr. Hicks. He had been re-elected for seven consecutive terms and was serving his fifteenth year as mayor when he died.

He owned and operated Badger Real Estate. His office was located on U.S. 1, which became My Grandmother's Restaurant, which was at the south end of the property, and at that time just north of the Frank Oberbeck Construction office. It has also been reported that Mayor Badger had a barrel factory in his backyard during the Depression and indicated that he could make a hundred barrels a day if necessary.

Mr. Badger died suddenly on January 5, 1940. He was survived by his mother, Mrs. Ida R. Badger of Sebastian; one brother, Dan R. Badger of Tampa; one sister, Mrs. Lillian R. Gates of Jacksonville; and numerous nieces and nephews, both in Florida and Georgia.

Leon O. Baughman, Sebastian Municipal Judge, 1940-1942

Leon Owen Baughman was born on January 12, 1902, in St. George, Georgia, and moved to Vero Beach in 1904. Leon's father, Walter F. Baughman, was born on August 25, 1869, in a log cabin on the 460-acre Baughman "home place" located on a tributary of the Savannah River near Dunbarton, South Carolina. Walter F. Baughman grew up on the home place and worked with his father on the farm and at the gin. Walter's father, Henry Baughman, owned one of the first cotton gins in that area. It was operated by mule power and later converted to steam power.

Leon's mother was Eva Isabelle Owen from the Dunbarton, South Carolina area. Initially, Mr. and Mrs. Walter Baughman settled on seventy acres, which Walter had inherited and farmed for themselves. Their first two children - daughter, Myrtice, and son, Cecil - were born in 1897 and 1899, respectively.

Around 1900, Walter and his family, together with his wife's relatives, the Owens, moved in covered wagons south across Georgia to the Big Bend of the St. Mary's River to Cutler, Georgia, now called St. George. Walter became the postmaster and was involved in the timber and cattle business. That is where son Leon was born, together with his brother, Alton "Monk" Baughman.

In 1904, when the family became restless and moved further south, they acquired land on the west side of the Sebastian River.

Several members of the Owen family came with the Baughmans, including Maude Muller Owen. Walter Baughman continued his interest in farming and timbering, and from his sugar cane made syrup and sugar. The family also grew citrus.

Walter's sister-in-law, Maude, applied for the position of postmaster of Sebastian and was awarded that on September 17, 1906, and served at various locations in that position in Sebastian for twenty-three years. She was succeeded by her niece, Myrtice Baughman Martin Hunter.

Later, Walter Baughman built from the timbers on his river property a two-story home at 1525 North Louisiana Avenue, later owned by John and Jackie DeVane. From there, the family operated the first dairy in Sebastian, with fresh milk (non-pasteurized) being delivered door to door. In 1912, Mrs. Walter (Belle) Baughman's sister, Maude Owen, married Fred Park, the youngest son of Sebastian pioneer, August Park.

Leon, known as "Skinny," worked at Sebastian's railroad station. He was also engaged in the citrus business, operated a dairy, and had cattle interests in Sebastian. For twelve years, he served on the city council. Leon Baughman was elected Mayor of the City of Sebastian in a special meeting of the city council on January 17, 1940. The vacancy existed because of the sudden death of then-Mayor George T. Badger. Mr. Baughman served until 1942.

Brother, Alton "Monk," married Clara Buchlie in 1908. Clara had been born in Switzerland. She and her parents lived in Roseland from 1918 to 1922. Monk had a daughter by an earlier marriage to Estelle Ingram, called Eileen, who lived in Vero Beach.

Leon's mother died in February 1947. Walter returned with his son, Monk, to revisit the old home place in South Carolina. While there, Walter died of a heart attack in May of 1950 and was returned to Sebastian to be buried beside his wife, Belle.

Leon was a veteran of World War II, serving in the United States Navy. He was a member of the John M. Nixon VFW Post 3918 of Vero Beach and a member of Fellsmere Masonic Lodge #232 F&AM. He was the initial Town of Sebastian Clerk.[491] He is listed in the St. Lucie County Directory of 1919 as a Clerk of the Post Office.

He passed away on December 31, 1970, and was survived by his brother, A. P. Baughman, and two nieces. Leon Baughman was buried in Sebastian Cemetery.

E. W. Vickers, Sebastian Municipal Judge, 1942-1945

Everett Western ("E. W.") Vickers was born in Hahira, Lowndes County, Georgia, on September 30, 1891. His father was Stephen Vickers, who was also born there, on May 18, 1852, and died on October 10, 1924, in Sebastian, Florida. Everett's mother was Sarah Folsom. Everett and his brothers, George and Frank, came to

Sebastian in 1908 from Hahira, which is just north of the Florida state line. Their sister was called "Bamma," who also moved to Sebastian.

Mary Edwards, the future Mrs. E. W. Vickers, was born in Portsmouth, Ohio, and came to Sebastian with her father, William C. Edwards (1858-1933), in 1911. Her father was head of the bookkeeping department for Selby Shoes, a national shoe company that had a factory in Portsmouth. He was also a teacher and purportedly a radical soapbox socialist who was fired from his job and thus came to Florida. He and his wife and daughters came first to Sopchoppy, Florida, in 1907. Mr. Edwards worked there as a teacher. Conditions were intolerable for the family, and Mrs. Edwards and the two daughters, Mary and Lydia Edwards, returned to Portsmouth for a time. When Mr. Edwards secured a job and a nice place to live, the rest of the family returned to Florida, Sebastian, in 1911.

The future Mrs. E. W. (Mary) Vickers taught school west of Sebastian (Collier Creek area) and then in Sebastian. Mr. and Mrs. E. W. Vickers were married in 1914. E. W. and Mary's first child, Lowell, died as a baby in Fort Pierce. The Vickers' first residence was on the west side of U.S. 1, about two and one-half miles south of downtown Sebastian. It is the piece of property where Dr. Fischer had his dental office.

Lydia Edwards married Chuck Gulledge in the 1920s in Sebastian. She passed away on January 4, 1988.[492]

The Vickers Brothers (George and Frank) Store was purchased by them around 1912 in Fellsmere. They later had a store on Main Street in Sebastian that was purchased from W. F. Cox, who is discussed under Chapter 12, Vero Mayor Judges. The Vickers brothers lived on the second floor of the Sebastian store and had the business on the first floor. The building later became a post office. The store was subsequently owned by Mrs. Mary Etta Roundtree and then became the City Hall at the end of World War II. She conducted the dry goods business in a store building, which is the present spot of the northbound lane of U.S. 1 on the corner of Main Street, where the Chamber of Commerce is located.

E. W. Vickers was appointed second city clerk to fill the unexpired term of resigned City Clerk L. O. Baughman.[493] The 1916 St. Lucie County Directory lists him as working for Vickers Brothers, General Merchandise. Mr. Vickers and his wife raised five children, all of whom were born in Sebastian. He was elected mayor of the City of Sebastian on October 20, 1942.

A chronological compilation of interesting historical facts about the Vickers, appearing in the City of Sebastian records, was done and is in a publication.[494]

E. W. Vickers was known throughout his life as a prominent citrus grower. His sister "Bamma" was active in civic affairs, and a bust of her is on display at the North County library. Mr. Vickers was an active member of the Mosquito Control Board and a member of the Sebastian Methodist Church, the Elks Club of Fort Pierce for thirty-seven years, and Fellsmere Masonic Lodge #232.

E. W. Vickers died on April 13, 1965, in Palm Beach, Florida. He was then survived by his wife, Mrs. Mary Edwards Vickers; two daughters, Mrs. Dorothy Rogers of Sebastian, and Mrs. Betty Foster of Hialeah; two sons, Jack and Donald Vickers of Sebastian; and three sisters, Mrs. Alma Hall of Homerville, Georgia, Mrs. Bamma Lawson, and Mrs. Mary Hall of Sebastian. He is buried in the Sebastian Cemetery.

Lee Mont Shafor, Sebastian Municipal Judge, 1945-1947

Lee Mont Shafor was born in Monroe, Ohio, on February 26, 1882. He was the son of Lee Shafor.

Lee Mont Shafor moved to Sebastian from Dayton, Ohio, in 1932. He was active in civic and political life in Sebastian, having served as Mayor from December 1945 to December 1947. He was also a citrus grower in the area. He passed away on November 15, 1953. He was survived by his wife, Daisy M. Shafor, of Sebastian, and a sister, Mrs. Charles Hughes of California.

Earl Roberts, Sebastian Municipal Judge, 1947-1949

Earl Roberts was born on June 7, 1897, in Pittsfield, Massachusetts. He moved to Indian River County in approximately 1940. He operated for many years the old Sebastian Inn, a hotel, cocktail lounge, and restaurant, which was built in the 1930s. It was located on the U.S. 1, now Indian River Drive, until it was torn down in 1968 by Art Corsi to make way for the Sportsman's Lodge. (The Sebastian Inn is not to be confused with the Sebastian Beach Inn, which is or was located on the barrier island in Brevard County.)

The Sebastian Inn was considered one of the best eating places between Jacksonville and Miami and drew crowds of diners on weekends. The hotel treated its overnight guests to trips on the Indian River on the hotel's sightseeing boat.

Mr. Roberts served two terms as Mayor of the City of Sebastian from December 1947 through December 1949. He owned and operated Earl's Hideaway Bar, which continues under the name of Earl's Hideaway Lounge.

Mr. Roberts died on December 23, 1980, in Melbourne, Florida, and was then survived by two daughters, Mrs. Evelyn White and Mrs. Cecelia Connelly, and one son, Frank Roberts. Earl Roberts is buried in the Sebastian Cemetery.

J. R. Middleton, Sebastian Municipal Judge, 1949-1951

J. R. Middleton was born in Modale, Iowa, on February 9, 1877. Mr. Middleton married the former Elbia Wagner, whom he met in Iowa. J. R. Middleton graduated from the University of Idaho in the early 1900s and later coached football at his alma mater. He then became a bank examiner for the State of Ohio. Thereafter, with a change in politics due to the "spoils system," Mr. Middleton obtained work in Michigan running an apple vending machine business in the Detroit area.

Mr. Middleton had two children, Arthur and John. Mrs. Middleton died when Arthur, who was born in 1914, was only four years old. Mr. Middleton then married Margaret Haberman.

In the mid-1930s, J. R. Middleton came to Florida, first to Grant and subsequently, Sebastian. He owned and operated several fish houses from West Palm Beach to Cocoa. They processed and shipped fish and crab meat. Mr. Middleton's son, Arthur, drove a truck delivering fish around the southeastern portion of the United States Arthur not only worked in the vending machine business and fish business with his father, he also worked for many years for FP&L, first in Sebastian as an apprentice lineman, and subsequently as a lineman, troubleshooter, and dispatcher for FP&L in Sanford, Florida. He retired in 1973. Son, John Middleton, served in and retired from the United States Navy, having worked particularly with submarines.

J. R. Middleton was Mayor of Sebastian from 1949 to 1951. Mr. Middleton was known for his financing wherewithal and his handling of certain bond issues for the City of Sebastian. Arthur Middleton has described his father's home as being the former McCain residence. (See Chapter 11).

In one of the city council elections prior to his becoming mayor, J. R. Middleton was re-elected to the city council, along with Charles Sembler and Archie Smith. That occurred on December 12, 1946. Mr. Middleton received 112 votes, Mr. Sembler received 105, and Archie Smith received 104. The fourth candidate, Frank Buckles, tallied 81 votes.[495] The long-lived Rodney Kroegel, the son of the first U.S. Wildlife warden, Paul Kroegel, has described J. R. Middleton as being "a well-off, smart man, like a lawyer!"

Son, Arthur Middleton, who had married Virginia Isabelle Glasgow of Sebastian, was married to her for over fifty-seven years. They had four children, Walter Arthur Middleton, an FSU graduate who worked for the City of Tallahassee, Barbara Sharp of Grovetown, Georgia, Raymond of Deland, Florida, who served his country in the 88th Airborne Division and who also worked for the Fire Department in Deland, Florida; and Grace E. Underwood who died in an industrial accident in the Charleston, South Carolina Navy Supply Depot.

J. R. Middleton died on February 7, 1966, just two days short of his 90th birthday. He died in Boise, Idaho. He predeceased his wife, Margaret, by about five or six years.

A. G. Shaffer, Sebastian Municipal Judge, 1951-1955

Alston G. Shaffer was born before 1908 in Buckhannon, West Virginia. He moved to Indian River County in 1949. He was married to May C. Shaffer, who predeceased him - Mrs. Shaffer having passed away on November 28, 1970. The Shaffers had two daughters.

The Shaffers lived next door to Mr. Bob Ware. In fact, Mr. Ware and his brother-in-law built and sold A. G. Shaffer his house, which was the second one in from the corner of Central Avenue and Main Street, behind the Video Doctor.

Mr. Shaffer defeated Henry P. Lyons for Mayor in December 1951 by a vote of 102 to 47. He was reelected to another 2-year term in 1953 by defeating former mayor, J. R. Middleton, 97-72. Mr. Ware remembers Mr. Shaffer as the Mayor of Sebastian. He and others have described A. G. Shaffer as being handicapped, using a wheelchair at all times, even when he served as mayor. Mr. Shaffer was self-employed as a watchmaker.

Mr. Shaffer died June 21, 1975, in Needham, MA, and was survived by 3 siblings. After a service in Sebastian at the United Methodist church, he was buried in Palm Beach Memorial Park in Lantana, FL.

C. E. Taylor, Sebastian Municipal Judge, 1955-1957

Charles Eli Taylor was born June 16, 1892, in Havelock, Iowa. Mr. Taylor married Bessie Elizabeth Williams on February 5, 1912, in Clarinda, Iowa. She had been his childhood sweetheart in Red Oak, Iowa. Immediately thereafter, he followed his grandfather, Charles Dukeshire, to Roseland, Florida.

Grandfather Dukeshire had been wanting to return to Florida since the Civil War, but could not enlist the consent of his wife, prior to her death, or that of his nine children. Mr. Dukeshire convinced his grandson, who in turn convinced his soon-to-be bride, to come to Florida.

When C. E. Taylor arrived in Florida with his wife and Grandfather Dukeshire, they stayed at a hotel in Roseland while ten acres were cleared. The pines were cut down, hauled to the Roseland Sawmill, and then brought back to the site where a four-room house and front porch were built. The grandfather and grandson team planted citrus and cedars.

Thereafter, Grandfather Dukeshire returned to Iowa for an operation but never recovered. C. E. Taylor inherited the land and $350.00 from his grandfather. The Taylors lived off the land and game from the surrounding areas.

The Taylors had four children: Rosalee Taylor Hume, Paul, Joel, and Irvin. It was after the third child that the Taylor family moved from Roseland to Sebastian in 1918. Mr. Taylor, who had apprenticed in Iowa as a barber, became the owner of Taylor's Barber Shop in Sebastian, but performed other work, including fishing, budding trees, picking guavas for a jelly factory, and grove care.

Mr. Taylor served as Mayor of Sebastian from Dec. 14, 1955, to Dec. 7, 1957. He was elected by defeating J. R. Middleton, with a vote count of 88 to 84.

On October 4, 1928, Paul Taylor was killed in a gun accident at home. Joel Dwayne Taylor died on September 19, 1966, and Mrs. Bessie E. Taylor died on October 8, 1973.

C. E. Taylor also preached and was a superintendent of the Methodist Church in Sebastian, and was later married to Mary Lawson, a parishioner of that church, when he was 86 years old. He died at age 93, on October 25, 1985, in Rockledge, Florida. Survivors included his son, Ervin W. Taylor of Rockledge, and one daughter, Rosalee Taylor Hume of Micco, who started the Sebastian River Art Club in 1937.

Paul Stevenson, Sebastian Municipal Judge, 1957-1959

Paul Stevenson was born in Syracuse, New York, on December 8, 1910. He worked in Bendix, New Jersey, and later purchased land in Sebastian. He moved to Sebastian in 1943 and married Hazel Tilton of New Jersey in 1946.

Mr. Stevenson worked a variety of jobs in the Sebastian area for years, as steady work was hard to come by. He was later employed with Piper Aircraft. Mr. Stevenson served on the Sebastian City Council for two terms, 1947 through 1949, and as mayor from December 1957 to December 1959. In that contest for mayor, he defeated Jack Baxter by a vote of 92 to 80. In 1958, Mr. Stevenson founded the Sebastian Chamber of Commerce.

It was as mayor that Mr. Stevenson persuaded the U.S. Government to give a large portion of land from a former military air base to the city in the 1960s for a city-owned airport. Then, Mayor Stevenson wanted the municipal airport to make it easier for businesspeople who lived in the area. He is also credited with the rocket that stood for many years on U.S. 1 at County Road 512 (the eastbound portion of the divided highway. (The rocket was meant to advertise a gas station he built on that corner and "symbolized performance like a rocket.")

He held court in the council chambers in City Hall. As to the mayor's capacity as a judge, Mrs. Stevenson related that Mr. Stevenson did not like judging others. Mrs. Stevenson was Postmaster from 1956 to 1970.

The Stevenson homestead was located at the corner of Coolidge Street and Indian River Drive. It is now considered a historic house in Sebastian. Plans were underway at one point to convert it to "The Angler Inn."

During Mr. Stevenson's lifetime, a monument was placed on the land that Mr. and Mrs. Stevenson donated to the City of Sebastian in 1977. It consists of that narrow strip of riverfront off Indian River Drive, between Coolidge Street and Fellsmere Road. It is a favorite spot where area residents can sit in the open pavilion and watch the activity on the river.

The Stevensons left the area and moved to Fernandina Beach in approximately 1987. "There had not been a great deal of growth in Sebastian until that point, but it seems to have boomed thereafter," Mrs. Stevenson related from her home in Fernandina Beach.[496] Mr. Stevenson died on July 5, 1992. He was survived not only by his wife, Hazel, but also by one daughter, Valorie, also of Fernandina Beach.

*In initially drafting this chapter, I had Robert Jackson starting in the mid-1960s as Municipal Judge, so I covered certain mayors post the

1959 timeframe, as per the above. So, the remaining mayors set forth below may not have been the sole municipal judges, but Judge Jackson would have worked with[497] and for them as the Municipal Judge.

Fred Rohme, Sebastian Municipal Mayor, 1959-1961

Frederick William Rohme was born on April 29, 1909, in Syracuse, New York. His father was Clarence Elmer Rohme, and his mother was Clara Bertha Kai.

Frederick William Rohme was married to Mary Elizabeth Schad in Syracuse, New York, on June 25, 1932. Mary Schad was born in Indianapolis, Indiana. They had one daughter, Jean. Mr. and Mrs. Rohme raised Jean in Schenectady, New York, until she was in the ninth grade, and then the family moved to Florida. They first lived in Delray and then in the West Palm Beach area. In Delray, Mr. Rohme worked in the building construction business. Mr. Rohme then operated a fish market in Riviera Beach and ultimately moved to Sebastian, being drawn by property in that area in 1955. The Rohmes lived on the river in Sebastian, adjacent to a warehouse and dock approximately four blocks north of Main Street. Mr. Rohme owned a bait and tackle shop and a smokehouse where he would primarily smoke shrimp.

On December 4, 1959, he was elected Mayor of Sebastian, defeating incumbent mayor, Paul Stevenson. Rohme didn't quite complete his term, but went on to be the Police Chief for Sebastian, which lasted for approximately ten years. He was a member of the local Lions Club and Masonic Chapter and a member of the First Baptist Church in Sebastian.

In approximately 1975, the Rohmes retired to Leesburg, Florida, to be with their daughter, Jean Wells, who had three children: Mary Ann, William, and Sandra. Mr. Rohme died on March 6, 1986, in Leesburg, and his wife, Mary, followed him in death some years later. The Rohmes' ashes were scattered by their daughter off the dock adjacent to where they lived in Sebastian.

Amos Simmons, Sebastian Municipal Mayor, 1961

Amos Simmons was born on November 15, 1926, in Perry, Florida, to Ollie Amos Simmons and Mary Rebecca (Poppell) Simmons. He was a veteran of the U. S. Navy and of the Baptist Faith. Amos Simmons started working for Florida Power and Light in Melbourne in 1949. Subsequently, he was transferred to Cocoa and then, as a lineman, to Sebastian. He was made foreman for FP&L in 1958. He worked for FP&L in the Sebastian area for approximately thirty-five years.

Mr. Simmons was appointed mayor, not elected, on June 26, 1961. He served for only a short period of time, as FP&L did not encourage its employees to be involved in politics. Mr. Simmons filled the unexpired term of Fred Rohme, who resigned to become the Chief of Police.

Mr. Simmons was married to Susie Lorene and raised two boys. The boys graduated from Sebastian Elementary School, the site of the present City Hall, and graduated from Vero Beach High School. Those boys are Robert Simmons of Lakeland and Richard Simmons of Perry. The Simmones lived in a home in front of the Methodist church on Main Street in Sebastian, just across the railroad tracks. The location became a furniture store.

Mr. and Mrs. Simmons retired and returned to live in Perry, Florida. He died on April 8, 2015, in Mayo, Florida. He was predeceased by his wife of 62 years, Susie Lorene, who died in 2011.

William E. Boone, Sebastian Municipal Mayor, 1961-1967

William Ervin Boone was born on May 15, 1913, in Jasper, Hamilton County, Florida. He was educated in Florida public schools, including the University of Florida. He served his country in the United States Navy during World War II. He moved permanently to Sebastian in 1959. He was married to the former Helen B. Meyer and had one daughter, Faye Sandra Cobb. Mr. Boone served as a deacon of the First Baptist Church in Sebastian.

Mr. Boone initially operated Boone Real Estate in Boynton Beach and then opened a branch office in Sebastian on U.S. Highway #1, just north of the present Chamber of Commerce in approximately 1955. He also worked for Piper Aircraft Company in Vero Beach. Mr. Boone closed the Boynton Beach office, making the Sebastian office his main office with another branch in Malabar. The Boone home was adjacent to the real estate office.

Mr. Boone was the Mayor of Sebastian for just over six years from 1961 through 1967. In 1965, he was reelected despite 2 opposing candidates in a record voter turnout of 298. He was the last of the mayor-municipal judges for Sebastian. Mr. Boone's daughter, Sandra, recalls Mr. Boone acting as municipal judge, handling and disposing of "violations."

Mr. Boone's daughter, Mrs. Eugene (Sandra) Cobb of Sebastian, had four children: Robin R. Brock of Columbia, South Carolina, William Mark Cobb of Williston, South Carolina, Craig Matthew Cobb of Roseland, and Timothy Brian Cobb of Vero Beach.

Mr. Boone died at age 57 on November 9, 1970, in Melbourne, Florida. He was survived by his second wife, Mrs. Wilma Boone, of Melbourne, Florida, and the daughter and grandchildren set forth above, two stepdaughters, his mother, two brothers, and three sisters. He is buried in Fountainhead Memorial Park in Grant – Valkaria, FL.

Robert Jackson, Sebastian Municipal Judge, 1959-1973

Robert Jackson was born April 13, 1932, in West Chester, Pa. He was raised in Washington, D.C. and attended Taft Junior High School and Calvin Coolidge High School, where he excelled in basketball and tennis. He moved to Brooksville, Florida, in 1947 and attended Hernando High School, where he continued his athletic successes, being on championship teams in football, baseball, and basketball. He then attended the University of Florida on a basketball scholarship. There, he was a member of Phi Delta Theta Fraternity, the university's Executive Council, the Blue Key honorary leadership fraternity, and was the student director of the intramurals program. He received his BS in Education in June of 1954.

Robert joined the United States Air Force and attended the Air Intelligence Service School in Denver, Colorado. He was then sent to Jordan and worked on briefing the commanding general, and later worked in the group headquarters. He was commissioned as a Second Lieutenant and served in South Korea as an investigator of POWs and did special projects throughout Korea. Thereafter, Robert returned to the U.S. and attended the University of Florida Law School on the G.I. Bill, graduating in May 1959, just after marrying Marjorie Ann Perritt in Vero Beach on March 19, 1959. Coincidentally, they were married by County Court Judge Miles B. Mank, II.

Prior to graduating from law school, Robert was a legislative aide to the state representatives from St. Lucie and Indian River Counties, Rupert Smith and L. B. Vocelle. Following law school, Robert was an associate at the firm of Vocelle and Vocelle in Vero Beach.

Jackson was a municipal judge for the City of Sebastian and also practiced law in the areas of real estate, probate, trust law, and tax, and became board-certified in real estate by the Florida Bar. He also served as an assistant state attorney prosecuting felonies in Indian River and Okeechobee Counties. Robert was a hospital trustee for the Indian River Hospital District for 12 years, a member of the Exchange Club of Vero Beach, and a deacon at the First Baptist Church in Vero Beach. He later became Board Certified in Tax, Trusts, and Estate Planning, as well as in Real Estate. Bob retired from the practice of law in 2007.

Robert Jackson died on March 27, 2024. Robert and Marjorie raised 3 children: Robert Neal Jackson, Karen Jackson, and Jennifer Jackson Pileggi.

Chapter 15 - City of Wabasso Municipal Court

Wabasso began its existence at least by 1894, when it was a fuel stop for the railroad.[498] Its name is believed to be taken from an Indian name spelled backwards or from Longfellow's poem, Song of Hiawatha. [499]

In 1925, it became the City of Wabasso after previously being organized as a town.[500]In the city charter, the mayor was given jurisdiction for the trial of all offenses against the laws of the city and was designated as judge of the municipal court.[501] The city council, however, was given the authority to provide for the election of a municipal judge to perform all the duties of the mayor with respect to the mayor's court. The act provided that when the city council acted, the mayor's court was to become the municipal court.

As of May 31, 1935, the City of Wabasso was abolished.[502]

Interviews with a couple of prominent pioneers from Wabasso failed to verify that a court for Wabasso was actually used.[503]

Chapter 16 - Town of Indian River Shores Municipal Court

A. History of Indian River Shores Municipal Court

The nature of municipal courts and their abolition[504] by the constitutional amendments of 1972 are discussed in more detail under the preceding chapter of City of Vero Beach - Municipal Court.

The Town of Indian River Shores was created in 1953 by a special act of the Legislature.[505] Article V, Section 3 provided in part: "At such organizational meeting, the town council may also appoint a ... municipal judge...." Article XI created the municipal court "for the trial of all offenders against the municipal ordinances." It was further stated that "the municipal court shall have a judge, an acting judge, a clerk and assistant clerk or clerks"[506] and that "the municipal judge shall be a practicing attorney-at-law... appointed by the council to hold office at the will of the town council, and need not be a qualified elector of the town."[507]

Article XI provided, "The Mayor shall be the acting municipal judge to preside over the municipal court in the absence or disqualification of the municipal judge."[508] Unlike the other municipal courts in Indian River County, this one started with a non-mayor judge.

Marshall O. Mitchell, the town attorney, was made the municipal judge at the organizational meeting of the town council. See endnote.[509] The first mayor, who could serve as acting judge in the judge's absence, was Fred Tuerk, who served as mayor from 1953 until 1968 (after which he was still on the town council). Mr. Mitchell was continually appointed as municipal judge for four-year terms until July 27, 1965, when he was succeeded as municipal judge by his law partner, G. Kendall Sharp, who likely served until the court's abolition in 1973. Another partner, Gordon Johnston, served as town attorney in 1967.

Alex MacWilliam, Jr., who became a council member on June 25, 1959, was subsequently appointed as clerk of the municipal court in 1962, and Elizabeth H. Mason was appointed as assistant clerk. Under Chapter 34 of the Ordinances of the Town of Indian River Shores, the judge and the clerks were to serve without salary or compensation. The ordinance also required the court to convene at 10 a.m. every Tuesday morning. However, prior council minutes of 2/8/61 showed the town attorney (Mitchell) to be paid $1,200.00 per year, and Ms. Mason, as secretary to the council, was paid $3.00 per hour.

MacWilliam was the son of Alex MacWilliam, Sr., whose biographical information is listed under the heading of the Municipal Court of Vero Beach. He was succeeded by Tom Begley in January of 1975. The municipal court was abolished by Ordinance No. 159 on May 1, 1975, and the jurisdiction was transferred to the county court of Indian River County effective May 1, 1975, in accordance with Florida Statute 168.031 and the Supreme Court of Florida Transition Rule 16.

The following is a list of the municipal judges and the time frames in which they served as municipal judges:

Mayor/Acting Judge:	
Fred Tuerk	1953 - 1962
Roland B. Miller	1963 - 1975+
Non-Mayor Municipal Judges:	
Marshall O. Mitchell	1962 - 1963
G. Kendall Sharp	1963 - 1973

B. Biographical Information on Municipal Judges of Indian River Shores

Fred Tuerk, Mayor 1953-1966 and Acting Judge in the Municipal Judge's Absence

Fred R. Tuerk was born in Chicago, Illinois, on October 26, 1905. He was the son of George E. Tuerk, who was born in Chicago in 1874, and Elizabeth Brennwald Tuerk, who was also a native of Chicago, born in 1879, and who resided for some time in Indian River

County. Tuerk's grandparents were German and Swiss immigrants who came to America in the middle of the 19th century.

After Tuerk's 1923 graduation from Crane High School in Chicago, he enrolled at the University of Chicago and graduated just three years later, in 1926. In 1928, he received his master's degree from Columbia University in New York City. In 1930, Tuerk returned to Chicago and became a partner in the investment house of Fuller, Cruttenden Investment Bankers (later changed to Cruttenden and Company). He was a member of the Chicago Stock Exchange from 1930 until 1947 and the governor from 1942 until 1947. He was also a member of the New York Stock Exchange during this period.

Refused for military service during World War II, Tuerk was president of the Utah Radio Products Company from 1940 to 1946. The company, with 5,000 employees, contributed to the Manhattan Project, which produced the atomic bomb. He received high honors from the U.S. Government for outstanding contributions to the war effort. In 1947, he moved to Pasadena, California, where he resided for three years while serving as director and active member of the William R. Staats Investment Company, as well as numerous other companies.

Tuerk moved to Vero Beach in approximately 1950 and became an active citizen and businessman. Continuing his work in investments, he also became active in farming and citrus. He also purchased extensive real estate holdings, including the Windswept Hotel, which became the Holiday Inn Oceanside, as well as 3,000 acres of river-to-ocean land north of Vero Beach that stretched for four and one-half miles. He designated the land as the site of the City of Indian River Shores, which was said to be larger geographically than the City of Miami Beach. In 1953, through his influence, the Florida Legislature created the Town of Indian River Shores. He served as mayor from 1953 until 1963 and as a town councilman.

Along with his other contributions to the development of Indian River County, Tuerk was also responsible for the drainage of over 30,000 acres of marshland west of Vero Beach, and for the organization of the St. Johns River Drainage District, which, in addition to bringing more land into valuable agricultural production, is also responsible for water conservation in the area.

It has been reported that Tuerk's interest in the United Fruit Company led to his acquisition of an estimated 70,000 acres in British Honduras. He also gave some 80 acres of land in Indian River Shores to St. Edward's School, a private preparatory school, but the school opted to acquire the old Riomar Country Club building for its campus.

Tuerk attended the First Presbyterian Church in Vero Beach and was a member of the Riomar Country Club and the Riomar Bay Yacht Club.

In August 1950, he married Adriana Kromhout in Vero Beach. Born in Long Island in 1932, Mrs. Tuerk was the daughter of Ysbrand and Lena Kromhout, who were both born in Holland. Mr. and Mrs. Tuerk were the parents of John E. Tuerk, born in 1951, and Adrianna Elizabeth Tuerk, born in 1954, each in Vero Beach.

They all survived Mr. Tuerk's death on February 2, 1967, in Vero Beach, as did two children from his first marriage, Mrs. Douglas F. Williamson, Jr., then of New York City, New York, and George R. Tuerk, then of San Diego, California. Son, Fred R. Tuerk, Jr., passed away in California in 1961.

Roland B. Miller, Mayor – Acting Municipal Judge 1963-1975+

Roland B. Miller was born in Lakeland, Florida, on October 4, 1914. He was the son of William T. Miller and the former Versa Donaldson. He was a 1933 graduate of Lakeland High School, where he played football. He was long associated with the Chevrolet Motor Division of General Motors, both in Jacksonville and for 23 years as an automobile dealer in Vero Beach.

Miller was active with real estate in Indian River County and was an incorporator of the Town of Indian River Shores. He served as its mayor for 14 years, from 1963 to 1977. He was instrumental in bringing about the Sebastian Inlet Bridge on A1A. He was also a trustee of the Indian River Memorial Hospital and a member of the

Vero Beach Rotary Club, the Moose Lodge, the First Methodist Church, and a charter and lifetime member of the Elks Lodge #1774.

Miller died on May 19, 1992.

Marshall O. Mitchell, Municipal Judge 1953-1965

Marshall Outhwaite Mitchell was born in Osceola, Missouri, in 1908. After he graduated from high school, he entered Baker University in Baldwin, Kansas, from which he graduated four years later. His advanced study was taken at the Washington University School of Law in St. Louis, Missouri, and upon his graduation in 1932, he was admitted to the Missouri Bar.

In 1938, after his admission to the Florida Bar, he joined his older brother, Charles A. Mitchell, in the practice of law at one of the first law firms in Vero Beach, Vocelle & Mitchell. Marshall Mitchell practiced in Vero Beach until the onset of World War II.

Mitchell was a lieutenant commander in the Navy and was involved in numerous actions in the Pacific. In his post-war civilian life, he was active in the Veterans of Foreign Wars, serving as post commander, Florida senior vice commander, and a member of the national Veterans of Foreign Wars legislative committee.

Among the many positions which Mitchell held in the community were attorney for the Indian River Memorial Hospital for many years, attorney for the Indian River County Board of Public

Instruction from 1950 until his death, and attorney for the Indian River Mosquito Control District. He was a member of the American Bar Association, the Florida Bar Association, and the Indian River County Bar Association. He was also a fellow in the College of Probate Counsel of the American Bar Association. Mitchell was one of the founders of Title Security Company.

Mitchell was the president of the Vero Beach-Indian River County Chamber of Commerce. In addition, he was a member of the Rotary Club and a founder of both the Vero Beach Little League and the Vero Beach High School booster club, the Indian Chiefs. He was a member of Trinity Episcopal Church, Phi Alpha Delta honorary legal fraternity, and Sigma Phi Epsilon social fraternity.

Mitchell and his wife, Hazel, were the parents of three daughters - Mrs. Lorne Cassel of Indian Harbour Beach, Judith Roberts of Vero Beach, and Mary Marshall Mitchell Jones of Birmingham, Alabama.

Mitchell died on August 20, 1968, in Coral Gables, Florida. Following his death, the Marshall O. Mitchell Scholarship Fund was organized through the then Indian River Citrus Bank to continue service to the community, a trait for which Mitchell was reportedly well known.

G. Kendall Sharp, Municipal Judge 1965-1975

See bio information under the chapter on Circuit Judges.

Chapter 17 - Town of Orchid Municipal Court

The Town of Orchid was initially formed in 1965, primarily at the urging of the Michael, Lier, and Ryall families. Attorney John Gould of Vero Beach set up the charter for the town. The special act creating the town was Chapter 2021 of the Laws of Florida, 1965.

Shortly thereafter, Darrell Fennell became the town attorney. Fennell said that there never was a municipal court in Orchid,[510] notwithstanding Article XI, which created a municipal court "for the trial of all persons charged with violating municipal ordinances." Similar to other special acts then in effect, the municipal judge was required to be a practicing attorney, appointed by the town council but not the electors of the town. The mayor would be the acting municipal judge in the absence of a municipal judge.[511]

The right to implement a municipal court was abrogated throughout the State of Florida by Article V, Section 20 (d) 4, Constitution of the State of Florida (1972).

Fennell also said that throughout the history of the town, at least until about 1989 when the Orchid Island subdivision development began, Orchid was the smallest municipality in the state.[512]

Conclusion

There has been a super majority of outstanding jurists. Many had provided military service to their country or at least provided community service to their local governments. Many went on to appellate courts, if not governorships.

It has been my humble pleasure to interview many and read much, and I apologize for any errors. This has been a disjointed project over 32 years, some of it being done before I was aware of, or had access to, the internet.

I had also come across what I'll call a conclusion at the end of Hellier's book, Indian River (cited in the bibliography). He wrote:

"A Last Word

A friend, Lawrence E. Will, an author living in Belle Glade, asked our good friend, Professor Tebeau of the University of Miami, if any money could be made in publishing a Florida History. To which Mr. Tebeau replied: 'About the most you get from a history book is the satisfaction of writing it.' To which Mr. Will says, 'Amen.'"

That quote did not discourage me since that is what I expect to get from my book. The fact that you are reading this proves that I have been able to make an arrangement for its publication.

To that, I also say amen and thank you.

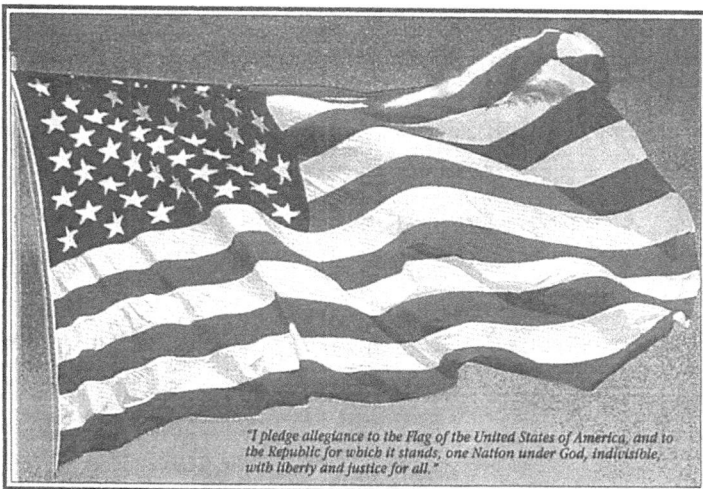

"I pledge allegiance to the Flag of the United States of America, and to the Republic for which it stands, one Nation under God, indivisible, with liberty and justice for all."

Veterans Day Parade
Courthouse &Opening Ceremonies

November 11, 1994

Honoring All Who Served
Army • Marine Corps • Navy • Air Force • Coast Guard

*"The administration of justice is
the firmest pillar of government."*
George Washington

Parade

Indian River County Sheriff's Color Guard

Chairman John Tippin, Indian River County Commission
Mayor Caroline Ginn, City of Vero Beach

Honorable Patsy Kurth, State Senator
Honorable Charles Sembler II, State Representative

L.B. "Buck" Vocelle, Chief Judge Circuit Court
Sherman N. Smith, Jr., - Ribbon Cutter Attorney Since 1935
Charles E. Smith, Circuit Judge

Ron Frankel, Florida D.V.A.
Conway Austin, President Veteran's Council

Indian River County Sheriff Gary Wheeler

City of Vero Beach Color Guard

City of Vero Beach Police Chief James Gabbard

Mayor Robert Schoen, Town of Indian River Shores

Mayor Arthur Firtion, City of Sebastian

James B. Balsiger, County Judge
Joe Wild, County Judge

James DelVecchio, Veteran WWI
Joseph DelVecchio, son of James DelVecchio

Frank Wallace, Veteran WWI
Florence Noonan, escort

Vero Beach Sr. High School Marching Band

Army Recruiter SSIC William Pass USA

John M. Mixon Post 3918, Veterans of Foreign Wars and Auxiliary
Michael DiGangi, Commander

Felix Poppell Post 39, American Legion and Auxiliary
Herb Nelson, Commander

Gene Evans Chapter 34, Disabled American Veterans and Auxiliary
Jake Gehrig, Commander

Indian River Chapter 494, Military Order of Purple Heart and Aux
Gordon K. Brown, Commander

Indian River Det. Marine Corps League and Auxiliary
William J. Owen, Commandant

WWI Barracks 598 and Auxiliary
Frank K. Wallace Sr., Past Commander

Indian River Ex-Prisoners of War
John Lachman, Commander

Vietnam Veterans of America Chapter 567
Bernie McGhee, President

American Veterans Post 6 and Auxiliary
Gary D. Purdy, Commander

Air Force Association
Robert B. Stiastny, President

Italian-American War Veterans
Adam Rossetti, Commander

TROA Color Guard and Members

Treasure Coast Chapter, American Merch; Marine Veterans
John J. Arthur, Commander

Jewish American War Veterans
Ralph Barunstein, President

Treasure Coast Unit of WAVES
Wilma Collins, President

Woman Army Corps Veterans Associatio
Delphine Oropesa

Treasure Coast Council 334, Navy League the U.S.
Walter P. Halstead, President

Air Force Jr ROTC Vero Beach Senior High School
Major, Don Bradley CM/SGT Joseph D'Ambrosio

U.S. Navy Sea Cadets
CDR. Robert Lightser

Jeffrey K. Barton, Clerk of the Circuit Cou

Bruce Colton, State Attorney 19th Judicial Circuit

Diamond Litty, Public Defender 19th Judicial Circuit

Indian River County Bar Association

Daughters of the American Revolution

Sons of the American Revolution

Girl Scouts of America

Elks Lodge

Indian River County EMS Unit

Indian River County Fire Department Hook & Ladder Truck

Ceremonies

WELCOME AND RECOGNITION OF DIGNITARIES .... County Commission Chairman John W. Tippin

VETERANS CEREMONIES .... Conway L. Austin, President, IRC Veteran's Council, LTC,USMC Retired

FLAG RAISING .... Indian River Detachment Marine Corps League

NATIONAL ANTHEM .... Vero Beach Sr. High School Band James Sammons, Director

INVOCATION .... Dean Donavan, American Legion Post 39

PLEDGE OF ALLEGIANCE .... C. Vincent McCann, Director IRC Veteran's Services

MOMENT OF SILENCE .... Rev. G.P. "Pete" LaBarre CDR USNR Retired

SHIPS BELL .... John Matthews, Indian River Detachment Marine Corps League

ECHO TAPS .... Frank Miller/Martha Van Gordon

FIRING SQUAD .... VFW Post 3918

LONE PIPER .... The Harp & Lion Pipes & Drum Band

VETERAN'S ADDRESS .... Ronald S. Frankel, General Counsel Florida Department of Veteran's Affairs

FREEDOM SHRINE .... Edgar Schlitt, Exchange Club of Indian River County

BAR ASSOCIATION .... President John H. Power, Attorney

DEDICATION SPEECH .... Judge L.B.Vocelle, Chief Judge Circuit Court

RIBBON CUTTING .... Judge L.B. Vocelle, Commission Chairman John Tippin, Sherman N. Smith, Jr., Attorney Since 1935

CLOSING REMARKS .... Conway L. Austin, Pres. IRC Veteran's Council

BENEDICTION .... Al Gates, Chaplain VFW Post 3918

PIPERS TROOP THE LINE .... Harp & Lion Pipes & Drum Band Barney Quinn, Pipe Major

In addition to the many fine people who are listed as participants in the
parade and the ceremonies, appreciation goes to:

Indian River County Commission
John W. Tippin, Chairman
Ken Macht, Vice-Chairman
Fran Adams
Richard N. Bird
Carolyn K. Eggert

Indian River County Courthouse Advisory Committee

City of Vero Beach Recreation Department

Johnson's Flower World Florist

Treasure Coast Tele Visions

WAXE 1370 AM

This program is printed courtesy of the Press-Journal

Event Coordinators: Carol K. Johnson, Vero Beach Indian River County Chamber of Commerce and
Reginald E. Wilcox, Esq., Indian River County Bar Association

Endnotes

1. <u>Jonathan Dickinson's Journal,</u> Florida Classic Library, Port Salerno, Florida, 1985. See also, McCoun, William E. <u>Southeast Florida Pioneers, The Palm & Treasure Coasts,</u> Pineapple Press, Inc., Sarasota, Florida, 1998, p 1-6.

2. Lyon, Eugene, <u>More Light on the Indians of the Ays Coast,</u> December, 1967 p 13- 15.

3. Gannon, Michael V., <u>Florida, A Short History</u>, University Press of Florida, Gainesville, Florida, 1993, p 4 & 5.

4. On February 23, 1512, Ponce De Leon received a patent authorizing him to discover and settle Bimini, supposed to be an island lying to the north of Cuba. Fuson, Robert H., <u>Juan Ponce de Leon and the Spanish Discovery of Puerto Rico and Florida,</u> The McDonald and Woodward Publishing Company, Blacksburg, Va. 2000, p 91. The expedition was delayed until 1513. Following his discovery of Florida, his patent was extended to Florida.

5. Cash, W.T., <u>The Story of Florida</u>, Volume II, The American Historical Society, New York, 1938, p 613.

6. <u>"Merits and Services of Captain Juan Velez de Medrano Notaries,"</u> Archive of Madrid (AHP) Protocolo 646 (1969), fol. 256-259vo., Translated by Eugene Lyon; Armstrong, Douglas R., 1996, French Castaways at Old Cape Canaveral, privately published, Palm Bay, Florida, p 46, 51 &122; and Ericksen, John M., <u>Brevard County, A History to 1955</u>, The Florida Historical Press, Tampa, Florida 1994, p 11. See also, Lyon, Eugene, <u>The Enterprise of Florida, Pedro Menendez de Aviles and the Spanish Conquest of 1565-1568,</u> The University Presses of Florida, Gainesville, Fla. 1990, p 130

7. Gannon, Michael V., <u>Florida, A Short History,</u> University Press of Florida, Gainesville,

Florida, 1993, p 15.

8. Id., p 8.

9. Id., p 17.

10. *Today in Florida History*, October 7, 1763. The Florida Historical Society and the Tebeau-Field library of Florida History.

11. Gannon, Michael V., Florida, A Short History, University Press of Florida, Gainesville, Florida, 1993 p 19. However, Tanner shows the population then as 3096, including garrisons. Tanner, Helen H., Zespedes in East Florida 1784 - 1790, University of Miami Press, Coral Gables, 1963, p 135.

12. Fairbanks, George Rainsford, The History & Antiquities of the City of St. Augustine, Florida, A Facsimile Reproduction of the 1885 Edition, Bicentennial Floridiana Facsimile Series, The University Presses of Florida, Gainesville, 1975, p170; Rasico, Philip D., The Minorcans of Florida: Their History, Language and Culture, Luthers, New Smyrna Beach, 1990, p 51, 53.

13. Griffin, Patricia, Mullet on the Beach: The Minorcans of Florida, 1768-1788, St. Augustine Historical Society, St. Augustine, Fla., 1991, p 35 and Panagopoulos, E. P., New Smyrna, An Eighteenth Century Greek Odyssey, Holy Cross Orthodox Press, Brookline, Ma., 1978, p 62. Fairbanks, George Rainsford, The History & Antiquities of the City of St. Augustine, Florida, A Facsimile Reproduction of the 1885 Edition, Bicentennial Floridiana Facsimile Series, The University Presses of Florida, Gainesville, 1975, p170.

14. Mirow, M. C., FIU College of Law, Miami, The Thistle, the Rose, and the Palm: Scottish and English Judges in British East Florida, Cambridge University Press, 2020, p 89.

15. Id. p 94.

16. Mowat, Charles Loch, University of California Publications in History, Volume 32: East

Florida as a British Province 1763-1784, University of California Press, Berkeley & Los Angeles, 1943, pp 163-165.

17. Claghorn, Charles E., Naval Officers of the American Revolution: A concise Biographical Dictionary, The Scarecrow Press, Inc., Metuchen, N. J., 1988, p 17.

18. Mirow, M. C., FIU College of Law, Miami, The Thistle, the Rose, and the Palm: Scottish and English Judges in British East Florida, Cambridge University Press, 2020, p 119 and Mirow, M. C., FIU College of Law, Miami, Judges for British Subjects in Spanish East Florida, 66 Washington University Journal of Law & Policy, The Law & Policy of Criminal Justice, 2021, p 13.

19. Historic Property Survey of Indian River County, Florida, Historic Properties Associates, Inc., St. Augustine, Florida, April 1989; Tanner, Helen H., Zespedes in East Florida 1784 - 1790, University of Miami Press, Coral Gables, 1963, p 139. Murdoch, Richard K., Governor Cespedes and the Religious Problem in East Florida, 1786-1787, Florida Historical Quarterly, Vol 26, No. 4, Article 5, p 5.

20. Drayton had a number of properties in the St. Augustine area. One author called his estate Oak Hill (Mowat, Charles L. (1943) The Enigma of William Drayton, Florida Historical Quarterly, Vol 22. No. 1, Article 3, p 6) and another called it Oak Forest. (Doggett, Carita, Dr. Turnbull and the New Smyrna Colony of Florida, Founders Publishing Company, Eustis, Florida, 1994, p 616). I don't know if that is different terminology or if there were two distinct properties. He also seemed to own Drayton Island within Lake George, west of Ormand Beach. However, his heirs had unsuccessful claims to a number of properties, allegedly the subject of British land grants. (See Mowat, immediately above, p6.)

21. Mowat, Charles Lock, East Florida as a British Province 1763 - 1784, Vol. 3, University of Cal. Publications in History, University of Calif. Press, Berkely and Los Angeles, Ca., 1943 p 162 and

Mirow, M. C., FIU College of Law, Miami, <u>The Thistle, the Rose, and the Palm: Scottish and English Judges in British East Florida</u>, Cambridge University Press, 2020, p 102 & 104.

22. Mirow, M. C., FIU College of Law, Miami, <u>The Thistle, the Rose, and the Palm: Scottish and English Judges in British East Florida</u>, Cambridge University Press, 2020, p 101.

23. Look at the endnote two back. Mowat says Drayton sold Oak Hill in February 1778 to the Chief Justice, Hume, who replaced him (on page 31).

24. The Governor's Council was the upper house legislature of the Province of East Florida and was founded in 1784, 17 years before its respective lower house, the House of Commons. It consisted of 12 members, with a quorum of 5. Fandom, American Revolutionary War, Wiki.

25. Wright, J. Leitch, Jr., <u>British St. Augustine</u>, Historical St. Augustine Preservation Board, St. Augustine, Fla., 1975, p28.

26. <u>Guide to the Microfilm Edition of the Forbes Papers</u>, The Forbes Family, Captain Robert Bennet Forbes House, Milton, Massachusetts, p 16.

27. Mirow, M. C., FIU College of Law, Miami, <u>The Thistle, the Rose, and the Palm: Scottish and English Judges in British East Florida</u>, Cambridge University Press, 2020, p 111.

28. Id.

29. This is the oldest masonry fort in the continental U. S., begun by the Spanish in St. Augustine in 1672. When the British gained control of Florida in 1783, the fort became known as Fort St. Mark. When transferred back to Spain in 1783, it became known by its original name. In 1819, when Spain ceded Florida to the United States, it was called Fort Marion in honor of Revolutionary War hero Francis Marion. It became a National Monument in 1924, and after 251 years of continuous military possession, was deactivated in 1933. In 1942, by an Act of Congress, the original name of Castillo de San Marcos

was restored.

30. Doggett, Carita, Dr. Turnbull and the New Smyrna Colony of Florida, Founders Publishing Company, Eustis, Florida, 1994, p 134.

31. Mirow, M. C., FIU College of Law, Miami, The Thistle, the Rose, and the Palm: Scottish and English Judges in British East Florida, Cambridge University Press, 2020, p 116, and Schafer, Daniel L., Plantation Development in British East Florida: A Case Study of the Earl of Egmont, Florida Historical Quarterly, Vol 63, No. 2, Art. 5, 1984, p 176.

32. Brown, J. A., Panton, Leslie and Company, Indian Traders of Pensacola and St. Augustine, Vol 37, Florida Historical Quarterly, 1959, p. 328.

33. The Oldest City, St. Augustine Saga of Survival, The Florida Historical Quarterly 1983, p 123.

34. Lockey, Joseph B., The St. Augustine Census of 1786, Volume 18, The Florida Historical Quarterly, Number 1, July 1939, p 20.

35. Tanner, Helen H., Zespedes in East Florida 1784 - 1790, University of Miami Press, Coral Gables, 1963, p 49 and Mirow, M. C., FIU College of Law, Miami, Judges for British Subjects in Spanish East Florida, 66 Washington University Journal of Law & Policy, The Law & Policy of Criminal Justice, 2021, p 13.

36. Mirow, M. C., FIU College of Law, Miami, Judges for British Subjects in Spanish East Florida, 66 Washington University Journal of Law & Policy, The Law & Policy of Criminal Justice, 2021, p 14.

37. Schafer, Daniel L., Plantation Development in British East Florida: A Case Study of the Earl of Egmont, Florida Historical Quarterly; Vol 63, No 2, Art 5, 1984, p 177.

38. Schafer, Daniel L., St. Augustine's British Years 1763-1984, The St. Augustine Historical Society, St. Augustine, 2001, p 22.

39. Born of the Sun, The Official Florida Bicentennial Commemorative Book, Worth International Communications corporation, 1975, p 112.

Chapter 2 - U.S. Territorial Florida

40. Commissions to Major General Andrew Jackson, by President James Monroe, March 10, 1821, Reprinted in Vol. 25 West's Florida Statutes Annotated 297 (1970), West Publishing Co.; Gannon, Michael V., 1993, Florida, A Short History, University of Florida Press, 1993, page 28.

41. Territorial Papers of the United States, Vol 22, The Territory of Florida, p 42. Manley, Brown, and Rise, The Supreme Court of Florida and Its Predecessor Courts, 1821-1917, University Press of Florida, Gainesville, Fla., 1997, p 14.

42. Ordinances of Major General Andrew Jackson, Pensacola, July 21, 1821, Reprinted in Vol. 25 West's Florida Statutes Annotated 305, West Publishing Co., 1970.

43. The Florida Historical Society List-Serv Today in Florida History, July 21, 1821.

44. Ordinances of Major General Andrew Jackson, July 21, 1821, Reprinted in Vol. 25 West's Florida Statutes Annotated 305, West Publishing Co., 1970

45. The Florida Historical Society List-Serv "Today in Florida History," May 27, 1822.

46. Wikipedia on William Grafton Delaney Worthington.

47. Act of Congress, March 30, 1822, 3 U.S. Stat. 654, Reprinted at Vol. 25 West's Florida Statutes Annotated 321, West Publishing Co., 1970

48. Farris, Charles D., The Courts of Territorial Florida, Florida Historical Quarterly, 19 (April 1941), p 347.

49. Act of Congress, March 30, 1822, 3 U.S. Stat. 654, Reprinted at Vol. 25 West's Florida Statutes Annotated 321, West Publishing Co., 1970.

50. Act of Congress, March 3, 1823, 3 U.S. Stat. 750, Reprinted at Vol. 25 West's Florida Statutes Annotated 327, West Publishing Co., 1970.

51. The Florida Historical Society List-Serv "Today in Florida History" for September 26, 1823.

52. American Insurance Company v. 356 Bales of Cotton, 26 U.S. 511 (1828).

53. Records of many of those appellate cases, starting in 1824, still exist, such as in the State Archives and even on microfilm at the Indian River County Main Library. However, the records are in cursive and sometimes very hard to read.

54. The Act of Congress, May 26, 1824, 4 U.S. Stat. 45, Reprinted at Vol. 25 West's Florida Statutes Annotated 333, West Publishing Co., 1970.

55. Richards, Florida's Hibiscus City of Vero Beach, Brevard Graphics, Melbourne, Fla., 1968 p 42; Gannon, Michael V., 1993, Florida, A Short History, University of Florida Press, 1993, page 30.

56. Act of May 23, 1828, Ch. 77, 4 Stat. 292, Referenced at Vol 25 West's Florida Statutes Annotated 344, West Publishing Co., 1970.

52. Rogers, William Warren and Brown, Jr., Cantor, Florida's Clerks of the Circuit Court, Their History and Experiences, Century Press, Tallahassee, Florida, 1996, p 7.

58. Id at p 10.

59. The Act of Congress, May 26, 1824, 4 U.S. Stat. 45, Reprinted at Vol. 25 West's Florida Statutes Annotated 333, West Publishing Co., 1970.

60. Florida State Archives, Record Group 00110, Series 985, Territorial Court of Appeals. See also Farris, Charles D., The Courts of Territorial Florida, Florida Historical Quarterly, 19 (April 1941),

p 346.

61. Rogers, William Warren and Brown, Jr., Canter, <u>Florida's Clerks of the Circuit Court, Their History and Experiences</u>, Sentry Press, Tallahassee, Fla., 1997, p 10, 11.

62. <u>American Insurance Company v. 356 Bales of Cotton</u>, 26 U.S. 511 (1828). This was an appeal to the Supreme Court of the United States from the Circuit Court of Appeals from South Carolina. The trial court in this case was established by the Florida Legislature and Governor, and not a federal constitutional court, for which the Supreme Court of the United States ruled was the exclusive court jurisdiction for admiralty cases.

63. Denham, James M., <u>A Rogue's Paradise, Crime and Punishment in Antebellum Florida, 1821-1861</u>, The University of Alabama Press, Tuscaloosa, Ala. 1997, p 142.

64. Article I, Section 87, First Division - Title II, Chapter III of the Compiled General Laws of Florida, 1927, Annotated which cites November 6, 1829, Section 1 as the reference for the above principle. See Florida Territorial Act of Nov. 6, 1829, section 1, p 8 & 9.

65. <u>The Supreme Court of Florida, A Reference Manual,</u> Sesquicentennial Edition, The Florida Supreme Court, 1995, p 18.

66. Id. p 22.

67. <u>United States vs. Fleming's Heirs</u>, 33 U.S. 478, 8 L Ed 1016 (1834).

68. My reference for this was "Tales of Old Brevard, Brevard Grant in litigation more than 100 years." However, Hoover wasn't yet president in 1926 and likely wasn't signing land patents as Secretary of Commerce in 1926. Also, I have seen references where Cain purchased 20 arces or had a claim as a settler.

69. Florida State Archives; Published in Shofner, Jerrell H., <u>History of Brevard County</u>, Volume

1, Brevard Conty Historical Commission, 1995, p 32 & 44.

70. Robison, Jim and Andrews, Mark, Flashbacks: The Story of Central Florida's Past, The Orange County Historical Society and the Orlando Sentinel, 1995, p 13.

71. Officers of Counties, 1827-1845, Vertical File, Series 259, Florida State Archives.

72. Hebel, Ianthe Bond, Centennial History of Volusia County, Florida, 1854-1954, College Publishing Company, Daytona Beach, Fla., 1955, p 1. Gold, Pleasant Daniel, "History of Volusia County, Florida" (1927). Text Materials of Central Florida. 112. P 47.

73. Robison, Jim and Andrews, Mark, Flashbacks: The Story of Central Florida's Past, The Orange County Historical Society and the *Orlando Sentinel*, 1995, p 18, and Act No. 15 of the Legislative Council of the Territory of Florida, approved February 2, 1838 (Repealed by Act No. XIII of the Council of the Territory of Florida, approved March 9, 1843). That same Legislative Council also authorized a courthouse for Mosquito County. Act No. XVII, of the Council of the Territory of Florida, approved March 9, 1843.

74. Cash, W. T. (State Historian), The Story of Florida, Vol II, The American Historical society, Inc., New York, 1938, p. 626 and 628; Series 259, Volume 3, Florida State Archives.

75. Id., p 628.

76. Burbey, Louis H., Our Worthy Commander, The Life and Times of Benjamin K. Pierce in Whose Honor Fort Pierce Was Named, Indian River Community College Historical Data Center, IRCC Pioneer Press, Ft. Pierce, Florida 1776, p 56 & 9-10.

77. Hebel, Ianthe Bond, Centennial History of Volusia County, Florida, 1854-1954, The Volusia County Historical Commission, Deland, Florida, College Publishing Co., Daytona, Florida 1955, p 1.

78. Section 5, Article V, Constitution of the State of Florida of 1838.

79. Mallon, <u>1840 Index to Florida Census</u>; Shaw, Aurora C., C.G., <u>1840 Florida U. S. Census Index</u>

80. Florida State Archives; Published in Shofner, Jerrell H., <u>History of Brevard County</u>, Volume 1, Brevard Conty Historical Commission, 1995, p 36.

81. Thompson, Arthur W., <u>Jacksonian Democracy on the Florida Frontier</u>, University of Florida Monographs, Social Sciences No 9, University of Florida Press, Gainesville, Florida, p 52, citing to House Journal (1842).

82. Denham, James M., <u>A Rogue's Paradise, Crime and Punishment in Antebellum Florida, 1821-1861</u>, The University of Alabama Press, Tuscaloosa, Ala. 1997, Appendix 1, 209-211.

83. *Today in Florida History*, August 4, 1842.

84. Rights, Lucille, Rieley, <u>A Portrait of St. Lucie County, Florida</u>, The Dunning Company, 1994 p 36

85. Van Landingham, Kyle, S., <u>Pictorial History of St. Lucie County 1565-1910</u>, Sun Bank of St. Lucie County and the St. Lucie Historical Society, p 9   in 1st and 2nd editions; p 7 in third edition.

86. Rights, Lucille, Rieley, <u>A Portrait of St. Lucie County, Florida</u>, The Dunning Company, 1994 p 71

87. Territorial Act of Florida approved March 14, 1844, Section 1.

88. An Act to designate the time and places for holding the county courts in certain counties in the Territory of Florida, Approved December 29, 1824.

89. Chapter 874, Florida Territorial Acts, "An Act to establish the County Site of Mosquito County," Approved January 29, 1835.

90. No IV An Act to establish a county site in Mosquito County, approved February 24, 1843.

91. Florida Territorial Acts, An Act to organize a county to be called St. Lucie County, March 14, 1844.

92. Act January 6, 1855, Laws 1855, Chapter 651.

93. Chapter 2021 [No 46] An Act to locate the Seat of Brevard County, approved February 9, 1874.

94. Laws of Florida, 1905, Chapter 5567.

95. Kjerulff, Georgiana, Tales of Old Brevard, The Kellersburg Fund of Brevard Historical Society, Inc., Florida Institute of Technology Press, Melbourne, Fla., 1972, p 21.

96. Territorial Acts of Florida 1842, p 8; Clemons v. Chase, 162 So. 917, (Fla. 1935). See also *Wikipedia*, Leigh Read; Wikipedia, Leigh Read County.

97. Robison, Jim and Andrews, Mark, Flashbacks: The Story of Central Florida's Past, The Orange County Historical Society and the Orlando Sentinel, 1995, p 30; Territorial Act of Florida, approved March 14, 1844, and No. XXXI, An Act to alter and change Mosquito County to that of Orange, approved January 30, 1845.

98. Record Group 101, Series 32, Letterbook 5, W. D. Moseley to Sir, July 3, 1845.

99. Cash, W. T. (State Historian), The Story of Florida, Vol II, The American Historical society, Inc., New York, 1938, p 635.

100. Tapping Reeve opened the first law school in the United States devoted to teaching students the practice of law in 1784 in Litchfield, Cn. Sheppard, Steve, The History of Legal Education in the United States: Commentaries and Primary Sources, Salem Press, Pasadena, Ca. 1999, p 184.

101. Doherty, Herbert J., Jr., Richard Keith Call, Southern Unionist, University of Florida Press, Gainesville, Florida, 1961, p 36 and 37.

102. In 2016, the Florida legislature agreed Edmund Kirby Smith, "a Confederate General shouldn't represent the state – especially one who moved away from Florida when he was 12." *Vero Beach Press Journal, Treasure Coast Newspapers*, 4/15/17, p.8A.

103. Manuscript autobiography of Judge Thomas Douglas, quoted in Rowland H. Rerick, Memoirs of Florida, The Southern Historical Association, Atlanta, Georgia 1902, Vol. 2, p 65 and quoted in Parks, Joseph H., General E. Kirby Smith, C.S.A. Louisiana State University Press, Baton Rouge 1954).

104. Manley, Brown, and Rise, The Supreme Court of Florida and Its Predecessor Courts, 1821-1917, University Press of Florida, Gainesville, Fla., 1997, p 29, which cites to Hall, Politics of Justice, 16, 23; Hall and Rise, From Local Courts to the National Tribunals, 12-13; Doherty, Whigs of Florida, 1-7.

105. Manley, Brown, and Rise, The Supreme Court of Florida and Its Predecessor Courts, 1821-1917, University Press of Florida, Gainesville, Fla., 1997, p 63.

106. Motte, J. R., Journey into Wilderness, University of Florida Press, Gainesville, Fla., 1963, p 113. See also Denham, James M., A Rogue's Paradise, Crime and Punishment in Antebellum Florida, 1821-1861The University of Alabama Press, Tuscaloosa, Ala. 1997, p 124.

107. Doherty, Herbert J., Jr., Richard Keith Call, Southern Unionist, University of Florida Press, Gainesville, Florida, 1961, p 81.

108. Mahon, John K., History of the Second Seminole War 1835-1842, Revised Ed'n, University of Florida Press, Gainseville, FL. 1985, P 266.

109. Quoting Fairbanks, George R., History of Florida, From its Discovery by Ponce de Leon in 1512 to the Close of the Florida War, in 1842, J. B. Lippincott & Co., Jacksonville, Fla., 1871, p (v).

Note: Bronson is in my book for his judicial service in the Eastern District of the Florida Territorial Court. After Statehood he became a Federal Judge of the District of Florida and subsequently the Northern District of Florida.

110. Rogers, William Warren and Brown, Jr., Canter, Florida's Clerks of the Circuit Court, Their History and Experiences, Sentry Press, Tallahassee, Fla., 1996 p 7 & 10.

111. Rogers, William Warren and Brown, Jr., Canter, Florida's Clerks of the Circuit Court, Their History and Experiences, Sentry Press, Tallahassee, Fla., 1996 p 7.

112. Douglas, Thomas, Autobiography of, Calkins & Stiles, New York, 1856. Excerpts from Dr. Carita Doggett Corse loaned to The Federal Writers, p 19/p106.

113. Denham, James M., A Rogue's Paradise, Crime and Punishment in Antebellum Florida, 1821-1861, The University of Alabama Press, Tuscaloosa, Ala. 1997, p 27.

114. The Florida Historical Society was founded in 1856 in St. Augustine but was forced into a hiatus with the Civil War and Reconstruction. Fairbanks saw the need to collect, preserve and publicize documents pertaining to Florida history. The society continues with a library, opened in 1997 as the Tebeau-Field Library of Florida History in Historic Cocoa Village, Florida. *Today in Florida History*, November 26, 1998, The Florida Historical Society and the Tebeau-Field Library of Florida History. Today the library is now known as The Florida Historical Society's Library of Florida History.

115. Addison Blockhouse now a Historic State Park. Not open to the public.

116. Coker, Edward Caleb, New Englander on the Indian River Frontier Caleb Lyndon Brayton and his view from Brayton's Bluff. Florida Historical Quarterly, Volume 70, No.3, January 1992.

117. Shofner, Jerrell H., History of Brevard County, Volume 1, Brevard County Historical Commission, 1995, p 52, but see Denham, James M., A Rogue's Paradise, Crime and Punishment in

Antebellum Florida, 1821-1861, The University of Alabama Press, Tuscaloosa and London, 1997, p 223.

118. Shofner, Jerrell H., History of Brevard County, Volume 1, Brevard County Historical Commission, 1995, p. 66.

119. The Historical Record Survey Division of Professional and Service Projects, Works Progress Administration, Spanish Land Grants of Florida, State Library Board, Tallahassee, Florida, Volumn II (Confirmed Claims) November 1940. P 234.

120. Strickland, Alice, Ormond-on-the-Halifax, A Centennial History of Ormond Beach, Florida, 1995, p 14.

121. Bockelman, Charles W., Six Columns and Fort New Smyrna, Halifax Historical Society, Daytona Beach, Fla, Printed by E. O. Painter Printing Co., DeLeon Springs, Fla., 1985 p22.

122. Burnham also went on to be the first sheriff of St. Lucie County in 1844.

123. Stanley, Eileen E, Pioneering Sebastian and Roseland, Arcadia Publishing, 2017, p 43.

124. McGoun, William E., Southeast Florida Pioneers: The Palm & Treasure Coasts, Pineapple Press, Inc., Sarasota, Florida 1998, p 21. Ranson, Robert, East Coast Florida Memoirs 1837-1886, Florida Classic Library, Port Salerno, Florida 34992; 1989 p 19. (Note Ranson has the death of Burnham in 1892, unlike McGoun, the latter being consistent with what is on Wikipedia.)

125. The Brevard Museum of History & Natural Science, 2201 Michigan Av., Cocoa, Florida 32926.

126. Conflicting information shows he could have been born in Eleuthera, Bahamas in 1810

127 Mount Oswald Plantation was created by Richard Oswald who acquired the twenty-thousand acres on the Halifax and Tomoka Rivers from the British Government in 1766. He was also known as a

signer of the preliminary peace negotiations at the end of the American Revolution for the British, at the time of giving up his plantation for the British exodus from Florida.

128. For an interesting history on James Darley of Tomoka's land grant claims, and the revolt of negroes on one of his ships, which killed some of his crew, see The Historical Record Survey Division of Professional and Service Projects, Works Progress Administration, Spanish Land Grants of Florida, State Library Board, Tallahassee, Florida, Volumn I (Unconfirmed Claims), August 1940, P55.

129. An Act to divorce Francis (sic) Dummett, Approved March 15, 1844.

130. Erikson, John M., Brevard County, A History to 1955, The Florida Historical Society Press, Tampa, Florida, 1994, p 64.

131. Shofner, Jerrell H., Nor is It Over, Florida in the Era of Reconstruction 1863-1877, The University Presses of Florida, Gainesville, Fla., 1974. P 132.

132. Bockelman, Charles W., Six Columns and Fort New Smyrna, Halifax Historical Society, Daytona Beach, Fla, Printed by E. O. Painter Printing Co., DeLeon Springs, Fla., 1985.

133. Motte, Jacob Rhett, Journey into Wilderness, University of Florida Press, Gainesville, Florida, 1963, p 152.

134. In 1801, Dr. Ambrose Hull from Connecticut attempted to start a new settlement on the coast to grow cotton and sugar, but his plans were delayed after Indians attacked his plantation. Eventually, Hull regrouped, called the area "Mount Olive," and built his house on top of what is now called the Turnbull Ruins. Hull's House was destroyed in 1812 during the Patriots' War. Ketcham, Sandra, Visitflorida.com

135. Denham, James M., A Rogue's Paradise, The University of Alabama Press, Tuscaloosa, Ala. 1997, p 75.

136. Denham, James M., A Rogue's Paradise, The University of Alabama Press, Tuscaloosa, Ala. 1997, p 21.

137. Davis, T. Frederick, History of Jacksonville, Florida and Vicinity, 1513 to 1924, Reproduction of the 1925 Edition, University of Florida Press, Gainseville, Florida 1964, p 58. His grave was initially, a thirty-five foot cairn-type tower built nine years before he died, but was desecrated years after his death and subsequently burned in the Great Fire of 1901. It was later relocated to the Evergreen Cemetery in Jacksonville. Today, it merely reads, THE FAMILY TOMB OF ISAIAH D. HART, THE FOUNDER OF JACKSONVILLE.

138. Van Landingham, Kyle, In Pursuit of Justice, Law & Lawyers in Hillsborough County, 1846-1996, Hillsborough County Bar Association, 1996, p 10.

139. Manley, Brown, and Rise, The Supreme Court of Florida and Its Predecessor Courts, 1821-1917, University Press of Florida, Gainesville, Fla., 1997, 283, which cites to 160 *Florida Reports*, xliv; Tampa Florida Peninsular, March 19, 1859, March 10, 1860, Brown, "Ossian Bingley Hart." 194-97; Brown, "Politics, Greed, Regulator Violence, and Race in Tampa." p 27.

140. Brown Jr., Canter, Ossian Bingley Hart, Florida's Loyalist Reconstruction Governor, Louisiana State University Press, Baton Rouge, 1997, p 276.

141. Shofner, Jerrell H., History of Brevard County, Volume 1, Brevard Conty Historical Commission, 1995, p 61.

142. Joseph S. Osborn Family Tree on Ancestry.com

143. McGoun, William E., Southeast Florida Pioneers, The Palm & Treasure Coasts, Pineapple Press, Inc., Sarasota, Fl., 1998, p 73.

Chapter 3 – Statehood – (1845) Through Pre-St. Lucie County (1905)

144. Denham, James M., Fifty Years of Justice, A History of the U. S. District Court for the Middle District of Florida, University Press of Florida, Gainesville, Florida, 2015.

145. The Supreme Court of Florida, A Reference Manual, The Supreme Court of Florida, 1995, p 26

146. Denham, James M., A Rogue's Paradise, Crime and Punishment in Antebellum Florida, 1821-1861, The University of Alabama Press, Tuscaloosa, Ala. 1997, p 35-36.

147. Chapter 4 [No. iv], Laws of Florida, 1845.

148. Chapter 49 (No. 22), Laws of Florida, 1845.

149. Chapter XXII, Territorial Laws of Florida, Approved February 27, 1845.

150. Territorial Act of Florida, Approved March 14, 1844, sect. 5.

151. Florida in 1845, From Mitchell's Universal Atlas, Copyrighted 1846.

152. Chapter 49 (No. 22), Laws of Florida, 1845.

153. Shofner, Jerrell H., History of Brevard County, Volume 1, Brevard Conty Historical Commission, 1995, p 62.

154. Dunn, Hampton, Historic Florida Courthouses, Hallmark Publishing Company, Gloucester Point, Va., 1998, p 215.

155. Denham, James M., A Rogue's Paradise, Crime and Punishment in Antebellum Florida, 1821-1861, The University of Alabama Press, Tuscaloosa and London, 1997, p 33 and particularly his cited footnote 29.

156. Rights, Lucille, Rieley, A Portrait of St. Lucie County, Florida, The Donning Company, Virginia Beach, Va., 1994 p 41; Van Landingham, Kyle, S., Pictorial History of St. Lucie County 1565-1910, Sun Bank of St. Lucie County and the St. Lucie Historical Society, p 12 (1st Edition and Revised

Edition – undated, and p 10 in the 3rd Edition, 2007.

157. <u>Carter v. Bennett</u>, 6 Fla. 214 (1852).

158. <u>Carter v. Davis</u>, 8 Fla. 182 (1858).

159. See for example, <u>Len-Hal Realty, Inc. v. Wintter Cummings</u>, 689 So.2d 1191 (Fla 4DCA 1997).

160. Van Landingham, Kyle S., <u>Pictorial History of St. Lucie County 1565-1910</u>, Sun Bank of St. Lucie County and the St. Lucie Historical Society; p 12 (1st Edition and Revised Edition – undated, and p 11 in 3rd Edition, 2007).

161. Chapter 651(No.42), Laws of Florida, 1855.

162. Rights, Lucille, Rieley, <u>A Portrait of St. Lucie County, Florida</u>, The Donning Company, Virginia Beach, Va., 1994 p 73. See also Raize, Erwin R. & Associates, <u>Atlas of Florida</u>, University of Florida Press, Gainesville, 1964 with map of Florida for the year 1860.

163. Rights, Lucille, Rieley, <u>A Portrait of St. Lucie County, Florida</u>, The Donning Company, Virginia Beach, Va. 1994, p 36, 73.

164. Eriksen, John M., <u>Brevard County, A History to 1955</u>, Florida Historical Society Press, Tampa, Florida, 1994, p 50; Rights, Lucille, Rieley, <u>A Portrait of St. Lucie County, Florida</u>, The Donning Company, Virginia Beach, Va., 1994, p 73.

165. Letter of Wesley W. Stout to Dept. Of State, Division of State Library Services July 18, 1970.

166. Ranson, Robert, <u>East Coast Florida Memoirs, 1837 to 1886</u>, Florida Classic Library. Reprint Edition, Port Salerno, Fla. 1989, p 9 & 19.

167. Journal of the Proceedings of the House of Representatives of the General Assembly of the

State of Florida, Seventh Session, November 28, 1854, December 21, 1854, and December 23, 1844, Tallahassee, Florida.

168. Van Landingham, Kyle S., Pictorial History of St. Lucie County 1565-1910, Sun Bank of St. Lucie County and the St. Lucie Historical Society, page 12 (1st Edition and Revised Edition – undated, and p 11 in the 3rd Edition, 2007).

169. Rights, Lucille, Rieley, A Portrait of St. Lucie County, Florida, The Donning Company, Virginia Beach, Va., 1994, Pages 43 & 51.

170. Chapter 890 (No. 32), Laws of Florida, 1859.

171. Taylor, Robert A., Rebel's Storehouse, University of Alabama Press, 1995, p 100, 101.

172. Record Group 101, Series 577 Governor Perry general correspondence 1860-1861, Box 1, Folder 8. See also Scripps Treasure Coast Newspapers, April 11, 2011m p 1.

173. Chapter 1,445 (No. 16), Laws of Florida, Approved 12/6/1864.

174. In 1863 and 1864 Union ships, including U.S.S. Roebuck, U.S.S. Sagamore, U.S.S. Honeysuckle, U.S.S. Gem of the Sea, and U.S.S. Beauregard seized Confederate vessels, including the sloop, Ann and the schooners, Caroline and Pride, as well as British blockade runners and salt works in general, along the Indian River between Haulover on the north and Jupiter Inlet on the south. More particularly, the seizures included the capture by the U.S.S. Sagamore of the Pride on February 4, 1863, near the Indian River Narrows, commonly thought to be present day Vero Beach. Today in Florida History, January 1,5,8,9,11,14,16,17,28, February 2, and 4, Florida Historical Society.

175. Taylor, Robert A., Rebel's Storehouse, University of Alabama Press, 1995, p 106; Eriksen, John M., Brevard County, A History to 1955, The Florida Historical Society Press, Tampa, Florida, 1994 p 79.

176. Shofner, Jerrell H., History of Brevard County, Volume 1, Brevard Conty Historical Commission, 1995, p 72.

177. Eriksen, John M., Brevard County, A History to 1955, The Florida Historical Society Press, Tampa, Florida, 1994, p 79 & 80 and Robison and Andrews, Flashbacks: The Story of Central Florida's Past, The Orange County Historical Society and the Orlando Sentinel, Orlando, Fla. 1995, p 225.

178. Cody, Aldus M and Robert S, Osceola County, The First 100 Years, Published by Raymond G. Cody for the Osceola County Historical Society, 1978, p 28.

179. Eriksen, John M., Brevard County, A History to 1955, The Florida Historical Society Press, Tampa, Florida, 1994, p 79.

180. Brevard County Historical Commission Archives; published in Shofner, Jerrell H., History of Brevard County, Volume 1, Brevard Conty Historical Commission, 1995, 152 & 177.

181. Chapter 1520 (No. 57), Laws of Florida, Approved 1/15/1866.

182. Bradbury and Hallock, A Chronology of Florida Post Offices, Handbook No. 2, The Florida Federation of Stamp Clubs, 1962, p 6.

183. Cash, W. T. (State Historian), The Story of Florida, Vol II, The American Historical society, Inc., New York, 1938, p 652.

184. Section 7, Article VI, and Section 3, Article XVI, Constitution of the State of Florida of 1868.

185. Florida State Archive Record Group 101- Series 577, Folder 18, Governor Reed correspondence Box 1.

186. Florida State Archive Record Group 101- Series 577, Folder 18, Governor Reed correspondence Box 1.

187. Eau Gallie had previously been known as Arlington, which is the name of the homestead that the Houston family gave it in 1859. https://rossetterhousemuseum.org.

188. Bradbury and Hallock, A Chronology of Florida Post Offices, Handbook No. 2, The Florida Federation of Stamp Clubs, 1962, p 10.

189. Brevard County Historical Commission Archives, published in Shofner, Jerrell H., History of Brevard County, Volume 1, Brevard Conty Historical Commission, 1995, 178 & 199.

190. Shofner, Jerrell H., History of Brevard County, Volume 1, Brevard Conty Historical Commission, 1995, p 131, with his footnotes omitted.

191. Gleason, W. Lansing, Vignettes of Eau Gaille as It Used to Be, A Portion of the Melbourne Centennial Book, Published by the Melbourne Area Chamber of Commerce Centennial Committee and Weona Cleveland, National Printing, Inc., Melbourne, Florida, 1980, p 67-68.

192. Eriksen, John M., Brevard County, A History to 1955, The Florida Historical Society Press, Tampa, Florida, 1994, p 83.

193. The Harry T. & Harriette V. Moore Judicial Complex opened in the City of Viera in Brevard County in 1996. It was named after pioneer civil rights activists, who were prominent in the NAACP, were active in the school system in Brevard County, and who were bombed in their home in Mims, Florida on Christmas Day, 1951.

194. Lake View had a post office from June 8, 1871 until May 13, 1875, although listed under one reference as being in Volusia County (Bradbury, Alford G., and Hallock, E. Story, A Chronology of Florida Post Offices, The Florida Federation of Stamp Clubs, 1962), the latter of which is likely incorrect in light of the Brevard County Commission's seat creation in 1875.

195. Minutes of Brevard County Commission, July 15, 1879 and Kjerulff, Georgiana, Tales of

Old Brevard, The Kellersburg Fund of South Brevard Historical Society, Florida Institute of Technology, Melbourne, Fla., 1972, p 29.

196. Eriksen, John M., Brevard County, A History to 1955, The Florida Historical Society Press, Tampa, Florida, 1994, p 80, 81 and Kjerulff, Georgiana, Tales of Old Brevard, The Kellersburg Fund of South Brevard Historical Society, Florida Institute of Technology, Melbourne, Fla., 1972, p 29.

197. Eriksen, John M., Brevard County, A History to 1955, The Florida Historical Society Press, Tampa, Florida, 1994, p 81, 82 and Robison, Jim and Andrews, Mark, Flashbacks: The Story of Central Florida's Past, The Orange County Historical Society and The Orlando Sentinel, Orlando, Fla., 1995, p 142- 145 and Tinsley, Jim Bob, Florida Cow Hunter, The Life and Times of Bone Mizell, University of Central Florida Press, Orlando, Fla., 1990, p 21.

198. Van Landingham, Pictorial History of St. Lucie County 1565-1910, and Horton, Jack B. Jr., Titusville, Fla. The First 50 years, 1867-1917, published in The Titusville Star Advocate, March, 1967; Ericson, John M., Brevard County, A History to 1955, The Florida Historical Society Press, Tampa, Florida, 1994, p69 and Newman, Anna Pearl Leonard, Stories of Early Life Long Beautiful Indian River, Stuart Daily News, Inc., Stuart, Florida, 1953, p 86.

199. Brevard County Commission Minutes, October 18, 1879.

200. Brevard County Commission Minutes, July 16, 1879.

201. Brevard County Commission Minutes, January 5, 1880.

202. Brevard County Commission Minutes, October 19, 1880.

203. Horton, Jack B. Jr., Titusville, Florida. The First 50 Years (1867-1917), published in The Titusville Star Advocate, March, 1967; Brevard County Commission Minutes of January 2 & 31, 1883, November 15, 1883 and January 25, 1884.

204. Horton, Jack B., Jr., <u>Titusville, Florida - The First Fifty Years, 1867-1917</u>, Titusville Star - Advocate, March, 1967.

205. Section 6(1) of Article V, Constitution of Florida, 1885.

206. Laws 1903, Chapter 5121, Section 8.

207. Brevard County Commission Minutes, September 5, 1887.

208. Bradbury and Hallock, <u>A Chronology of Florida Post Offices</u>, Handbook No. 2, The Florida Federation of Stamp Clubs, 1962, p 57 & 69.

209. Newman, Anna Pearl Leonard, <u>Stories of Early Life Long Beautiful Indian River,</u> Stuart Daily News, Inc., Stuart, Florida, 1953 p 9.

210. President Theodore Roosevelt Executive order No. 1014, dated January 26, 1909, enlarging Pelican Island.

211. Clerk of the Circuit Court for Brevard County, Florida, Docket Bench 1897-1954.

212. Cash, W. T. (State Historian), <u>The Story of Florida</u>, Vol II, The American Historical society, Inc., New York, 1938, p 669.

213. In 1898, Jones left the Brevard County Court role for the 7th Circuit bench. See bio later in this chapter.

214. Denham, James M., <u>A Rogue's Paradise, Crime and Punishment in Antebellum Florida, 1821-1861</u>, The University of Alabama Press, Tuscaloosa and London, 1997, p27 ; Denham, James M., <u>From a Territorial to a State Judiciary, Florida's Antebellum Courts and Judges</u>, Vol 73 Florida Historical Quarterly, April 1995, p451 and 452.

215. Cash, W. T. (State Historian), <u>The Story of Florida</u>, Vol II, The American Historical society, Inc., New York, 1938, p 638.

216. Cash, W. T. (State Historian), The Story of Florida, Vol II, The American Historical society, Inc., New York, 1938, p 638.

217. Sebastian Sun, May 26, 1989, p 9-A.

218. Taylor, Robert A., Rebel's Storehouse, University of Alabama Press, 1995, p 78.

219. Carter v. Davis, 8 Fla. (1858).

220. Shofner, Jerrell H., Nor Is It Over Yet: Florida in the Era of Reconstruction 1865-1877. University of Florida Press, Gainesville, 1974 p 88.

221. Shofner, Jerrell H., Nor Is It Over Yet: Florida in the Era of Reconstruction 1865-1877. University of Florida Press, Gainesville, 1974 p 14.

222. Davis, William Watson, The Civil War & Reconstruction in Florida, University of Florida Press, Gainesville, Fla., 1964, p 355.

223. Id. p 535.

224. James, John G., Southern Student's Hand-book of Selections for Reading and Oratory, A.S. Barnes & Co., New York, 1879. P.305.

225. Cocke's name does not appear as a judge of the Second Circuit in the *Florida Reports*. *Wikipedia* shows him being appointed by Govenor Harrison Reed to the First Judicial Circuit in 1868. He reportedly served until January 16, 1873, when newly elected Governor Ossian B. Hart appointed him Florida Attorney General, allegedly because of Cocke's support for Hart and Republican President Ulysses S. Grant during the 1872 election.

226. William H Gleason was from New York, lived in Miami (then Ft Worth), and developed Eau Gallie, Florida. He was a Lieutenant Governor of Florida and served briefly as Governor in Governor Harrison Reed's stead when the latter was facing impeachment, but Gleason was later thrown

out of office as Lieutenant Governor. He also started the first Florida Agriculture College in Eau Gallie. One building was completed, but it was never used for the intended purpose.

227. Shofner, Jerrell H., Nor Is It Over Yet: Florida in the Era of Reconstruction 1865-1877. University of Florida Press, Gainesville, 1974, p 280.

228. Wallace, John, Carpetbag Rule in Florida: The Inside Workings of the Reconstruction of Civil Government in Florida After the Close of the Civil War, University of Florida Press, Gainesville, Fla., 1964, originally published in 1888.

229. The JP&M Railroad fraud was a post-Civil War scheme by George Swepson and Milton Littlefield, who seized control of several Florida railroads, including the Jacksonville, Pensacola & Mobile Railroad, and profited by selling fake bonds and state certificates.

P 164. Add endnote re Blackstone. Sir William Blackstone was an 18th-century English Jurist who wrote Commentaries on the Laws of England, which provided an overview of the English common law and which was used by the American Founding Fathers.

230. Shofner, Jerrell, Florida in the Balance: The Electoral Count of 1876, Florida. Historical Quarterly, XLVII Oct. 1968.

231. Shofner, Jerrell, Florida Portrait, A Pictorial History of Florida, Florida Historical Society, Tampa, Florida, and Pineapple Press, Inc., Sarasota, Florida, 1990, p 88.

232. *Today in Florida History*, November 23, 1883, The Florida Historical Society and the Tebeau-Field library of Florida History.

233. Sir William Blackstone was an 18th century English Jurist who wrote Commentariies on the Laws of England which provided an overview of the English common law and which was used by the American Founding Fathers.

234. Shofner, Jerrell H., History of Brevard County, Volume 2, Brevard County Historical Commission, 1996, p 195.

235. Van Landingham, Kyle S., In Pursuit of Justice - Law and Lawyers in Hillsborough County 1846-1996, Hillsborough County Bar Association, 1996, p 47.

236. McGoun, William E., Southeast Florida Pioneers, The Palm & Treasure Coasts, Pineapple Press, Inc., Sarasota, Fl., 1998, p 90-92. It is also interesting to note that Tom Tiger was the father of DeSoto Tiger, who was killed by John Ashley. Id. P.136. The later event triggered the Ashley Gang feud with the sheriff of Palm Beach County, that ultimately resulted in the death of John Ashley at the foot of the Sebastian Bridge, mentioned in Chapter 13 of this book.

237. Disney v. State, 72 Fla. 492, 73 So. 598 (Fla. 1916).

238. Shofner, Jerrell H., History of Brevard County, Volume 1, Brevard County Historical Commission, 1995 p 228.

239. Rights, Lucille, Rieley, A Portrait of St. Lucie County, Florida, The Donning Company, Virginia Beach, Va. 1994, p 47.

240. Cocoa Tribune, September 13, 1923, p 1.

241. https://www.facebook.com/atropicalfrontier/posts/bell-family-of-fort-pierce-part xviii.

242. Shofner, Jerrell, H., History of Brevard County, Volume 1, Brevard County Historical Commission, 1995, p 73.

243. Cohen, M.M., Notices of Florida and the Campaign, University of Florida Press, Gainesville, Florida, 1964, p 95.

244. Shofner, Jerrell H., History of Brevard County, Volume 1, Brevard County Historical Commission, 1995, p 62.

245. Shofner, Jerrell H., History of Brevard County, Volume 1, Brevard County Historical Commission, 1995, p 63.

246. Shofner, Jerrell, H., History of Brevard County, Volume 1, Brevard County Historical Commission, 1995, p 71.

247. Richards, J. Noble, Florida's Hibiscus City of Vero Beach, Brevard Graphics, Incorporated, Melbourne, Florida, 1968, p. 148.

248. Not only did E. L. marry into the Michael family, and have terrific citrus groves on the east side of the Indian River, but one of the Michaels, John C., married brother James T. Gray's daughter, and by 1900 James T. Gray and his wife and Mr. & Mrs. John C. Michael and family were living next to each other in Precinct 9, Brevard County and by the 1910 Census, they were next to each other again, in the Oakland area of Orange County, Florida. E. L. Gray died before 1900, and James T. Gray died in 1911. In 1939 James T. Gray's headstone for serving as a Sgt. In the 3rd Ga. Bat. of the Ga. Infantry in the Confederacy was applied for by his daughter, Mrs. J. C. Michael. Ironically, this white Jas. T. Gray seems to be buried in the Oakland, African American Cemetery. In comparing the two prominent James T. Grays, since the white James T. Gray was in the area of the Narrows by 1883 and the black James T. Gray swears on his homestead application that he has occupied his land since 1894 (although it is possible he was here sooner), and the Justice of the Peace dates were 1887 and 1889, the Justice of the Peace was likely James T. Gray of Georgia.

249. This was built by L. C. Moore on Moore's Point and President Grover Cleveland would be a guest at that hotel.

250. Hemming was a Colonel in the Civil War, and he towed ships up the St. Johns River, along with his son Charles, to avoid seizure and scuttled them south of Palatka by Dunn's Creek. These ships

were used in blockade running and included the yacht, America, which was the celebrated winner in the 1851 challenge with Great Britain, and it was the namesake for the America's Cup. The other boat was the steamer, St. Mary's. Waters, Zack C., <u>Florida's Confederate Guerillas: John W. Pearson & the Oklawaha Rangers</u>, Florida Historical Quarterly, 1991.

251. Peck, William H., <u>Titusville Star</u>, 1887, as quoted from the Hutchinson, Janet, <u>History of Martin County</u>, Historical Society of Martin County, Stuart, Florida, 1998, p 35.

252. Record Group 150 - Series 1325, Secretary of State incoming correspondence, 1831-1917, Box 2, Folder 6, 1853-1857

253 John C. Houston was born on Big Talbot Island, Duval County, in August of 1813. He married Mary Virginia Hall in Pablo Beach (the former Jacksonville Beach), on Sept. 22, 1836. They lived in Duval County until 1842. They moved south to Enterprise, where he was Sheriff of Mosquito County, as mentioned on page 50, and the Houstons were looking to settle under the Armed Occupation Act. They ended up in Eau Gallie, formerly known as Arlington. His daughter has purportedly said it took five days to move there with an ox team, mule team and several horses. Their house became a refuge for Confederate blockade runners in the Civil War. Houston is considered the first permanent settler of Eau Gallie and was a Brevard County Commissioner during Reconstruction 1864-1874 and he established the second post office in Brevard in 1871. He was a Justice of the Peace in 1872. He died in 1875. Son, John C. Houston, IV (1842 – 1918) was mayor of Eau Gallie three different times, starting in 1897. Each Houston are buried in the Houston Pioneer Cemetery in Eau Gallie. (Eau Gallie was absorbed into the City of Melbourne in 1969.)

254. Florida State Archives. Series S 1284, State and County Directories, 1845-1969, Brevard County, p 2.

255. Hanna, Alfred Jackson and Hanna, Kathryn Abbey, Florida's Golden Sands, The Bobbs-Merrill Company, Inc., New York, 1950, p 166-169.

256. Horizons, A publication of the Tebeau-Field Library, Issue 1, Number 1, September 1998, p 13.

257. The Florida Star, Volume 1, No. 19, September 1, 1880.

258. The so-called Republican hegemony during Reconstruction did not last long. It consisted of enfranchised African Americans and a divided Republican party of northern carpetbaggers and scalawags (under the federal military rule), which suffered from infighting, who, in a short time (by 1877), were starting to be overtaken by the Democrats. (In the disputed election of 1876, Rutherford B. Hayes was given the presidency through the Compromise of 1877, but federal troops were removed from the South in return.)

259. Augustus or Autgust Oswald "George" Lang wasn't a judicial figure, but lived an interesting life in this area, including being a keeper of the Jupiter Inlet Lighthouse, before he was murdered. For more information consult Stanley, Ellen E., Pioneering Sebastian and Roseland, Arcadia Publishing, 2017, p 65.

260. Van Landingham, Kyle, S., Pictorial History of St. Lucie County 1565-1910, Sun Bank of St. Lucie County and the St. Lucie Historical Society; p 42 (1st Edition and Revised Edition – undated, and p 52 in 3rd Edition, 2007, p 33.

261. Shofner, Jerrell, H., History of Brevard County, Volume 1, Brevard County Historical Commission, 1995, p 63.

262. Author, Ellen E. Stanley has him coming from Maine. Stanley, Ellen E., Pioneering Sebastian and Roseland, Arcadia Publishing, 2017, p 44.

263. Ranson, Robert, East Coast Florida Memoirs, 1837 to 1886, Florida Classic Library. Reprint Edition, Port Salerno, Fla. 1989, p16. However, I don't see where either Pecks, Samuel or son, William, were doctors, and Samuel Peck supposedly left the area in 1845.

264. Cohen, M. M., Notices of Florida and the Campaigns, A Facsimile Reproduction of the 1836 Edition, University of Florida Press, Gainesville, Florida, 1964, p 95.

265. Florida State Archives, Series S 1284, Directory of Elected and Appointed Officials, Brevard County 1870-1969, p 1.

266. Shofner, Jerrell H., Nor is it Over Yet, Florida in the Era of Reconstruction, The University Presses of Florida, Gainesville, Fl. 1863-1877, 1974, p 96.

267. Florida Today, September 25, 1998, as Published in Cleveland, Weona, Cross Towns Remembered, Florida Today, Melbourne, 1994, p 25.

268. The Florida Star, Volume 1, No. 19, September 1, 1880. Florida State Archives Series S 1284, Directory of Elected and Appointed Officials, Brevard Co, 1870-1969, p 4.

269. Id. p 4 & 5.

Chapter 4 - St. Lucie County through the Creation of Indian River County

270. Van Landingham, Kyle, S., Pictorial History of St. Lucie County 1565-1910, Sun Bank of St. Lucie County and the St. Lucie Historical Society; p 42 (1st Edition and Revised Edition – undated, and p 52 in 3rd Edition, 2007.

271. Rights, Lucille Rieley, A Portrait of St. Lucie County, Florida, The Donning Company, Virginia Beach, Va. 1994, p145.

272. Miley, Charles S., Miley's Memos, The Indian River Community College Historical Data Center, 1980, p 18-20.

273. Chapin, George M., <u>Florida 1513-1913, Past, Present and Future</u>, The S. J. Clarke Publishing Company, Chicago, Illinois, 1914, p 620 and via Hathi Trust, p 644.

274. Id., Hathi Trust p 657.

275. *Fort Pierce News*, August 13, 1915, p 1.

276. Chapter 7592 - (No. 334), Laws of Florida, 1917.

277. The Florida Historical Society List-Serv, *Today in Florida History*, September 6, 1920.

278. Continued as Circuit Judge, but no longer applicable to our then circuit.

279. Continued to serve in the Fifteenth Judicial Circuit (no longer applicable to the new Indian River County) until his murder in 1955.

280. Continued as a circuit judge, but no longer applicable to our new Fifteenth Judicial Circuit.

281. Reese, Joseph H., <u>Florida Flashlights</u>, The Hefty Press, Miami Florida, Florida State Library, 1917, p 110.

282. *Fellsmere Tribune*, June 4, 1921.

283. Continued to serve in the Fifteenth Judicial Circuit, but no longer applicable to the new Indian River County and the new Twenty-First Judicial Circuit, until his murder in 1955.

284. Weiss, Murray and Hoffman, Bill, <u>Palm Beach Babylon, Sins, Scams & Scandals</u>, Carol Publishing Group, New York, 1992, Chapter 10.

285. McGoun, William E., <u>Southeast Florida Pioneers: The Palm & Treasure Coasts</u>, Pineapple Press, Inc., Sarasota, Florida, 1998, p 40-45.

286. The Twenty-First Judicial Circuit became the Ninth Judicial Circuit in 1935. See Chapter 5.

287. In January 1999, two sections of the house which were moved to the Indian River by the site of the old Merrill Barber Bridge at the east end of Royal Palm Blvd. On January 11, 1999, the first

section was barged south on the river to Harbor Branch Oceanographic Institute in St. Lucie County.

288. *TCPALM.COM; Vero Beach Press Journal*, April 20, 2018, p 3D.

Chapter 5 - Indian River County Courthouses

289. Chapter 10148 (No. 126), Laws of Florida, 1925.

290. The City of Vero had its name changed by the legislature on November 23, 1925, to Vero Beach. Chapter 11779, Laws of Florida, 1925.

291. Chapter 8377 (No. 595), Laws of Florida, 1919.

292. Chapter 10148 (No. 126), Laws of Florida, 1925.

293. See chapter entitled Pre-County Courts.

294. Chapter 10148 (No. 126), Laws of Florida, 1925, and Chapter 10180 (No. 158), Laws of Florida, 1925.

295. Id. and Chapter 7351, Laws of Florida, 1917.

296. Chapter 10079 (No. 57), Laws of Florida, 1925.

297. Chapter 17085 of the Laws of Florida, 1935.

298. Chapter 195 of the Laws of Florida, 1967; F.S. 26.164 (1967).

299. This is the same Judge C. E. Chillingworth who was murdered years later and which resulted in the book entitled The Murder Trial of Judge Peel, by Jim Bishop, that was presided over by Nineteenth Judicial Circuit Judge D. C. Smith. See Circuit Judges infra. Remember also that in the first five months of 1925 this area was a part of the Fifteenth Judicial Circuit which included Palm Beach County. See also Vero Press of April 2, 1925, p 1, concerning the April 1925 term of the circuit court in Fort Pierce, being covered by Judge Chillingworth and it lists all the Vero residents being called to jury duty.

300. *The Vero Press*, March 26, 1925, p 1.

301. The community of Quay located in Indian River County was South of Wabasso and North of Toledo and Gifford near Old Dixie Highway. Quay was originally named Woodley and renamed Quay after United States Senator Quay who was a winter visitor and was able to get the channel dredged. During the boom Quay was renamed to Winter Beach because of a contest when developer C. C. Braswell ran a contest to rename the area. Mrs. Robert Brown of Fort Pierce was the lucky winner. Winter Beach application beat out more than 3,000 other suggestions from around the country. Mrs. Brown won a $1,000.00 lot in the new development for submitting the winning name. (Vero Beach Press Journal, September 17, 1995 (70 years ago)). The boom ended just about when Winter Beach was to develop 8,000 lots along the Old Dixie Highway. "Quay Dock Road" still exits. It was never an approved municipality under the Florida laws. It once was a part of St. Lucie County, and there was a special act of the Legislature which created the Quay Bridge District in 1921. (Chapter 8826 of the Laws of Florida, 1921). However, the District was abolished in 1927. (Chapter 12891 of the Laws of Florida, 1927). Toledo had a post office established on 9 March 1894, which was discontinued in favor of Quay on 15 June 1918. Woodley had a post office established on 8 March 1894 and discontinued on 17 March 1902 in favor of Quay, which in turn was discontinued in favor of Winter Beach on 16 Nov 1925. See Bradbury, Alford G., & Hallock, E. Story, A Chronology of Florida Post Offices, The Florida Federation of Stamp Clubs, 1962.

302. See the Resolution of Commissioner LaBruce described in the County Commission minutes of April 24, 1931, more fully discussed in the next chapter.

303. These businesses can be discerned from their signs in photographs of the Seminole Building dating back to 1926.

304. Both law firms had advertisements in the January 15, 1925 edition of The Vero Press.

305. *Scripps Treasure Coast Newspapers, IR* June 7, 2009, p B6 (80 years ago column).

306. Vero Beach Press Journal, August 25, 1933, p 1; See also Minutes of County Commission, August 21, 1933, Page 462.

307. *Vero Beach Press Journal*, September 8, 1933, p 1.

308. *Vero Beach Press Journal*, September 15, 1933, p 1. This same edition had an article about C Mudge of Fellsmere joining the IRC Co. Comm'n, and it was his second stint, having previously served before the County's creation.

309. Minutes of County Commission, October 3, 1933, Page 476.

310. Minutes of County Commission, October 3, 1933, Page 476.

311. *Vero Beach Press Journal*, October 6, 1933, p 1.

312. Minutes of County Commission, October 11, 1933, Page 478.

313. *Vero Beach Press Journal*, October 20, 1933, p 1.

314. Lockwood, Charlotte, Florida's Historic Indian River County, MediaTronics, Inc., Vero Beach, Fla. 1975, p 110.

315. Minutes of County Commission, March 6, 1934, Page 498.

316. Minutes of the County Commission, July 5, 1934, Page 517.

317. *Vero Beach Press Journal*, February 1, 1935, p 1.

318. Minutes of County Commission, February 5, 1935, Page 548.

319. *Vero Beach Press Journal*, July 12, 1935. P 1.

320. Minutes of County Commission, September 3, 1935, Page 580.

321. Minutes of County Commission, December 7, 1935, Page 10.

322. *Vero Beach Press Journal*, December 20, 1935, p 1.

323. Minutes of County Commission, April 3, 1936.

324. *Vero Beach Press Journal*, July 31, 1936, p 1.

325. Minutes of County Commission, July 28, 1936, Page 53.

326. Minutes of County Commission, March 12, 1937, Page 99 and *Vero Beach Press Journal*, March 12, 1937, p1.

327. *Vero Beach Press Journal*, March 19, 1937, p 1.

328. Minutes of County Commission, March 19, 1937, Page 102.

329. The bridge over the Sebastian Inlet was named after Mr. Graves.

330. The same Commissioner who was Chairman when the initial courthouse on 14th Avenue was started in 1936. He was known as "Jess Hamilton". He came from Winter Beach and was a farmer.

331. Interview of Mrs. J. Hubert (Beverly) Graves by Eugene J. O'Neill on February 8, 1995 and February 11, 1995.

332. Sick Building Syndrome is common in Florida since buildings are often enclosed and have air conditioning. The terminology describes health symptoms like headaches, irritation of the eyes, nose, or throat, coughing, dizziness, and/or fatigue, which occur after spending time indoors with poor air quality, such as mold, dust, and/or chemical contaminants.

333. E.g. Indian River County v. E. T. O'Neill & Son, Case #80-107. This was a three-day jury trial before a panel of 12, decided in December 1980 on the third floor of the 2001 Building.

334 The referenced jury trial was the last in the circuit court. The last county court jury trial was handled by Charles A. "Chuck" Sullivan, Jr. before judge Balsiger.

335. *Vero Beach Press Journal* December 19, 1990, p 1.

336. See Minutes of the Meetings of the Board of County Commissioners of Indian River County

of February 11, 1992 and February 25, 1992.

337. Dunn, Hampton, Historic Florida Courthouses, Hallmark Publishing Company, Gloucester Point, Va., p 113.

338. A procession was led from the lodge, by Master of the Lodge, Robert Clark. He was a member of the bar association for many years, whose office was last across from the new courthouse on the corner of 16th Avenue and State Road 60. The Masons ceremonially installed the cornerstone to the new courthouse on that date.

339. *Vero Beach Press Journal*, October 9, 1994, p 4A.

340. See for example *Vero Beach Press Journal* June 23, 1994.

341. The dedication occurred following a parade on a sweltering day. Sherman Smith confined his comments to fit the occasion and then presented Judge Vocelle's words at a public county commission meeting on the following Tuesday, which was televised.

342. *Vero Beach Press Journal*, January 12, 1990, p 1.

343. Ibid.

344. Ibid. Ironically, years later, Mr. Nall would have his office in the beautifully refurbished courthouse executive center.

Chapter 6 – Florida Courts in General in the 20th Century

345. Allen Morris published a series of the handbook. He was the Florida House Clerk from 1966 to 1986 and thereafter was the Clerk emeritus/Historian until 1995.

346. The Supreme Court of Florida Reference Manual, The Supreme Court of Florida, 1995, p 44

347. Vol 18 U of F Law Review, 1965 p 109

348. Fla. Const. Art V, sect. 1

349. *Vero Beach Journal*, November 5, 1926, p 1.

350. State Archives Series S 1284, State and County Officers Elected or Appointed, Indian River County, p 5.

351. List of Registered Voters 1914, St. Lucie Tribune, Oct. 23, 1914, as compiled by W:\Pam Cooper\MyDocuments\Indian River History\DIRECTORIES AND LISTS\1914 Registered Voters St. Lucie Co..doc page 2 4/1/14

352. Chapter 29150 of the Fla. Laws, 1953.

353. *Vero Beach Press Journal*, November 4, 1954, p 1. The vote was 680 to 318 with one precinct, Wabasso, missing in that report.

Chapter 7 - Circuit Court In and For Indian River County

354. Chapter 10079 Acts 1925, Section 2; Chapter 10148 Acts 1925, Section 2; Chapter 10180 Acts, 1925, Section 2.

355. Compiled General Laws of Florida 1927 Annotated, Sections 4888 through 5129.

356. Section 1, Ch. 17085, Laws of Florida, 1935.

357. Section 6, Ch. 67-195, Laws of Florida, amending Florida Statute 26.164.

358. Ch. 105, Fla. Stats (1971); Ch. 71-49, Laws of Florida.

359. S.J.R. #52-D, adopted at the Third Special Session of the Legislature, 1971 and approved by the voters of a special election on March 14, 1972, eff. Jan. 1, 1973.

360. Ankona had a post office in 1886 which was discontinued in favor of Fort Pierce in 1953. Eldred had a post office in 1904 which was discontinued in favor of Fort Pierce in 1942. Eldred was a mile or two south of Ankona, the latter being 8 miles south of Fort Pierce.

361. For a nice summary of the history of the Braford Bull at the Adams Ranch, See Enns, Gregory, <u>Cow Creek Chronicles, The Rise and Fall of an Early Florida Cattle Ranch,</u> University Press of Florida, Gainseville, Flordia, 2025 p 133, 134.

362. Adams, Alto, <u>The Fourth Quarter</u>, Privately published by Judge Alto Adams, 1976 and Adams, Alto, The Rule of Law, Florida Flair Publishing. Miami, Florida, 1980.

363. <u>State v. North St. Lucie River Drainage District</u>, 3 So. 2d 500(Fla 1941)(affirmed); <u>Moye v. State</u>, 3 So. 2d 403 (Fla 1941)(affirmed); <u>Florida Publish Co. v. Stroemer</u>, 4So. 2d 518 (Fla. 1941)(affirmed); <u>Knapp v. Fredricksen</u>, 4 So. 2d 251 (Fla 1941)(affirmed); <u>St. Lucie County v. Nobles,</u> 5 So. 2d 855 (Fla 1942)(affirmed); <u>United Land & Investment Co. v. Baker,</u> 5 So. 2d 266 (Fla 1941)(affirmed); <u>Palm Shores v. Nobles,</u> 5 So. 2d 52 (Fla. 1941)(reversed).

364. State Road 76 is also known and signed as Kanner Highway, is a 31,504-mile-long northeast-southwest (signed east-west) state highway connecting Port Mayaca on the shore of Lake Okeechobee at the intersection with US 98-441 (Sr 400-SR 15) with Stuart on the shore of the St Lucie River near the Atlantic Ocean and the Treasure Coast at an intersection with US 1 (SR 5). *Wikipedia.*

365. Judge Smith did not like to publicize the fact that he was born in McAlisterville, Pa., but rather that he grew up in Wabasso, to which he moved 6 weeks after his birth. See also *Scripps Press Journal* November 12, 2000, p C1.

366. Bishop, Jim, <u>The Murder Trial of Judge Peel</u>, A Trident Press Book, Simon and Schuster, New York, 1962, p 56.

367. *Ft. Pierce Tribune*, June 17, 1991.

368. A *Vero Beach Press Journal* article on February 11, 1971, reports on Judge Trowbridge handling three different murder trials, pending in the circuit court for Indian River County, as well as a

multiple defendant rape case.

369. The Supreme Court of Florida, A Reference Manual, The Supreme Court of Florida, 1995, p 30.

370. When I first met Judge Nourse after a hearing in the late 1970s, he told me of his ancestor, Rebecca Nurse, an alleged witch from Salem, Massachusetts, who was hung as a witch in 1692. This ancestry was confirmed by Jimmy Anne Haisley when she eulogized her sister LeVan on September 30, 2025. What is even more fascinating about the witch story is that she did not have a lawyer and was first acquitted by a jury, but then the jury changed their verdict, and she was hung. Her conviction was reversed in 1711.

371. (Stone v O'Brien), Murphy, Dennis, NBC News App., Dec 23, 2005. See also TCPalm.com, June 5, 2008.

Chapter 8 - Clerks of the Circuit and County Courts for Indian River County

372 On or about March 4, 2025, Judge Warner notified Governor Ron DeSantis that she would retire from the Fourth District Court of Appeal on September 30, 2025, after serving on the court for over thirty-six years.

373. This changed in the 1990s to have a central state depository for the child support and alimony payments.

374. See the biographical information under Judge Andrews in the St. Lucie County chapter for details on this historical house.

Chapter 9 - County Court in and for Indian River County

375. Richards, J. Noble, Florida's Hibiscus City Vero Beach, Brevard Graphics, Melbourne, Fla.,

1968, p 182.

376. Morris, Allen, The Florida Handbook, 1967-1968, The Peninsular Publishing Company, Tallahassee, Fl. 1967, p 117.

377. Morris, Allen, The Florida Handbook, 1977-1978, The Peninsular Publishing Co., Tallahassee, Florida, 1977, p187.

378. *Vero Beach Press Journal*, April 27, 1994 at p 4. See also Wild v. Dozier, 672 So.2d 16 (Fla. 1996).

379. Section 3, Chapter 10072, Laws of Florida, 1925.

380. Section 34.021, Fla. Stat. (1977). Laws of Florida, 1978 Chapter 346.

381. Section 34.021, Fla. Stat. (1977).

382. Laws of Florida, 1971, Chapter 49.

383. Temporary judge.

384. Appointed to unexpired term.

385. B. W. Ketchum was one of the youngest judges appointed in Florida, at age 22. His father, C. H. Ketchum. was a noteworthy politician from Key West, being a Grand Dragon of the KKK for Florida, from which position he resigned circa the time his son became the judge. The father was also a state representative from Monroe County. B. W. Ketchum was also the Indian River County Coroner and a Commissioner of the Circuit Court for Indian River County in 1925. He was defeated when trying to retain his county court judge position in 1926 by Otis Cobb. He was also known as the "Marrying Judge," having married 70 couples in just over a year in office. Ironically the front page of the *Vero Beach Press Journal* of January 22, 1932 notes him as a confirmed bachelor.

386. Scripps Treasure Coast Newspapers, August 22, 2010 (80 years ago column).

387. Honeywell was also the first female deputy sheriff in the state, not assigned to desk duty, by her appointment in January 1925.

388. *Vero Beach Press Journal*, June 5, 1931, p 1.

389. Knight v. Atkin, 95 Fla. 526, 116 So.2d. 239 (Fla. 1928).

390. *Vero Beach Press Journal*, September 11, 1969.

391. Richards, J. Noble, Florida's Hibiscus City of Vero Beach, Brevard Graphics, Melbourne, Fl., 1968, p 182.

392. Wild v. Dozier, 672 So.2d 16 (Fla. 1996).

Chapter 10 - Small Claims Court

393. Morris, Allen, The Florida Handbook, 1967-1968, The Peninsular Publishing Co., Tallahassee, Florida, 1977, p 122.

394. Chapter 26920, Laws of Florida, 1951; Chapter 42 of the Florida Statutes (1951).

395. Chapter 30369 of the Laws of Florida, 1955.

396. 10 Fla. Jur. 2d Constitutional Law, Sections 428.

397. *Vero Beach Press Journal*, January 12, 1961, Page 1D.

Chapter 11 - Fourth District Court of Appeal

398. Amendment No. 1 to Article V of the Florida Constitution, approved by 79.52% of the voters of the State of Florida on November 6, 1956.

399. Ch. 57-248, Laws of Florida, which became Chapter 35 of the Florida Statutes.

400. Ch. 65-294, section 2, Laws of Florida.

401. Ch. 65-294, section 4, Laws of Florida.

402. Id. Section 2.

403. Section 35.042, Florida Statutes (1995).

404. Section 26.021(15), Florida Statutes, section 26.021(17), Florida Statutes and section 26.021(19), Florida Statutes (1994).

405. Ch. 65-294, section 1, Laws of Florida (Florida Statute 35.05 (1965)).

406. *Today Newspaper*, July 23, 1968.

407. *Vero Beach Press Journal*, November 18, 1955.

408. *Vero Beach Press Journal*, November 11, 1965. P 1.

409. *The Florida Bar Journal*, Volume 50, No. 3 March of 1976.

410. Chapter 105, Florida Statutes (1971); Ch. 71-49, Laws of Florida.

411. Because of disagreements over Article V, Article V was excluded by the Legislature from the proposed amendments to the Florida Constitution 1968 which was approved by the people of the State of Florida. In 1970 the proposed Article V revisions to the Constitution adopted by the Legislature on July 5, 1969, (S.J.R. No. 36) was defeated in the general election by the populous in November 1970 by a vote of 526,328 to 503,992. Another revision to Article V was proposed by S.J.R. #52-D at the 1971 Third Special Session of the Legislature and was adopted by the voters at a special election on March 14, 1972, effective January 1, 1973. Article V of the Florida Constitution in 1972 also accounted for the abolition of the municipal courts, discussed in the next chapters.

412. *Vero Beach Press Journal*, February 2, 1967, p 1.

413. 67-11, Laws of Florida, which amended Section 35.06 of the Florida Statutes.

414. Section 2, 67-29, Laws of Florida, which amended Section 35.05 of the Florida Statutes.

415. *Today Newspaper*, July 23, 1968.

416. The Supreme Court of Florida, A Reference Manual, The Supreme Court of Florida, 1995,

p 42.

417. McCain resigned from the court rather than face impeachment charges. The Florida Bar v. McCain, 361 So.2d 700, (Fla. 1978). He also was disbarred. Id. See also *TC Scripps Treasure Coast Newspapers*, Oct 31, 2011.

418. See for example Smith, Len Young and Robertson, G. Gale, Business Law, West Publishing Co., St. Paul, Minn., 1977, p 148.

419. McCain was a fugitive on drug charges since 1983. He skipped out on a $1 million bond while awaiting federal and state charges in Louisiana for allegedly conspiring to smuggle and sell 30,000 pounds of marijuana. *The News Tribune*, December 28, 1986.

Chapter 12 - City of Vero Beach Municipal Court and Justices of the Peace

420. See for example Article 3, Section 21 (S.J.R. 81, 1937; adopted 1938).

421. Morris, Allen, The Florida Handbook, 1967-1968, The Peninsular Publishing Co., Tallahassee, Florida, 1967, p 122.

422. Fla. Stat. 168.01 (1947).

423. Chapter 8377, Laws of Florida, 1919.

424. Id. Section 14.

425. Chapter 6, An Ordinance Prescribing the Jurisdiction Procedure of the Municipal Court, and for other purposes, July 17, 1919, City of Vero Beach, Florida.

426. Chapter 14439, Laws of Florida, 1929.

427. Id. Section 19.

428. Chapter 319, Ordinances of the City of Vero Beach, Approved November 28, 1934.

429. Chapter 416, Ordinances of the City of Vero Beach, Approved November 13, 1941.

430. Chapter 21613, Laws of Florida, 1941, section 19.

431. Chapter 22500, Laws of Florida 1943.

432. *Vero Beach Press Journal*, July 11, 1947, p 1.

433. *Vero Beach Press Journal*, July 11, 1947, p 1.

434. *Vero Beach Press Journal*, January 16, 1948, Page 1.

435. Chapter 515, Ordinances of the City of Vero Beach, Approved September 27, 1949.

436. Fla. Stat. 92.142 (Section 506 Ch 95-147).

437. Laws of Florida, 1951, Chapter 27943, Section 95.

438 Id., Sec. 96.

439. Chapter 672, Ordinances of the City of Vero Beach, Approved January 18, 1955.

440. The Municipal Courts in Florida were abolished as of January 3, 1977. Article V, Section 20(d) 4, Constitution of the State of Florida (1972).

441. *Vero Beach Press Journal*, December 13, 1935, p 1.

442. Mr. James L. Boring, a 1964 graduate of the University of Florida Law School, went on to practice law in Vienna, Virginia.

Chapter 13 - Town of Fellsmere Municipal Court and Justices of the Peace

443. There is no recorded plat of Cincinnatus Farms during 1892-1900 in Brevard County. Possibly, lots may have been sold in Section 16, Township 315, Range 37 East since that section was excepted in the sale of the Russell property but that section was not accessible by rail.

444. Cleveland, Weona, Crossroad Towns Remembered, A Look Back at Brevard & Indian River Pioneer Communities, Florida Today, Melbourne, Florida 1994, p 80. Chapter 7154, Laws of Florida, 1915, Section 35.

445. Lecture of Dr. Gordon Patterson, Professor of History at Florida Tech given at the North Indian River County Library in Sebastian on March 26, 1996. See also Fellsmere Tribune, January 27, 1917.

446. Burnett, Gene M., Florida's Past, People and Events that Shaped the State, Sarasota, Florida, 1986, Volume I, p 210.

447. Interview on April 20, 1996, with Professor Gordon Patterson by Eugene J. O'Neill.

448. *The Vero Journal*, October 15, 1926.

449. Notwithstanding the mysterious ending of Chief Commissioner Piffard's term, which you will read about as the book continues, there is an inconsistency during his term when the March 5, 1921 Fellsmere Tribune shows in a front page legal notice that Charles H. Gifford is Chief Commissioner, yet in the same edition, on page 2, it is C. H. Piffard.

450. But see clarification of this time frame under his biography in this same chapter.

451. Was acting mayor 12/21/36 to 6/114/1937, filling the unexpired term of H. C. Watts, who left during his term.

452. Mayor Barnes died in office and the council, in his honor, did not appoint an acting Mayor to fill his unexpired term. Votapka, Richard B., Fellsmere Commissioners and Mayors, as Revised on January 5, 2022.

453. The Municipal Courts in Florida were abolished as of January 3, 1977, the latest and some courts were sooner. Article V, Section 20(d) 4, Constitution of the State of Florida (1972). See more on this in the Chapters on Sebastian and Vero Beach.

454. Votapka, Richard B., Fellsmere Historian, History of Fellsmere, June 13, 2024, p 22.

455. T.J. Braniff v. Henry F. Baier and Charles A. Baier, 101 Kan. 117, 165 P. 816 (S.Ct. Ks.,

1917).

456. *Ft. Pierce Tribune*, August 31, 1920. P 3.

457. *Ft. Pierce Tribune*, September 14, 1920 (which published a photo of the team from 1904.

458. *Ft. Pierce Tribune*, November 2, 1920.

459. *Ft. Pierce News*, August 13, 1915.

460. *Ft. Pierce News*, March 11, 1927.

461. *Ft. Pierce News*, August 13, 1915, p 28.

462. City of Fellsmere Council Meeting Minutes, December 4, 1925.

463. *The Vero Press*, July 23, 1926.

464. Votapka, Richard, Fellsmere Historian, History of the Charles and Helen Piffard Home, January 18, 2024.

465. *The Vero Press* (St. Lucie County), April 27, 1922.

466. An ancestry.com family tree shows that Mr. Young's first wife was Florence, who he married September 17, 1902, in New Haven, Connecticut. He had a son, Russell B. Young, in 1904, but died at age sixteen in Connecticut.

467. Smiley, Nixon, Florida: Land of Images, E.A. Seamann Publishing, Inc., Miami, Florida, 1972, p 81.

Chapter 14 - City of Sebastian Municipal Court and Justices of the Peace

468. I would also note that he was a County Commissioner for Indian River County for at least 1950-1953.

469. Transcript of proceedings of meeting held at town hall of the Town of Sebastian, St. Lucie, Florida on the 8th day of December 1924 on record in the clerk's office. See also Vickers, Ramona,

More Tales of Sebastian, Sebastian River Area Historical Society, Inc., 1992, p 60.

470. Stuart, Hix C., The Notorious Ashley Gang, St. Lucie Publishing Co., Stuart, Florida, 1928, p 72; More Tales of Sebastian, Sebastian River Area Historical Society, Inc.; 1992, p 235-238; Adams, Judge Alto Lee, The Fourth Quarter, 1976, Privately published by Judge Alto Adams; Miley, Charles S., Miley's Memos, Indian River Community College Historical Data Center, 1980, p 78.

471. More Tales of Sebastian, Sebastian River Area Historical Society, Inc., 1992, p 77.

472. Vero Beach Press Journal, Nov. 5, 1926.

473. Florida State Archives, Series S 1284, State and County Directories, 1845-1969, St. Lucie and Indian River County.

474. More Tales of Sebastian, Sebastian River Area Historical Society, Inc., 1992, p. 9.

475. See second endnote on page 495 for references for more information on the controversial capture and killing of the Ashley Gang.

476. Chapter 11155 of the Laws of Florida, 1925, Approved May 18, 1925.

477. Chapter 11735 of the Laws of Florida, 1925.

478. Chapters 11733 & 11734 of the Laws of Florida, 1925.

479 City of Sebastian Catalogue List of 1924-1987, p 172.

480. Chapter 2256 of the Laws of Florida, 1965.

481. Id, Section 1.

482. Died in office.

483. Ordinance No I-73, City Council of the City of Sebastian, dated May 31, 1973.

484 See Photo of the plaque on his monument under the Fultz Biography on p. 254.

485. More Tales of Sebastian, Sebastian River Area Historical Society, Inc., 1992, p 77.

486. *Vero Beach Press Journal*, Nov. 5, 1926.

487. Florida State Archives, Series S 1284, State and County Directories, 1845-1969, St. Lucie and Indian River County.

488. I found the name Lisbon Futch by coming across a social column in the Sebastian News portion of (likely) the *Vero Beach Press Journal* of August 27, 1952, with the name of Mrs. Lisbon Futch. That got me off the search for Fistok, but on to Futch. Lisbon Futch was born August 20, 1897, in Sebastian. He was the son of William Edmund Futch and Rachel Ida Hooten. Lisbon was a veteran of both World War I and World War II, and his son mentioned below was a World War II hero.

Lisbon Futch married Margaret Anna Hepp on October 22, 1921, in Philadelphia. They lived in Philadelphia for a while and had at least two sons, Charles Leslie Futch and Nelson Hepp Futch. The Futches came to Sebastian by at least 1940 where he subsequently was Justice of the Peace. Lisbon Futch was a Sebastian Inlet Commissioner from 1951 – 1976 and also a member of the Real Eight Company. Mrs. Lisbon Futch was a Postmaster in Sebastian, succeeding Myrtice Baughman Martin.

Son, Charles Leslie Futch was killed in World War II while on his eleventh bombing mission over St. Nazaire, France. His plane was a B-17 Flying Fortress, known as the Queen of the Skies and he was the Top Turret Gunner and Engineer of the craft.

Lisbon Futch died in Melbourne, Florida on April 3, 1978, at age 80, and is buried in the Sebastian Cemetery. (The social article of 1952 alluded to indicated that Mrs. Lisbon Futch was spending several weeks with her son, Nelson Futch and his family in Philadelphia.)

489. More Tales of Sebastian, Sebastian River Area Historical Society, Inc., 1992, p 66.

490. Williams, Ada Coats, Florida's Ashley Gang, Florida Classics Library, Port Salerno, Florida, 1996, p 37.

491. Old City Records 1924-1932. <u>More Tales of Sebastian</u>, Sebastian River Area Historical Society, Inc., 1992, p 60 & 61.

492. Vickers, Ramona, & Gulledge, Lydia Edwards, <u>More Tales of Sebastian</u>, Sebastian River Area Historical Society, 1992, p 52.

493. Vickers, Ramona, Old City Records 1924-1932, <u>More Tales of Sebastian</u>, Sebastian River Area Historical Society, Inc., 1992, p 62.

494. Vickers, Ramona, Facts about Vickers from City Records 1924-1932, <u>More Tales of Sebastian</u>, Sebastian River Area Historical Society, Inc., 1992, p 51.

495. *Vero Beach Press Journal*, December 15, 1946.

496. Interview with Mrs. Stevenson by Eugene J. O'Neill on January 29, 1996

Chapter 15 - City of Wabasso Municipal Court

497. House Bill No. 1905 which became law on June 25th 1966 provided for a practicing attorney judge, but also that the municipal court shall have an acting judge who shall be the mayor.

498. *Vero Beach - Indian River County Newsweekly*, December 19, 2012, P 8.

499. *Vero Beach – Indian River County Newsweekly*, October 24, 2012, P 11.

500. Chapter 11792 of the Laws of Florida, 1925, Approved December 1, 1925.

501. Id. Section 14.

502. Chapter 17689, section 2 of the Laws of Florida, 1935.

503. Interview with Judge D.C. Smith by Eugene J. O'Neill on November 3, 1994 and 9/6/96; Interview with Gerald Pryor by Eugene J. O'Neill on November 4, 1994; Interview of Thomas Cadenhead Jr. by EJON on 10/6/96; Interview of Bobby Longaker by EJON on 10/6/96; Interview of Jean Powers Shaw by EJON on 10/6/96; and Interview of Audrey Osteen Erickson Hanson by EJON

on 10/15/96.

Chapter 16 - Town of Indian River Shores Municipal Court

504. The Municipal Courts in Florida were abolished as of January 3, 1977. Article V, Section 20(d) 4, Constitution of the State of Florida (1972).

505. Chapter 29163 of the Laws of Florida, 1953.

506. Id. Article XI, Section 1.

507. Id. Article XI, Section 2.

508. Id. Article XI, Section 3.

Chapter 17 - Town of Orchid Municipal Court

509. Town of Indian River Shores, Resolution No. 3, June 25, 1953.

510. Interview of Darrell Fennell by Eugene J. O'Neill on December 1, 1995.

511 Chapter 2021, Laws of Florida 1965, Article XI, Section 2.

512. Ibid.

Bibliography

Adams, Judge Alto Lee, <u>The Fourth Quarter</u>, 1976. Privately published by Judge Alto Adams.

Argo, Don David, Canaveral Light, Florida Historical Society Press, Cocoa, Fl, 2001.

Armstrong, Douglas R., <u>French Castaways at Old Cape Canaveral</u>, privately published, Palm Bay, Florida, 1996.

Bacon, Eve, <u>Orlando, A Centennial History</u>, The Mickler House, Publishers, Chuluota, Florida, 1975.

Bartram, William,<u> Travels Through North and South Carolina, Georgia, East and West Florida</u>, 1791, Literary Classics of the United States, New York, New York, 1996.

Bishop, Jim, <u>The Murder Trial of Judge Peel</u>, A Trident Press Book, Simon and Schuster, New York, 1962.

Blackman, William Fremont, Ph.D., LL.D., <u>History of Orange County, Florida</u>, The E. O. Painter Printing Co., Deland, Florida, 1927.

Bockelman, Charles W., <u>Six Columns and Fort New Smyrna</u>, E.O. Painter Printing Co., DeLeon Springs, Florida 32028, 1985.

Born of the Sun, The Official Florida Bicentennial Commemorative Book, Worth International Communications Corporation, 1975.

Boyd, Joseph A., Jr., and Reder, Randal, A History of the Florida Supreme Court, University of Miami Law Review, September 1981.

Bradbury, Alford G., and Hallock, E. Story, A Chronology of Florida Post Offices, The Florida Federation of Stamp Clubs, 1962.

Brown, Canter, Jr., Fort Meade, 1849-1900, The University of Alabama Press, Tuscaloosa, and London, 1995.

Brown, Canter, Jr., Ossian Bingley Hart, Florida's Loyalist Reconstruction Governor, Louisiana State University Press, Baton Rouge and London, 1997.

Brown, Canter, Jr., Justice Ossian Bingley Hart, Florida Supreme Court Historical Society Review 4 (1991-1994):1-3, 16-17.

Brown, J. A., Panton, Leslie and Company, Indian Traders of Pensacola and St. Augustine, Florida Historical Quarterly, Vol 37, 1959, p. 328.

Brown, Raymond Richards, Memories of Eden, Brut Printing, Jacksonville, Florida, 1996.

Burbey, Louis H., Our Worthy Commander, The Life and Times of Benjamin K. Pierce in Whose Honor Fort Pierce Was Named, IRCC Pioneer Press, Fort Pierce, Florida, 1996.

Burnett, Gene M., Florida's Past, People and Events That Shaped the State, Volume I, Page 210, Pineapple Press, Inc., Sarasota, Florida, 1986.

Cash, W.T., The Story of Florida, Volume II, The American Historical Society, Inc., New York, 1938

Cemeteries of Indian River County, The Indian River Genealogical Society, Inc., 1987.

Chapin, George M., Florida 1513-1913, Past, Present and Future, The S. J. Clarke Publishing Company, Chicago, Illinois, 1914.

Claghorn, Charles E., Naval Officers of the American Revolution: A concise Biographical Dictionary, The Scarecrow Press, Inc., Metuchen, N.J., 1988.

Clerk of the Circuit Court, A Public Trustee, Established by the Florida Constitution of 1838, Prepared and published by the Florida Association of Court Clerks and Comptrollers.

Cleveland, Weona, Crossroad Towns Remembered, Florida Today, Melbourne, Florida, 1990.

Cody, Aldus M., and Robert S., Osceola County, The First 100 Years, The Osceola County Historical Society, 1987.

Cohen, M.M., Notices of Florida and The Campaigns, Introduction by O. Z. Tyler, Jr., Floridiana Facsimile and Reprint Series. Gainesville: University of Florida Press, 1964; originally published 1836.

Coker, Edward Caleb, New Englander on the Indian River Frontier. Caleb Lyndon Brayton and his view from Brayton's Bluff. Florida Historical Quarterly, Volume 70, No.3, January 1992.

Collins, LeRoy, Forerunners Courageous, Stories of Frontier Florida, Colcade Publishers, Inc., 1971.

Compiled General Laws of Florida

Constitution of the State of Florida

Covington, James W., The Billy Bowlegs War, 1855-1858, The final stand of the Seminoles against the whites, The Mickler House Publishers, Chuluota, Florida, 1982.

Davis, Frederick T., History of Jacksonville, Florida and Vicinity, 1513 to 1924, 1925, Reprinted by San Marco Bookstore, Jacksonville, Florida, 1990.

Davis, William Watson, The Civil War and Reconstruction in Florida, A facsimile reproduction of the 1913 edition, Quadricentennial Edition, Florida Facsimile Reprint Series, University of Florida Press, Gainesville, 1964.

Denham, James M., A Rogue's Paradise, Crime and Punishment in Antebellum Florida, 1821-1861, The University of Alabama Press, Tuscaloosa and London, 1997.

Denham, James M., From a Territorial to a State Judiciary, Florida's Antebellum Courts and Judges, Vol. 73 Florida Historical Quarterly, April 1995.

Dewhurst, Wm. W., <u>The History of St. Augustine, Florida</u>, Academy Books, Rutland, Vt., 1968. Reprinted from the 1885 Edition by G. P. Putnam's Sons of New York.

Doggett, Carita, <u>Dr. Andrew Turnbull, and the New Smyrna Colony of Florida</u>, The Drew Press, Florida, 1919.

Doherty, Herbert J., Jr., <u>Richard Keith Call, Southern Unionist</u>, University of Florida Press, Gainesville, 1961.

<u>Douglas, Thomas, Autobiography of</u>, Calkins & Stiles, New York, 1856. Excerpts from Dr. Carita Doggett Corse were loaned to The Federal Writers.

Dovell, J. E., Ph.D., <u>Florida, Historic Dramatic Contemporary</u>, Volume II, Lewis Historical Publishing Company, Inc., New York, 1952.

Dunn, Hampton, <u>Historic Florida Courthouses</u>, Hallmark Publishing, Inc., Gloucester Point, Virginia, 1998.

Enns, Gregory, <u>Cow Creek Chronicles, The Rise and Fall of an Early Cattle Ranch</u>, University Press of Florida, Gainesville, FL. 2025.

Eriksen, John M., <u>Brevard County, A History to 1955</u>, The Florida Historical Society Press, Tampa, Florida, 1994.

Fairbanks, George Rainsford, <u>The History & Antiquities of the City of St. Augustine, Florida</u>, Bicentennial Commission of Florida, 1975.

13 Fla. Jur. 2d, <u>Courts and Judges</u>

Farris, Charles D., <u>The Courts of Territorial Florida</u>, Florida Historical Quarterly, 19 (April 1941).

Fitzgerald, T. E., <u>Historical Highlights of Volusia County</u>, The Observer Press, Daytona Beach, Florida, 1939, reprinted by Volusia County Historical Preservation Board, 1993.

<u>The Florida Bar Journal</u>

<u>The Florida Historical Society Quarterly</u> Periodical

The Florida Historical Society List-Serv "Today in Florida History"

<u>Florida Statutes</u>

<u>Florida Statutes Annotated</u>

<u>Laws of Florida</u>

<u>Florida Becomes a State</u>, Florida Centennial Commission, Tallahassee, Florida, 1945.

Forbes, James Grant, <u>Sketches, Historical & Topographical of the Floridas, More Particularly of East Florida</u>, A Facsimile Reproduction of the 1821 Edition, University of Florida Press, Gainesville, Florida, 1964.

Francke, Arthur E., Jr., Gillingham, Alyce Hockaday, and Turner, Maxine Carey, <u>Volusia, The West Side</u>, E. O. Painter Printing Co., Deleon Springs, Florida, 1986.

Fusion, Robert H., Juan Ponce de Leon and the Spanish Discovery of Puerto Rico and Florida, The McDonald & Woodward Publishing Co., Blacksburg, Va., 2000.

Gannon, Michael V., 1993, Florida, A Short History, University Press of Florida.

Gannon, Michael V., The New History of Florida, University Press of Florida, Gainesville, Florida, 1996.

Gibson, Lillian Dillard, 1558-1978, Annuals of Volusia, Birthplace of Volusia County, 1978, R. Alex Gibson, Volusia, Florida.

Gleason, Lansing W., Vignettes of Eau Gallie As It Used To Be, a Portion of the Melbourne Centennial Book, Melbourne Chamber of Commerce, Centennial Committee, and Leona Cleveland, National Printing Inc., Melbourne, Florida, 1980.

Gold, Pleasant Daniel, "History of Volusia County, Florida" (1927). Text Materials of Central Florida. 112.

Griffin, Patricia, Mullet on the Beach: The Minorcans of Florida, 1768-1788, St. Augustine Historical Society, St. Augustine, Fla., 1991.

Hall, Kermit L., And Rise, Eric W., From Local Courts to National Tribunals, The Federal District Courts of Florida, 1821-1990, Carlson Publishing Inc., Brooklyn, N.Y. 1991.

Hanna, Alfred Jackson, and Hanna, Kathryn Abbey, Florida's Golden Sands, The Bobbs-Merrill Company, Inc., New York, 1950.

Hanna, Kathryn Abbey, <u>Florida Land of Change</u>, The University of North Carolina Press, Chapel Hill, 1948.

Hawks, J. M., M.D., <u>The East Coast of Florida. A Descriptive Narrative</u>, Lewis and Winship, Lynn, Mass., 1887.

Hebel, Ianthe Bond, <u>Centennial History of Volusia County, Florida, 1854-1954</u>, College Publishing Company, Daytona Beach, Florida, 1955.

Hellier, Walter R., <u>Indian River, Florida's Treasure Coast</u>, Hurricane House, Publishers, Inc., Coconut Grove, Florida, 1965.

Hutchinson, Janet, <u>History of Martin County</u>, Historical Society of Martin County, Stuart, Florida, 1998.

Henshall, James A., <u>Camping & Cruising in Florida</u>, Robert Clarke & Co., Cincinnati, 1884, Reprinted by Florida Classics Library, Port Salerno, Florida, 1991

Hethering, Alma, <u>On the River of the Long Water</u>, The Mickler House Publishers, Chuluota, Florida, 1980.

Hine, C. Vickerstaff, <u>On the Indian River</u>, Charles H. Sergel & Company, Chicago, 1891.

<u>Historic Properties Survey of Indian River County, Florida</u>, Historic Property Associates, Inc., St. Augustine, Florida, April 1989.

<u>History of Florida, Past and Present</u>, Vol III, The Lewis Publishing Company, Chicago and New York, 1923.

Horton, Jack B., Jr., <u>Titusville, Florida - The First Fifty Years, 1867-1917</u>, Titusville Star - Advocate, March, 1967.

<u>Huguenot Emigration to Virginia</u>, Virginia Historical Society, Genealogy Publishing Co., Baltimore, 1966.

<u>Jonathan Dickinson's Journal</u>, Florida Classic Library, Port Salerno, Florida, 33492; 1985.

James, John G., <u>Southern Student's Handbook of Selections for Reading and Oratory</u>, A.S. Barnes & Co., New York, 1879.

Johns, John E., <u>Florida During the Civil War</u>, University of Florida Press, Gainesville, Florida, 1963.

Kjerluff, Georgiana Greene, <u>Tales of Old Brevard</u>, The Kellersberger Fund of the South Brevard Historical Society, Inc., Florida Institute of Technology Press, Melbourne, Fla. 32901, 1972.

Knott, James R., <u>Palm Beach Revisited, Historical Vignettes of Palm Beach County</u>, 1987.

Lockey, Joseph B., <u>The St. Augustine Census of 1786</u>, Volume 18, The Florida Historical Quarterly, Number 1, July 1939.

Lockwood, Charlotte, <u>Florida's Historic Indian River County</u>, Media Tronics, Inc., Vero Beach, Florida, 1976.

Lyon, Eugene, <u>More Light on the Indians of the Ays Coast</u>, December 1967.

Mahon, John K., History of the Second Seminole War 1835-1842, Revised Edition, University Presses of Florida, Gainesville, Florida, 1985.

Makers of America, Florida Edition, Vol III, The Florida Historical Society, Jacksonville, Florida, A. B. Caldwell, Atlanta, Ga. 1909.

Manley, Walter W., Brown, E. Canter, Jr., and Rise, Eric W., The Supreme Court of Florida and Its Predecessor Courts, 1821-1917, University Press of Florida, Gainesville, Florida, 1997.

Matthews, John Harry, Law Enforcement in Spanish East Florida, 1783-1821, UMI Dissertation Service, 1987.

McGoun, William E., Southeast Florida Pioneers: The Palm & Treasure Coasts, Pineapple Press, Inc., Sarasota, Florida, 1998.

Michaels, Brian E., The River Flows North, A History of Putnam County, Florida, The Putnam County Archives and History Commission, Palatka, Florida, 1976.

Miley, Charles S., Miley's Memos, Indian River Community College Historical Data Center, 1980.

Minutes of the Board of County Commissioners of Indian River County

Mirow, M. C., FIU College of Law, Miami, Judges for British Subjects in Spanish East Florida, 66 Washington University Journal of Law & Policy, The Law & Policy of Criminal Justice, 2021.

Mirow, M. C., FIU College of Law, Miami, <u>The Thistle, the Rose, and the Palm: Scottish and English Judges in British East Florida</u>, Cambridge University Press, 2020.

Moore, Gary, <u>A March of Centuries, Lawyers and the Law in Jacksonville, 1564 to 1997</u>, The Jacksonville Bar Association, 1997

Motte, Jacob Rhett, <u>Journey into Wilderness</u>, University of Florida Press, Gainesville, Florida, 1963.

<u>More Tales of Sebastian</u>, 1992, Sebastian River Area Historical Society, Inc.

Morris, Allen, <u>The Florida Handbook</u>, 1967-1968, Eleventh Edition, The Peninsular Publishing Co., Tallahassee, Florida, 1967.

Morris, Allen, <u>The Florida Handbook</u>, 1975-1976, Fifteenth Edition, The Peninsular Publishing Co., Tallahassee, Florida, 1975.

Morris, Allen, <u>The Florida Handbook</u>, 1977-1978, Sixteenth Edition, The Peninsular Publishing Co., Tallahassee, Florida 1977.

Mowat, Charles L. (1943). The Enigma of William Drayton, Florida Historical Quarterly, Vol. 22. No. 1, Article 3

Mowat, Charles Lock, <u>East Florida as a British Province 1763 - 1784,</u> Vol. 3, University of Cal. Publications in History, University of California Press, Berkeley and Los Angeles, CA., 1943.

Murdoch, Richard K., <u>Governor Cespedes and the Religious Problem in East Florida, 1786-1787</u>, Florida Historical Quarterly, Vol 26, No. 4, Article 5.

Nelson, David Paul, <u>General James Grant, Scottish Soldier and Royal Governor of East Florida,</u> University Press of Florida, Gainesville, Florida, 1993.

Newman, Anna Pearl Leonard, <u>Stories of Early Life, Long Beautiful Indian River</u>, Stuart Daily News, Inc., Stuart, Florida, 1953.

<u>North Florida Living Magazine</u>, January 1984.

Oliva, Jose R., Speaker, <u>The People of Law Making in Florida, 1822-2019</u>, floridamemory.com, February 2019 Edn.

Panagopoulos, E.P., <u>New Smyrna, An Eighteenth Century Greek Odyssey</u>, Holy Cross Orthodox Press, Brookline, MA., 1978.

Parks, Joseph H., <u>General E. Kirby Smith, C.S.A.</u>, Louisiana State University Press, Baton Rouge, Louisiana, 1954 (1962 ?).

Pierce, Charles W., <u>Pioneer life in Southeast Florida</u>, University of Miami Press, Coral Gables, Florida, 1970.

Pratt, Theodore, <u>The Barefoot Mailman</u>, Hawthorne Books, Inc., New York, New York, 1943.

Proctor, Samuel, <u>Napoleon Bonaparte Broward, Florida's Fighting Democrat</u>, University of Florida Press, Gainesville, Florida, 1950.

Raize, Erwin R. & Associates, <u>Atlas of Florida</u>, University of Florida Press, Gainesville, 1964

Ranson, Robert, <u>East Coast Florida Memoirs 1837-1886</u>, Florida Classic Library, Port Salerno, Florida 34992; 1989.

Rasico, Philip D., The Minorcans of Florida: Their History, Language and Culture, Luthers, New Smyrna Beach, 1990.

Reese, Joseph H., Florida Flashlights, The Hefty Press, Miami, Florida, Florida State Library, 1917.

Remini, Robert V., The Life of Andrew Jackson, Penguin Books, New York, NY, 1988

Rerick, Rowland H., Memoirs of Florida, 2 vols., Southern Historical Association, Atlanta, 1902.

Richards, J. Noble, Florida's Hibiscus City of Vero Beach, Brevard Graphics, Incorporated, Melbourne, Florida, 1968.

Rights, Lucille, Rieley, A Portrait of St. Lucie County, Florida, The Dunning Company, 1994.

Robison, Jim and Andrews, Mark, Flashbacks: The Story of Central Florida's Past, The Orange County Historical Society and The Orlando Sentinel, 1995.

Rogers, William Warren and Brown, Jr., Cantor, Florida's Clerks of the Circuit Court, Their History and Experiences, Century Press, Tallahassee, Florida, 1996.

Ruster, William J., The History of the Polk County Court System, 1861-1995, Associated Publications Corp., Bartow, Fla., 1995.

Schafer, Daniel L., Plantation Development in British East Florida: A Case Study of the Earl of Egmont, Florida Historical Quarterly; Vol 63, No 2, Art 5, 1984.

Schafer, Daniel L., St. Augustine's British Years 1763-1984, The St. Augustine Historical Society, St. Augustine, 2001.

Shepard, Steve, The History of Legal Education in the United States: Commentaries and Primary Sources, The Salem Press, Hackensack, New Jersey, 1998.

Shofner, Jerrell, Florida Portrait, A Pictorial History of Florida, Florida Historical Society, Tampa, Florida, and Pineapple Press, Inc., Sarasota, Florida, 1990.

Shofner, Jerrell H., History of Brevard County, Volume 1, Brevard County Historical Commission, 1995.

Shofner, Jerrell H., History of Brevard County, Volume 2, Brevard County Historical Commission, 1996.

Shofner, Jerrell H., Nor Is It Over Yet: Florida in the Era of Reconstruction 1865-1877. University of Florida Press, Gainesville, 1974.

Short, Carolyn, Theater Plaza "A Historic Sense of Place."

Smiley, Nixon, Florida: Land of Images, E.A. Seamann Publishing, Inc., Miami, Florida, 1972.

Spanish Land Grants of Florida, The Historical Record Survey Division of Professional and Service Projects, Works Progress Administration, State Library Board, Tallahassee, Florida, Volume I, unconfirmed claims, August 1940, and Volume II, confirmed claims, November 1940.

Stanley, Eileen E., and Decker, Carol, Micco & Grant, Settlements in the Florida Wilderness, America Through Time, Fonthill Media, Inc., www.through-time.com, 2025.

Stanley, Ellen E, Pioneering Sebastian and Roseland, Arcadia Publishing, 2017.

Stone, Elaine Murray, Brevard County, From Cape of the Canes to Space Coast, Windsor Publications, Inc., Northbridge, CA.

Strickland, Alice, Ormond-on-the-Halifax, Alice Strickland, Ormond Beach, 1980, p. 14.

Stuart, Hix C., The Notorious Ashley Gang, St. Lucie Printing Co., Inc., Stuart, Florida, 1928.

The Book of Florida, The Florida Editors Association, The James O Jones Company, 1925.

The Supreme Court of Florida, A Reference Manual, The Supreme Court of Florida, 1995.

Tales of Sebastian, 1993, Sebastian River Area Historical Society, Inc.

Tanner, Helen H., Zespedes in East Florida 1784 - 1790, University of Miami Press, Coral Gables, 1963.

Taylor, Robert A., Rebel's Storehouse, University of Alabama Press, 1995.

Tepper, Roberta L., Esq., and Art Bernardino, Art, <u>Two Hundred Years of Justice: The Courts in Gaston County</u>, Commission on the Bicentennial of the United States Constitution.

<u>The Book of Florida</u>, The Florida Editors Association, The James O. Jones Company, 1925.

<u>The East Coast of Florida, Personal and Family Records</u>, Volume III, The Southern Publishing Company, Delray Beach, Florida, 1962.

Thompson, Arthur W., <u>Jacksonian Democracy of the Florida Frontier,</u> University of Florida Monographs, Social Sciences No. 9, Winter 1961, University of Florida Press, Gainesville, Florida.

Thompson, Dave, <u>The Space Coast: Launchpads, Beach Made It Unique, The History of Brevard County, Florida</u>, compiled by Alpha Theta Chapter of Delta Cappa Gamma, 1972.

Tinsley, Jim Bob, <u>Florida Cow Hunter, The Life and Times of Bone Mizell</u>, University of Central Florida Press, Orlando, 1990.

Van Landingham, Kyle, S., <u>Pictorial History of St. Lucie County 1565-1910</u>, Sun Bank of St. Lucie County and the St. Lucie Historical Society, 1988.

Van Landingham, Kyle S., <u>In Pursuit of Justice, Law & Lawyers in Hillsborough County, 1846-1996</u>, Hillsborough County Bar Association, Drawing Board Publishing Services, 1996.

<u>Vero Beach Press Journal</u>, 1994, My Grandpa's Scrapbook (Videotape).

Wallace, John, Carpetbag Rule in Florida: The Inside Workings of the Reconstruction of Civil government in Florida After the Close of the Civil War, University of Florida Press, Gainesville, Florida, 1964; originally published in 1888.

Weiss, Murray, and Hoffman, Bill, Palm Beach Babylon, Sins, Scams & Scandals, Carol Publishing Group, New York, 1992, Chapter 10.

Will, Lawrence E., Okeechobee Boats and Skippers, Great Outdoors Publishing Co., St. Petersburg, Florida, 1965.

Williams, Ada Coats, Florida's Ashley Gang, Florida Classics Library, Port Salerno, Florida, 1996.

Whitfield, James B., Florida State Government, An Official Directory, Florida Steam Book and Job Office, Tallahassee, Fla. 1885.

Whitfield, James B., Revised by Morris, Allen, Legal Background of the Government of Florida, Reprinted from the Florida Statutes, West Publishing Co., St. Paul, Minn.

Wright, J. Leitch, Jr., British St. Augustine, Historical St. Augustine Preservation Board, St. Augustine, Fla., 1975.

Wynne, Lewis N. and Horgan, James J., Florida Pathfinders, Saint Leo College Press, Saint Leon, Florida, 1994.

Wynne, Lewis N. and Horgan, James J., <u>Florida Decades, A Sesquicentennial History, 1845-1995</u>, Saint Leo College Press, Saint Leo, Florida, 1995.

<u>Florida Becomes a State</u>, Florida Centennial Commission, Tallahassee, Florida, 1945.

<u>Newspapers</u>

East Coast Advocate

The Fellsmere Farmer

The Fellsmere Tribune

The Fort Pierce News

The Fort Pierce Tribune

The Titusville Star

The Titusville Star Advocate

The Vero Press

Vero Beach Press Journal

Index of Names

C

Cocke, Mary Magdeline Chastain … 157
Cocke, Richard … 156
Cocke, William Archer … 138,156,157, 158,159,160,161
Collins, Edith E. … 454
Collins, Geoff Glover … 454
Collins, George G. Jr. "Joe" … 432,453,454
Collins, Leroy … 315,317,321,324,326, 327,382
Collins, Mary Schmidt … 454
Collins, R. Scott … 454
Collins, William … 10,15
Cone, Gov. Federick Preston … 233,309,312,313
Connelly, Cecelia … 514
Conner, Burton C. … 306,354,355
Conner, Deborah … 355
Conner, Ralph … 458
Coppinger, Gov. Jose Maria … 45
Cook, William … 140

Cooksey, Byron T. … 261,263,331,396,426, 450
Corbin, Brenda … 367
Corsi, Art ... 514
Cossin, Diane … 418
Cossin, Karen … 418
Cox, Cynthia L. 306,352,353,354
Cox, Fannie … 445
Cox, Harry … 352
Cox, Wiley Festus … 427,430,437,445
Crane, Henry … 50,90,119,140,173
Crane, Henry Lafayette … 90
Crane, Sophia Allen … 90
Crittenden, John … 57
Crooks, H.E. … 224
Crosby, J.C. …267
Crosby, Oscar … 455
Cross, Cleve … 415
Cross, Estelle … 415
Cross, Spencer C. … 406,407,413,416
Crouse McKinley … 240
Crunch, Leslie Andrews … 243

Diamond, David ... 380
Diamond, Earl ... 380
Diamond, Emory G. ...
380
Diamond, James Henry
... 379
Diamond, John T. ...
380
Diamond, Samuel I. ...
380
Diamond, Sarah ... 379
Diamond, Walker ...
380
Didlake, W. P. (Young)
... 438
Dickinson, Jonathan ...
2
Disney, D. J. ... 167,249
Dittman, A.C. ...
142,174,175
Dittman, Cora Irene
Hood ... 175
Dixon, Mrs. Ida Green
... 476
Dixon, Orville "Dick"
... 476
Doggett, Carita ... 27
Dole, Elisabeth Irene ...
469,470
Dole, Frank W. ...
458,459,461,469,470

Dole, John Wesley ...
469
Dole, Joseph ... 469
Dole, Leona Pearl
Loftiss ... 469
Dole, Marie Ellen ...
469
Donnell, Ballard ... 236
Donnell, Elizabeth ...
236
Donnell, Ezra Ballard
... 229,232,233,234
Donnell, Freda ... 236
Donnell, James Peter ...
233
Donnell, Mary Frances
Bass ... 233
Donnell, Rena Roberts
... 235
Donnelly, J.B. ... 233
Donoghue, Gregory J.
... 289
Douglas, Hannah
Sanford ... 143
Douglas, Thomas ...
60,61,70,120,138,143,
145,149,151
Douglass, John Ballard
... 143
Drake, Sir Francis ... 5
Drayton, Mary Grote ...
18

McKinley, William … 243

McLean, aka McLane, Charles … 130,139,197

McLemore, Robert Jordan … 430

McMillan, William J. … 142

McNair, Anne Marie … 380

Medici, Elia … 6

Medlin, Candy Lee … 484

Medlin, Frances … 483

Medlin, M.L. … 462,483

Medlin, Virginia "Lillian" … 484

Medlin, W.T. … 483

Menendez de Aviles, Pedro … 4

Menendez de Valdez, Pedro … 4

Mensh, aka Mensch, Max … 459

Mensh, aka Mensch, Sam … 459,492

Merriman, Ida B. … 376

Merriman, Ingram A. … 376

Merriman, Jeanette Bazler … 378

Merriman, Luster Mason … 266,373,375,376,377, 378,444

Merriman, Richard M. … 378

Merriman, William B., IV … 377

Merriman, William … 376

Metz, Linda Lou … 364

Michael, John C. …567

Michael, Margaret Emma Gray … 178,567

Middleton, Arthur … 515,516

Middleton, Elbia Wagner … 515

Middleton, Mrs. Margaret Haberman … 515

Middleton, John … 515

Middleton, J.R. … 499,515,516,517

Middleton, Raymond … 516

Middleton, Virginia Isabelle, Glasgow … 516

Middleton, Walter Arthur … 516

Wright, Abner ... 191
Wright, Annie C. Jones
... 167
Wright, Benjamin ...
74,258,267,304,305,
306,379
Wright, Freda ...
358,366,367

X

Y
Yates, Mrs. Earl S.
Ketchum ... 374
Young, Albert
Huntington ... 480
Young, Albert
Huntington Curtis Sr. ...
481
Young, A.W. ...
425,426,431,437,438,
442
Young, Alice Geraldine
Barbour ... 479
Young, George Toohey
... 437
Young, Gladys Wallis
Wahaples ... 479
Young, Guilford Dudley
Sr. "G.D." ...
462,479,480

Young, Guilford Dudley
Jr. ... 480
Young, Irene Daley ...
436
Young, Christine Jensen
... 325
Young, J.D. ...
266,270,271,274
Young, John ... 325
Yulee, David Levy ...
75,76,77,150,152

Z
Zacharakis, Cynthia ...
341
Zespedes ...
11,19,25,26,29
Zeuch, Herman ...
243,436
Zorc, Frank L. ... 290

About the Author

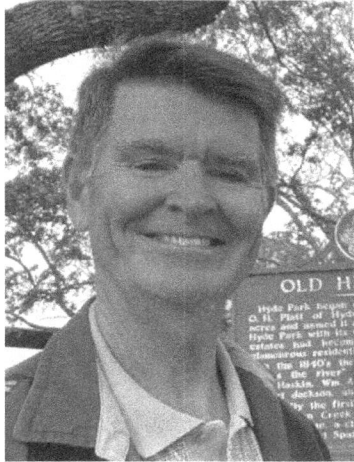

Eugene J. O'Neill was born in Holyoke, MA., on Oct 9, 1950. He obtained a B. S. in Civil Engineering from Merrimack College in 1972 and a J. D. from Western New England University in 1976, and an LLM there in 2021 in Elder Law & Estate Planning. He practiced for forty-four years with the firm of Gould Cooksey Fennell in Vero Beach, Florida, where he was a triple board-certified lawyer in Civil Trial Law, Business Litigation Law, and Construction Law. He was president of the Indian River County Bar Association in 1993-1994 and was an AV-rated lawyer by Martindale-Hubbell and was recognized as a Super Lawyer in Construction for many years.

www.ingramcontent.com/pod-product-compliance
Lightning Source LLC
Chambersburg PA
CBHW070613270326
41926CB00011B/1679